12-11-61

Goals and Values in Agricultural Policy

Other publications of the Center for Agricultural and Economic Adjustment are available as follows, from the source indicated below:

Problems and Policies of American Agriculture, Iowa State University Press, Ames, Iowa, 1959.

Demand for Farm Products, Center for Agricultural and Economic Adjustment, Iowa State University, Ames, Iowa, 1959.

Adjustment and its Problems in Southern Iowa, Center for Agricultural and Economic Adjustment, Iowa State University, Ames, Iowa, 1959.

The Feed-Livestock Workshop, Center for Agricultural and Economic Adjustment, Iowa State University, Ames, Iowa, 1959.

Consumer Preferences and Market Development for Farm Products, Center for Agricultural and Economic Adjustment, Iowa State University, Ames, Iowa, 1960.

Adjustments in U.S. Agriculture: A National Basebook, Iowa State University Press, Ames, Iowa, 1961.

Dynamics of Land Use: Needed Adjustments, Iowa State University Press, Ames, Iowa, 1961.

Goals and Values in Agricultural Policy

Assembled and published under the sponsorship of the

IOWA STATE UNIVERSITY CENTER FOR
AGRICULTURAL AND ECONOMIC ADJUSTMENT

Iowa State University Press, *Ames,* Iowa, U.S.A.

Preface

1173147

THE PAPERS INCLUDED IN THIS BOOK were presented
at a conference on Goals and Values in Agricultural Policy,
sponsored by the Center for Agricultural and Economic Adjustment of Iowa State University. The need for holding the conference was suggested by many persons over the United States.
The professional input represented by the conference and the papers contained in this book, like other conferences and activities
of the Center, should be looked upon as a joint enterprise of the
professional staffs of the entire complex of land grant universities, the United States Department of Agriculture and other research and educational institutions, rather than as a specific activity of Iowa State University.

While goals and values in agricultural policy have long concerned social scientists, little effort has been devoted to systematic treatment of the associated problems. The purpose of this
conference was to bring agricultural economists, political scientists, sociologists, general economists and other social scientists
together in an interdisciplinary approach to problems of goals
and values. The structure of the conference was generally this:
First, papers were designated to review and analyze the development of the value-goal system of American society generally,
without reference to agriculture in particular. Second, papers
were assigned to identify current major goals of American society. Next, papers were assigned which would review the goals of
American society for agriculture in particular, and the goals of
farm people for their own industry. A paper was assigned to
deal with the goals and values held by American society for general economic organization, supposing that this paper would provide a framework for analyzing goals for economic organization
of agriculture. Finally, major attention was focused on agriculture through papers assigned to deal with the particular structural and goal-value problems of agriculture. Two papers (Chapters 14A and 14B) were assigned to outline agricultural policies

which were consistent with the goal-value orientations of American society.

This particular conference structure was employed in order that the problems of agriculture might be better analyzed in the broad context of American society. With continued growth in population and the national economy and a relative decline in the resources employed by agriculture, this framework becomes extremely relevant for future decades. While the papers presented did not always follow the general conference outline, important progress was made in coming to grips with the goal and value problems of the industry. Solutions to the major economic problems must have their roots in goal-value phenomena. The basic economic and physical cause of the agricultural problem is now well understood. Agriculturists and economists can suggest a half dozen ways to solve it. But solutions immediately confront problems in goals and values, the deeply imbedded beliefs of particular individuals, groups and organizations in respect to "what is right" or "what ought to be." In some cases, disagreement rests on goals themselves. In other cases, conflict arises in respect to the appropriate means of attaining particular goals. Until goal and value positions for agriculture are more clearly articulated, and until it is recognized that progress to solution of the income problem rests on resolution of apparent conflicts in goals and values, progress in solving major structural problems of agriculture may be small.

This conference was only a beginning. The topic under consideration is broad and complex. Further analyses, conferences and workshops are needed. It is hoped however, that the conference at which these papers were presented will serve as a catalyst for this purpose.

EARL O. HEADY
Iowa State University
Director, Center for Agricultural
and Economic Adjustment

Table of Contents

Chapter 1

EARL O. HEADY
LEE G. BURCHINAL

Iowa State University

The Concern
With Goals and Values
in Agriculture

T HE MAJOR PROBLEMS in farm policy evidently are those
of goals and values. Agriculture has been burdened with
surpluses, declining income and low resource returns for
the last decade. The situation is not new. Aside from depression
and war which temporarily concealed it, the tendency towards
surplus capacity and tardy income growth has existed since the
1920's. But the problem is now approaching crisis magnitude.
Mammoth government stocks are growing in embarrassment to
farm people and in cost to the general public. Yet farm prices
and income still decline. The problem continues not because
economists lack general understanding of its causes or alternatives which could alleviate it, but because public agreement is
generally lacking on the appropriate means and, to an extent, on
the proper objectives of farm policy. Economists can suggest a
half dozen effective means for eliminating the problem, whether
the criterion be one of improving farm income, equalizing resource returns with other industries, bettering the allocation of
resources between agriculture and other industries for national
benefit or eliminating surplus stocks and production.

Numerous methods exist for attaining any one of these as an
end per se. However, even where farm and nonfarm publics can
generally agree on an end or objective, such as restricting the
rate of growth and cost of surplus stocks, there is lack of agreement on the methods and timing for doing so. The build-up in and
cost of stocks could certainly be eliminated through strict marketing quotas or free market prices, or several alternatives between these extremes. Incomes could be better supplemented and
at lower public cost by policy means other than those now employed. But even though several means clearly exist for attaining
agreeable ends, appropriate legislation has not been accomplished,
evidently because of value conflicts. Too, the ultimate ends or
objectives of farm policy, particularly in relation to national
economic and foreign policy, evidently involve values.

1

Because the basic issues in farm policy are value oriented, and are not purely problems of economic science, it is necessary to bring the problem of values explicitly into focus in order that research workers, educators, administrators, and the public will better understand the nature and importance of the complex issues which are involved. The program has been structured in an interdisciplinary manner because the problems involved relate to fields of sociology, anthropology, political science, social theory, psychology and economics. The critical problems facing agriculture, as is also true for our society generally, in the 1960's include those related to value orientations. An even greater need is to appraise our values and chart a policy course which is consistent with general societal goals. In this context, a near-crisis exists in farm policy. Recent and current policies apparently have failed, not only to solve the basic farm problem, defined as it may be related to alternative objectives or ideal types, but also failed to provide any great satisfaction to any major economic or political group.

INFORMATIONAL NEEDS

Thus we establish a starting point in facing the basic issues; we are not expected to provide answers to all questions of values in agricultural policy. The planning committee hopes, however, that it will stimulate further research, thought and discussion in respect to goals and values as these relate to agricultural policy. But effort should not stop here. The goal and value conflicts which serve as obstacles to solution of major farm problems will not be resolved through exchange of ideas or improved hypotheses by a few score of professional persons. Neither will they be resolved by increased knowledge on the part of a few congressmen. Both national and farm policy are decided largely and ultimately by the public through the voting mechanism. Hence, goal and value conflicts may best be resolved through extended education.

In particular, land grant colleges and universities need to put much more emphasis on public affairs in extension and other educational programs. Perhaps not more than a dozen state extension services, covering only a small fraction of the nation's voters, now have as much as one full-time person assigned to public affairs education. National policy is not determined by the people of a dozen states, and increased public investment in this area is needed.

The specific objective of such education is not, of course, to impose values or value judgments on people. Instead, it is to provide objective facts and information and intelligent discussion so that: individuals can better identify alternative goals and formulate their values accordingly; they can better understand conditions of conflict and complementarity among various goals and ends; they can better evaluate the consequences of following different policy means; they can more effectively identify the most efficient and effective means for attaining particular policy ends; and they can even make improved distinction between ends and means.

Leaders among both farm and nonfarm publics are intelligent. Experience in states with broad social science and public affairs extension programs indicates that, given facts and information, people can better order and articulate their values, can better associate themselves with public goals, and can make more intelligent appraisal of policy means. However, there will continue to be too little basis for these steps important to public policy formulation and national purposes until more public educational institutions develop programs and devote more resources to this general area. Some may refrain from doing so because they fear the subjects involved are controversial. But again, experience of those states with broad extension education programs in social sciences indicates that this need not be so, if educators are objective and do not try to impose value judgments on the public they serve. In fact, the public image of land grant colleges and universities likely is larger, and public financial support is probably broader, where extensive educational programs in public affairs are carried on with the vigor of education in the production technology. The public image of the land grant colleges and universities needs to be broadened substantially beyond that of purveyors of production technology if these colleges and universities are to fulfill their role in helping people to understand the urgency of better defining our public purposes and in developing appropriate policy elements; then, if the contribution of further improvement in technology is to be understood better in terms of contribution to long-run national objectives, broad financial support should be made available for this program.

We hope to provide a more substantial basis than previously has existed for developing further hypotheses and research, as well as public knowledge and understanding, relative to the value conflicts in agricultural policy. It would be unfortunate, however, if organized effort in this direction were to cease with this perhaps small and tardy beginning.

VALUE AND POLICY CONFLICT

Not all answers will be given here to the goals and values problems because the phenomena are too broad and complex. In the first place, conflict does not arise over a set of near-ultimate goals or ends such as life, liberty and happiness. Western society agrees more or less unanimously on these "high level" or generalized ends, although as American society has become increasingly affluent and wealthy it has found itself more undecided and less unanimous on the means most appropriate to attain maximum happiness. But the operational problems confronting the public in deciding future farm policy involve ends which are not so easily identified and articulated. To a large extent the ends of life, liberty and happiness are complementary or noncompetitive. Over a fairly wide range, more of one may be attained without sacrifice of another, or even with a gain in another. Still, custom and legislation place restraints on liberty in order that freedom on the part of some individuals does not lessen the life and happiness of others.

But these issues are much sharper at the level of farm policy. Freedom of decision and action as a policy objective is directly competitive with production control as a policy means for attaining the intermediate policy end of increased prices or improved farm income. As mentioned previously, conflict on acceptable means exists even where we have agreement on such direct or intermediate goals as reducing the size of the farm surplus. Conflict is over the means, or the collection of means, to attain this specific goal in conjunction with other goals. On the one hand, we could use free market prices for this purpose, but at a particular short-run sacrifice in income and people in segments of farming. On the other hand, we could set marketing quotas for all products, but with particular restraint on the efficacy of prices and the decision freedoms of farmers. Here the conflict may be over specific means as they are tied to ends one step higher in the means-ends hierarchy. The means and ends themselves become intertwined and it becomes difficult for the public to distinguish among them. But in other cases the means take on the immediate characteristics of ends, as they almost always do in the means-ends chain, and public disagreement or conflict arises directly over the means themselves. Disagreement over means, which momentarily become ends of debate, has come into sharp focus over such agricultural policy mechanisms as direct payments, free market prices and cross compliance paired against their policy alternatives. Disagreement among these alternative means exists evidently because of differences in values in respect to what method ought to be used to alleviate a particular problem and attain a specific goal.

Intermediate goals in respect to number and size of farms and magnitude of the farm population also give rise to policy conflicts because of the heterogeneous values among segments of farm and nonfarm publics. A policy or market mechanism which leads to larger and fewer farms is, within the value structure of some farm people, the antithesis of all that has been good in the American way of life, even if nonprice mechanisms must be used to retain these conditions. Values which lead others to believe that greater play of prices is most consistent with the American way of life, even if substantial changes must result in size and number of farms and in magnitude of the farm population, are held just as deeply by others.

In general, then, means and ends are not discrete. Neither do ends or goals serve entirely as discrete alternatives with constant marginal rates of substitution. In the realm of human satisfaction and acceptance, the problem is not one of determining which discrete goal or end should be selected over another or all others. Instead, it is a problem of determining what mix or combination of goals, at the various levels in the means-ends hierarchy, is optimum, desirable or acceptable. This is true since the value system of an individual, community or society is not represented by an indifference map wherein the individual indifference curve is linear, denoting that each unit gain towards one goal causes an equal sacrifice in satisfaction for all units of other goals foregone. Instead, the indifference lines serving as the counterpart of social values in respect to goals for public policy are curved, denoting that a combination of competing goals or ends is necessary for maximizing quantities which are relevant both for the individual and the community. Under these conditions, one goal is seldom selected to the exclusion of all others. Instead, there exists some combination of competing goals, with some of one being sacrificed to gain part of another, which must be decided upon by society. Policies need to be melded accordingly and, even though the process is difficult, it is hoped that later papers can suggest the processes and feasibilities for doing so.

It is difficult to systematize and organize means for resolving all conflicts in public policy because the public itself is so heterogeneous. Except for crises such as those representing threats to national existence and continuance of the main thread of our social system, we do not attach ourselves to a single national purpose, with policies devoted mainly to this singular end. There is, in fact, not one public but many publics, each with a different goal for, or special interest in, economic structure and policy for agriculture. The policies most beneficial to one of these publics or special interest groups is often in contradiction to that most beneficial to another public or economic sector. Pressures develop accordingly around agricultural policy. Thus the firms which sell inputs to farmers, those which store surpluses or those who process farm products have interest in particular types of farm programs, some in conflict with each and some in conflict with programs directed towards solution of the farm income and surplus problems. Or, programs which serve to curtail output or adjust the labor force and population of agriculture, as a means of price improvement and surplus control, are not those which correspond to the particular interests of local businesses and public institutions in rural communities. But even at the farm level, numerous publics exist and have interest in different types of farm policies or, in some cases, different goals for policy. Some farmers sell feed and are interested in high support prices for grain; others use it as a livestock input and are interested in buying it at a low price. Farm publics also differ in interest by geographic and commodity groupings, or even by size and scale of operations. In general, the consuming public may desire abundant and cheap food while the farm-producing public might prefer greater scarcity and higher prices.

Out of this maze of interest groups must be melded agricultural policy elements which allow reasonable attainment of broader national purposes and goals. The task is not impossible and perhaps is easier than our current maze and the sometimes inconsistent set of farm policy elements would lead us to believe. Some, but certainly not all, of the conflicts in agricultural policy arise because the public lacks information before action programs are put into effect. In important cases, the public is unaware that two policy elements, existing side by side, are in opposition in respect to attainment of particular objectives or goals. Sometimes it does not realize that greater attainment of one goal requires sacrifice in another.

Our present agricultural and food policy structure abounds with elements which conflict as ends or as means of attaining a particular objective. On the one hand we have programs which pay farmers to use inputs which increase output. Payments, under the label of soil conservation, for irrigation or soil amendments used on level land are examples. On the other hand, we have used direct payments to farmers to lessen land and related inputs as a means of decreasing output. Other conflicting policy elements and goals are less apparent or arise unwittingly. An example may be the desire for abundant and low cost food for consumers. A century back, with higher demand elasticities for food, this goal may have been entirely consistent with improved incomes for farmers. But gradually over time, as per capita income has increased and demand elasticities have declined, abundant and low cost food for consumers has come to conflict with farm income, at least starting from the structure in number and size of farms that has existed. Even in academic circles, land grant colleges and universities find that the "close at hand" goals, with which they have believed themselves to serve the public, also may conflict. The efficiency of the research and extension education departments, for example, in providing the foundation for a new structure of farming, has caused the resident teaching departments to wonder why they have fewer undergraduate students to service.

LEVELS OF GENERALIZED VALUES

An important question on goals and values is: At what level of generalization can we identify goals or values which have broad acceptance by the diverse publics or sectors of our society? The goals of life, liberty and happiness are too broad and general to be used in formulating acceptable and workable farm policies. Even at this level of generalization, however, we could not obtain agreement by all sectors on farm policy. While all sectors of agriculture undoubtedly would agree on liberty for our society — in the sense of freedom for the nation to govern itself without interference by an outside country — they do not agree similarly on complete liberty in production and marketing decisions. On the one hand, we have strong insistence by some organized groups that this freedom of decision be retained or returned to the farm industry. But just as vigorously, other groups campaign for more control over production and marketing. Some farm groups have democratically voted production controls and sacrifice of some liberty in decisions. Examples are those of tobacco and wheat. But even farmers who are homogeneous in the sense that they derive their income from cattle do not agree in respect to liberty in decisions. Cattle ranchers stump strongly for freedom, but dairy farmers in major milk sheds willingly accept quotas and marketing orders.

At a somewhat lower level in generalization are the more mechanical goals of economics. Two general goals exist in welfare economics and are directed toward maximization of utility or satisfaction by a society. These are efficiency in production and efficiency in consumption and the optimum allocation of resources and income respectively among persons, commodities, time periods and locations. Criteria exist, in marginal terms, as a means of specifying subgoals or conditions which must exist if the two over-all welfare economic goals are to be attained. These criteria recognize also that reorganization of economic activity and structures which result in gain to the community or society may cause sacrifice and diminished utility to particular sectors of it. However, because of the inability to make exact interpersonal utility comparisons, principles of compensation are specified to assure that when some persons or groups are made "better off," none are made "worse off."

In a general way, society has subscribed to these general goals in economic organization. When it condemns land for public buildings or highways, it compensates the owners. Through the Sherman Act and other antitrust legislation, attempts were made to assure a degree of competition which is reasonably consistent with the subgoals or marginal conditions which must exist for the more general goal of efficiency of production. To assure some minimum level of consumption, roughly consistent with necessary marginal conditions for an optimum allocation of income, we have provided unemployment compensation, public schools, food distribution to the needy and have endorsed the progressive income tax. For farm policy in particular, the various subsidy schemes used over the last three decades probably are a societal reflection of the compensation principle. The public investment in making food abundant depresses income under the low price elasticities of demand which prevail for farm products. Hence, we might interpret the various farm price and income support devices as an act of society to compensate farmers for the income sacrifice which they experience under our policy of abundant and low cost food as a product of our efficient public research and education institutions and certain other policies in agriculture.

But obviously, society has not subscribed fully to the over-all goals, or to the particular subgoals and marginal conditions, of modern welfare economics. To do so might be considered interference with other value-goal orientations. It has placed restraints on extremes in monopoly power, but it has not reduced industry organization, even where increasing scale returns are unimportant, to the pure competition model in order that the appropriate marginal conditions prevail. To do so would conflict, perhaps, with liberty or freedom in decision, or even with the "American business way."

At a less general goal-value level in economics, we have such goals as economic progress, equity in income distribution and stability in income, the latter being a reference to maintenance of business stability and employment opportunities. These goals are "less strenuous," in the sense that they do not require the "tight" marginal conditions associated with the text in welfare economics. Society may simply define the degree to which these goals are desirable, or failure to attain them is undesirable. Maximum and/or minimum restraints are expressed accordingly through social policy. Evidently most individual publics or groups which make up American society desire economic progress. Yet we have no evidence that the maximum rate of economic growth is desired.[1] Any leading economist or businessman could mention a dozen ways in which obstacles to progress could be lessened and the rate of economic growth accelerated. Greater public investment in education, improved counseling and employment services, aid to underdeveloped communities and elimination of featherbedding and particular monopoly restraints in use of technologies are examples. Still we accept a less-than-maximum rate of growth, even though economic progress is an obvious national purpose, because it is not an ultimate goal and is not valued discretely at a higher level than all other goals. Perhaps in agriculture we are even indicating that the rate of progress exceeds that acceptable relative to other goals and values. The adjustment in size and number of farms and the size of the farm population has promised to be more rapid than can be assimilated by rural communities, given the particular value orientation around previous agricultural structures. This possibility is suggested in the income transfer payments we make to farmers, tending to hold them to agriculture and the rural community when the flow of new technology and the pressures of the market would detach more of them from these bases.

Another step down the ladder of goal generality is represented by those rooted in economics, political science and sociology and tied directly to farming. To mention a few, we have: preservation of the family farm; the Jeffersonian doctrine of a large rural population to insure democracy; or even the sometimes-stated policy goal of guarantee that not all the social cost stemming from the share of national progress attributable to agriculture falls on farm people. But again, while society may have accepted these more specific goals for agriculture, it has not attempted to "maximize" them because they fail to serve as discrete goals substituting at a high and constant marginal rate for goals of other orientation.

---

[1] Too, while American society has reflected a goal of some equity in income distribution, it has not tried to maximize this goal. Rather, it more nearly has tried to provide a minimum in level in availability of consumption opportunities.

Agricultural scientists have themselves espoused less general goals for agriculture which represent value judgements. In the technical fields, at the time surpluses began to become continuous and permanent, some have attempted justification of their efforts with the value-loaded statement, "but we will always want efficiency," referring to efforts to increase output from our agricultural resources. Similarly in economics, while less so now than a decade back, some agricultural policy experts evidently selected the economic efficiency model as an end. Supposing the marginal conditions for equilibrium, they have said, "we ought to move people from farms in order that marginal productivity of farm labor might be increased." There are, of course, two ways in which the marginal productivity of labor in agriculture might be increased and selection of one over the other itself requires a value judgement. Given the inelastic demands for farm products, increased supply control or monopolistic marketing practices are an alternative to reduction of the agricultural labor force as a means of increasing the marginal return of farm work. Used in a degree in certain nonfarm industries, production quotas and monopolistic output and price policies evidently are not in major conflict with the basic value system of American society. Yet one of the major conflicts in agricultural policy is over this very issue.

Apparently, then, it is difficult to identify a level of generality in goals and values which might remove all conflicts in farm policies. If it were impossible to do so, we could throw up our hands and go home. But the "guts" of the farm problem lies in the area of goals and values and we believe important progress here is possible. The situation is confused because the problem has not been sufficiently and specifically recognized as one of goals and values. We have not, in fact, spelled out goals for policy and structure of agriculture with any specific content. Largely we have tried to use "patch up" policies, attempting programs which simply take care of the "problems of this planting season," without examining their longer-run effect. We have done little to decide where we want to go in agricultural structure, given the prospects and pulls of national economic growth and our growing challenges in world society. It is not impossible that the diverse economic sectors with interest in agriculture could agree on some general goals for the agriculture which should exist for 1970 or 1975. Then we could use short-run policies which alleviate problems of the moment but do not lead us far astray from the longer-run target. From study, for example, it appears that many farm couples who wish income supports so that they may remain in agriculture do not hold firmly to this goal and policy for their sons.

Too, progress will be made when the many opposing groups in
farm policy recognize the problem as one of goals and values,
with conflict being at particular levels in goal-value generality.
In communication, they might well find themselves in agreement
for certain goals of high generality and greater length of time.
With differences arising over more specific goals and short-run
policies, greater agreement would be possible. Then recognizing
that values and goals are not discrete, substituting at constant
rates and entirely for each other, the optimum mix of policy elements might be more nearly attained, recognizing the particular
values of each sector. Unfortunately, at the present, groups differing in respect to major farm policy elements seem to be shout-
ing at each other and to the general public: "... only our values
and goals should prevail; yours should be submerged."
    The real positive prospect is that the farm problem will be
recognized as one in goals and values, and education and communication will be developed accordingly. Progress will then be in
sight and citizens will have a foundation for more clearly seeing
the basis and consequences of particular policy courses. In their
own minds, they will have information for formulating and articulating goals which are meaningful to themselves, to the growth
trends of the national economy and to the nation's world responsibilities.
    We adhere to this hypothesis. The public has not been given
the probable outcome of particular policies, even where these
were quite apparent. They have not been sufficiently informed of
the compatibility or conflict among different agricultural policy
elements, or between these and other developments such as national economic development. Often they cannot visualize the
outcome of a particular program because the universe with which
they are acquainted is too small. Too frequently, policies have
been enacted in an informational void. This is true for several
important national policies, as well as those for agriculture specifically. Foreign policy is no exception. Generally we have
been short of funds for certain national purposes in this respect.
But still there has been no systematic and organized informational effort to explain objectively the needs and consequences of
these investments. Their purposes and outcomes are only held
vaguely in the minds of most people.

PERSPECTIVE IN AMERICAN SOCIETY

    Partly, the need for a basic examination of goals and values
for agricultural organization and policy has, as is true for our

growing concern for better defining our national purposes, simply "crept up on us." The physical and economic structure of agriculture has been changing rapidly, largely as a result of (a) the rapid flow of new technology into the industry and (b) continued national economic growth, affecting both the relative rewards of resources used in different industries and the consumption opportunities open to people. Agricultural production is oriented increasingly toward and highly integrated with the dominant commercial-industrial interests and social systems of our total society. Modern agriculture, its changes and its problems, must be analyzed and explained in terms of the major developments in American society. Its value systems, goal patterns, social organization, technical development, and its recurring social, political and economic crises are inseparable from those of our total society. For these reasons, we are approaching the examination of one contemporary American social problem — that of agriculture — from the broad perspective of development in American society, not just the agricultural sector per se. Attention is focused upon general value-goal patterns of American society, and then within this context, upon value-goal patterns which pertain to the structure and functioning of the American agricultural industry.

To many students of society, this approach is the only reasonable one in analysis of any social phenomena because value patterns define which developments should be construed as "problems" or "progress." Furthermore, general value systems prescribe the legitimate or acceptable means which can be used to ameliorate conditions otherwise precluding the attainment of societally desirable goals. Unfortunately, however, in the analyses of variables which have led to the present imbalance between the agricultural and nonagricultural sectors of our society and which may contribute to the solution of this imbalance, value or goal patterns are frequently assumed or ignored. Even where they are recognized, seldom are they clearly articulated.

This conference has as one objective an explicit examination of value-goal patterns as these impede or facilitate current and future developments designed to bring incomes in agriculture to levels comparable with nonfarm economic activity, or to adjust resource use in the directions expressed through the pulls of the market. Of course, that either of these ends should be attained is itself a value judgement.

We live in the midst of an international crisis requiring us to re-examine our national values and goals, as well as the policies for attaining these goals. The present ferment and discussion on national goals and values has direct relevance for agricultural

policy, rural community development and farm family living. In
turn, examination of the value-goal patterns as these relate to
the agricultural sector of our society can contribute to a clarification of our national goals and values. However, the problem of
clarifying goals and values for American agriculture is complicated by at least two sets of conditions, both of which have been
referred to previously: (1) the rapid shift in relative demand for
farm and nonfarm labor, with consequent changes in population
and in the American social structure and (2) the increasing heterogeneity of the American society. Later participants in this
program will examine these and related factors in greater detail.
However, brief consideration of them is appropriate at this point,
to further indicate the need and urgency for examining the value-
goal systems of American agriculture specifically.

Relative Composition of Labor Force and Population

First, we have become fond of comparing the relatively isolated farm community of the pre-twentieth century era, with its
essentially closed social system and local marketing arrangements, with the contemporary rural scene which has and still is
undergoing vast technical and social change. However, these
comparisons are generally focused upon overt technological and
social differences. Profound changes in value systems also have
been involved. In the relatively isolated, self-sufficient community of the last century, values were integrated around the institutions of the local community: the farm family, the church and
local government. Under impact of the technological, demographic and social changes of this century, a new agriculture,
closely integrated with industries and businesses supplying its
inputs and receiving its outputs, has been emerging. These
changes are expressed in an increased number of large commercial farms, as well as an increase in part-time farming. It also
is expressed in such developments as: contract farming or vertical integration; growth of farmers' cooperatives which integrate
agricultural production with many other functions of production,
marketing and consumption; and marketing arrangements and
orders designed to maintain price differentials. Agriculture has
become increasingly dependent on both government programs and
the "agribusiness" sector of the economy. These changes have
required a reintegration of values, a process which is not fully
completed and which is weighted with economic and political
motivations.
        While these technical, demographic, economic and value-goal

changes have taken place at rapid pace, value premises upon which public pronouncements have been based concerning the state of agriculture and the ideas and beliefs regarding the social, moral and personal values of rural life, have been less dynamic. Clearly the values associated with the appeal of urban-centered conveniences and the acquisition of the goods and services of the "good life" are binding both farming operations and the aspirations of farm families closer to the business-industrial economy of the United States. At the same time, however, values associated with the tenacity of ideas rooted in Jeffersonian democracy and rural idealism are still reflected in appeals of agricultural policy. Failure to adjust our image of rural America and to adapt policies, which are expressions of value statements, consistent with the economic, technological and social characteristics of modern agriculture is probably a main cause of our inability to make demonstrable progress in solving the pressing surplus and income problems of the industry.

Our inability to identify a set of values and goals for American agriculture which is consistent with our national and international goals is, in part, a reflection of the characteristics of values themselves: value systems provide internalized guides, invested with a high degree of affect and meaning for participants. Goal-directed behavior associated with values is felt to be binding for the personality, conscience, life goals, preferred material acquisitions and subjective states of various kinds. These characteristics change slowly, both at the individual level and at the institutionalized or group level. These emotionally laden characteristics of value-goal systems need to be kept in mind constantly as agricultural adjustment proposals are made.

Heterogeneity of Society

The second point for discussion in clarifying goal-value systems as they relate to solutions of agricultural problems is the heterogeneous character of American society. At one time, perhaps prior to the Civil War, generalized American values and goals were those of an agricultural people. But today, the basic orientation for economic, political and social activities in the United States is that of gesellschaft integration based on industrial production and commercialism, as well as bureaucratic organization. This orientation is opposed to the earlier gemeinschaft character of personal relations which dominated the economic, political and social life of rural society. Because of the gesellschaft character of the American society and the varied social and ethnic composition of our population, it is not surprising to find that American society does not have a completely consistent and integrated value structure. Rather, the total society is characterized by diversity and varying rates of change in value patterns. This is true within agriculture, as well as for the total society. Understandably, then, the farm policies which appeal to one sector of agriculture do not appeal to other sectors. Some of our major policy conflicts stem from the fact that the different sectors of agriculture do not recognize this condition and attempt to cause all of agriculture to embrace their policy proposals, and hence their construct of values.

The complex division of labor, regional differentials in economic growth, overlapping of farm and urban areas of residence and socialization and the proliferation of special interest institutions and organizations themselves give rise to value-goal differentials. These developments tend to increase the saliency of value-goal patterns around which institutions are formed and to insulate different value-goal patterns from one another. Potential conflict and strain, as well as potential reinforcement and integration, are thereby avoided. Yet such insulation is difficult to maintain in the open system of the American social order. A foremost characteristic of the American social order is its integration around economic and political foci and the delicate interdependence of these two structures. Because of this high degree of interdependence, groups holding differing and frequently incompatible values not only become aware of one another, but interact directly. In the national social system, this awareness and interaction lead to political struggle.

The recurring farm policy debate is ample evidence of this process. The debate continues because values relative to economic and political action in American society in general and for American agriculture in particular are not clearly defined. At this point, it is redundant to say that the degree to which government should be involved in American agriculture is a controversial question. But this controversy continues because there are value differences between farm and urban interest groups and within the farm sector of society. There is diversity of value systems directly in relation to the desired structure and functioning of American agriculture. Frequently large commercial farmers or owners adhere to different value-goal patterns for agriculture, at least over their commodity grouping, than do smaller farm owners and operators. Different commodity groups have value-goal patterns which reflect their particularistic interests, rather than the universalistic agricultural or national interests. Still other value-goal patterns for American agriculture are endorsed by the representatives of the "agribusiness" organizations. This diversity complicates the analysis of values and goals of or for American agriculture. However, it is essential to maintain this comprehensive view of values if policy is to be analyzed effectively. We do not infer that value-goal systems held by these and other groups are static and operate in isolation as separate units. Instead, value frames of reference are constantly shifting and recombining in configurations stemming from the processes of change, interdependence, conflict, adaptation and reformulation. Agricultural policy prescriptions by persons in action groups in and related to agriculture, as well as by nonfarm persons and groups, are involved in this ferment of social interaction. Eventually this interaction is reflected in the political process, the only means which we have for melding the aspirations of the various groups and for correcting policy voids or excesses accordingly.

GENERAL SOCIAL VALUES

Emphasis above was on the heterogeneous character of groupings in American society and the concomitant value differences. We do not wish to imply that there are no more or less general values of American society. Without some degree of value integration, even if only at a high level of abstraction, no society could function inter-generationally, assimilate new elements, adjust to internal and external demands and still maintain its distinctive character. American society, as all societies, does have some degree of value integration. These generalized values provide one basis for appeal for resolving conflicts which prevent solution of the most pressing problems of American agriculture. Generalized values are especially characterized as those which are complementary among the various publics or interest groups of society. Hence, a starting point, in obtaining agreement on farm policy, might be identification of these areas of complementarity in goals and values. Following this, compatible adjustments and compensation to minimize sacrifice of particular groups or to cause no group to be made "worse off" for the gain of others, might be made where competitive goals and value systems are involved. It is an ambitious hope that this volume may sow seeds leading in this systematic direction.

Some dominant values in American society can be identified at a high level of abstract inference. Among generalized value sets which might be mentioned, Robin Williams suggests the dominant value themes of American society to be the following:[2] (1) active mastery of the natural world, rather than passive acceptance; (2) interest in the external world of things and events rather than the internal world of meaning and affect; (3) an open rather than closed world view, with emphasis on change and personal types which are outgoing and assimilative; (4) faith based in rationalism as opposed to traditionalism, with de-emphasis on the past and orientation based towards the future; (5) acceptance of a universalistic rather than a particularistic ethic; (6) preference for "horizontal" rather than "vertical" interpersonal relations: peer-relations, not superordinate-subordinate relations, equality rather than hierarchy; and (7) emphasis on individual personality rather than group identity and responsibility.

Such generalized value patterns include specific orientations which guide behavior in the economic, political and social arenas of interaction. Specific orientations characteristic of American society include a set of work-related values such as achievement and success, activity and work, efficiency and practicality, material comforts and science and secular rationality; and a set of political-related variables such as respect for individual personality, equality, freedom, democracy and humanitarianism. Conflicts among these goals are obvious in application to specific aspects of American behavior or farm programs, again largely because goals are not discrete with constant marginal rates of substitution.

RESOLVING VALUE CONFLICTS FOR AGRICULTURE

To the extent that generalized value orientations can be identified for American society, given the rapid change taking place in economic and social structure and the particular adaptations that other resource and production groups have made for themselves, agriculture and the community in general must resolve certain value conflicts as they relate to farming. Some of the more important ones appear to be the following:

1. To what extent can farm policies, determined democratically, depriving farmers of individual choice of compliance or noncompliance be reconciled with freedom?

2. Should farmers be given as much control over price as other major economic sectors of American industry, given the forward progress in economic and technical development of

---

[2] Robin Williams, American Society. Knopf, New York. 1951. Pp. 388-442.

agriculture, or should the agricultural environment be re-
strained to one of pure market competition among farmers?

3. To what extent can we afford to give priority to value and goal
patterns focused on material comforts as compared to maintaining a sufficient posture for protecting values inherent in
our desire for freedom and equality?

4. Will our success in emphasizing efficiency in agricultural
production, as implemented by science, technology and secular
rationality, require that values associated with work and activity or achievement and success be adjusted in the direction
of greater leisure?

5. To what extent can we resolve the desire for security and stability in economic affairs and the rapid rate of technical progress and structural change in agriculture?

6. Do values associated with achievement and success and work
and activity make us less sensitive to values associated with
humanitarianism? United States agricultural surpluses and
world food shortages come to mind as a concrete example.

Other questions could be raised, but we leave these to persons presenting the remaining chapters.

In this discussion we have attempted to indicate the importance of analyzing general values and goals in relation to those of
agriculture. If progress is to be made in the solution of current
agricultural problems, value and goal patterns with respect to
the structure and functioning of agriculture, held by various sub-
groups of American society with conflicting value-goal patterns
in respect to American agriculture, must be articulated as
clearly as possible. Probable consequences of these value-goal
patterns must be analyzed as objectively as possible.

We hope this presentation will contribute to these ends.
Chapters by Nelson Foote, Harry Jaffa and Don Martindale provide the broad framework for viewing value and goal patterns of
American society. Values and goals for economic organization
of American society are viewed by Jesse Markham. John Brewster next deals with societal values and goals in respect to agriculture. This is followed by Olaf Larson's chapter on the goals
and values of farm people, and Dale Hathaway's on goals for
economic organization of agriculture. Goal conflicts associated
with various agricultural programs as seen from the frame of
reference of different groups of farm and nonfarm related persons are analyzed by Don Kaldor, Ward Bauder and Howard Hines.
Ross Talbot focuses on the trends in the political position of agriculture.

The foregoing chapters are essentially analytical. Attention is shifted from the level of analysis to that of projection or inference in the remaining chapters. The first of this last group, by Kenneth Bachman and Ed Bishop, describes the structure of agriculture if it were made consistent with societal values and goals for economic organization. Lyle Shannon assesses the rates of change in agricultural production which may be tolerable in terms of their impact on the structure and functioning of other segments of our society and in terms of the value and goal orientation for the proper structure and functioning of family, community and national social systems. Farm policy programs which are acceptable in terms of the values of farm people are described by Lauren Soth. Finally, Boris Swerling and John Schnittker, using the preceding material as a base, attempt to formulate agricultural policy elements for the 1960's which are most consistent with the basic economic and social values for agriculture and for the total society. The various able discussants will "fill in the gaps" and extend the analyses in these general areas, with George Mehren tying them together in the final chapter.

The authors provide the frame of reference for discussion. One of the contributions, we hope, will be the stimulating and critical questions which will be raised by their presentations. Active participation by all persons in this field will contribute to providing a broad frame of reference for the direction of education, research and action programs related to the adjustment of agriculture in the 1960's.

JAMES G. MADDOX
North Carolina State College

Discussion

AFTER SETTING forth the thesis that the major problems of farm policy are in the realm of goals and values, Professors Heady and Burchinal center their attention on three problems: (1) the sources of value and policy conflicts; (2) the level of generalization at which goals and values that will be acceptable to various sectors of society can be identified; and (3) the need for analysis, discussion and extension education as a basis for resolving conflicts among goals, values and policies.

Their effort is commendable. There has often been a disposition among agricultural economists to try to close their eyes to value problems. This tendency appears to stem from two sources:

(1) the fear economists have of being branded as unscientific or partisan, and (2) uncritical acceptance of the view that economists should limit their studies to alternative means of achieving predetermined ends. A corollary of the latter view is that the choice of ends should be left to such dubiously qualified people as philosophers, moralists, statesmen and run-of-the-mill politicians, or to that vaguely defined entity called "society." Heady and Burchinal provide a forceful argument for the agricultural economist to recognize goals and value judgments as a necessary part of the grist to be ground in his mill.

In the section pertaining to "Value and Policy Conflict" they make at least three instructive points. First, they contend that conflicts about farm policy arise mainly over intermediate goals, as distinguished from higher order or more ultimate goals, and over means by which goals can be achieved. Second, they point out that means and ends are not discrete, and that important problems arise in determining the mix, or combination, of goals which is optimum, desirable or acceptable. Third, they point out that "there is not one public but many publics, each with a different goal for, or special interest in, economic structure and policy for agriculture."

In a later section entitled "Perspective in American Society," where they examine some of the general patterns of values in American society and the relationship of these to values which pertain specifically to agriculture, they are, in effect, continuing their analysis of sources of conflict between values and policies. Here they point to the complications which have arisen because of: "(1) the rapid shift in relative demand for farm and nonfarm labor, with consequent changes in population and in the American social structure and (2) the increasing heterogeneity of the American society." As a result of the former, a new, highly commercialized and specialized agriculture is rapidly emerging, but changes in value judgments are lagging. We have a situation in which 18th and 19th century values are being applied to 20th century problems. The increasing heterogeneity of our social structure brings value conflicts between urban and rural sectors and between various groups, regional and economic, within agriculture.

All of the major points in these sections seem to me to be both valid and valuable. In a sense they are elementary, but they are also fundamental. Once we recognize the existence of numerous "publics," each with a combination of goals, no one of which is held to the exclusion of others, and each combination of which may in fact be means of attaining higher order goals, and once we recognize the numerous conflicts which arise from the disparities between rates of change in values and rate of change in the technological and structural characteristics of society, the problem of resolving policy conflicts becomes extremely complicated. The ordinary procedure of the economist in choosing one fairly clear-cut goal and describing the conditions necessary for its maximization appears to be a rather puny effort alongside of the "real McCoy." Indirectly, therefore, the authors of this first chapter have humbled us, if not humiliated us, to the point where we should be eager to study the subsequent chapters. Hopefully, the latter will provide us with guides out of the forest.

When Professors Heady and Burchinal turn to a discussion of what I believe to be their second main problem, they appear to be less fruitful than in other parts of their discussion. In that section entitled "Levels of Generalized Values," they pose as important the question: "At what level of generalization can we identify goals or values which have broad acceptance by the diverse publics or sectors of society?" After discussing several types of goals, and various difficulties of resolving conflicts that are associated with each, they conclude: "... it is difficult to identify a level of generality in goals and values which might remove all conflicts in farm policies. If it were impossible to do so, we could throw up our hands and go home." They eschew this alternative, however, by asserting a faith that progress can be made. They buttress this position of optimism in two ways: first, by a few critical swipes at our tendency to use "patch up" policies and our failure to spell out "goals for policy and structure of agriculture with any specific content;" and second, by the prospect, or perhaps it is the hope, "that the farm problem will be recognized as one in goals and values, and education and communication will be developed accordingly."

All of this seems to me to be less than satisfactory. I may read into this discussion implications which are unwarranted, but this part of their chapter seems to be searching for a will-o'-the-wisp — for some kind of a magic, verbal statement of goals which "might remove all conflicts in farm policies." This is reminiscent of the Knights of the Round Table searching for the Holy Grail. I believe that the difficulty arises from an erroneous view of the policy-making process. Therefore, I want to suggest an alternative view to that which I think is implied by Professors Heady and Burchinal. In a very sketchy form it is as follows:

1. In the society in which we live conflicts about values, and hence about policies, are endemic, widespread, continuing and complex in origin.

2. They have to be resolved and re-resolved in a continuous

process of adjustment and redefinition of values, goals and policies.

3. With our pluralistic form of social organization, conflicts are commonly resolved by horse trading and bargaining, that is, by negotiation and renegotiation, the results of which are a continuing series of temporary armistices.

4. The principal negotiators are the officials of large organizations such as corporations, trade associations, labor unions, associations of farmers and government.

5. This process of bargaining is dynamic and continuing. Thus, there is a never-ending stream of temporary armistices issuing forth as results.

6. Government officials — legislators, administrators and jurists — play a double role in this process. They function both as negotiators and as command givers. They are, therefore, of key importance.

7. Some of the temporary armistices may develop into permanent peace treaties. To the extent that this occurs, it is likely to be discovered by the historian several years after the fact.

8. When a cluster of these temporary armistices about issues which significantly alter the allocation of power among various groups and classes in society crystallize into permanent peace treaties within a relatively few years, we have one of those rare "watersheds" or "turning points" in history. We often call these "revolutions."

With this sketch of a conceptual model before us, we ask: What is the role of the social scientist in resolving policy conflicts? I am by no means sure that I know the answer, but I do not believe that it is to search for some idealized level of generalization in the statement of goals and values which is supposed to remove policy conflicts. A more fruitful endeavor, I suggest, is to explore the characteristics of the processes which both originate and resolve conflicts about particular goals, values and policies, and from such explorations to accumulate knowledge which will enable him to suggest specific social techniques that will aid in bringing about temporary armistices.

Let me try to illustrate how this general line of thinking might be applied to a specific policy problem. One of the important present conflicts revolves around the extent to which national bargaining versus free market prices is to be used as a mechanism for pricing farm products and allocating agricultural

resources to different uses. Former Secretary of Agriculture
Benson, many businessmen and the top officials of one of the
farm organizations are on the side of the free market mechanism. A good many important legislators and the officials of
other farm organizations view national bargaining, at least for
some farm products, in a very favorable light. Other people, including not a few agricultural economists, are on one side or the
other. Various and sundry types of arguments are used in support of each view. For several years, progress toward an armistice has been blocked mainly because the pertinent leaders of
the legislative and executive branches of government are on opposite sides of the issue. While the bargaining goes on, the farm
income situation worsens, and the growing size of the surplus
stockpile brings embarrassment to all of us.

Faced with this situation, what should the agricultural economist do? Clearly, we must permit him to write papers and read
them before his colleagues. If we deny him this opportunity, he
will come apart at the seams and the profession will disappear.
I suggest two broad, and admittedly rather vague, areas in which
he might fruitfully exercise his paper-writing predilections.

First, the nature of the problem needs to be sharply defined
so that the principal negotiators can bargain about common issues. As a first step in this direction, I suggest that the problem
pertains mainly to the delegation of authority. It can be stated as
follows: To what extent should the citizens of this country delegate the authority to price farm products to individual producers,
consumers and traders in market places, and to what extent
should they delegate this authority to organized groups and to
government?

Other people may see the problem from different perspectives, and have other definitions. But, at least, here is an area
which needs further exploration by the social scientists. We
need to educate the negotiators to visualize clearly what they are
bargaining about. I suspect that they are now bargaining about
two quite different issues, each of which is based in different
sets of traditional values. Those who support national bargaining
as a substitute for free market pricing appear to do so on the
ground that it is a mechanism for putting farmers in a position of
greater equality with other groups in society. Their goal is
equality of pricing power for farmers. A good deal of their argument, however, runs in terms of the level at which farm products
should be priced. The opponents of national bargaining on the
other hand, are not apparently really concerned about the level of
prices. They fear the reallocation of power in society, especially
the role which government would play, if national bargaining were

substituted for free market pricing. The values on which their
views are based are essentially those associated with the concept
of laissez faire.

After the nature of the problem is clarified, and bargainers
are in this way encouraged to negotiate about common issues, the
second major area in which the social scientist can contribute is
to outline the forms of organization and the principles of action
which are consistent with each of the alternative pricing mechanisms. Agricultural economists have done considerable work
which is relevant to questions of consistency. There is, however,
much unworked ground. I will mention only two examples. First,
too little attention has been given to the kinds of authority which
should be delegated to the executive branch, if government organization is to be consistent with national bargaining as a pricing mechanism. Likewise, too little attention has been given to
questions of how the two types of pricing mechanisms, and the
level and degree of stability in prices which is likely to be associated with each, will probably affect different sizes and types of
farms in various regions. These are but two examples. I am
sure that many more questions of consistency merit the analytical attention of social scientists.

In the preceding paragraphs I have tried to sketch out a view
about the policy-making process, and to offer a few tentative
suggestions about the way in which social scientists can make a
contribution to understanding, and hence resolving, policy conflicts. I was moved to attempt this because I felt that Professors
Heady and Burchinal were on the wrong track in trying to identify
a level of generalization in the statement of goals and values
which would eliminate policy conflicts. In my view, we will never
eliminate policy conflicts in any meaningful sense of that term.
However, I see much valuable work which the social scientist can
perform in helping the participants in the policy-making process
move from temporary armistice to temporary armistice. This
may not be an appealing role to many agricultural economists. I
only suggest that those who insist on finding an ultimate solution
ask themselves if they haven't defined their problem incorrectly.

Goals and Values and Social Action: A Model With Complications

A S IT IS nowadays the fashion to say, let us take a simple model and then complicate it.

Several years ago, with two colleagues, I had occasion to review the annual reports of a large number of family-serving agencies in the Chicago metropolitan area. Most annual reports of nonprofit institutions consist simply of a list of activities, buttered with self-praise and including discreet allusions to needed finances. By contrast, most annual reports of profit-making institutions consist mainly of financial data, with little examination or evaluation of activities. But among the several hundred reports we studied, a few stood out as sophisticated instruments for self-scrutiny. Among these, one in particular appealed to us, which furnishes the beginning model here.

It was the annual report of a famous maternity hospital, one that has influenced maternity hospitals and maternity wards everywhere. This hospital was established about a half century ago on the novel proposition that giving birth is not a disease; therefore, mothers and new infants should be treated as such, in facilities more precisely appropriate to their characteristics.

The founders of this hospital were especially concerned with the reduction of mortality, which they hoped to reduce first of all by separating mothers and infants from diseased hospital patients. Health, in a word, was their most generalized value, maternal and infant health a more specific form of this value, and the reduction of maternal and infant mortality, their concrete objective. There are a few problems of definition in calculating mortality rates — for example, how should the hospital count miscarriages and premature births — but usually deaths are easy to count, a quantitative index that is both convenient and valid. And once in possession of such a workable index, the hospital was prepared to specify definite goals for each year of its operation. The two mortality series in its annual report show a steady decline toward a steady low level at present.

25

ACHIEVEMENT OF PREVIOUS GOALS GIVES RISE TO NEW

In the early years, these goals were expressed in reaching so many deaths per thousand; in later years, by virtue of repeated success in achieving goals, further goals in reducing mortality have had to be expressed in tenths. And here we come to the first major complication of our model: As time has gone on, and further reductions of maternal and infant mortality have become more and more difficult to obtain, even in tenths, the hospital, by virtue of its long record of success, has been forced to define new goals, and even new specific values. Even so, its newer goals and values have developed consistently with its original commitment to health. To illustrate, its staff has worked hard to ascertain and correct the causes of blindness among premature infants; the hospital now operates one of the leading clinics for treating infertility; its well-baby clinic keeps track of infants long after they leave its walls; and for several years it has been experimenting with classes for expectant fathers.

What can be witnessed in the black-and-white statistical series showing the decline of mortality rates over the years among mothers and babies in this hospital is not only a magnificent story of medical achievement, but an equally interesting example of how values and goals and social action can be conceived scientifically.

There is little direct evidence in the annual report of the hospital to prove my next point, apart from the meticulous measurements that are recorded, but in my judgment the inference is justified that systematic self-scrutiny by the hospital itself contributed importantly to the regular progress that is still going on. A second inference is more arguable: To judge from the histories of other agencies, it seems to me that without such a built-in device for knowing at all times where it is going, the hospital would long since have dropped into the slumber of routine which claims most institutions after they have satisfied their original impulses; perhaps by now it would have been superseded by some new institution set up to realize new goals.

In other words, our simple model is not as simple as it may have seemed when first stated. For our contemporaries who like to talk of models as representations of systems, we have already pointed out that the hospital is an open-ended system, stretching through time. The new goals and values which emerge may appear retrospectively to flow logically out of the original statements of purpose, but in fact they were not predictable by deduction. There has been repeated uncertainty as to which way to turn; alternatives have been numerous and possible; mistakes

have occurred, and opportunities have been wasted. The hospital
has critics, for example, who are not loath to denounce it for ne-
glecting the approaches of natural childbirth, rooming-in and
psychotherapy. Its scheme of rational self-direction is as open
to uncertainty and controversy as any other institution, but it is
a scheme which proceeds by putting its practices — both present
and proposed — continually to the test of objective measurement
of results.

PRACTICES ARE EVALUATED BY RESULTS

Another complication already implicit in the practice of the
hospital is that its commitment is not to its practices but to their
results. It is the results which are sacred, not the practices.
And this aspect, however innocuous it may sound, is a radical
difference between the maternity hospital and most other agencies and institutions, which concentrate more on effort than effect. Where most annual reports abound with florid descriptions
of their activities — nowadays often with pictures in four colors —
this hospital's fairly brief report abounded in tables and charts,
showing rates of change in various indices, in comparison both
with the past and with regional and national contemporary norms.
The activities and the facilities are described, to be sure, but
they are taken to represent the effort put forth. The value of
such effort is not judged by its volume nor by the good intentions
which motivate it, but by the effect. Only after both effort and
effect have been specified can one begin to calculate efficiency,
which is where costs and revenue properly enter the picture.

The matter of good intentions deserves some skeptical analysis. Every group and institution seems to profess some kind of
generalized values by which it justifies its actions. But as far as
words go, it very often happens that another group or institution
which acts quite differently will nonetheless profess identical
values. And meanwhile, as found especially in politics, groups
professing quite different values may yet agree on specific actions. These few common-sense observations would suffice to
demonstrate that the link between values and actions is at best
very difficult to establish. But there are other and more sophisticated reasons to distrust any model of social action which simply predicates values as the springs of action.

The first of these reasons is that most values are quite difficult to measure operationally. The second is that, when the effort
is made, the terms in which values are usually expressed splinter
into many meanings, none of which is acceptable as a definition to

more than a few of those who profess the value. Jefferson, for example, thought slavery to be incompatible with the belief in equality set forth in the Declaration of Independence, so his views on slavery were excised from his original draft — to be reinstated in the Constitution nearly a century later, after civil war. Despite this painful example, which is not fully resolved after a second century of contention, the most hopeful way of dealing with the second difficulty is through struggling to solve the first. That is, the way to resolve conflicts over the meaning of general values is through trying to define them in terms of action.

Let us go back to our simple model for the progressive improvement of maternal and child health. Like the Emancipation Proclamation, merely setting up a separate maternity hospital was not deemed to be enough. At best it was conceived as a helpful precondition for reducing certain kinds of mortality. Indeed, with the invention of various of these methods, it was found that they could be adopted in conventional hospitals; hence it can now be argued that separate maternity hospitals are no longer required, if they ever were. But the main goal was to lower the mortality rate, and the institution and its practices and instruments were to be evaluated by their contribution to this result.

Let us suppose that in 1863, coincident with the extinction of legal slavery, some kind of social action had been undertaken by the federal government with the objective of adding some measurable improvement each year to the economic and social status of the former slaves, comparable to the program of school integration "with all deliberate speed" which the Supreme Court initiated in 1954. I think steady movement over the past century might have culminated in a far different picture from that which exists today.

Between our example of maternal and infant health, which will seem noncontroversial to most, and the program of integration pursued by our Negro citizens, which may seem controversial to some, many in-between examples could be introduced, but they all come within the scope of the more complicated model of social action we have adduced thus far. In the case of the major subject matter which brings this audience together — agricultural policy — it must fall somewhere near the middle of the range bounded by the values of health and equality. Agricultural policy is justified by relatively noncontroversial values like productivity on the one hand, and by fighting words like restriction and overpopulation on the other.

If we are to get out of the realm of clashing platitudes, the best way to do so is to start transforming our values into goals, our words into numbers and to tie these to definite periods of time. Intentions thus become intended effects, which are gauged by comparison with the outcomes of efforts in previous periods of action.

THE SETTING OF GOALS AFFECTS MOTIVATION

Values stated in the abstract, while they may evoke strong feelings of group loyalty, rarely offer the steady stimulation to their achievement that comes from organizing action to achieve them in the form of successive interim goals. There is something both realistic and stimulating about setting goals in fairly close reference to prior accomplishment. This peculiar adjustment of motivation to exceed prior accomplishment, but within a range which is reasonably possible, is what is meant by challenge. If there were some way to test the motivating effect of goal setting, it would be found that for any group or individual there is some optimum level of performance at which to place the goal of each period of performance. If it is set too high, the effect is fear of failure and discouragement. If it is set too low, the consequence is overconfidence, slackness and reduced effort. When set just right, it generates a benevolent spiral of success, enhanced aspiration and extended powers. In athletics, a good coach becomes very skilled in judging just when a player or team is ready to attempt some bigger challenge, and in communicating this expectation. Leadership in any organization must likewise repeatedly assess when it can assume a responsibility beyond its previous powers and performance. Considering how well recognized the phenomenon of challenge is, it is somewhat strange that the essentially quantitative comparison which it implies has not been more carefully worked out in annual reports, manuals of administration and leadership training. Even in studies of the planning process, much less attention is given to the social psychology of optimal goal setting than the pay-off seems to deserve. Perhaps the reason is the lack of development of the appropriate measures, which is a technical task that the ordinary group member should not be expected to handle.

EXPECTATION AND OUTCOME ALWAYS DIFFER

Just as it is reasonable to expect goals to be set at some level possible of achievement, so is it reasonable to assume that there will always be some discrepancy between the goal set and the outcome actually experienced. The goal is simultaneously a target of effort and a prediction of outcome. As an inevitably erroneous prediction, it deserves intensive study. As a prediction, it may either overestimate or underestimate the final result. Because of hope and optimism, there is always some tendency to overestimate what can be done in the next period of action. On the other hand, with failure and inpediments, the outcome may be underestimated. In either case, one question always raised is whether the goal should be raised or lowered the next time.

The discrepancy between intention and outcome is only partly a consequence of setting goals too high or too low: it may often be due to untoward circumstances which were not taken into account in making the prediction embodied in the goal. But whether the discrepancy arose from yielding to impulses of hope or fear, or from incorrectly assessing the effects of circumstances which could not be controlled, it can be studied for further insights into both the environment and the actors. It is as important to know the one as the other. The nature of both is revealed progressively by repeated testing, but it is never wholly revealed; surprises continue, as do mistakes and disappointments. Yet given the mechanism of periodic appraisal, and the basing of goals for the next period on experience in the last one, there is unmistakable progress in coping with the sources of error. Some would like to call this mechanism for self-correction "feedback," after the mechanical analogy, but I think the physical analogy demeans the human features of learning from the utilization of mistakes, as well as ignoring the open-ended feature of purposive social action to which we referred earlier.

Finally, in summary, the process of intelligent action can be said to become an object to itself in the same way that the primitive goals of the organization did. The list of goals and their appropriate measures is lengthened or shortened, modified and refined, year by year. Annual reports themselves are improved by critical scrutiny and systematic comparison. I am personally eager to promote the full-time professional employment of sociologists as collaborating technicians in the production and sophisticated development of annual reporting by all types of institutions. There is already much more known than can be said here about the structural relations of the people in organizations who perceive, proclaim and execute lines of action, as against those who observe and measure it, or the external clienteles and audiences who suffer or enjoy the consequences.

At this point, however, more of the purposes of this conference may be served by applying the model as sketched thus far than by adding further details. It is now time to stand back from it and ask if it is approrpiate for organizing analysis of goals and values and social action in agriculture.

THE APPROPRIATE UNIT OF ACTION

The first challenge to the utility of this model is sure to come from those who perceive that it starts from the assumption of action as organized by a single institution, an institution which is only a part of the total society. The model does not contemplate goals and values and social action from the standpoint of society as a whole, and advisedly so. The numerous reasons for insisting that the single institution is the appropriate unit for our model can be specified under two heads: (1) criticisms of the notion of the whole society as the appropriate unit and (2) arguments for the institution as the appropriate unit.

Especially in regard to agriculture, toward which both the federal and state governments forthrightly assert a large measure of responsibility, there is a constant temptation to conceive agricultural policy as somehow reflecting the public interest in a comprehensive way, just as the state as an institution is often unreflectively assumed to possess a comprehensive concern with every aspect of society and department of culture. Since everyone must eat and wear clothes, and thus everyone is dependent on agriculture, agricultural productivity is easily taken as a universally-shared value. Our public school system, capped by the land grant colleges and universities and the extension services, also foster this assumption. Yet it does not take much pondering of the matter to bring such an easy assumption into doubt.

Abstractly and sociologically, we know that the state is simply that institution which possesses the monopoly of force within a territory. Its scope is defined by the taxing power and its geographical boundaries. Like every other institution, its personnel are inclined to attribute pre-eminent importance to its claims on the public at large, and to identify its welfare with that of the whole society. Modern democratic ideology has given the claims of nationalism a peculiar intolerance, as the historians and students of comparative government have repeatedly pointed out. Under more tyrannical regimes, people feel far less moral obligation to recognize the claims of the state on their lives, their fortunes and their sacred honor. They therefore quite conscientiously exert themselves to frustrate the tax collector, the recruiting officer and the political police, and we of course applaud them. It is illogical, however, to accept as absolutely right the same claims on the person of the citizen when they come from government officials who have obtained their jobs through the medium of election. Majority rule can be just as tyrannical and immoral as minority rule, and all the philosophers of democracy have recognized this possibility, as the historians have noted its recurrent actuality up to the present. Democratic theorists, at least those concerned with society as a whole and the individual as a whole, have generally sought to keep the state as an institution in its proper place, as one among many institutions, each of which is only a part, though it serve the whole. They have sought to limit the power of the state to certain minimum functions, on performance of which there is a close enough approach to unanimity to justify imposing reciprocal requirements on the citizenry uniformly. In the case of agriculture, for example, because land is finite in amount, and all of it is vested in some owner, one cannot obtain more of it without receiving it from another. Thus the state is universally accepted as the arbiter on disputed claims to possession of land.

For a tragi-comic contrast, we might note the legal and moral anomalies of the wet-back situation in southern California, in which farm labor unions and farming corporations vie over how the restrictions on immigration will be applied, with the interests of both the public and the wet-backs pretty much lost from sight in the scuffle. The issue of how government payments for restriction of production should be shared between landlord and tenant likewise makes it clear that public policy is ultimately defined by the outcome of conflicts of interest among competing groups.

There is no group, not even the Supreme Court, which rides the clouds far above the clash of all other groups in society. What we have in democratic government is at best a mechanism consisting of elections, courts and continuous legislation, by which conflicts may be resolved in a more satisfactory manner than by some other mechanisms. And the same generalization may be said to apply to any of our other institutions: they are not innately good or finally perfect but merely appreciably better, for the time being, than available alternatives. Indeed, this tentative, limited view of institutions, as instrumental rather than sacred, which springs from our view of government, is indubitably responsible for the relative success we have enjoyed in resolving differences among the many competing, relatively autonomous groups and institutions which compose our pluralistic society. The few outbreaks of overt conflict and violence we have suffered have usually arisen from challenges by groups irreconcilably committed to fixed principles of absolute rule by one institution or another.

Coming back from this disquisition on the pluralism of our
society to agriculture, we find in American agriculture one of the
most pluralistic arrays of groups and interests and competing
segmental institutions imaginable. Who would suppose that the
grain farmers of the Midwest and the dairy farmers of the Northeast are united in their goals and values simply because both are
engaged in agriculture? Sheep raisers and cattle raisers have
historically feuded. When the public finally quits smoking, does
anyone expect the cotton planters to invite the tobacco planters to
join their throng? If we look away from the conflicting interests
of the producers of various commodities and at the various social
groupings in rural society, we observe contests between the family farm and the corporation, the tenant and the landlord, Negro
and white, small and large, cooperative and independent, Farm
Bureau and Farmers Union and countless alliances with nonagricultural groups. There is such a crisscrossing of these interests
— allies in one respect are so often rivals in another — that the
programs of political parties, when they come to agriculture, depend more on obscuring differences than on clarifying and recon-
ciling them. Indeed, it is in the political approach to goals and
values that the greatest emphasis is put on finding the broad
platitudes, the encompassing compromises, the muffled formulations of intended effects and the emotional appeals to widely
shared sentiments.

For all these reasons, and more which could be readily cited,
it seems wise to turn away from any model of social action which
takes as its unit society as a whole, or the government, or even
the United States Department of Agriculture. I have been employed in both the USDA and in a state college of agriculture and
know I do not have to remind this audience of how pluralistic they
are, of how policy emerges from the pulling and hauling of contending groups.

Now when we come to the positive reasons for adopting the
single institution as the basic unit for interrelating goals and
values and social action in a model appropriate for the analysis
of agricultural policy, the most impressive reason for recom-
mending the dynamic model of the annual cycle of review and
planning is that it fairly well represents reality already, while
offering a guide to more self-conscious recognition of those interrelations.

Even if not at regular intervals, there are moments in the
career of any institution when its principals pause, or are made
to pause, to reflect on the meaning of its past performance for
future goals and values and performance. Such intermittent sessions of evaluation, alternating with sessions of action, may be

infrequent, hasty, unsupported by formal reports and measures
and budgets for the coming year, yet they seem to arise from the
natural tendency of human beings to structure their behavior in
distinguishable units, each with a beginning, middle and end, as
the social psychologists say. Some sentimental advocate of spontaneity and informality might argue more or less plausibly for
letting action find its own organization, without attempting to
regularize it in explicit periods. Their sentiment might constitute a minor argument against adoption of our model. But again,
experience itself is on the side of making the planning process as
explicit and regular as possible.

Experience tells us, for example, that when the actions of
large numbers of people must be coordinated — and surely they
must if social action is to be effective — there is much virtue in
regular routines and schedules. The unavoidable irregularities
get placed in relation to the regularities and are thereby made
more manageable. Without routines, every action is an emer-
gency, but no one can live long or maintain consistent direction
in the midst of perpetual emergencies. The very idea of goals
and values implies policy stretching over time and encompassing
some fairly organized universe of particulars. Agriculture pre-
eminently and originally has based its routines on the cycle of
the seasons; in this respect, the influence of agriculture is still
written heavily over the practices of all other institutions of
every society.

In terms of widening conceptions of what has been called
methodology, our model is uniquely adapted to the application of
scientific method to social action. By utilizing quantitative
measures of performance over regular intervals, it permits exact comparisons of results in one period with those in another.
Hence trends can be validly compared. Moreover, the actions of
one institution can thereby be validly compared with those of another, one of which can be construed quite legitimately as the experimental and the other as the control group. From the experimental standpoint, any new practice can be considered as a
hypothesis or as the independent variable in a hypothesis, its
effect to be measured by the variation it causes in the measures
of accomplishment — the annual goals — of the institution.

Additional virtues of the model could be adduced. Also, there
are other models of social action, such as the numerous versions
of an equilibrium model, with which it could be compared as to
relative advantages and disadvantages. An equilibrium model,
for example, is not only essentially a static model, but represents a closed system. From this point on, probably the most
welcome question which might be raised is how the conception of

1173147

goals and values and social action here presented works when it is applied to agriculture.

Perhaps the most satisfying way to answer this question is to attempt to apply the model to the operations of the institution which is sponsoring this conference, the college of agriculture at Iowa State University. I do not have at hand its annual report, although I feel safe in assuming there is one. I also feel safe in assuming that it falls short of being the kind of sociological document which a thorough application of our model might make it.

For example, how accurately is this institution able to appraise both the productivity of Iowa agriculture and the contribution of the university to this productivity year by year?

To what extent does the college of agriculture assess year by year the ratio of ownership to tenancy among the farmers of the state, making predictions beforehand on the basis of cumulative understanding of the conditions governing this changing ratio, and then analyzing the discrepancies between expectations and outcomes in order better and better to grasp — and potentially manipulate, or enable others to manipulate — these conditions?

How current is our picture of full-time family farming and how is it faring in terms of acreage and income, in comparison to corporation farming and part-time farming? How far has the farm population of the state been analyzed with a view to distinguishing its various values and motives for being in agriculture? One hears on every hand that even with the steep decline of recent years there are still too many people on our farms. If this be true, has anyone identified those who ought to leave? By what criteria? Are these the ones who are actually leaving? How much effect, if any, does their leaving have on production and productivity? Over the years, can the rural sociologists' findings about the composition of migrants from farm to city be reconciled in some intelligent pattern with the kinds of loan policies of credit institutions, the educational policies of the secondary schools in rural areas and the kinds of service and advice given to the smaller producers? The farm population is very heterogeneous and its motives for staying on the land are mixed. If this population were regularly classified into several relevant categories by the college of agriculture, and the differential rates of migration for each category were predicted and then checked against actual moves, the running picture of how much or how little population behavior is affected by the policies of this and related institutions would probably moderate the strong opinions heard from both sides of the issue. The most productive probably migrate least of all.

Even in the realm of the pure technology of productivity,

despite its ostensible noncontroversiality, I wonder what might
be learned and what policies might be altered by studying the
relative contributions to rising productivity from chemical manufacturers, machine manufacturers, agricultural educators and
biological researchers.

If we look at the control of overproduction in terms of the
distribution of acreage among alternate land uses, I wonder if
anyone is maintaining a continuous flow-chart which shows in
percentages of the total land surface of Iowa how the ratios are
changing. For example, it seems to me that road building and the
growth of suburbs are taking land out of the production of basic
commodities faster than legislation is.

Most important of all, I wonder if a more objective scrutiny
of the practices and policies of the college of agriculture, with
respect to production and productivity, comparing intended and
actual effects year by year, might not bring this institution to the
point reached by our introductory example, the maternity hospital. The college of agriculture has striven mightily over the
years to increase the productivity of Iowa agriculture. The year-
by-year quantitative record of achievement of goals has been
magnificently impressive. But now the very holding of this conference, and the note of crisis which pervades many of the papers,
make evident that disturbing doubts are emerging as to whether
the more basic value of farmer welfare is being served by further
enhancing the output of corn and hogs and wheat and milk and the
other major commodities. So far most of the political discussion
has been concerned with disposal of surplus and adjustment of
prices to producers. There is no evident disposition, however,
among the multiple contending proponents of divergent interests
or within the college itself to slow down or halt the pursuit of
higher productivity. The problem of overproduction which the
college is now gingerly approaching with its left hand is still being vigorously aggravated by its right.

Frankly, I do not sympathize more than moderately with the
notion that the college of agriculture's most appropriate role in
the current situation is to engender at every crossroads the kind
of discussion of public affairs which would imitate the clash of
interests in Congress or before public hearings of decision-
making bodies. Academic discussion by definition does not make
decisions. Decisions are made either by constituted decision-
making bodies, subject to pressures from contending advocates,
or by separate organizations with respect to their own actions
only. Since the college of agriculture is neither in a position to
advocate a specific political proposal, nor is it a forum in which
the conflicts between groups can actually be resolved, it can at

best pursue its traditional, nonpartisan educational role. And that would not be to bring all its talents and capacities to the support of agricultural welfare in Iowa.

There is a certain limited analogy between the uncomfortable situation of Iowa farmers and those mass producers of durable goods who have seen their products descend, if you will pardon the expression, to the status of commodities, indistinguishable from those of other producers, all thrown into an overproduced market in which every move each makes to increase his productivity or productive capacity drives down the prices of all. In this situation, the way out that is being pursued by the mass producers of industrial commodities might also serve as an enlightening analogy for Iowa farmers, and possibly suggest an appropriate revision of its goals by the Iowa State University College of Agriculture. Without abandoning the value of productivity, the new value becomes innovation, the search for new products. If too many corn and hogs are being produced for the good of producers, let new uses be found for the land and the people, instead of trying either to remove them from production or find ways of taxing consumers to perpetuate redundancy. I cannot help believing that if the human and material resources of the college of agriculture were systematically oriented to developing new farm products, such a reorientation would be welcomed on every hand, and the crisis of goals and values would subside.

The problem then would be execution. Success could hardly be expected to come at once, but as we described the concept of challenge, success in achieving such a new goal seems possible. The technical problems would call on the talents of many specialists, but even to an amateur and spectator, numerous opportunities for new farm products seem to be obvious. We also have a few real examples from which to take heart.

Right here in Iowa, to illustrate, we have the example of hogs specially reared to produce superior bacon, that commands at the consumer level a premium of twenty cents per pound.

Looking forward, the upgrading of consumer diets that is going on at a tremendous rate indicates an array of opportunities of unprecedented scope. The whole banana industry, it is said, has been reconstituted by the development of dwarf varieties. But perhaps the most interesting opportunities for agriculture lie in other directions than food production. Except for minerals, it appears that agriculture could actually produce its own fertilizer. The vast growth in the uses of paper, plastics and synthetic films and fibers suggests an immense array of possibilities for agricultural products in making these. All the trends in building materials, construction and the manufacture of major consumer

durables plainly indicate a series of huge markets for wood substitutes here. The volume of imports of organic materials from
abroad and the pressure on domestic supplies of fossil materials
suggest, in fact, that the capacity of Iowa farmers to synthesize
them year by year from solar energy may before this century is
out prove all too insufficient.

I see no reason for worry over goals and values, if alongside
productivity, on which all agree, we write in also new products,
and get on with action.

LEONARD BROOM

University of Texas

Discussion

DR. FOOTE'S PAPER is predicated on one fundamental value —
rationality. It is a value so basic to the contemporary academic
mind that it is taken for granted and it is, furthermore, expressed in a form familiar and attractive to scholars. It calls
for objectivity and, preferably, measurement. The underlying
model implied in the empirical case of the maternity hospital,
and off and on in the paper, is an input-output type, one that
lends itself to quantification and exactness once the preliminary
problems of unit definition and the like have been solved. He
makes unit definition as easy as possible by setting productivity
as the specific and single objective measure against which effort
is to be assessed. But at the very outset, and despite his dis-
claimers, the normative presupposition of his paper should be
recognized. His preference for interim goals against values ar-
bitrarily moves the point of focus but does not really simplify the
problem.

Dr. Foote has warned against obscuring and confusing the
evaluation and formation of policy by paying attention to values.
He has said in effect, "Take care of productivity and the values
will take care of themselves." (As a matter of fact, I think that
the notion of the market place, whether it be for goods, political
candidates or ideas, is a major theme in the American value
system, and that it deserves far more attention than the lip service it usually gets. Note, however, that his implicit use of the
marketplace principle makes fundamental value assumptions that
are bound to affect the rest of his analysis.)

Let me reflect for a moment on the problem of how open the
market place of ideas ought to be. The scholar assumes that it
ought to be as open as possible and this conference is founded on

an article of faith: that the best way to resolve conflicts is to make differences explicit. Scholars are not politicians and cannot be expected to approach problems as do politicians. Where the scholar strives for clarity even at the cost of exacerbating tensions, the politician in a plural society may strive for obscurity in order to mute tensions that may be disruptive to the social order. The politician can assume social functions for ignorance; the scholar cannot. As we go about our business we ought to remind ourselves from time to time that we are talking about the conditions of action, not action itself.

Dr. Foote says that values are hard to specify, that they won't hold still, and that they tend to come apart under scrutiny. All these observations are to a degree true, but to be useful guides for analysis or action, models must admit the relevant variables. A simpler world would be a happier world for social scientists, and a large part of our job is to discover simplicity and order in the welter of apparent disorder. Model building is one of the ways to approach order, but the social scientist cannot impose order on the world; he must discover it. A model is never more than a plausible first approximation. By eliminating values from inquiry, or rather by restricting himself by implication to one value-invested goal — productivity — Foote has built a spurious order into his model, and it must fail in the face of reality unless the implicit is made explicit.

What happens if we accept, for the sake of argument, the value criterion of productivity? What kind of productivity is meant:

The maximum number of units?
The maximum number of units of highest value?
The maximum monetary return?
The maximum return with a minimum of capital investment?
... with the minimum of labor, etc., etc.?

Dr. Foote knows that productivity is capable of many interpretations, depending on the underlying value system. Indeed, we can confidently guess what value criteria he prefers. But we cannot assume that the same value criteria are taken for granted in American agriculture, even Iowa agriculture. Let me illustrate by quoting from the Wall Street Journal of June 21, 1960:

FOREIGN BUYERS complain about the poor quality of U.S. cotton, tobacco and flour.

The charges hurt some export sales, though the extent of the impact can't be precisely figured. A Federal study shows foreign importers and

spinners are disappointed by the condition of U.S. cotton. It's poorly packaged, dirty and thus more expensive to use, foreign buyers say. A big
complaint is tattered covers caused by frequent sampling by wary buyers
each time U.S. bales change hands. Spinners said surface cleaning was
necessary on 76% of U.S. bales. The foreigners rated American cotton
among the "poorest packaged." Russian cotton was listed among the best.

Foreigners claim U.S. tobacco quality is slipping. Britons in particular sound warnings over maleic hydrazide, a chemical used to control
growth of leaf-depleting "sucker" branches. The chemical is said to affect
taste and burning quality. Canada and Rhodesia, other U.K. suppliers,
have cut use of the chemical. Some buyers say U.S. leaf is poorer because
of too-close planting and use of too much fertilizer.

As for flour, changed European baking habits call for a higher quality
product. Some buyers find U.S. quality inconsistent even within the same
grade. The Soviets deliver a consistent, state-controlled product.

This is a rather polite quote to read in Iowa: cotton, tobacco and
flour. The state of affairs described obtains under conditions of
high unit productivity. Clearly, productivity as a criterion needs
to be qualified by other value criteria.

Furthermore, if the Wall Street Journal story is a true story,
a question is raised about the viability of certain underlying
values that are conditional to the achievement of consistent productivity, however defined. In a competitive world economy can
American agriculture succeed if pride of workmanship is lacking? If what is frequently called the work ethic is no longer sufficiently strong to insure good performance and good quality in
some parts of American agriculture, can it be revived? Or can
another set of motivating values be substituted? These may be
preliminary questions but their answers are absolutely essential.
I shall leave to others who are informed and wise about American
agriculture to say what its goals ought to be. But whatever goals
are accepted, they must be assessed against an understanding of
the underlying values of the operators of American farms.

It might seem that I have concluded that Dr. Foote's model is
defective and that its application is useless. This is not the case.
He has given us many insights, and the analysis that he proposes
of such service institutions as the college of agriculture (I would
add the department of agriculture) deserves to be undertaken, although, as I have said, I am skeptical about the monolithic productivity criterion. I do feel that the first and last unit of analysis
is the producing unit, not the auxiliary control and guidance machinery, and that value analysis would loom large in such inquiry.

Dr. Foote touched upon another line of investigation which
may be mentioned here in the form of a postscript. You will recall his observation about road and suburb building taking land
out of production. This is an important problem, not merely for

its immediate effects, but because it is an essentially irreversible phenomenon. Let me underscore the theoretical significance of this. If a given choice or action forecloses other important alternatives, it must obviously be approached with far greater care than if the action may be reversed. For example, building a factory on farm land may ruin the land for farming; this would be an irreversible act. On the other hand, the experimental introduction of a new crop, even though it might disrupt farming routine, would obviously be easy to reverse. It seems to me that the purposes of wise planning would be served if policies were labelled as reversible or irreversible or, even better, according to their ease of reversibility. Because I am a former resident of southern California, the relation of industrial building to farming struck a familiar note in my memory. In the 40's and 50's irreplaceable alluvial fans of great agricultural productivity became the sites of housing developments, aircract factories and freeways. There is nothing unique about the southern California case. It has been going on all over the world ever since Man decided to live in cities and to place his cities on the alluvial plains and along watercourses. The southern California case impresses us because of its recency and rapidity of development and because it happened when its cost was understood. To prove that the short-run market place model needs the restraint of a longer perspective, we need only observe that the southern California incident is continuing and is now being replicated in the San Francisco Bay area, a region that would not demean itself by learning from southern California. A countervailing value, conservation, and its organizational embodiment, conservationism, is one expression of society's reservations about the market place model. Many lessons may be drawn from this example. I choose this: that the goals and values of agriculture are inextricable from the goals and values of whole societies. And I would add that the assessment of the interaction of competing values is essential to scientific understanding and the development of informed policies.

JOHN C. GREENE

Iowa State University

Discussion

IN KEEPING with the structure of Mr. Foote's chapter, I shall comment (1) on his model of social action; (2) on his rejection of society-as-a-whole as a legitimate unit for the discussion of goals and values and social policy, and (3) on his application of his model of social action to the agricultural college.

The only difficulty with Mr. Foote's model of social action, so far as I can see, is that it has very little bearing on the problems of goals and values in agricultural policy. It certainly is true that if one knows in a general way what he wants to accomplish, it is very helpful to specify intermediate objectives and establish quantitative measures of year-by-year progress toward the achievement of the goal. In the insurance business, this method of incitement to accomplishment has been developed into a fine art, an art slightly amusing to the outsider in some of its aspects, but highly effective in selling insurance.

But the problem is not primarily to establish intermediate goals on the way to the accomplishment of some generally accepted objective of agricultural policy, but rather to arrive at a consensus concerning the objectives themselves. Thus, Professors Heady and Burchinal state that there is a "need to appraise our values and chart a policy course which is consistent with general society goals." The basic problem, they add, is one of "determining what mix or combination of goals, at the various levels of the means-ends hierarchy, is optimum, desirable or acceptable." "There exists," they assert, "some combination of competing goals . . . which must be decided upon by society." In view of these statements by the organizers of the conference, I cannot but question the relevance of Mr. Foote's model, which, as he himself says, "does not contemplate goals and values and social action from the standpoint of society as a whole."

This would seem to dispose of Mr. Foote's model, but we cannot leave the matter there. Mr. Foote defends his rejection of the general societal viewpoint vigorously. If his argument is sound, this conference may as well close shop and go home. But is it sound?

He begins by asserting that "public policy is ultimately defined by the outcome of conflicts of interest among competing groups." From this he jumps to the conclusion that we must reject "any model of social action which takes as its unit society as a whole, or the government, or even the United States Department of Agriculture." I submit that the conclusion does not follow from the premise. It is undeniable that public policy is determined to a very considerable extent by the pulling and hauling of competing interest groups. The purpose of public policy is precisely to reconcile conflicting interests and points of view, to establish some harmony of purpose amidst the welter of interests. But how is this possible? It is possible in a democratic society only because (and to the extent that) the government officials who formulate policy and the individuals comprising the competing interest groups are capable of being influenced by conceptions of national interest transcending their particular interests.

If individuals and groups and government officials were incapable of entertaining and being influenced by conceptions of national interest, there could be no public policy, for there would be no public. It would make no sense to speak, as Professors Heady and Burchinal do, of "melding" out of the maze of interest groups the elements of an agricultural policy which would allow reasonable attainment of broader national purposes and goals. Mr. Foote misses the point of the democratic process when he accuses political parties of doing more to obscure issues than to clarify them. The "broad platitudes," the "muffled formulations," the "encompassing compromises" which irritate him are inevitable concomitants of the effort to find a common basis of action amid the welter of divergent views and interests.

The essential unsoundness of Mr. Foote's argument against taking the general societal viewpoint can be shown by applying his pluralistic analysis to the single institution which he selects as a proper unit for the application of his model of social action. This unit is the agricultural college, by which I presume he means a land grant institution like Iowa State University. As he himself recognizes, a college or university is itself a collection of interest groups, each seeking to influence administrative policy. The power politics of the academic world is too familiar to most of us to require documentation. By Mr. Foote's own argument, then, it makes no sense to talk of college policy as if it represented a concerted effort to achieve certain educational objectives. Far from interrelating goals, values and social action, the college would be, on this view of things, a chaos of conflicting goals, values and interests, many of which would have only the remotest connection with education. But Mr. Foote does not apply the pluralistic argument to the case of the college. He assumes, quite sensibly in this case, that a college cannot only have general values and goals, but can specify intermediate objectives on the road to attaining those goals.

Unfortunately, however, Mr. Foote's conception of the goals proper to an agricultural college is much too narrow. It is several decades out of date. He overlooks the fact that there are no more agricultural colleges in the sense of colleges composed primarily of farm students and concerned primarily with teaching methods of agriculture. Iowa State is now a university of science and technology. The majority of its students do not come from farms; the majority will not go into farming after college. Even if one restricts the argument to the agricultural college proper, i.e., to that part of the college or university specifically concerned with agriculture and related subjects, Mr. Foote's ideas are still too narrow. The college certainly should concern itself with the things he mentions — productivity, new products, careful analysis of conditions, problems and trends in agriculture. But, as Messrs. Heady and Burchinal point out, these efforts may prove self-defeating unless they are balanced by equally strenuous efforts to teach the farm population to think in national and international terms. The crisis of goals and values cannot be eliminated by the simple expedient of developing new farm products, as Mr. Foote seems to think. It may be somewhat alleviated, however, if the state colleges will stop thinking of themselves as agricultural colleges and set out to inculcate in all of their students, whether farm or nonfarm, a broad range of knowledge and information and a profound sense of responsibility as citizens of a great world power. It is not necessarily true that, as Charles Wilson is reputed to have asserted, "what is good for General Motors is good for the country," but it is undoubtedly true that, in the long run, what is good for the country will be good for General Motors, for the farmer and for everyone else.

Chapter 3

HARRY V. JAFFA

Ohio State University

Agrarian Virtue
and Republican Freedom:
An Historical Perspective

W E ARE ALL hearing and reading a great deal these days
about the "national purpose." The occasion, of course, is
the deepening crisis in our relations with the Communist
world, and the sense that we are declining, if not falling, in the
contest for all the world. The sense of urgency intensified during
the presidential campaign with the conviction that the country is
at a kind of crossroads, and that we all have a measure of responsibility for the decisions about to be made.

In reading through the remarkable series of essays published
by the New York Times and Life I was struck above all by one
thing. Although the series was announced to be a debate, there
was in fact no striking disagreement or conflict of views on the
announced theme. The authors differed in their emphasis, and
sometimes wrote about very different things; but what they said
complemented each other. That we had a "national purpose," and
that that purpose was most excellently defined for us on an appropriate level of generality by such documents as the Declaration
of Independence, the Preamble to the Constitution, the Gettysburg
Address, and some other of the more notable speeches of our
greatest presidents, no one really questioned. Walter Lippmann
seemed to think we needed new purposes, that we had fulfilled
much of the programmatic expectations of the "national purpose"
as conceived in the nineteenth century. But what he seemed to
mean, was that we had to re-think the concrete demands in our
own time of our traditional purposes, not that we needed anything
to replace or supplement the commitment to freedom expressed
on the level of abstraction of, say, the first two paragraphs of the
Declaration of Independence.

With all this I have no quarrel. And yet I think the tone of the
"debate" has been rather too much determined by present exigen-
cies to fulfill our genuine needs. Confronted by the overwhelming
purposefulness of the Communist world — that is, by its absolute
conviction of its rightness, and unwavering pursuit of a single

end — we seek to reassure ourselves by looking backward to a
time when America's revolutionary spirit flamed high. In effect,
we hope to reproduce a decent version of Communism's monolithic dynamism, not so much because we are dissatisfied with
what we have, as because we think we will not keep what we have
unless somehow we change a little. We hope to control the future
by recapturing the past. I believe something very like this is the
only policy by which we will be saved, if we are saved. But we
will not succeed by means of a synthetic past mirroring back to
us only what we want to find in it.

We will never discover, for example, an America firmly
united simply by the inspirational conviction of a great purpose,
so that without coercion it wheeled and marched as efficiently as
a modern totalitarian regime. The American people were probably as deeply divided upon the question of independence in 1776
as upon, let us say, intervention in the European war of 1939, and
probably much more deeply divided than they are today upon a
more drastic approach to the Communist peril. In the gravest of
all our crises, the American Civil War, the division of the American people passed all visible boundaries. The greatest of all
expressions of national purposes came from the gravest moments
of doubt and conflict over those very purposes. The passion that
found its consummation in, for example, the Gettysburg Address
is inseparable from the tragedy that produced it. I do not mean
to suggest that we must become tragic figures ourselves before
we can understand a pronouncement like the Gettysburg Address,
but I do think that if we are to have a vicarious salvation, we
must understand in a far more profound way than we hitherto
have, the integrity of the Gettysburg Address and the tragedy it
expressed.

Each age has its own urgent reasons for division as well as
for unity. The American people are not today divided in the sense
that they were in 1776 or 1861. We are restless and discontented
and we are worried, but these passions afflict all of us together.
The question of more or less government spending, of flexible or
rigid price supports, of whether medical support for the aged
shall or shall not be undertaken within the framework of the
social security system, are not questions for the sake of which
we seize the standards of righteousness, and embark upon cru-
sades. There is nothing here for which to pledge our lives,
fortunes and sacred honor, or to give the last full measure of
devotion. We now know what popular government means. It
means government by the consent of the governed, and we know
that this consent must be expressed in such things as frequent
elections with secret ballots, accompanied by freedom of speech,

press, association and religion. No considerable group, pressure, interest, faction, sect or opinion must be denied access to a major party, or be denied the possibility of forming itself into a party. One-party politics is morally unthinkable, because without competition between at least two parties, minorities are at the mercy of majorities, and the majority itself is at the mercy of the oligarchy which controls the organization of the majority. Knowing all this so well, we are at a loss to see anything but massive evil in a massive world movement which, while frantically calling itself democratic and egalitarian, denies it all. And yet, if we look into our own past, to ponder and to learn, and not merely to overcome moral enervation, we will find divisions as deep as any that now divide us from the Communists. If we would draw inspiration from men of the stature of the founding fathers, or of Lincoln, we must draw it as much from encountering the deep and justifiable doubts and anxious difficulties that they encountered, in fashioning a national purpose for us, as in professing devotion to that purpose as a shaped and finished thing.

Reflection upon the nature of our "national purpose" begins, of course, with the Declaration of Independence. It was there announced that governments are instituted to secure certain rights, and that by their adequacy in securing these rights they are to be judged; and judged not by privileged orders, but by the people, by and for whom alone they may be rightfully instituted. But the rights for whose security the American government was instituted were not regarded as being in any sense uniquely American. They were, on the contrary, believed to be rights held in common with all mankind, rights held in virtue of the self-evident truth "that all men are created equal." The United States was the first nation consciously dedicated to the security of rights so conceived; it was the first nation to link its own welfare in this way with the welfare of all nations, by announcing that what it sought for itself was the birthright of all other peoples as well. Paradoxical as it may seem, the uniqueness of America's national purpose lies in its universality. Other nations might follow the banner of equal human rights, but we alone had raised it, and our claim to distinction as the exponents of the creed inscribed upon that banner could never be rivalled so long as we remained faithful to it. To paraphrase Webster, in the great drama of human affairs we had been placed at the head of the system of representative and popular governments, and as long as we fulfilled the duty incumbent upon ourselves "to preserve the consistency of this cheering example," and took care that nothing weakened "its authority with the world," no one could share with us this post of honor. This nation has had no other past to celebrate paramount

to that constituted by the events of the American revolution.
From the moment of the revolution its more remote past could
be looked upon as no more than a preparation for independence.
By contrast, for example, the reaction which followed the revolution in France could find in France's monarchical past — in the
story of Joan of Arc, for example, and all that that story symbolized — another and different explanation of France's claim to
greatness. But there has never been any similar possibility here.
Only in this country have all possible claims to national superiority and national uniqueness subsisted both in logical and psychological harmony with the assertion of the common and equal
rights of all people and all nations.

It is not to be supposed, because of America's dedication to
the political creed set forth in the preamble to the Declaration of
Independence, that conflicts as to national purpose were thereby
to be avoided. Not only did equality as a principle hold out great
promises of moral and material improvement; it also made demands not unlike those which made the rich young man in quest
of the kingdom of heaven turn sadly from Jesus. Lincoln often
compared it to the Gospel injunction, "Be ye perfect as your
Father in heaven is perfect." It held up a standard that was, in a
sense, beyond attainment. In inviting men to aspire to what they
could never wholly attain it engendered frustrations which could
not but embitter political life. Like the Gospel, in the name of
peace it brought not peace, but a sword. The Civil War is not
only the gravest crisis this nation has had to undergo; it is at
once an epitome of all the great conflicts in American history and
represents them in sharper focus. For it is important to realize
that, in the Civil War, not only did both sides read the same Bible
and pray to the same God, but both believed they were fighting for
the cause for which Washington fought. Still more important is it
to realize that both were, in a profound sense, correct. According
to the revolutionary faith, because all men are created equal,
governments derive their just powers from the consent of the
governed alone. But that consent may rightfully be withdrawn
whenever in the opinion of the governed the government no longer
protects their unalienable rights to life and to liberty. There
never was a time from the moment of independence that white
Southerners in an overwhelming majority did not believe that
their lives and liberty would be terribly endangered by large-
scale emancipation. Jefferson, even as he condemned in un-
measured terms the wrong of slavery, confessed, "Justice is in
one scale and self-preservation in the other." And he always insisted that even gradual emancipation, if it were pursued, as he
believed it should be, must be accompanied by deportation of the

emancipated slaves. Meanwhile, many good men doubted that deportation, even if it were feasible, would be more humane or just than slavery. In this, Southerners may have been wrong, but it is important to remember that government in accordance with the opinion or consent of the governed does not require that the governed be right. Sooner or later the experiment in popular government had to face the question of just how wrong the opinion of the governed might be, and still continue to constitute the foundation for the just powers of government. From this you will see that the Declaration of Independence, while it propounded a purpose, propounded a problem as well.

In my opinion, the Civil War became as inevitable as any human event can be from the moment that the war with Mexico, hard upon the annexation of Texas, added great new territories to the country in the South and West. It was not so much a question of the extension of slavery, although that assuredly was involved, as it was a question of political control of the new states and territories by either the old slaveholding, or the old free, states. In 1860 the election of Lincoln meant that the free states had won; for with that election it became practically certain that there would never in the future be a majority in both houses of Congress who would vote to admit, and a president who would approve, the admission of another slaveholding state. From this moment the time was not far distant when the control of the relation of the races in the South could, and probably would, be taken from the hands of the white Southerners. No protests by Lincoln could be convincing that he did not mean to interfere with slavery in the states where it already existed. He could not commit the new and growing antislavery majority as to the future. It would not have required a constitutional amendment to have given the death sentence to slavery in the slave states. Recent studies bear out the view that federal interference with the interstate slave trade would have subjected slavery to economic strangulation, and the power so to interfere could easily be inferred from the commerce clause of the Constitution. It was only a matter of time until the North had the naked power to enforce such restrictions upon the South through the federal government. But to the South the American revolution meant nothing if it did not mean that the control of the safety of home and hearth should never be out of the power of the people or their immediate representatives. In 1861 the South saw the government of the Union they had done so much to create becoming an instrument of the deadliest kind of hostility against themselves. The great error of the South, although it was never committed by some of her noblest sons, was in denying the tenet of equality itself. If the

South had continued to stand upon the right to security of life and
liberty, and the right to judge of the means indispensable to that
security, rights truly sanctioned by the idea of equality,[1] her case
would have been well-nigh irrefragable. Goaded on by the abolitionists' appropriation of the great proposition she came to believe, and even demand that the North believe, that slavery was
not merely a necessary evil but a positive good. In denying the
principle in virtue of which her own consent might be required as
a basis of the common government, the wheel of contradiction
came full circle. In terms of abstract logic, here was one answer
to the question of what limits there might be to the errors of the
governed. As the abolitionists had forgotten the requirement of
consent, the disciples of Calhoun and Fitzhugh had forgotten why
there must be consent. As Lincoln interpreted the Civil War,
both sides had sinned against a common faith; both had to make a
common atonement to achieve a common redemption. The denials
of either side were like Peter's denials of his Lord. They were
somehow necessary for the passion both were to undergo that
they might both become witnesses of a single truth, a truth which,
like the house built upon it, had in a sense become divided against
itself.

To understand the fatal polarization of conflict in American
politics in the Civil War we must go back to the period of the
founders, and to the subsequent party politics of the Jeffersonian
and Jacksonian eras. The founders, whatever their differences,
were agreed that popular government might become practicable
now, only because of recent discoveries and improvements in
political science, discoveries and improvements which would
strengthen the rational powers of the people, and hence strengthen
the popular capacity for just government. This, indeed, helps to
account for the annunciation of the principle of equality, the
principle of popular government, only so late in human history as
the last quarter of the eighteenth century. The famous tenth
Federalist catalogues some of the vices of "the American con-
stitutions," notwithstanding their "valuable improvements" on
popular models, both ancient and modern. That popular government is inherently unstable, given to excess factionalism, and
that the rights of property and person under it are notoriously
insecure, was the view of Madison, and it was a view he expected
his public to share. Yet he and they believed its inherent evils

---

[1] For an extended discussion of the idea of equality in the Declaration of Independ-
ence, see Chapter XVII, "The Meaning of Equality: Abstract and Practical," in my
Crisis of the House Divided: An Interpretation of the Issues in the Lincoln-Douglas
Debates. Doubleday, New York. 1959.

might be overcome, and overcome in such a way as to make it preferable to every other form of government. Why?

The means of improving popular government fall, broadly speaking, into two categories. First, the means for the direct improvement of the people by education, particularly education in science, that science of which, in the eighteenth century, Newton was the most celebrated exponent; science was the key to all progress and the enemy of all the medieval superstitions which buttressed feudal class distinctions and false pretensions to merit; education would teach men to know and assert their rights, and to recognize the men and measures that truly advanced and secured them. Second, the construction of a constitutional order in which impulses to action would come from majorities, but in which there would be many different majorities, in whose differences would lie many inducements to impartiality and reasonableness. The very idea of majority rule would be transformed from a numerical to a qualitative concept.

The transformation of majority rule from a quantitative to a qualitative concept: Hoc opus, hic labor est. Yet this is the work that the founders set out to achieve, and upon which the truth of the proposition of equality, for all its self-evidence, depended. How Jefferson sought to achieve this transformation, with particular reference to the first of the means above mentioned, may be indicated by what he wrote to John Adams in 1813:

For I agree with you that there is a natural aristocracy among men. The grounds of this are virtue and talents .... May we not even say, that that form of government is best which provides the most effectually for a pure selection of these natural aristoi into the offices of government?

According to Jefferson, the best form of government is democratic precisely because it is also aristocratic, in the true sense of the latter word. In a democracy we "leave to the citizens the free election and separation of the aristoi from the pseudo-aristoi, of the wheat from the chaff." But since these citizens differ among themselves as much as the wheat does from the chaff, it is not surprising that, as Jefferson confesses, "in some instances wealth may corrupt and birth blind them." To minimize this, Jefferson had drawn up the laws abolishing primogeniture, entail and the alliance of church and state in Virginia, laws which, he says, "laid the axe to the foot of the pseudo-aristocracy." But, he added, "had another which I prepared been adopted by the legislature, our work would have been complete."

This measure, which is here said to complete Jefferson's scheme for uniting the principles of democracy and aristocracy,

was his bill for the general diffusion of learning. It would have
provided free primary, secondary and university education. But
it would not have opened all to all students. Only primary education would have been universal. Only a select number of gifted
scholars would have gone to high school, and a still more select
number of the more gifted to the university. This scheme Jefferson called the "keystone of the arch" of the form of government
he advocated, and it is impossible to overestimate its significance
in understanding the original expectations in regard to democracy
by the man who, more than any other, laid the foundations of
democratic thought in America. The purpose of this class of
university men, co-opted out of the mass of their fellows on the
basis of ability and achievement alone, is to demonstrate the difference between an aristocracy of merit, a natural aristocracy
and the pseudoaristocracy of birth, wealth or other fictitious
claims to distinction. The existence of this intellectual aristocracy would, in practice, considerably narrow the task of the citizens in separating the wheat from the chaff, for I do not doubt that
Jefferson expected most if not all public officials to be chosen
from it. And I think it worth noticing that, violently as Jefferson
condemned Plato's Republic, membership in one or another of
Jefferson's three educational classes would be determined by a
process not unlike that in which membership in one or another of
the three classes — whose souls are gold, silver and brass — is
determined in the Republic. Educational "government" is from
the top down, even as the authority for political government is
from the bottom up. Yet Jefferson's scheme is not the less au-
thentically egalitarian: genuine equality of opportunity necessarily leads to inequality of reward. Superior talent deserves
superior training and superior recognition. And this kind of recognition supplies to merit the prestige it needs if the ordinary
citizen is to be guided by it in choosing those who are really able
to fulfill the public trusts.

Next we come to those discoveries and improvements in political science which cause even the bad effects of the popular
principle to have beneficent consequences. Democracy in 1800
had a bad name in America, not only because of the French revolution, but because it was still understood in its ancient sense of
direct rule of the people in a community small enough for the
sovereign authority to consist of the assembled citizens. We have
already adverted to the fact that Madison, in the tenth Federalist,
rejects such a form of government — apart from the fact that it
would be impracticable for a modern nation — because it is tur-
bulent and unjust to minorities. The concentration of all the
powers of government, as in a direct democracy is, according to

Jefferson, "the definition of despotic government," and it is "no alleviation that these powers will be exercised by a plurality of hands and not by a single one." The poor may despoil the rich with their votes, or the largest religious sect may persecute lesser ones. The fundamental remedy of the founders is derived from the following familiar (Federalist #51) Madisonian proposition:

> In a free government the security for civil rights must be the same as that for religious rights. It consists in the one case in the multiplicity of interests, and in the other in the multiplicity of sects. The degree of security in both cases will depend on the extent of country and number of people comprehended under the same government.

The theory of the extensive republic is the main contribution of the celebrated Federalist to the solution of the problem of the tyranny of the majority. This theory depends upon the idea of representation. It is true that representation must be supplemented by separation of powers and checks and balances, but in the Federalist the most vital checks and balances are not the legal ones, but those brought into play by representation in an extensive republic. Now representation, like Jefferson's educational plan, itself implies an aristocratic modification of democracy, as that term was anciently understood. It substitutes the discretion of an elect — because elected — few, for that of the people at large. In the famous tenth Federalist, Madison is explicit that, in the large republic, because the representatives are far fewer in proportion to the population — e.g. congressional districts are much larger than state assembly districts — they will in all probability be abler and more disinterested men. More important, because the variety of interests that they will be called upon to reconcile will be much larger, they will have much more freedom to follow the rules of justice instead of the interests of factions.

But what did Madison mean, when he spoke of following the "rules of justice and the rights of the minor party?" In my opinion, "rules of justice" and "rights of the minor party" are distinguishable but inseparable. Justice means giving to everyone his due, and is supremely concerned with that irreducible minority, the individual. But individuals differ. Hence justice involves a concern for, and liberation of, individual differences. There is, Madison says, "a diversity in the faculties of men from which the rights of property originate," and this diversity is "sown in the nature of man." Because it is, it must also be patronized by the "Laws of Nature and of Nature's God." Indeed, says Madison,

laying down a proposition of incalculable weight for the understanding of our constitutional tradition, "The protection of these
faculties [viz., the "different and unequal faculties of acquiring
property"] is the first object of government." That the emancipation of natural human talents from artificial class barriers
meant primarily the liberation of the acquisitive faculties did not
mean that these were regarded as the most important or valuable
human faculties; but it did mean that they were politically the
most important. The passion for material well-being is the
dominant passion of the mass of men precisely when they are
freed from the restraints of a feudal class system and feudal
religion, which invite most men to forego their claims to justice
in this world, in exchange for promises to be fulfilled in another.
Jefferson understood this — somewhat distastefully, to be sure —
when he wrote during the revolution: "From the conclusion of
this war we shall be going downhill ... the people ... will forget
themselves but in the sole faculty of making money." Again, in
the tenth Federalist Madison wrote: "A landed interest, a manufacturing interest, a mercantile interest, a moneyed interest,
with many lesser interests, grow up of necessity in civilized
nations ...." Finally: "The regulation of these various and
interfering interests forms the principal task of modern legislation, and involves the spirit of party and faction in the necessary
and ordinary operations of government." I have underscored the
word "civilized" to make clear that the emancipation of acquisitiveness, the loosing of the spirit of faction, even though this is
something intrinsically bad — as indicated by the famous definition
of faction — is the very characteristic of civilization. And the
task of modern legislation — meaning legislation in a civilized
society — consists in regulating the interests which arise from
the different species of property, which themselves arise, be it
remembered, from a diversity of faculties sown in the nature of
man.

In the paragraph following the one we have just quoted from,
in the tenth Federalist, Madison says that "most important acts
of legislation [are] so many judicial determinations, not indeed
concerning the rights of single persons, but concerning the rights
of large bodies of citizens." He has already observed that no
man can be a just judge in his own cause, and he now observes
that in legislation "the different classes of legislators [are
nothing but] advocates and parties to the causes which they
determine." He follows this with three examples. The first has
to do with private debts, the second with protective tariffs and
the third with the apportionment of taxes on various descriptions
of property. Let us quote the central example, that concerning
the tariff:

Shall domestic manufactures be encouraged, and in what degree, by restrictions on foreign manufactures? These are questions which would be
differently decided by the landed and manufacturing classes, and probably
by neither with a sole regard to justice and the public good.

Now all three examples, but this one pre-eminently, define the
struggle then going on, but much more the struggle that was to go
on throughout the Jeffersonian and Jacksonian eras, between the
agricultural interest and all other interests in American politics.
What is of immense importance in understanding the politics of
these eras, from the perspective of the Philadelphia convention
of 1787, is that the Madison of the Federalist held that the question above propounded could be far more justly judged by the
representatives of the extensive republic. In 1798 Jefferson formulated, and Madison explained and defended, the republicanism
of the Virginia and Kentucky resolutions. According to this latter
doctrine, it is the representatives of the states, and not those
assembled in the national legislature, who can best be entrusted
with judging infringements of the rights of the minor parties.
State rights and strict construction became the supreme dogmas
of the party of which Jefferson and Jackson were the greatest
leaders, and of which Madison was a most notable chieftain. But
they arose in massive contradiction to the theory of the extensive
republic, which was the most important theory underlying the
Constitution of 1787, of which Madison is rightly known as the
father.

Although Madison in the Federalist clearly envisaged the
question of a protective tariff arising under the Constitution, and
equally clearly thought that it was a question that could be decided
best in the national congress, it later became Democrat party
dogma that any protection of manufactures not incidental to revenue, was not "protection" for one class of acquisitive faculty,
but exploitation of others for the benefit of one. The same attitude came to be held in regard to a national bank and internal
improvements by the national government.

Let us for the moment consider the latter, internal improvements, since in some respects it was the most characteristic of
the issues dividing the parties before the slavery issue came to
dominate everything else. The Whigs felt that building roads and
canals, clearing and deepening rivers and harbors and encouraging science and invention were things that at once emancipated
the initiative and talents of individuals and enabled the whole
country to grow more prosperous. But it was impossible to appropriate money from the federal treasury, to which the whole
country contributed, to build a road or canal without spending it

in some part of the country, where some few individuals or groups would gain particular advantages. The characteristic Whig view was that the improvement of the part was simultaneously the improvement of the whole. According to that theoretician of state-rights republicanism, John Taylor of Carolina, Congress had no more right to confer economic benefits that were not simultaneously enjoyed by all, than to confer benefits upon a particular religious sect. It could no more lay a tariff to encourage the manufacture of woolens than to lay a tax to promote membership in the Congregational Church.

Nothing is clearer, from the famous tenth Federalist, than that all economic interests as such are on the same moral, or rather immoral, level. In view of the fact that in 1787, and indeed until after the Civil War, the "landed" interest remained the interest of the overwhelming majority of Americans, the problem of controlling faction was practically the problem of enabling interests other than those of farmers to have an equal chance to survive and to grow. The constitutional convention is frequently looked upon in the histories as a Thermidorean, or conservative reaction against the democratic radicalism of the revolution. This thesis has been very persuasively controverted recently.[2] But whatever validity it has must be seen against the background of agrarian "radicalism" as against the alleged "conservatism" of other interests. That agrarians should then have been radical democrats is not surprising, when we consider that farmers were the overwhelming majority, and the greater the moral weight attributed to the majority as such, the greater the moral weight of the interests of farmers in their struggles with conflicting interests. There is no question in my mind that the movement for the Constitution was in concrete terms a movement to neutralize the overweening power of agrarian forces, which frequently rode roughshod over banking, commercial and manufacturing interests in the states. Nor do I have much doubt that Hamilton's program, from the funding of the debt and establishment of the National Bank, to the Report on Manufactures, was a logical extension of the movement that engendered the Constitution, although it may have been a greater extension than anyone envisaged in 1787. Certainly the acquisitive faculties that found protection, and

---

[2] "Democracy and The Federalist: A Reconsideration of the Framers' Intent," by Martin Diamond, in Amer. Polit. Sci. Rev., March, 1959. I am indebted to Professor Diamond for a clearer understanding of the role of the large or extended republic in the theories of The Federalist, as set forth in his unpublished essay on "The Federalist's View of Federalism," Institute for Studies in Federalism, Claremont Men's College, February, 1960.

enjoyed growth, under the aegis of the national banks and the tariffs, could never have had such an efflorescence under the Articles of Confederation. And yet the whole movement of Jeffersonian democracy — and in this respect the Jacksonians only sought
to restore the pristine Jeffersonianism from which Jefferson's
heirs had fallen away — was a movement to restore the full force
of the numerical majority, the agrarian majority, which the federal system designed in 1787 was intended to fragment and divide.
The purpose of party organization, Jeffersonian and Jacksonian,
was to bring together the latent agrarian majority in the whole
country, and enable it to be "united and actuated by [the] common
impulse of passion, or of interest," that distinguished them from
the moneyed, manufacturing and commercial interests. Why was
it that Jefferson did not think, as did the Madison of the Federalist,
that such a passion and interest, no less than the passion and interest of any other economic group, would be "adverse to the
rights of other citizens [and to] the aggregate interests of the
community? "
     The answer is to be found in the agrarian ideology which was
part of Jefferson's thought from the outset, and which subsisted
in uneasy relation to those other elements upon which we have
already dwelt. Let us hear the great thematic passage in the
Notes on Virginia:

The political economists of Europe have established it as a principle, that
every state should endeavor to manufacture for itself; and this principle,
like many others, we transfer to America, without calculating the difference of circumstance .... In Europe the lands are either cultivated, or
locked up against the cultivator. Manufacture must therefore be resorted
to of necessity not choice, to support the surplus of their people. But we
have an immensity of land courting the industry of the husbandman. Is it
best then that all our citizens should be employed in its improvement, or
that one-half should be called off from that to exercise manufactures and
handicraft arts for the other? Those who labor in the earth are the chosen
people of God, if ever he had a chosen people .... Corruption of morals
in the mass of cultivators is a phenomenon of which no age nor nation has
furnished an example. It is the mark set on those who, not looking up to
heaven, to their own soil and industry, as does the husbandman, for their
subsistence, depend for it on the casualties and caprice of customers.
Dependence begets subservience and venality, suffocates the germ of virtue, and prepares fit tools for the designs of ambition ....

     Here we uncover a deep stratum of early American party
conflict. Jefferson hated Hamilton not so much for his ultramon-
tane constitutionalism, or alleged monarchism, as because the
financial and commercial interests Hamilton promoted, and the
manufacturing he would promote, produce the wrong kind of
human being. John Miller notes that "of the Tory property

confiscated by Virginians during the Revolutionary War, one third belonged to the hated Scotch merchants of Norfolk."[3] I have little doubt that Jefferson felt an ancestral dislike for the "bastard brat of a Scotch peddler" who later stood for the protection and promotion of these same commercial interests, as well as defending Tory claims to restitution under the Treaty of Paris and Jay's Treaty. Equality of opportunity could not legitimately demand a bank or tariff, not because the power to do these things was not enumerated in the Constitution, but because banking and manufacturing were not morally healthy activities for the citizens of a republic.

But Jefferson was mistaken when he spoke of the husbandman not depending on the casualties and caprice of customers. I do not think an argument is necessary at this date to support the proposition that agriculture in the United States, then as now, has been emphatically a commercial operation. In fact, the idea of independence which Jefferson here expresses is an adaptation of the aristocratic contempt for those who are "in trade." But this idea is not only aristocratic, but in its hostility to commerce is hostile to the very foundations of a democratic order. Jefferson wished America's workshops to remain in Europe. Yet so long as this remained the fact, not only would the sources of political independence remain remarkably fragile, for obvious reasons, but American farmers would continue to be, as Jefferson himself once said that Virginia planters were, "a species of property annexed to certain mercantile houses in London." More profoundly, commerce (whose home was the cities) was, historically, the very engine of that personal liberty reaching political fruition in the American republic. A purely agrarian society once subsisted upon the soil of western Europe, and its system was known as feudalism. Primogeniture, entail and all the other props of the artificial aristocracy Jefferson so loathed, were the logical and necessary concomitants of a society based exclusively upon the ownership of land. And no society ever exhibited greater "corruption of morals," in Jefferson's own sense of that term. The mass of cultivators, in that most agrarian of regimes, were serfs, that is, in the decisive sense, slaves.

Because of the supposedly superior virtues of farmers, Jefferson would

let our workshops remain in Europe.... The mobs of great cities add just so much to the support of pure government, as sores do to the

---

[3] John C. Miller, Origins of the American Revolution. Stanford University Press, Stanford, California. P. 17

strength of the human body. It is the manners and spirit of a people which preserve a republic in vigor.

Yet in another passage in the same Notes, Jefferson indulged his most famous denunciation of slavery, as a "perpetual exercise of the most boisterous passions, the most unremitting despotism on the one part, and degrading submission on the other," concluding that "the man must be a prodigy who can retain his manners and morals undepraved by such circumstances." Yet Jefferson did not seem to realize the extent to which, in constantly seeking to strengthen agriculture, not with other elements making for a balanced economy, but at the expense of other elements, he was acting to strengthen slavery.

A remarkable, if not wholly accurate clue to the relation of the ideological and material elements in the early American party struggle is given in the following passage from Henry Adams' John Randolph:

Between the slave power and states' rights there was no necessary connection. The slave power, when in control, was a centralizing influence, and all the considerable encroachments on states' rights were its acts. The acquisition and admission of Louisiana; the embargo; the war of 1812, the annexation of Texas "by joint resolution;" the war with Mexico, declared by the mere announcement of President Polk; the fugitive slave law; the Dred Scott decision — all triumphs of the slave power — did far more than either tariffs or internal improvements, which in their origin were also southern measures, to destroy the very memory of states' rights as they existed in 1789. Whenever a question arose of extending or protecting slavery, the slaveholders became friends of centralized power, and used that dangerous weapon with a kind of frenzy.

I think Adams is less than fair in characterizing measures of Jefferson's and Madison's administrations as measures to extend slavery. I do not think they were meant to be, yet in the perspective of history we must observe the extent to which they in fact had that tendency and effect. It should be noted, for example, that before Iowa was admitted as a free state in 1846, every state admitted to the Union from territory acquired since the revolution was a slave state. These included Louisiana, Missouri, Arkansas, Florida and Texas; and it was provided in the resolution of annexation that Texas might be subdivided into four more slave states. The parties of Jefferson and Jackson, profoundly influenced by the agrarian ideology of which Jefferson was the chief architect, had as their supreme practical objects, the acquisition and protection of land — land plentiful and cheap. Next to this came low taxes — cheap land and cheap government. The powers of the national government might be construed to the limit — and even beyond, for Jefferson himself did not believe there was any constitutional power to purchase Louisiana — if the object was to gratify farmers. At the same time, these same powers were construed in the strictest manner in order to veto things like internal improvements, which might require the government to raise taxes for any other purpose than to buy, annex or conquer land, land which might be sold to poor farmers at nominal prices, although more often it went to land speculators.

Jefferson may not have intended it, but the agricultural interest he strengthened was primarily a southern agricultural interest. The Louisiana Purchase gave slavery a territorial foundation it otherwise would have lacked, when the invention of the cotton gin, and the British power looms, called the great ante-bellum cotton kingdom into existence. And there certainly was never a commercial operation which begot such subservience upon a market, over which the producer himself had little or no control, or which begot such venality and ambition as the cotton kingdom.

The fate of the Jeffersonian agrarian ideology in the South is poignantly illustrated by a passage in John Taylor's Arator, first published in 1803. Taylor, be it remembered, was a disciple of Jefferson, and Jefferson wrote in 1820, that he "rarely, if ever, differed in any political principle of importance" with Taylor. Taylor still accepts the view that slavery is, in the abstract, an evil. But, in the Notes on Virginia, he cannot accept the condemnation of slavery as a corrupter of morals. He tries to explain away these passages by saying that they were written in the somewhat excessive heat of the revolution, a war for liberty, and hence were a kind of generous excess. And then we hear the first, not so faint beginnings, of the "positive good" school concerning slavery.

> Slavery was carried farther among the Greeks and Romans than among ourselves, and yet, these two nations produced more great and good patriots and citizens, than, probably, all the rest of the world....
> To me it seems, that slaves are too far below, and too much in the power of the master, to inspire furious passions; that such are nearly as rare and disgraceful towards slaves as towards horses ... that children from their nature are inclined to soothe, and hardly ever suffered to tyrannize over them; and that fewer good public characters have been raised in countries enslaved by some faction or particular interest, than in those where personal slavery existed.
> I conjecture the cause of this to be, that vicious and mean qualities become despicable in the eyes of freemen from their association with the character of slaves. Character, like condition, is contrasted, and as one contrast causes us to love liberty better, so the other causes us to love virtue better.

Slavery, like agriculture, is now seen as a school of good

manners and morals, and the characters resulting from it are
held to be more favorable to true republicanism than where all
men are more or less on a level of equality. The "submission
and flattery of slaves" Taylor says, makes free men despise
flattery. But the "submission and flattery of freemen," which is
what happens when politicians court votes in free states, "fills
men with the impudent and wicked wish to dictate." Slavery makes
men gentle, and equality makes them despotic! I think there is no
little truth in the contention that the flattery of politicians can
corrupt voters. But, it seems to me, the truest remedy for this
is something like the educational scheme Jefferson proposed,
carried out on a national scale. Here we have the view that the
degradation of one class of human beings may be desirable in
order to elevate the characters of another class. This was, as
Taylor seems to be aware, of the essence of the aristocratic republicanism of the ancient world, but it was the denial of the
democratic republicanism of ours.

   The attempt of the Jeffersonians, following one strand in their
Protean leader's[4] Protean thought, to shore up democratic egalitarianism against the corruptions of a nascent capitalism, resulted in a mistaken elevation of agriculture, as a peculiarly
moral occupation. In the aristocratic ancient world, there was an
affinity between virtue and agriculture. Land was held to be the
only stable kind of wealth, and inherited wealth to be the precondition for that disinterested and educated concern with political
affairs which was the essence of statesmanship. But the application of science to production, as advocated by no one more than
Jefferson, made it possible for all men to aspire now to a level
of material well-being, and hence to leisure and education, that
had heretofore been possible only for a few. Technology and the
division of labor would result in an economy which would implement this much higher level of material well-being. Such an
economy, however, required the whole paraphernalia of commerce, finance and industry. This is why Madison, in the tenth
Federalist, referred to this complex of interests as the mark of
a civilized nation. The immortal part of Jeffersonian democracy
lies in its perception of the need for virtue as the indispensable
ingredient of a republic, modern as well as ancient. But virtue
could never again mean quite the same thing in a world

---

   [4] What one might call the Jefferson problem is amusingly symbolized by a story
told in Nathan Schachner's biography of Jefferson. After receiving the British ambassador in homespun and carpet slippers — and being mistaken for one of the
servants — President Jefferson would retire to Monticello and, in the intimacy of his
domestic circle, dress like a grandee of the pre-revolutionary Paris he had once
adorned.

revolutionized by science. Perhaps Jefferson's very greatness
lies, in a way, in his comprehensive inability to abandon those
aristocratic elements in the definition of virtue that his commitment to democracy required. The quasi-feudalism of the ante-
bellum South was greatly fortified by its inheritance from Jefferson of an agrarian ideology. Although quixotic and anachronistic,
it endowed America's great "lost cause" with more than a touch
of the antique glory it recalled. But such a cause could not be
permitted to survive in a nation devoted more profoundly and
truly to that flaming proposition, of which Jefferson was also the
author, that all men are created equal.

PAUL MEADOWS
Syracuse University

Discussion

THIS CHAPTER is well worth rereading. Its relevance to the
harried and hurried head-lining news of agricultural policy lies
not so much in its valuable historical detachment as in the particularly deft manner by which its author suggests the nature of
public policy — whether agricultural or not — as an historical-
social process. I think the point is especially pertinent. As a
person who for a good many years has taught a sociology course
in American farm movements, I have often been struck with the
fact that agricultural policy in the past has seldom if ever had
the neat, machined precision of mathematics, but rather has dis-
played a dramatic situational dialectic in which ideology and
sentiment and oftentimes sheer idiocy have weighted the balances
of decision making. Indeed, the historical narratives seem to
have few econometric models.

   · Since I am not the least bit a professional historian, I shall
not pass judgment on the reliability of Professor Jaffa's "re-
capture" of the past. I must add, however, that as a devoted
admirer of Henry Nash Smith's volume Virgin Land, I was a
trifle puzzled by Jaffa's sentence: "Jefferson may not have intended it, but the agricultural interest he strengthened was primarily a southern agricultural interest." This is to me a strange
reading of the aftermath of the Louisiana Purchase. Be that as it
may, not at all puzzling was his presentation of an historical
analytical model which describes some neglected dimensions of
agricultural policy, which may in its developmental aspects be
conceived of as a birthing process aided by the obstetrical services of group ideology, politicized interests, and logicizing

activities — a formidable paramedical team for a patient needing care.

As I interpret his main point, with respect to the goals and values in agricultural policy, he is emphasizing the modes and pathologies of an historical process by which the dialectics of differences are stated and resolved, perhaps wrongly, but nonetheless resolved. The image evoked by his perspective is the Toynbee concept of "challenge and response." He writes: "The greatest of all expressions of national purposes come from the gravest moments of doubt and conflict over these very purposes." He presents and analyzes several such moments, and in so doing he is underlining the twin themes that (a) some such conflictive and transcending process is at work with respect to current agricultural policy as surely as it has been present in earlier great debates about the "national purpose," and (b) some of the modes and hazards of definition of policy as we find them in our own national history are powerful agents in our collective behavior today. By returning to the early decades of our national history, he is asserting, as do some child psychologists and sociologists about the developing person, that the nation-as-child is indeed father to the nation-as-man.

Perhaps I am reading too much into Jaffa's words. I hope not. Perhaps there was less of a pronounced analytical model in his intentions than in his writing. Nevertheless I was impressed with the role that analogy played in the organization and development of this chapter. There is, of course, nothing strange about this. All models are analogies, and generalizations from models are analogical extensions. The value of his analytical model — the value to me at least — is that it renews its strength when it reestablishes contact with history, exactly as did Antaeus, son of earth.

American agriculture today is surely in a minority position. Professor Jaffa returns in history to a time when the position of agriculture was exactly reversed, when the American farm population was a decisive majority. Defining and rationalizing the interest, the role, the significance of the agricultural establishment with respect to the whole nation involves considerations and criteria no different now than then. The problem may be described in Gestalt psychology terms, as the part-whole relation. Whether the part is large or small with respect to the whole, there is always the tyrannizing tendency of the part (any part, mind you!) to identify itself with the whole, indeed as the same as the whole: thus, for example, agrarian virtue as republican freedom. This mode of moralizing one's interest is, of course,

not confined to farmers and agricultural economists. With no
difficulty at all, one can say that what is good for the AAUP is
good for the country!

This bit of rhetoric, this synecdoche of ideology, in which the
part stands for the whole, can be a vicious and dangerous thing,
whether it occurs in the form of Communist monolithic dynamism
or in the form of American corporate dynamism. Professor
Jaffa's sympathies, as he works out the solution of the part-whole
relation, lie with Madison, it appears, and much less with Jefferson. Jefferson's passion for democratic egalitarianism led him,
as Professor Jaffa points out, to the absurd elevation of agriculture as a peculiarly moral occupation. Madison, propounding the
theory of the extended republic, approaches the problem from the
other end of the relation, from the whole to the part. Here, it
might be pointed out, Jaffa outlines two great, two very conflictive concepts of justice: the Platonic and individualistic concept
of justice embodied in the phrase, "to each his own," as against
the Aristotelian and collective concept of justice as the bond
between man and his community.

Professor Jaffa's sympathies seem to lie with the latter. And
so do mine. For the alternative is ultimately an Hobbesian world
in which the hand of all is raised against all. The demanding and
infantile isomorphism of the one regarded as the many, of the
minority as the same as the majority, of the majority as the same
as the total in the end seems to wind up in some holocaust of conflict in which all must come to make atonement in order that all
may have a common redemption. This kind of historical process
is humanly wasteful, culturally destructive. There is surely
some other solution.

Each part proclaims its identity as the whole; this is indeed a
classic instance of Harry Stack Sullivan's concept of the paratac-
tic distortion of social reality. Professor Jaffa points, however,
to a process of situational transcendence — to use Kenneth Burke's
arresting phrase — by which the doctrine of the extended republic
comes to replace the omnipotent infantilism of the overdetermin-
ing part, be that part agriculture, or manufacturing, or labor, or
a state or a region. Such transcendence is not easy to achieve; it
is, as he points out, always enmeshed in a web of conflict of some
kind and some intensity. For the process of transcendence of
individual differences and irreconcilability is often blocked by an
irrationality, the irrationality of an illusion which succeeds, un-
happily for the part, only very ineffectively to screen the reality.

To be specific: American enterprises of all species and
types, agriculture no more than the others, pretend to a kind of
protestive innocence, to a kind of historical virtue, to a kind of

"down-underneath-we-hate-all-these-compromises" rationalization, while voting themselves more and more bureaucratization, more and more central direction, more and more involvement with administered rather than market decision making. The real world has changed, but the illusory image of freedom, of uniqueness, of special virtue persists. In time, the irrational refusal to accept the reality of an other-controlled existence ends in the pseudoschizophrenic posture, in which the offended but innocent self-styled victim complains, "I am damned if I do, and I am damned if I don't." This double bind — as Gregory Bateson and his colleagues call it — is characterized by the most hopeless confusion of literalness and metaphoricness. Like the schizophrenic patient, the embattled and confined and angry and anxious part, persisting in his metaphorical identity with the collective good, seems doomed to some permanent rupture with reality. He may, paranoiacally, blame the market, or the administration, or technology, or somebody, for his ailment. He may, hebephrenically, mimic what everybody else is saying or doing — or what he thinks they are saying or doing. Or he may, catatonically, retreat into a world of dumb and injured rejection.

I have taken liberties with Professor Jaffa's analytical model, because I think the agricultural establishment in the United States exhibits a number of parallels with the disturbed and anxious condition of the schizophrenic patient. (After all, for many years now, I have been hearing that American agriculture is sick.) Like any analogy or model, this one has its limitations, its own distortions of reality. But it serves a useful purpose: there are many perspectives on reality; sometimes the most profitable one is the incongruous perspective. However, as in psychiatry so in history, salvation lies along a road of transcendence. This process of transcendence may be called by many names. Professor Jaffa's fine phrase, from the Federalist, the doctrine of the extended republic, is surely one of them. It is, of course, not the sole dimension of public policy. But in its wonderful accent on integrity, it is by all means a very important dimension of public policy.

Chapter 4

DON MARTINDALE

University of Minnesota

The Status of American Goals and Values

I N THEIR INVITATIONS to participate in this discussion, the
organizers propounded a series of provocative questions to
each contributor. Those posed to me were: (1) Does America
have a unique set of goals and values? (2) How much discrepancy
between ideal and real goals is permissible? (3) How can conflicts be resolved?

In a general way these questions may be answered very
quickly and easily. First: Does America have a unique set of
goals and values? Yes. In fact it has a number of them. Second:
How much discrepancy between ideal and real goals is permissible? If real goals differ from ideal goals in that they are actually pursued, there is no reason why the discrepancy between
the two should not be infinite. The amount of difference that is
tolerable is measured only by the limits of tolerance itself.
Third: How can conflicts be resolved? If the conflict is between
ideal and real goals, it is most conveniently solved by dropping
the ideal; that is, if there is any reason in solving this sort of
conflict in the first place. If, however, the conflict is between
discrepant actual goals of different people, the solution found in
fact will usually express the precise ratio of strength of the interested parties. It is seriously doubtful whether any other solution will prove to be stable.

These remarks are not intended to dismiss the issue, but to
indicate the need to fix the terms of the discussion if it is to cut
beneath current stereotypes.

THE COMMUNITY AS THE
BASIS OF GOAL-VALUE SYSTEMS

This paper rests on the assumption that the objectives men
pursue in the course of their interhuman activities are fixed by
the character of their communities. We take "goals" to mean the

qualities men secure by their social activity and "values" to mean
the principles which organize their goals into systems and determine appropriate means. Communities are total ways of life
arising out of the human requirements for stable and consistent
interhuman activities which are complete enough to take care of
the normal needs of the ordinary life. The goal-value systems
which arise in social life represent the array of means and ends
appropriate to particular communities. The empirical sociology
of value — that is the study of the system of means and ends in
any given pattern of interhuman activity — is assumed to rest on
the relativity of any given goal-value system to community type.
In the past such goal-value systems as tribalism, agrarianism,
cosmopolitanism and nationalism have been anchored in the communities of the tribe, peasant village, city and the nation.

While America gradually evolved a more or less "dominant"
goal-value system and while this is undergoing change at present,
America has at no time sustained a single, exclusive goal-value
system. The multiplicity of American goal-value systems is
anchored in the plurality of its communities. Even in colonial
days three distinct types of communities with fragments of a
fourth had appeared. At this time America had evolved plantation
communities in the South, village communities and cities in the
northern colonies. Moreover, there were some small settlements
of peasant communities at this time. Each of these types of communities continued to develop throughout the 19th century. To
them, after the American revolution, was added the national community which grew slowly at first, but evolved more rapidly as
time went by. Moreover, beginning in the 1830's there was an
increasing tendency for blocks of ethnic aliens to form in the expanding cities, adding pluralities of ethnic ghettos to the other
community types operating as semiclosed, semiautonomous systems within the framework of American society. Each one of
these communities was in process of evolving its distinctive
goal-value system.

The First National Synthesis of an American Goal-Value
System — The Rise of the Yankee as the Distinctive
American Type

In the conflict of the many subcommunities with one another
that has marked the increasing consolidation of American society,
there is a tendency for the more powerful, which is usually also
the more comprehensive community, to win out. The town grows
at the expense of the village, the city at the expense of the town

and the nation at the expense of the city. Moreover, sometimes where a conflict between two different subcommunities occurs, the arena for the conflict is shifted to a community more comprehensive than both. For example, the conflict between Negro and white communities of the American South after the Civil War took place within the framework of the region. The conflict between the farm communities of the Old Northwest and the eastern industrial-financial centers prior to the Civil War shifted to the framework of the growing nation. So, too, did the conflict between the plantation-dominated South (technologically backward and resting on slave labor) and the industrial and farm-village communities of the North (resting on a progressive technology and free labor). This is no place to trace in detail all the forms that community conflict may assume. However, it should perhaps be noted that not all forms of such community conflict have the components of alienness and prejudice peculiar to ethnic and majority communities.

However, with the tendency for each conflict to shift to the arena of most comprehensive power, a transvaluation of goals occurs. When former rural communities are replaced by the city, there is simultaneous redefinition of goals. Though their private preferences were at opposite ends of the scale, the agrarian mystic Oswald Spengler[1] and the cosmopolitan sophisticate Georg Simmel[2] were agreed that the European peasant rural communities and the city differed in characteristic ways: the core of economic life shifted from agricultural to nonagricultural pursuits; a subsistence economy was replaced by a money and market economy; property in land ceased to be the main type of wealth; the organic rhythms of the natural year were replaced by artificial clock and calendar schedules; the family and age grades declined in importance as the clique and social class arose; and even the very modes of thought were changed as a traditional outlook was thrust aside in place of a logical and rational point of view.

The transfer of the arena of community conflict to the next higher level of power[3] is an aspect of a process which in the

---

[1] Oswald Spengler, The Decline of the West. Alfred A. Knopf, New York. 1926. Vol. II. Pp. 85 ff.

[2] Georg Simmel, The Sociology of Georg Simmel. (Trans. by Kurt H. Wolff.) The Free Press, Glencoe, Illinois. 1950. "The Metropolis and Mental Life." Pp. 409 ff.

[3] This, to be sure, is not always voluntary. The conflict between two communities may be utilized by a third with more power than either to improve its own situation the easy way. It may offer its services as moderator as a part of a long-range program of taking over both.

community at large directly parallels the formation of economic consolidations and mergers and the increasing domination of an area of economic life by a few giant concerns. These two kinds of consolidation are merely a specific and a general form of the same process. In fact, the community framework within which the giant economic concerns of contemporary North America operate is provided not by the rural community, the ethnic community, or even the city, but by the nation. The social historical phenomena of greatest importance on the American social scene — more important than any of the conflicts of American sub-communities — is the growth of the nation at the expense of all local forms.

The growth of the American nation, the most comprehensive and powerful community of American society, has been accomplished by the destruction of subcommunities and the reincorporation of their fragments into a new system. To a considerable extent the integration of the nation and the predominance of its goal-value system are to be measured by their capacity to create new and special social types. A social type is an individual whose behavior epitomizes the goal-value system of his community. The communities of hunters and gatherers created the tribesman; rural subsistence communities sustained the peasant; the urban community supplied the social foundation for the citizen; and the new community of the nation-state has created the "national."

In other contexts, on the basis of a review of much of the literature on American character, the following formulations[4] were made:

All major observers agree that American character tends to manifest great practicality, considerable anti-intellectualism, a genius for organization, a strong materialism, a tendency to conceptualize social and political affairs in moralistic terms, a manifestation of great faith in individual initiative, and a sense of civic responsibility. These are the major clues to American character, and the Yankee emerges as the central and unique American type.

This list of traits and trait combinations is about as near to a general characterization of the uniqueness of the American "national" as it is possible to formulate. Moreover, the general historical process by which these American traits arose out of American subcommunities can be traced.

The social composition of the eastern seaboard of colonial

---

[4] Don Martindale, American Social Structure. Appleton-Century-Crofts, New York. 1960. P. ix. For comparative purposes, see Bradford Smith, Why We Behave Like Americans. J. B. Lippincott, Philadelphia. 1957. Pp. 77-98.

North America was initially fixed by the the fact that the majority
of its inhabitants were north Europeans (predominantly English),
middle and lower middle-class townsmen of a variety of Protestant faiths. There was no extensive peasant contingent among
them; there was only a comparatively thin strata of upper middle-
class and royalist elements. Though the primitiveness of frontier traditions forced a rural way of life on the majority of the
colonial Americans, their "natural" community was the town
rather than the rural village, and they were dominated by a
"civic" rather than by a traditional "agrarian" mentality.

Moreover, the pioneer farmer in America later derived from
the seaboard did not have a peasant's attitude toward the land.
His orientation to the wilderness was more that of the miner or
extractor. With great frequency he was derived not from peasant
but from middle-class urban stock.

The particularism of townsmen (which would raise loyalties
to the local community above all loyalties to interlocal combinations) was strong in the days following the American revolution.
In the teeth of the obvious fact that the national government was
in their own hands, the colonists retained a powerful suspicion of
central government. The Bill of Rights is a monument to this
suspicion. That in the face of this particularism the new nation
could thrive at all is a tribute to good sense and practical necessity. The world was, after all, entering a period of national consolidations of economic, political and social life. Economic,
financial and political concerns were in considerable measure
national and international. Hamilton represented those economic
and financial interests in the new state that seized the economic
and financial opportunities that had been forcefully vacated by the
British. Secondly, the threat of a reinvasion of the state by the
British made it militarily advisable to strengthen the central
government. Finally, a newly rising society on the frontier was
raising problems which it was unable to solve by its own resources and was pressing the state and central governments for
assistance. The chief frontier problems requiring federal help
were transportation and the Indians. Hence, while the mentality
of townsmen remained dominant, a new national mentality was
rising. The townsman was the clearest voice within the latter.

Between the period of the forming of the new state and the
Civil War, the evolving community structures of the United States
were shaping into three regional groupings — the Northeast, the
South, and the Old Northwest. The contrast between the northern
village communities and the southern plantation communities has
already been sketched. In both North and South the agricultural
husbandman was evolving into a farmer, though in different ways.

However, of greater importance for the moment was the existence of two sets of class tensions, the resolution of which eventually tended to strengthen the national community as against all of the regions.

The lesser of the class tensions in the early state period were between the eastern capitalist, banker, businessman and western frontiersman. It is a mistake to view this as a rural versus urban conflict, for the frontiersman was often rural only from necessity. He was often motivated by the desire for speculative profits. He mined the land for its superficial resources, and often left a semiruined farm behind him. Only gradually during the course of the nineteenth century, when genuine peasant types (such as the Germans and Scandinavians) settled on the land abandoned by the pioneer farmers, was the same land improved and brought under intensive cultivation. Meanwhile, the original "Old Yankee" pioneer farmer had often cannily moved into the newly forming towns, organized the banks, businesses and enterprises. The pioneer farmer of the Old Northwest was derived from middle-class elements of the eastern seaboard, even as his forefathers on the coast had been derived from middle-class elements from north European countries. Between the Old Northwest and the Northeast a drama was played out somewhat similar to the previous drama between the colonists and England. This time, however, the eastern banker and businessman played the role parallel to the Tories of the colonial period. However, between the eastern and midwestern groups there was a more fundamental kinship than in their colonial counterparts. The psychology of both groups was essentially middle class, for they represented the upper and lower sections of the middle classes; they were its creditor and debtor sections. The mentality of both groups was essentially that of middle-class townsmen. The easterners were Episcopalians, Congregationalists and Unitarians; the midwesterners were Presbyterians, Baptists and Methodists. The moment their situation improved and their indebtedness declined, the midwesterner behaved precisely like his eastern cousins. In fact, as soon as their fortunes improved, they liked nothing better than to send their daughters to Boston finishing schools and their sons to Harvard.

The social classes of the Northeast and the Old Northwest tended, each in its own peculiar way, to carry their problems to a national level. The easterners sought federal support of tariff policies which would protect their new businesses, and they also wanted to establish a national banking system. The midwesterners sought federal support to bring the Indians under control, to finance the building of roads and canals and, later, the railroads. They also sought federal support of liberal land policies and cheap money schemes. As Northeast and Old Northwest carried their contests to a national level, each helped strengthen those aspects of the federal government which would take care of its particular needs.

The major class tension joined the Northeast and Old Northwest in opposition to the South. The plantation communities were tied to the other regions in a number of ways. The northeast manufacturing area was one of the primary markets for southern cotton. Whenever the slave plantation system began to dominate an area, it either drove the non-slave-owning farmers to migrate or to retreat to marginal lands. The Old Northwest was one of the main export areas for the excess southern population. The South was a traditional low tariff area, which put it in tension with the North. The protective tariffs resorted to by the North for the benefit of budding industries guaranteed the high price of southern imports. As an area resting on a wasteful system of agricultural practices, the South contested with the West in the attempt to extend the plantation system. This ran counter to the drive from liberal, small, individualized land holders of the West. Eventually the advanced technology and free labor system of the North clashed with the unprogressive technology and slave labor system of the South.

Here, too, the contest was shifted to the national scene. The Civil War tremendously strengthened the national community, and led to a reconstitution and simplification of an emerging national character. The war greatly reduced the role of the goal-value system of the South in the emerging national scheme. The war forced a fusion, with many mutual compromises developing between the Northeast and the West. In the newly constituted Republican Party the mentality of the middle-class Protestant townsman was lifted above the regional formations that contributed most to it and placed in a dominant position on a national scale. The concessions made by the East to the West in the course of this development were notable, including the Homestead Act, the Morrill Act and the formation of the U.S. Department of Agriculture. Meanwhile, the Civil War not only represented a great shared national experience but created fabulous markets for both manufactured and agricultural products. It accelerated the movement toward mass production in industry and toward mechanization and commercial orientation in agriculture.

From the Civil War period to World War I, the South was occupied with the problems of reconstruction and race. The region was too riddled by internal tensions to enter very deeply

into other events sweeping the country forward. Between the reorganized Northeast and Midwest, which had been fused by war
and industrialization, and the areas farther west, a new drama
developed somewhat similar to that which had earlier split asun-
der the Northeast and Old Northwest. The West was still the
debtor region, still in need of transportation facilities, still inclined to take political action to promote its economic interests
(in Populism, the Free Silver Movement and the Greenback Movement). However, the West as a whole presented new problems.
The Southwest had a special major set of problems in its Spanish
components. The arid west presented special problems for agricultural and social technology. Among other things, it not only
rendered irrelevant the farm techniques successful in the East
and Midwest, but also many of its social and political arrangements. The Homestead Act, for example, promoted a fragmenta-
tion of holdings which was extremely uneconomic in many areas
of the arid west. The settlement of the West first leaped over the
arid west to the coast, where the Oregon Territory to some degree enacted a drama similar to the settlement of the Old Northwest. Major events on the Great Plains included the destruction
of the buffalo and the brief flowering for two decades of the heroic
period of the cattle industry before the windmill, barbed wire,
dry farming, winter wheat and irrigation began to convert the
area to agriculture. By 1890 a frontier line had ceased to exist,
and all the free land had been taken up.

Though new elements were beginning to appear on the national
scene that did not fit the main pattern, there is little doubt that
the last two decades of the nineteenth century and the first 10
years of the twentieth century were the period of the first inclusive synthesis of the American character. It was even experienced by many Americans as a kind of age of awakened self-
consciousness. In the 1880's, as Kazin notes, America was ready
for a truly national literature.

However, it was not alone in its literature that America was
coming to a new self-consciousness. In the pragmatism of Charles
Pierce, William James and John Dewey, American thought for the
first time produced a distinctive philosophy of its own. In the sky-
scraper, Americans were making a unique contribution to the
architecture of the world. In the prarie style of Sullivan and
Wright, America was developing a style of domestic architecture
of its own. In this period, a national self-consciousness was even
manifest in the attempt to regulate population through immigration control designed to conform to its emerging concept of an
ideal population composition.

The Decline of the Yankee as the Distinctive
American Type

At the very time when American character came to its first
full synthesis (around 1890) and elevated the Yankee into its distinctive national type, major events were in process which seriously upset the trial balance of the American national community.

By 1890 the frontier line had come to an end. America was a
land of small towns. The Yankee with his Puritanism, his capacity for hard work, his mechanical ingenuity, his strong self-
reliance and moral confidence (which permitted him to view success as the natural reward of virtue), his civic consciousness,
his town-meeting democracy, was the epitome of the small Protestant town. Intuitively, he viewed the country as a whole as a
sort of federalism in which his small town was the one solid and
dependable unit.

The three great processes which arose outside the first synthesis of community and character in the United States were: (1)
the gradual assimilation of the mass migrations from the period
of the 1880's to the first world war; (2) the rise and partial integration of the city; and (3) the formation of powerful complexes
of mass industry and government.

The influences of these forces have not yet been completely
assimilated. Many students, for example, have even come to believe that they have rendered archaic much of American liberalism and conservatism. For American liberalism and conservatism became fixed with respect to the first synthesis of American
community and character in ways blinding them to emerging prop-
erties of the changing national community.

The set of characteristics listed earlier as typifying the
American character represent its first synthesis. They were
more true during the period 1880-1910 than they have been since
that time. While they still hold, in considerable degree, they
seem to hold less true as time goes by. The American character
is changing, and it is not yet clear where the change will end.

SAMUEL W. BLIZZARD

Princeton Theological Seminary

Discussion

THE PAPER PREPARED by Professor Don Martindale is most commendable for the breadth and perspective in which it presents the goals and values of American society. He has used the historical method rather than the analytical method of science, and this choice of method may have influenced the selection of substantive materials about goals and values he has included. This does not imply any desire on my part to deprecate the historical method and to applaud the scientific. However, by definition the former is more appropriate for the study of the origin and development of basic goals and values in American society, and the latter for the study of the current status and content of goals and values.

When values are studied, especially if it is assumed that they have changed or are changing, one may expect much disputation. The debate that has ensued the publication of the Jacob report on Changing Values in College is a present reminder of this fact.[1] Much of the discussion about that report has tended to focus upon the meanings to be attached to terms like values and the methodology used in studies of values. The Hazen Foundation, the sponsor of the research, has published two critical essays about the Jacob report, one by a philosopher[2] and another by a sociologist.[3]

Reference to the importance of methodology is made for nonpartisan rather than partisan motives. The study of goals and values is an emotionally overburdened enterprise. The methods of philosophy, history and behavioral science would each appear to be needed. The philosopher has much to contribute to an understanding of the ontology of values. The historian is the master of a methodology that permits a description of the development of values in a given society. The behavioral scientist would appear to have a special responsibility in describing the present status and content of values in society. The behavioral scientist and the

---

[1] Philip E. Jacob, Changing Values in College. Harper and Brothers, New York. 1957.

[2] John E. Smith, Value Convictions and Higher Education. The Edward W. Hazen Foundation, New Haven. 1958.

[3] Allen H. Barton, Studying the Effects of College Education. The Edward W. Hazen Foundation, New Haven. 1959.

75

historian are concerned with the "isness" of values as distinguished from the "oughtness" described in philosophy, or perhaps
it is the difference between values abstractly and concretely described.

I had hoped that Professor Martindale, a sociologist, would
present a discussion of the current status of goals and values
based on the empirical data now available. Admittedly much of
these data are derived from research on microcosmic situations.
For example, the Goldsen et al. report "What College Students
Think" may be cited.[4] The rural life studies of Landaff, New
Hampshire and Harmony, Georgia, etc., reveal much about values
in specific communities.[5] In addition the extensive literature of
attitudinal and public opinion studies should offer a theoretician
much empirically derived material for the development of a mac-
rocosmic analysis of the present status and content of goals and
values of American society.

The distinction that Professor Martindale makes between
goals and values is useful because it highlights the fact that the
two concepts are frequently used interchangeably in the literature.
Goals are "the qualities men attempt to secure in the course of
their activities," according to Martindale's definition. I assume
that the term is used as a synonym for a value as used by Laswell
and Kaplan which they call "a desired event – a goal event."[6] In
any case, the eight values used by Laswell (power, respect, rectitude, affection, well-being, wealth, skill, and enlightenment)
correspond closely to the goals cited by Martindale. The Goals
of Life Inventory, developed as a project of the Cooperative Study
in General Education, evaluates twenty goals that are more specific than those of Martindale, although it appears to have the
same connotation for the term goal.[7] It includes self-development,
serving the community, serving God, peace of mind, etc.

Values, according to Martindale, are "principles in terms of
which men arrange their goals in axiological systems and fix the
relations between means and ends." His use of the word "evaluated" in this context raises a question about the clarity of his
terms. Gunnar Myrdal avoids using the term "value" because it

[4]Rose K. Goldsen, Morris Rosenberg, Robin M. Williams, and Edward A.
Suchman, What College Students Think. D. Van Nostrand Company, Princeton, New
Jersey. 1960.
[5]Carl C. Taylor, et al., Rural Life in the United States. Alfred A. Knopf, New
York. 1949. Pp. 495-509.
[6]Harold D. Laswell and Abraham Kaplan, Power and Society. Yale University
Press, New Haven. 1950. Pp. 16-28.
[7]Harold E. Dunkel, An Inventory of Student's General Goals of Life. Education
and Psychological Measurement, 4:87-95, 1944.

has a loose meaning.[8] He finds the terms beliefs and valuations useful. The former are ideas people have about how reality actually is or was; the latter are ideas they have about how it ought to be, or ought to have been.[9] "Evaluations" appears to be a synonym for Martindale's use of the term values. It may be inferred from his discussion that the culture of American society permits great and wide diversity in the principles by which means and ends are evaluated, or by which evaluations are made. However, it is not clear what these principles are. In fact, the most disappointing feature of the whole discussion about the current status of "values" (to use Martindale's term) is his apparent failure to be specific about what the principles of evaluation are. His discussions of liberalism and conservatism give some hints, and his discussions of the major American goal-value systems that have developed historically are exciting. However, the reader is left to write his own postscript about the current status of goals and values.

The temptation of a discussant is to overplay his role, especially with reference to negative criticisms. To compensate, the following postscript is attached to Martindale's excellent historical development of American goals and values.

Professor Martindale has organized his discussion of goals and values around the development of community life: tribalism, agrarianism, cosmopolitanism, and nationalism. History helps us understand who we are, and it gives us a perspective on our present status. However, a discussion of the history of community life in relation to goals and values is apt to overshadow the fact that goals and valuations are shaped by and shared in patterns that we call institutions. Also the socialization of the individual person is closely related to, and in a sense is a product of, the interaction of personality system and institutions or social systems. In our monolithic society with its propensity for conformity to the mass image, institutions perform a major function in aiding the individual in identifying himself and the goals and values to which he is committed. Hence such diversity as there exists in the goals and values of our society is maintained by the role the person performs and the status he has in such institutional structures as the family, the educational system, the economic system, the political system, and the religious system. Variability regarding goals and values are found within each of these institutional structures. Available evidence would seem to

---

[8]Paul Streeter, Editor, Value in Social Theory, A selection of essays on methodology, by Gunnar Myrdal. Harper and Brothers, New York. 1959. P. 77.

[9]Ibid., p. 71.

support the notion that variability in goals and values is greater with reference to institutional systems than to community systems. Professor Martindale seems to suggest this in his discussion of conservatism and liberalism. An understanding of the current status of goals and values in American society requires an analysis of the function of institutions in maintaining diversity of goals and values.

I confess considerable skepticism about using variability in community life as a model for ordering goals and values in American society. Studies of community life suggest that the relation of local community groups and institutions to their respective regional and national organizations and institutions is far more important and decisive than is the interrelationship of these groups within the local community in which they are located. Vidich and Bensman[10] document this in their microcosmic research on a New York State rural community. Nisbet[11] and Stein[12] in their review of literature in the sociology of the community place the same ideas in larger perspective.

I can illustrate this by reference to the several institutional structures that are usually represented in the rural community. The economic enterprises are a case in point, whether they are oriented to production or distribution of goods and services, or whether they are organized as private enterprise or cooperatives. The producer is not producing for a local market, nor is the distributor interested only in local decisions for the products or services. Rather, both evaluate opportunities in terms of alternative prices in relation to supply and demand in other communities. The choice to produce or not, to sell or not, to buy or not, is part of an over-all production and distribution mechanism that is ordered by corporate enterprise (a trade association, a manufacturing association, labor union or other groups) beyond the local community that structure the decision-making processes.

Even the local church, an institution that is proud of its individualism and autonomy, is influenced in its decisions about goals to a greater degree by the regional or denominational class to which it belongs than it is by the wishes of the local congregation. In Protestant denominations, for example, national goals regarding

---

[10] Arthur J. Vidich and Joseph Bensman, Small Town in Mass Society — Class, Power and Religion in a Rural Community. Princeton University Press, Princeton. 1958.

[11] Robert A. Nisbet, The Quest for Community — A Study of the Ethics of Order and Freedom. Oxford University Press, New York. 1957.

[12] Maurice R. Stein, The Eclipse of Community — An Interpretation of American Studies. Princeton University Press, Princeton. 1960.

benevolence giving are far more determinative of budget askings in a local church than is the economic potential. The promotion of the clergyman is far more likely to be determined by the degree to which his church fulfills the national goals than locally derived goals.[13]

The same may be said with equal validity for educational, welfare, and political goals and evaluation. In fact, in our society we seem to have allocated this type of leadership to high priests in each institution who articulate the goals and values of that institutional structure. Lawyers are the high priests of the political structure.[14] Physicians are the high priests of the health system, the theologian of the religious institutions, and the schools have a similar small professional group that performs this function.[15] Professional schools train these high priests in the formulation and articulation of acceptable goals and values.

I suspect that among the high priests of the institutions the basic goals in American society are much more uniform and pervasive than Professor Martindale's review would suggest. A hint of this is suggested by a study conducted by Skolnick and Schwartz on the students enrolled in Yale University Professional Schools.[16] Law and divinity students are budding high priests for the political and religious institutions, respectively. It might be theorized that prospective lawyers are concerned with power goals, ministers with rectitude and moral issues, physicians with well-being, etc. Contrary to expectations Skolnick and Schwartz found that law and divinity students both emphasize power or decision making in their personal and professional life as a primary goal. To be sure, many selective factors are probably operating to make this similarity possible. However, it is most surprising to find that future clergymen see rectitude or morality as a secondary goal.

The difference in goals that are apparent in American society may be closely related to the institutional structures through which persons seek to fulfill their goals. If so, then the differential means for fulfilling goals are more important in explaining variability than are the differential goals. For example, the segment of the economy in which the farmer functions may be

[13]Vidich and Bensman, op. cit., pp. 227-57. Paul M. Harrison, Authority and Power in the Free Church Tradition—A Social Case Study of the American Baptist Convention. Princeton University Press, Princeton. 1959.

[14]Donald R. Matthews, The Social Background of Political Decision-Makers. Doubleday and Company, New York. 1954. Pp. 30-32.

[15]Neal Gross, Who Runs Our Schools? John Wiley and Sons, New York. 1958.

[16]Jerome H. Skolnick and Richard D. Schwartz, Power Perspectives of Divinity and Law Students. A paper presented at the Eastern Sociological Society Annual Meeting, Boston, Massachusetts. April 22, 1960.

important in how he evaluates the means available to him in fulfilling his goals. The farmer, and his high priests, articulate an
ethic to which they are committed, which guides choices he makes
between "good" and "bad" means for goal fulfillment.
There is another aspect to the relative uniformity of basic
goals in American society that is easily overlooked. A number
of recent works suggest the importance of personality in the
political process. [17] I am of the opinion that the personality variable is an important, but relatively unexplored variable, in relation to the purposes of this conference. The recent research on
an upstate New York rural community, to which we already referred, discusses the personality variable in relation to community integration. The authors [18] state:

> While integration thus exists at the institutional level, there is always
> the possibility that it does not reach down into the personal lives of the
> community member.... Adhering to publicly stated values while at the
> same time facing the necessity of acting in immediate situations places a
> strain on the psychological makeup of the person.

In a concluding chapter of their report, they examine the dilem-
mas faced by the residents of the small town and the modes of
personality adjustment that these residents use to minimize their
personal conflicts. There is a new urgency in the need for research on personality as a factor in goals and values as they relate to agricultural policy, especially because, I believe, the
valuations of the American farm public have been radically re-
structured.
Clarification as to who the high priests are and what their
roles are varies within the different institutions in American
society. It is rather clear that in political, religious and health
systems technically trained high priests are available and that
their role differs from that of other functionaries in these systems. In other systems technically trained high priests are not
available in great numbers and their role has not been universally
accepted. Agriculture is one of the systems in which the role of
the high priest is still being defined and his technical competence
being established. A resolution of the ambiguities involved in the
role of the high priest will do much to clarify the goals and values
of agriculture.

[17] T. W. Adorno, et al., The Authoritarian Personality. Harper and Brothers,
New York. 1950; Harold D. Laswell, Power and Personality. W. W. Norton and
Company, New York. 1948; Alfred H. Stanton and Stewart E. Perry, Personality and
Political Crisis. The Free Press, Glencoe, Illinois. 1951.
[18] Vidich and Bensman, op. cit., p. 285.

FRANK GRACE

University of Michigan

Discussion

PROFESSOR MARTINDALE has presented what I consider to be as thorough and scholarly a treatment of the status of American goals and values as one could in the scope permitted him. It is something of a brief intellectual and social history of the United States, tracing as it does some of the main themes in our development.

Professor Martindale's approach and emphasis, however, are those of a sociologist. I do not by this statement insinuate criticism or disagreement. On the contrary, I am, to the extent of my knowledge of the subject, in quite firm agreement with him, but as a political scientist concerned primarily with the development of political thought it is perhaps only natural that my approach and emphasis be somewhat different from his. I wish therefore as a student of political theory to raise some further questions with reference to the status of American goals and values. Perhaps these questions are all raised either explicitly or implicitly by Professor Martindale, but here we shall attempt to come at them in a somewhat different manner.

From its beginnings western civilization has embodied two fundamentally opposing traditions. These may be described or characterized in a number of ways, but there is hardly a more apt way to describe them than to say that one tradition has made God the measure and the other has made Man. One has accepted the existence of a transcendental order while the other has insisted that order is man made and exists only within the immanent realm. The tension between the two traditions may be observed in the debate between Socrates and Thrasymachus as to whether justice is natural or conventional. We can also see its outlines in the high Middle Ages in the conflict of Scholastics and Nominalists — Thomas Aquinas on the one hand and Marsilio of Padua on the other. We observe it again in Machiavelli and his critics, or in Hobbes and his critics. In the eighteenth century, Burke has become heir to the position of Socrates, and Robespierre to the tradition of Thrasymachus. In our own century the struggle continues with perhaps the best representatives of the God-the-measure tradition being the British and American liberal democracies and the best representatives of the Man-the-measure tradition being the new totalitarianisms of Nazi Germany and Soviet Russia.

81

Now I confess to gross oversimplification. At the level of reality, if not at the level of theory, the two traditions are commingled, and this is particularly true of the modern period. Bodin, the father of the modern concept of sovereignty, was troubled by the demands of a transcendental justice. The Marxist may deny with great vigor and in total sincerity the existence of a transcendental realm or the capacity of man to transcend existence, but in his denial he uses the language and symbolism of transcendence. The examples one could give of this commingling are endless, but one more might be in order. We speak constantly of our form of government as one in which both the principles of majority rule and minority rights operate, and it is true that they do. What we do not always realize is that majority rule makes man the measure whereas the minority rights principle appeals to a belief in man's capacity to experience transcendence. Taken alone the majority rule principle in effect holds that all opinions or desires are of equal worth, that the highest authority is the human will, and that social order demands that we count heads rather than make it necessary for the majority to resort to force. The minority rights principle, on the other hand, ascribes to the person a dignity and a worth independent of human opinion and authority, and although it may well serve utility and social order, it is not their creation.

These two traditions are, of course, functions of different views as to the nature of man and different philosophies of history. I will not bore you with any discussion of the nature of man or philosophies of history except to point out that in one tradition man has been regarded as a blend of spirit and body, reason and passion, good and bad. The higher elements of his nature are constantly opposed and thwarted by the lower with the consequence that his reach will always exceed his grasp and that his institutions will always fail to serve in full the purposes for which they were established. In the other view man has generally been regarded as a uniquely highly developed animal with an unparalled capacity for adaption. He is the master of his own fate and in good season he will perfect himself and establish within history a just and lasting peace when neither fear nor want will be known.

Today, as in the past, the great line of demarcation runs between these two traditions, or, in symbolic terms, between the City of God and the City of Man. This was pointed up not so long ago by one of the most distinguished of contemporary political philosophers, Professor Eric Voegelin of the University of Munich. According to Voegelin:[1]

---

[1] Eric Voegelin, "The Origins of Totalitarianism," Rev. of Polit., Vol. 15, No. 1, p. 75 (January, 1953).

The true dividing line in the contemporary crisis does not run between liberals and totalitarians, but between the religious and philosophical transcendentalists on the one side, and the liberal and totalitarian immanentist sectarians on the other.

Substantially the same idea is offered by Professor Leo Strauss.[2]

Looking around us, we see two hostile camps, heavily fortified and strictly guarded. One is occupied by the liberals of various descriptions, the other by the Catholic and non-Catholic disciples of Thomas Aquinas.

Further explication of the idea is contained in one of Reinhold Niebuhr's more recent books with the suggestive title of Pious and Secular America.[3]

Returning now to the task at hand — a discussion of the status of American goals and values — I should like to suggest again that in America from our beginnings both traditions have operated simultaneously. I have already made reference to our commitment to both majority rule and minority rights. There is also our great faith in the people coupled with such nonpopular institutions as the senate and judicial review. We have separated church and state, and for good reason, but yet we say that we are one nation under God and that in Him we trust. We have said that the business of our government is business, yet we tax ourselves to serve the underprivileged of the world. We have fought a war to end wars and make the world safe for democracy, and then have withdrawn to a selfish and blind isolation. We fought another war to secure a world free from fear and want, but we are not a nation devoid of realism. We have evidenced an almost unbounded optimism and faith in progress, yet we are cautious, conservative and intent upon constructing as many dikes against contingencies as is possible. We have admired the philosophy of revolutionary France, but our institutions owe much more to 1688 than to 1789.

The point is, I trust, abundantly clear. We have accepted both the City of God and the City of Man and have been a nation with a divided loyalty. But there is reason to believe that throughout most of our history most of us have made our loyalty to the City of Man subordinate. We have acted as if man is endowed with a spark of the divine, as if there is an objective standard of justice, and as if we have obligations extending beyond time. And, too,

---

[2] Leo Strauss, Natural Right and History. University of Chicago Press, Chicago. 1953. P. 7.
[3] Charles Scribner's Sons, New York. 1958.

most of us have been prepared to accept something less than perfection and have agreed with Walt Whitman that probably each fruition of success will bring forth something to make a greater sacrifice necessary.

I would submit that goals and values are — in the last analysis, if not more immediately — functions of how we conceive of man and his destiny. This may be trite, but it is too often forgotten that attempts to establish heaven on earth have only succeeded in creating hells. Such attempts result from our failure to appreciate the nature of the human materials with which we must work or from becoming too immersed in the tradition of man the measure.

To the degree that these observations are correct, the question becomes one of the relative strength of the two traditions today. Will we continue to try to build the best city that is humanly possible, aware that it will always incorporate injustice and suffering, or will we abandon the oldest knowledge of man, our finiteness, assume ourselves to be gods and attempt the establishment of our particular version of heaven? Of course I do not know the answer to the question I have raised, but the evidence that we are rapidly turning to the secular, immanentist creed is sufficient to justify genuine concern. I will indicate only some of the developments, but they are sufficient to give us pause.

There is, for example, reason to believe that our values are increasingly materialistic. The unparalled creature comforts of our age and the leisure which has attended our industrial and technical advances do not seem to have inclined us any more toward the life of the spirit or of the mind. Rather they appear only to have sharpened our appetites and accentuated our baser natures. I need not elaborate upon the dangers of excessive materialism. They are known to us all as are the signs of excess, but I would like, for the sake of emphasis, to point to two. Materialism can be and is the enemy of liberty. One need only point to Russia or China. We might well ask ourselves, however, whether we are prepared to accept the sacrifice involved in what we hope will be a successful prosecution of the Cold War. It is not without significance that the percentage of our gross national produce expended for public purposes has been declining for some time although our responsibilities and our resistance to taxation have never been greater.

Materialism, however, is perhaps a greater threat to our unity than to our liberty. Professor Roland Pennock, in an excellent study of liberal democracy,[4] has termed it the greatest danger,

...partly because it leads to a devaluation of liberty but chiefly because of its divisiveness. The possibilities of increasing total production are severely limited.... On the other hand, the possibilities for increasing the material well-being of one group at the expense of others are almost without limit.

The implications of these facts are obvious.

Another danger, paradoxically, has its origin in one of the great sources of our strength. I refer to our dedication to the principle of equality. It is an ancient principle, dating at least from the Stoics, but in relatively recent times it has undergone a vast change in meaning, the change being from an abstract to a literal content. It is one thing to assume that men are equal before their Creator and that therefore they should be equal before the law, that they are entitled to the respect of their fellows, and that equally they should have the opportunity of developing their capacities. It is quite another thing, however, to assume that because men are equal in some respects they are equal in all. To make them equal in fact involves nothing less than totalitarianism. A literal equality is incompatible with human voluntarism, spontaneity, liberty and excellence. It is compatible with mediocrity, anti-intellectualism, enforced conformity, and the deadening of the human spirit. Of necessity it is established only at the level of the lowest common denominator.

Is there any evidence that we are tending in this direction? I believe there is. I believe it is to be seen in the growing demands for conformity and social integration, in the increasing intolerance of intolerance and individualism and in our retreat from republicanism to majoritarianism. Tocqueville, with amazing insight, foretold the dangers of democratic equality 125 years ago, and our subsequent history has to a distressing degree sustained his prophecy. It is worth remembering that historically democracy is a form of government which has met with reasonable success only in those societies disciplined by belief in a transcendental order. When it becomes a social philosophy — or as we put it "a way of life" — the essence of which is egalitarianism, it is likely to be total in its demands.

Another danger stemming from our immanentism is our unrealistic optimism. It is not necessarily true that virtue always

[4] J. Roland Pennock, Liberal Democracy. Rinehart and Co., New York. 1950. P. 370.

triumphs, that right will prevail. The years since World War II
provide many examples of the type of behavior I have in mind. In
retrospect our rapid demobilization in 1945-46 was a dangerous
mistake, but it was a mistake made on principle rather than because of lack of foresight. I am aware that this action can in
large part be attributed to political pressures, but I would insist
that it must also be attributed in part to our naive belief in an inevitable progress toward a permanent peace. The League of
Nations had failed in large part because of our nonparticipation,
but with the United Nations it would be possible to beat our swords
into plowshares. And there are those of us naive enough to have
believed that what the U.N. failed to do could be done by four men
at the Summit. At the University of Michigan we have a Center
for Conflict Resolution. The men who staff it are perhaps de-
serving of every encouragement, but I am inclined to think there
is more than a suggestion of utopianism in their goal. There is
no magic formula for the achievement of peace, and there is
little likelihood that a group of academicians will meet with more
success than a group of politicians. Conflict inheres in our
natures, and peace remains the product of a balance of existential forces. To obscure this truth is only to serve conflict, not
resolve it.

A final danger I will point to is the cynicism, frustration and
sense of despair that can and often do attend our failures in
reaching for the impossible. One need only point to Nazi Germany to see the force of such sentiments. They are the stuff
upon which demagogues feed.

I have not attempted to do more than suggest some of the chief
dangers which, in my opinion, attach to a thorough-going anthro-
pocentric orientation. I am also aware of the dangers which arise
from the opposite direction, but I believe these to be negligible in
today's world.

Perhaps I could do no better by way of summary than to fall
back upon one of our most eminent intellectual historians, Professor Crane Brinton.[5] As he sees the matter, the great problem
facing us is how to bridge the gap between the desirable and the
attainable —

how to find the spiritual resources needed to face hardship, frustration,
struggle and unhappiness — all the evils [we] have been taught to believe
would be banished shortly from human life.

---

[5]Crane Brinton, Ideas and Men. Prentice Hall, New York. 1950. P. 539.

Professor Brinton then suggests that:[6]

> ...a realistic, pessimistic democracy — a democracy in which ordinary
> citizens approach morals and politics with the willingness to cope with
> imperfection that characterizes the good farmer, the good physician, the
> good holder of the cure of souls, be he priest, clergyman, counselor, or
> psychiatrist — such a democracy would demand more of its citizens than
> any human culture has ever demanded.

Such a democracy as he here describes does not bridge the
gap between the desirable and the attainable. Rather it takes the
tragic view and accepts the inevitability of the gap. But what
does such acceptance involve? In Professor Brinton's answer[7]
is to be found the essence of my remarks.

> The mass of mankind, even in the West, have never been able to take
> the tragic view without the help of a personal religion, a religion hitherto
> always transcendental, supernatural, other worldly.

My concern today is that we are less well prepared than at
any time in our history to take the tragic view. We may have
abandoned in some measure our faith in human perfectibility and
inevitable progress, but we have found no adequate substitutes.

---

[6]Ibid., p. 550.
[7]Ibid., p. 543.

Chapter 5

JESSE W. MARKHAM

Princeton University

Goals for Economic Organization: A Theoretical Analysis

ECONOMISTS HAVE GENERALLY AGREED that the economic goals of society are efficient resource allocation and a high rate of economic growth. They have, at least in the twentieth century, agreed that marginal analysis is a powerful tool for diagnosing these goals, irrespective of the political instrumentation through which they are sought.[1] To be sure, political economists differ sharply on which political instruments hold out the greatest promise for attaining these goals, but even a Soviet economist and an ardent proponent of a free market economy are likely to find themselves in substantial agreement on the goals themselves.

But while economists may agree on economic goals, even those who favor a free enterprise market economy do not always agree on the forms of industrial organization which hold out the greatest hope for attaining them. They may also disagree on the legal and social institutions that best preserve and nurture the forms of industrial organization they prefer.

These disagreements were much in evidence among the founders of the American Economic Association. Most of them had inherited from the classical economists a preference for competitive market organization. Yet to Professor Henry Adams, monopoly was an example in "harmony of control and unity of direction," and often produced goods more efficiently than competitive enterprise.[2] Professor Seligman stated at the Saratoga Conference on the Association's platform that[3]

---

[1] For example, compare George J. Stigler, The Theory of Price. Rev. ed. Macmillan, New York. 1952; and Abba P. Lerner, The Economics of Control. Macmillan, New York. 1946.

[2] Henry C. Adams, Relation of the State to Industrial Action. Publications of the American Economic Association, Vol. 1, No. 6 (January, 1887). Pp. 38-39, 42, 49.

[3] Ibid., p. 27.

competition is not in itself bad. It is a neutral force which has already
produced immense benefits, but which may, under certain conditions, bring
in its train sharply defined evils. Modern economics has, however, not yet
attained that certainty in results which would authorize us to invoke increased governmental action as a check to various abuses of free competition.

Professors J. B. Clark, Irving Fisher and Frank Taussig had a
stronger faith in competitive organization but misgivings about
the nascent antitrust policy in the form of the Sherman Act as a
means of preserving it. Clark viewed the act with outright hostility and Fisher and Taussig regarded it as inferior to positive
trust regulation.[4]
The separate roads of economists on the desirability of competitive market organization as a goal have since converged. The
postwar hearings on antitrust issues are replete with economists'
testimony extolling the merits of competition. But while economists may now be surer of their ground, reservations — some
made explicit and others implied — remain. Schumpeter's innovating monopolist is a sophisticated current counterpart of the
technologically superior monopolist of an earlier era; competition is often considered as unworkable for agriculture and is still
occasionally charged with creating "sick" industries and with
leaving monopoly power uncountervailed; proponents of the "new
competition" call for a new appreciation of big enterprise and
less insistence on vigorous antitrust effort to maintain the economists' version of workably competitive market structures.
In the face of such lingering doubts, can economists who
champion the goal of a reasonably competitive economy find sus-
tenance in the logic of their discipline? There is little doubt that
the antitrust principle has experienced a renaissance in the
1950's. In the United States antimonopoly legislation and enforcement machinery have been significantly strengthened; countries
of Western Europe have initiated new and stronger anticartel
policies; and treaties establishing the European Coal and Steel
Community and the European Economic Community contain provisions for limiting private monopoly power. While such policies
are a product of politics they envision economic goals. For this
reason they should periodically be tested against the accumulated
stock of relevant economic logic. Should they test out to be compatible with such logic the present course of industrial policy

---

[4] J. B. Clark, The Control of Trusts. Macmillan, New York. 1901. P. 12; Irvin
Fisher, Elementary Principles of Economics. Macmillan, New York. 1912. P. 330-
32; F. W. Taussig, Principles of Economics. 3rd ed. Macmillan, New York. 1921.
P. 458.

stands unchallenged. If not, the canons by which private industrial enterprise is governed need critically to be re-examined. The essential purpose of this essay is to subject the goal of a reasonably competitive market organization to such a test.

IDEAL OUTPUT AND THE STATIC STATE

The logical starting point for inquiry into the case for a competitively structured society is Professor Pigou's "ideal" output[5] — that output which yields the highest total satisfaction to a community. Under conventional assumptions concerning the shape of a community's transformation curve (concave to the origin) and indifference map (each indifference curve convex to the origin), the ideal output occurs where the transformation curve is tangent to one of the community's indifference curves. Point E (Fig. 5.1) where $T_1 T_1'$ is tangent to $I_3 I_3'$ illustrates such an output — move away from E in either direction along $T_1 T_1'$ and the community is taken toward $I_2 I_2'$, a lower indifference curve where by definition the community is worse off. But point E is also where a perfectly competitive economy is in equilibrium. The slope of the transformation curve, as measured by a tangent to it at any point, indicates the ratio of the social marginal costs of outputs X and Y — the amount of one of them which society must forego in order to obtain a small increase in the other. And consumer equilibrium requires that the price line must be tangent to one of the community's indifference curves, otherwise consumers can move to another point on the price line and reach a higher indifference curve. Hence, the tangent to the community's transformation curve at point E (the ideal output) must also be the same as the price line tangent to the highest indifference curve the community can possibly reach. This follows from the equation of prices with marginal costs under competitive equilibrium, making the ratio of the prices of commodities X and Y, given by the slope of $P_3 P_3$, equal to that of their respective marginal costs, also given by the slope of $P_3 P_3$ (Fig. 5.1). Thus, in equilibrium, a perfectly competitive economy yields the ideal output E.

---

[5]See A. C. Pigou, The Economics of Welfare. St. Martins, New York. 4th ed., 1929. Esp. Part II; R. F. Kahn, "Some Notes on Ideal Output," Econ. Jour. (March, 1935). Pp. 1-35; William J. Baumol, Welfare Economics and the Theory of the State. Harvard University Press, Cambridge. 1952; and Joan Robinson, The Economics of Imperfect Competition. Macmillan, London. 1948. Chap. 27. The discussion here is cast in terms of community indifference and transformation schedules rather than Marshall-Robinson firm revenue and cost schedules to simplify the graphic display and to facilitate the introduction of several minor adaptations. The presentation follows closely that employed by Baumol, ibid., Chap. 3.

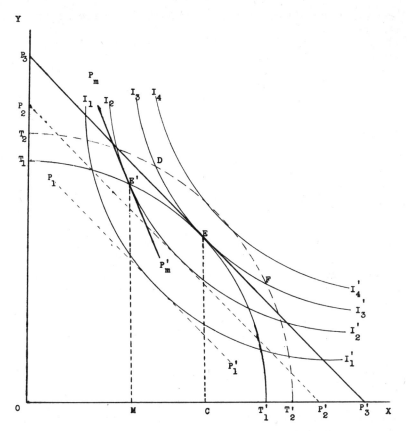

Fig. 5.1. Relationship of a community's transformation curve and indifference curve in establishing point of ideal output.

A monopolist in the midst of competitive industries prevents an equilibrium at the ideal output. For example, if X (Fig. 5.1) were produced by a monopolist and Y by a host of competitors, the monopolist would not maximize profits by producing OC of X (the competitive output) but rather by producing some smaller output OM and selling it at the highest possible price represented by the slope of the price line $P_m P_m'$.[6] The community then no

---

[6]If the monopolist were sufficiently powerful to avoid paying competitive rents to factors of production, it would produce more of X than if forced to pay such rents, but if it could avoid all payments of rent the monopolist would never find it profitable to produce more of X̄ than the competitive rate of output. This point is explained lucidly by Baumol, op. cit., pp. 40-42.

longer receives the ideal output E, but is driven to a lower indifference curve $I_2 I_2'$ and hence to a less desirable output E'. In Marshallian terms, the price-to-marginal cost ratios for monopolized industries are higher than those for competitive industries or, stated somewhat differently, monopolized industries have Lerner indexes $\left(\dfrac{P - MC}{P}\right)$ with values exceeding zero. The value of the national product can therefore be increased by shifting resources from competitive to monopolized industries.

The implications the "ideal" output argument holds for the goals of public policy — granting for the moment the assumptions on which it rests — are clear: Monopolies should either be prevented or made to behave "as though" they were competitive industries. The antitrust laws frustrate incentives to monopolize which if left unproscribed would inflict on society avoidable social costs calculated in terms of departures for the ideal output. Public utility regulation, through the agency of regulatory commissions, can eliminate the difference between the "natural" monopolist's price and its marginal cost; it can do so by confronting the monopolist with an appropriately fixed price which eliminates the relevant portion of the downward sloping demand curve the unregulated monopolist confronts.

But the foregoing familiar argument for competitive market solutions rests on a set of highly restrictive assumptions. First, it assumes no divergency between marginal social and marginal private costs. If, through external economies and diseconomies, the private costs incurred by the firm are different from those borne by society, it follows that competitive firms do not equate social marginal costs with prices when they maximize their profits. Conceptually, therefore, the resulting price lines may intersect the transformation curve at any point and hence the competitive output may possibly be less ideal (on a lower indifference curve than $I_2 I_2'$ at E' in Fig. 5.1) than that resulting from monopoly. [7]

Second, it assumes that the national income is uniquely distributed to members of society, and that the intrusion of monopoly

---

[7]Some of the earlier literature on the ideal output attributed the external economies of one industry to the internal economies of some subsidiary industry, and hence concluded that if external economies existed the system must contain some monopolies of scale. cf. R. F. Kahn, op. cit., p. 11; E. A. G. Robinson, Structure of Competitive Industry. Chicago University Press, 1959. P. 138; and Frank Knight, Fallacies in the Interpretation of Social Cost. Quarterly Journal of Economics, 1924. Pp. 582-606. But it has been correctly pointed out that external economies may arise from other sources. cf. Piero Shraffa, The Laws of Returns Under Competitive Conditions. Economic Journal, 1926. Pp. 535-50; Baumol, op. cit., p. 34; Joan Robinson, op. cit., p. 341.

does not alter the community's indifference map, either through its effect on income distribution or by affecting the degree of perfection of demand for finished products.[8] It is through the indifference curves and transformation curve that the ideal output can be identified. If two families of indifference curves are involved, one each for two different income distributions, or one each for two different states of consumer knowledge, comparisons between monopoly and competitive outputs become ambiguous.

Third, it assumes that a given amount of resources[9] is employed as efficiently as the given "state of the arts" permits. More especially, it implicitly assumes that the transformation curve itself is unaffected by how industries are organized; that is, a given transformation curve is used for comparing equilibrium outputs for perfect competition throughout the economy and for the same economy containing at least one monopolist.

Subject to these assumptions[10] the static case for competitively structured industry has gained strength as it has undergone frequent critical re-examination. Professor Kahn, in one of the first comprehensive inquiries into what has become known as the "proportionality thesis," concluded:[11]

The abandonment of the assumption of perfect competition does not entail any alteration in the condition for the maximization of the national dividend. "The amount of a factor in any use will be ideal when the value of the marginal product of each marginal unit (of resources) is the same in that use as in the alternative occupation."

---

[8]The more usual assumption is that market demand must be perfect. cf. Baumol, op. cit., p. 25. This raises no problems if defined simply as the inability of any buyer to affect price. However, it also implies perfect buyer knowledge. But consumer knowledge is affected by the totality of past experience, and is perfect only after the consumer has experienced all possible combinations of goods at all possible prices. cf. Nicholas Georgescu-Roegen, The Pure Theory of Consumer's Behavior. Quarterly Journal of Economics, August, 1936. Pp. 545-93; Choice and Constancy of Economic Laws. Idem, February, 1950. Esp. pp. 127-28, 133, 135. The assumption of perfect knowledge is therefore unnecessarily restrictive and the weaker assumption that the degree of consumer knowledge is unaffected by the structure of the supply side of the market serves essentially the same purpose.

[9]The assumption of a given level of resource employment, instead of the traditional assumption of full resource employment, was introduced by Baumol, op. cit., p. 25. Baumol's assumption is equally as useful and formally less abstruce.

[10]The assumptions made here do not exhaust the customary list. For example, community indifference curves assume the additivity of individual consumer preferences, and it must be assumed that such community indifference curves do not intersect. While these assumptions have raised skepticism about the entire community indifference approach, they are not especially germane to the competition-monopoly analysis.

[11]Kahn, op. cit., p. 20 (italics in the original).

But if the maximum dividend is to depend on the <u>proportionality</u> rather than the <u>equality</u> of prices and marginal costs, Joan Robinson's "world of monopolies" conceivably can allocate a given amount of resources as efficiently as a world of perfectly competitive enterprises.[12] Subsequent inquiries greatly weakened the proportionality thesis and, in the process, strengthened the argument for competitive resource allocation.

Lerner has pointed out that if workers' wages are not <u>equal</u> to the value of their marginal products they will not supply the ideal quantity of labor;[13] i.e., they will equate the marginal utility of added hours of leisure with that of the hourly wage rate, which will not be the same as the value of the marginal product the hour of labor creates. The same holds for other productive factors which may be used either inside or outside of business firms, and for goods which are both consumer goods and productive factors.[14]

Lerner also introduced,[15] and Professor McKenzie developed,[16] the argument that the proportionality thesis does not hold for an economy in which final products are produced by vertically disintegrated firms under variable combinations of factors. Consider for example a sheet-rolling mill which sells steel sheet to a steel fabricator, each of which is operated independently of the other and both have price-to-marginal-cost ratios of 110. The withdrawal of a unit of a productive factor from the steel fabricator will reduce total product by 110 times the unit cost of the factor. The employment of the unit of the productive factor in the sheet-rolling mill will increase its output by the same amount, and the subsequent employment of this output by the fabricator will increase total output by 110 times 110 times the unit cost of the factor. Hence, when all firms sell at prices proportional to marginal costs, it is possible to transfer some resources from later stages to earlier stages of a productive process and produce more of an intermediate product than is required to offset the output lost at the later stage. This possibility does not exist when the prices of goods and services are equal to their marginal costs and the prices of productive factors are equal to the value of their marginal products.

---

[12] Mrs. Robinson had reached this conclusion earlier, but had condemned monopoly principally on the grounds that it exploited productive factors by paying them a wage less than the value of their marginal product. See Joan Robinson, op. cit., p. 310.

[13] A. P. Lerner, The Economics of Control. Macmillan, New York. 1946. P. 103.

[14] Cf. I. M. D. Little, A Critique of Welfare Economics. Oxford University Press, New York. 1950. P. 136.

[15] A. P. Lerner, The Concept of Monopoly and the Measurement of Monopoly Power. The Review of Economic Studies, June, 1934. P. 172.

[16] Lionel W. McKenzie, Ideal Output and Interdependence of Firms. The Economic Journal, December, 1951. Pp. 785-803.

Finally, the proportionality thesis loses its appeal for a less elegant but pragmatically more persuasive reason. The price-to-marginal-cost ratio is determined by the elasticity of demand at the point where the marginal revenue and marginal cost schedule confronting the firm intersect. In order that the ratios be uniform throughout the economy it would be necessary for all firms to have the same elasticity of demand at the rate of output that maximizes their respective profits. There are no logical reasons for supposing that this will be the case. Hence, even if a given quantity of resources conceivably were ideally allocated when prices were proportional to marginal costs, a world of monopolies would be expected to bring about this result only through a fantastic accident.

To recapitulate, it can be demonstrated through a system of formal logic that a given quantity of resources is allocated to best satisfy consumer demand when the conditions of perfect competition prevail. It cannot be demonstrated through this or any other system of logic that an economy partly monopolistic and partly competitive, or one entirely monopolistic, can be expected to bring about an equally desirable allocation of resources. This conclusion is reached, and its validity usually left to rest, on a set of assumptions which are generally regarded as the imponderables of the economic system. It is proposed here to extend the analysis to the assumptions themselves. Divergencies between private and social costs, imperfect demand, and certain economies of size all may exist, and the fact that they do conceivably could weaken, strengthen or leave essentially undisturbed the case for competitive resource allocation that follows from the ideal output analysis as far as it has yet been carried.

MONOPOLY, COMPETITION, AND THE
TRANSFORMATION FUNCTION

Of the three basic assumptions underlying the logical case for a competitively structured economy, the validity of that concerned with the transformation function has precipitated widest debate. The formal ideal output model makes no allowance for how the form of business organization may affect the production possibilities open to society; it is assumed that firms are organized so as to use the given resources as efficiently as the state of the arts permits, but that neither efficiency nor the state of the arts is affected by the intrusion of monopoly on the competitive economy. If monopoly is generally a more efficient form of industrial organization, the argument for competitive resource allocation is significantly weakened; the reorganization of competitive industries into monopolies may increase the production possibilities of given resources by more than enough to compensate for any departure from the ideal output the presence of monopoly in the system may entail. In graphic terms (Fig. 5.1), if through monopolistic organization the transformation curve could be shifted from T_1 -T_1' outward to T_2 -T_2' society could reach the higher indifference curve I_4 and thereby be made better off than under competition. But it should be noted that this follows only if the economy is equilibrated on T_2 -T_2' somewhere between points D and F. If equilibrium should occur at any point to the left of D or to the right of F, society would still be worse off under monopoly in spite of its beneficial effect on production possibilities. In short, it is possible that monopoly produces goods and services more efficiently than competition, but it does not necessarily follow from this that society should, purely on economic grounds, prefer monopoly over competition. The output mix of the more efficient monopolists may be less desirable than that competitive firms would produce.

There are two reasons why monopoly may possibly be technologically more efficient than a large group of competing firms. The first is the familiar case of declining long-run average costs, or economies of scale.[17] The second is the case where the dynamism of innovation is contingent upon monopoly, the case put forward most cogently and with the greatest sophistication by the late Professor Schumpeter.[18] Both possibilities have cast serious doubts on the validity of monopoly-competition output comparisons, but on logical grounds they may very well tend as much to cancel out as to reinforce each other. The downward sloping average total cost schedule is a static concept which postulates that, under given factor prices and technology, large firms, (large relative to total market demand) may be more efficient than small ones. Hence, in time, producers will be relatively few. But an incessant attack on existing technology is the essential characteristic of Schumpeter's explanatory hypothesis of the dynamic capitalistic process. The perennial gale of creative destruction that unceasingly assaults prevailing cost functions tolerates no perennial lull for their full exploitation.[19] If the static apparatus of the ideal output analysis loses some of its relevancy for public

---

[17]Cf. Jacob Viner, Cost Curves and Supply Curves. Zeitschrift für National Okonomie, 1931. Reprinted in Readings in Price Theory (George J. Stigler and Kenneth Boulding, editors). Richard D. Irwin Press, Chicago. Pp. 212-16.

[18]Joseph A. Schumpeter, Capitalism, Socialism and Democracy, 2nd ed. Harper & Bros., New York. 1947. Chaps. vii and viii.

[19]Ibid., pp. 83-84.

policy by failing to take account of the dynamics of the innovating monopolist, it is not then greatly weakened by the possibility of ceteris paribus downward sloping long-run average cost functions.

The matter need not rest in quite this indecisive state. As Schumpeter himself put it, his refutation of inferences drawn from classical theory only yielded another theory — another principle by which to interpret economic facts.[20] As such it reduced to a persuasive system of logic much of what those who earlier had suspected that monopoly grew out of its own efficiency, and those who now extol the social beneficence of the "new competition,"[21] accepted on faith. Even so, Schumpeter's system does not sanction all forms of monopoly and trade restraints: Tacit and overt agreements to raise prices and limit output,[22] ordinary cartels bent only on preserving price structures,[23] and monopolization that deadens the drive to innovate, all fall under the classical theorem; and Schumpeter recognized that an all-pervading cartel system could as conceivably sabotage all progress as it could produce a larger and better bill of goods than perfect competition.[24] In truth, differences in practical policy inferences to be drawn from the logic of Schumpeter's alternative principle and classical theory are a matter more of degree than of kind. The one argues against "indiscriminate trust-busting or the prosecuting of everything that qualifies as a restraint of trade";[25] the other (presumably) for rigorous (but not necessarily indiscriminate) prosecution of monopoly and restraints of trade.

In short, the most serious challenge to the classical rationale for maintaining a competitively structured economy argues that any such policy should be administered with discrimination. This raises the factual question of whether monopoly should generally be considered, on technological grounds, a means or a barrier to the attainment of a larger and better national product. Schumpeter also appealed to facts, principally those found in the histories of the rayon, automobile, aluminum and petroleum industries.[26] These highly concentrated industries, he argued, rank high in terms of performance in the public interest. But it is also an important fact that they registered their impressive performance under a national policy of preserving competition, and the performance and the policy may not be unrelated. The old Standard

---

[20]Ibid., pp. 91-92.

[21]For a critical appraisal of the literature on the subject, see Edward S. Mason, The New Competition. Yale Review, August, 1953. Pp. 37-48.

[22]Schumpeter, op. cit., p. 85.

[23]Ibid., p. 102.

[24]Ibid.

[25]Ibid., p. 91.

[26]Ibid., pp. 89-90.

Oil Company was dissolved in 1911. Four of the oil companies created by the dissolution decree were among the top 35 firms in terms of research and development personnel in 1955.[27] The great period of growth, product improvement and price reductions in the rayon industry came in the 1920's, after American Viscose had lost control over the industry through its patent holdings and as 30 new competitors entered the field.[28] Between 1947 and 1954 the primary aluminum industry went through its greatest peacetime period of growth in history, with value of shipments increasing from $161 million to $604 million.[29] The growth followed the 1945 Aluminum Company[30] decision and the entry of three new competitors to the field. The automobile industry grew from infancy to maturity between 1916 and 1929; no less than 111 automobile companies, many of them small, had a hand in the growing process, and in reducing prices to the modest level of $700. Such isolated facts scarcely establish either the classical or Schumpeterian hypothesis concerning competition as a welfare goal, but they clearly do not call into serious question the logical case for a competitively structured economy.

Proponents of the "new competition" rest their case entirely on facts, which, they contend, show the large firm to be the principal source of economic growth and research effort.[31] However, what these facts are and precisely how they reveal this image of big business, are not entirely clear. If big firms have grown in proportion to the economy as a whole, then statistically they have "accounted for" much of the economy's growth. But this is neither relevant nor what those who state the case for bigness appear to have in mind. If big firms have grown at a more rapid rate than the economy as a whole it may mean that they have contributed relatively more to the economy's growth than other firms, or that they have grown at the expense of other firms. But if big firms have grown in size relative to the economy then

---

[27]James A. Worley, Industrial Research and Development and the New Competition. Unpublished Ph.D. thesis, Princeton University, 1958.

[28]Jesse W. Markham, Competition in the Rayon Industry. Harvard University Press, Cambridge. 1952.

[29]The Proportion of the Shipments (or Employees) of Each Industry, or the Shipments of Each Group of Products Accounted For by the Largest Companies as Reported in the 1954 Census of Manufactures. Bureau of the Census, United States Dept. of Commerce, July, 1957. P. 14.

[30]United States v. Aluminum Company of America. 148 F. 2d 416, 1945.

[31]Cf. David E. Lilienthal, Big Business: A New Era. Harper & Bros., New York. 1953; Frederick Lewis Allen, The Big Change. Harper & Bros., New York. 1952; A. D. H. Kaplan, Big Enterprise in a Competitive System. The Brookings Institution, Washington, D. C., 1954.

over-all concentration should have increased, and this both facts[32] and proponents of the "new constitution" deny.

Similarly, the facts recently analyzed by James Worley do not argue persuasively that research effort is highly correlated with size of firm.[33] It is true that research effort is highly concentrated, with the top 50 firms in 1955, in terms of research and development personnel employed, accounting for 33 per cent of such employees, and the top 100 firms for about 40 per cent. But only 26 of the 50 largest employers of research and development personnel appear on *Fortune's* 1955 list of the largest 50 firms in terms of assets, and only 33 of the largest employers are listed among the largest 100 firms. Worley correlated research and development personnel employed with total assets by firm for eight 2-digit Standard Industrial Classification industry groups.[34] If firms employed research personnel in proportion to their size as measured in terms of assets, the correlation coefficients should tend toward the value +1; they actually tend to fall between the values +0.5 and +0.6. While correlations on a 2-digit industry basis assume a higher degree of homogeneity of data than in fact exists, the coefficients provide little in the way of a factual basis for identifying intensity of innovational effort with mere size.

The facts also cast considerable doubt on the tendency for very large enterprise competitively to destroy established market power, a tenet of Schumpeter's theory essential to reasonably competitive performance, and a point given considerable emphasis by proponents of the "new constitution."[35] No doubt there are some striking examples where destruction of existing market positions has gone hand in hand with the creative process: Automobiles and trucks displaced the horse-drawn vehicle and, with the aeroplane, made heavy inroads on the railroads; synthetic fibers virtually destroyed the silk market; and television significantly reduced the markets of motion picture producers and exhibitors. The list could be extended. Membership in the group of leading American corporations by broad industry group has nevertheless shown an extraordinarily high degree of stability,[36]

---

[32] For what has become the standard reference on trends in concentration, see Morris A. Adelman, The Measurement of Industrial Concentration. Review of Economics and Statistics, Nov., 1951. Pp. 269-96.

[33] Worley, citing the Fortune Directory of the 500 Largest U. S. Industrial Corporations, July, 1955; and the National Research Council — National Academy of Sciences, Industrial Research Laboratories, various issues.

[34] Worley, op. cit.

[35] Schumpeter, op. cit., p. 84; A. D. H. Kaplan, op. cit., esp. p. 132.

[36] See Jesse W. Markham, review of A. D. H. Kaplan, Big Enterprise in a Competitive System. American Economic Review, June, 1955. Table on pp. 450-51.

and membership in the largest 50, irrespective of industry, apparently has been characterized by a declining rate of turnover.[37] The corporation's "continuity of life" and almost unlimited authorized activities (ultra vires is a very nearly obsolete legal phrase) account for some of the low turnover on the list of the largest 50 — companies can change industries without losing their corporate identity — but do not explain why the "Big Three" and the "Big Four" tend to be the same companies for decades. The gales unquestionably blow, but they are something less than perennial and often have the force of zephyrs — a possibility Schumpeter himself recognized in his assessment of 20th century trustified capitalism. [38]

For reasons which need no elaboration here, statistical derivations of ceteris paribus long-run firm cost functions have yielded little in the way of valid generalizations about efficiency and size of firm,[39] and there is little prospect that they shall ever do so. Milton Friedman has suggested study of the temporal behavior of the size distribution of firms as a more promising approach,[40] a variation of which may be described as follows: If, over time, increases in demand are met by proportionate increases in the number of firms, it can be assumed either that firms in operation at the beginning of the period confronted upward sloping cost curves or some other positive check on growth; if increases in demand are met by no increases and possibly by decreases in the number of firms, it can be concluded either that firms in operation at the beginning of the period could produce the additional output at a lower cost than new entrants or that potential entrants confronted some positive barrier to entry.

Comparisons of changes in output — assumed to be in response to changes in demand — and changes in firm population — for total manufacturing and for various subsectors — between 1935-39 and 1951, lead to intermediate conclusions (Table 5.1). For all

---

[37] Seymour Friedland, Turnover and Growth of the Largest Industrial Firms 1906-1950. Review of Economics and Statistics, February, 1957. Pp. 79-83.

[38] See Joseph A. Schumpeter, The Instability of Capitalism. Economic Journal, September, 1928. P. 384; and Business Cycles. McGraw-Hill, New York. 1939. Vol. II, p. 1044.

[39] See Cost Behavior and Price Policy. Committee on Price Determination, Conference on Price Research, National Bureau of Economic Research, New York. 1943; Caleb A. Smith, Survey of the Empirical Evidence on Economies of Scale; and comment by Milton Friedman, in Business Concentration and Price Policy, National Bureau of Economic Research. Princeton University Press, Princeton. 1955. Pp. 213-238; Richard C. Osborn, Efficiency and Profitability in Relation to Size. Harvard Business Review, March, 1951. Pp. 82-94; Hans Staehle, The Measurement of Statistical Cost Functions: An appraisal of some recent contributions. American Economic Review, June, 1942. Pp. 321-33.

[40] Business Concentration and Price Policy. Op. cit., p. 237.

manufacturing the increase in output was more than two times the increase in firms; in textiles, leather, lumber, stone, clay and glass, firms increases greatly exceeded output increases; in food, printing and publishing, chemicals and paper, increases in output substantially exceeded increases in firms. A host of factors other than the shape of ceteris paribus firm cost functions obviously influence the results of such comparisons — mergers, patent holdings, capital costs, factor and product price movements, new products, trade restraints and shifts in the cost functions, to mention only a few. Moreover, the industries shown are themselves aggregates comprising a heterogeneity of economic activity. Nevertheless, the increases in firms induced by increases in demand are, on the whole, large enough to refute any hypothesis that manufacturing generally is characterized by significant unexploited economies of scale.

Finally, neither the facts nor the logic of large-scale enterprise argue strongly that the profits maximizing motive should stimulate innovations, or even the full exploitation of scale economies, in preference to alternative activities which offer financial reward. Business firms, especially large firms, must weigh

Table 5.1. Percentage Change in Number of Firms and in Index
of Physical Volume of Production for All Manufacturing
and for Major Manufacturing Groups, 1935-39 to 1951

Industry	Change in Physical Volume Production	Change in Number of Firms
	(per cent)	(per cent)
All manufacturing	131	59
Textiles and textile products	85	102
Leather and leather products	-1	128
Lumber and lumber products	53	119
Paper and allied products	108	63
Printing and publishing	71	18
Chemicals and allied products [1]	191	70
Stone, clay and glass products	139	160
Food and kindred products [2]	57	10
Metal and metal products [2]	N.A.	104

[1] Includes products of petroleum and coal.
[2] Per cent increase, 1947 over 1935-39; firm population data not available for later years.

Sources: Changes in production calculated from Federal Reserve Board Indexes of physical volume of production. Changes in firm population calculated from Department of Commerce series appearing in various issues of the Survey of Current Business. The Department of Commerce considers the data for the various industry groups to be considerably less accurate than the data for total manufacturing.

the relative marginal profitability of research, advertising, new
plant construction and expansion by merger, among others.   And
although Schumpeter defined innovation broadly enough to include
most of this wide variety of activities, clearly all of them do not
necessarily make for greater economies in the use of resources.
It is surely possible, for example, that a $1 million increase in a
firm's advertising budget to alter existing community preferences, even if made at the expense of research and development,
may be entirely consistent with the logic of profits maximization.
It also is apparently consistent with the facts. In 1956 total research and development expenditures, including that contracted
out to private firms by the federal government, was estimated at
$6.1 billion, and total advertising expenditures at $9.9 billion.[41]
In 1955 the 50 largest corporations in the United States in terms
of assets included 26 of the largest 50 firms in terms of research
and development employees and 19 of the largest 50 firms in
terms of advertising expenditures (Table 5.2); the 100 largest
firms in terms of assets included 51 of the 100 largest in terms
of research and development employees and 44 of the largest 100
in terms of advertising expenditures. The largest firms in terms
of research and development generally were not the largest in
terms of advertising. The largest 50 on the research and development list included only 12 of the 50 largest advertisers, the
largest 100 only 24 of the 100 largest advertisers.

It is not to be inferred from this that research and development activity necessarily brings greater economic benefits to
society than advertising. As will be shown below the effects of
advertising are to be judged in part on whether it overcomes imperfect buyer knowledge or merely exploits it. But it does follow
that any random sample of firms drawn from the largest 100 is
likely to contain almost an equal number of the largest advertisers and the largest employers of research personnel, that the
sample's total advertising expenditures will equal its research
expenditures, and hence that the large firm is preoccupied as
much with altering the demand for existing products as with developing new products and processes.

The most serious challenge to the classical basis for a competitively organized industry may call to question a ruthless attack on all market power, temporary or enduring and however
attained. But the Schumpeterian principle falls far short of laying to rest the general presumption against monopoly, and clearly

---

[41] Research and development expenditures from Business Plans for New Plant and
Equipment. Economics Department of McGraw-Hill, New York. 1957. P. 12; advertising expenditures compiled from Printers Ink, August 23, 1957. P. 55.

Table 5.2. Cross-Classification of Largest 50 and Largest 100 Corporations According to Assets, Advertising Expenditures and Research and Development Personnel, 1955

	Largest 50		
	Assets	Advertising	Research and Development
Assets	50	19	26
Advertising	19	50	12
Research and Development	26	12	50
	Largest 100		
Assets	100	44	51
Advertising	44	100	24
Research and Development	51	24	100

Sources: *Fortune* Directory of the 500 Largest United States Industrial Corporations, July, 1955; Printers Ink, August 24, 1956. P. 73; and Worley, cited in footnote 27.

establishes no logical basis for a public policy favoring it. As an ideology it accepts most of the substance of antitrust policy, and may very well exaggerate both the scope and effects of the portion it rejects.[42] The industries to which it appeals for empirical verification may have performed laudably because of antitrust policy rather than in spite of it. Furthermore, the facts on large-scale enterprise reveal no high correlation between innovational activity and mere business size, but instead a complex intermixture of bigness, research effort and large advertising outlays. Accordingly, they suggest a major modification of the Schumpeterian hypothesis: On balance, advertising and innovational effort are two of several alternative paths to size and market power, and to retaining them, once achieved. Among the largest firms the traffic over one path appears to be no heavier than that over the other. Hence, it is equally as defensible to hold that big business threatens the existence of its rivals through attacks on the community's preferences as to hold that it does so through the new product, the new process and the new technology. This is an attack of a different character, and determination of its public policy implications requires analysis of its possible effects on the state of consumer knowledge.

---

[42] Cf. Edward S. Mason, Schumpeter on Monopoly and the Large Firm. Review of Economics and Statistics, May, 1951. P. 144.

MONOPOLY, COMPETITION, AND CONSUMER KNOWLEDGE

Analysis of the effects of market structure on the equilibrium output mix of the economy has concentrated heavily on conditions of supply, very likely because the taxonomy of markets has been built on the number and size distribution of sellers industries comprise. But there are persuasive reasons for supposing that demand for given final goods and services may differ between competition and monopoly: (1) Under perfect competition the "invisible hand" at work in the market integrates and organizes the bits and pieces of knowledge dispersed in the minds of many buyers and sellers.[43] Under monopoly and oligopoly sellers must communicate directly to buyers on such matters as price and quality. There may be no a priori grounds for concluding that one communication system is more efficient than the other, but they would very probably not allocate resources the same way. (2) As soon as the assumption of pure competition is dropped, as Chamberlin has explained,[44] selling costs such as advertising become an important determinant of the equilibrium of the firm through their effect on demand and costs. The introduction of selling costs as a variable in the equilibrating mechanism makes it inadmissible to assume that the firm's demand and cost functions are independent of each other; firms confront a family of such functions, a cost and demand function for every outlay of selling costs. (3) Because demand for goods and services is affected by the state of consumer knowledge, it follows that it is affected by actions firms take which make knowledge less imperfect, or less perfect.

But because imperfect knowledge is associated with departures from competition, it does not follow that its costs to society are attributable to monopoly. In truth, contemporary theory holds that imperfect knowledge is an important source of monopoly power rather than the other way around.[45] It does follow, however, that the communication methods and strategies sellers use in markets characterized by imperfect buyer knowledge can affect the magnitude of such costs, and herein lies a legitimate public concern. Much has been said on the wastes of advertising, such as that of competing oligopolists which all could profitably

---

[43] Cf. G. B. Richardson, Imperfect Knowledge and Economic Efficiency. Oxford Economic Papers, June, 1953. Pp. 140-41.

[44] E. H. Chamberlin, The Theory of Monopolistic Competition. 5th ed. Harvard University Press, Cambridge. 1946. Chaps. vi and vii.

[45] Cf. Tibor Scitovsky, Ignorance as a Source of Oligopoly Power. American Economic Review, May, 1950 supplement. Pp. 48-53; and Chamberlin, op. cit., p. 118.

discontinue collusively but none could profitably do alone.[46] This
misses the essential point. The "advertising message" created
on Madison Avenue, however abrasive on the ears, can impart
information as well as misinformation, and which it does is of
greater public concern than whether it is a defensive or offensive
strategem.

This point can be illustrated by reference to the demand side
of the welfare diagram used earlier to define the ideal output
(Fig. 5.2). Consider the case where the buying public is highly
informed on the relative amounts of satisfaction given by alternative combinations of commodities X and Y, and let the points of
indifference with this state of knowledge be represented by the
solid curves I-I and I_1-I_1. With the price ratio given by P-P, the
public would maximize its total satisfaction at B, taking OD of X
and OE of Y. Now suppose the producer of Y had misinformed
the public, advertising desirable qualities of Y it did not possess,
and as a consequence shifted the indifference curves I-I and $I_1 I_1$
to I'-I' and I_1'-I_1' respectively. At the same prices the public
would, ex ante, consider itself best off at C, taking OD' of X and
OE' of Y, but ex post would find itself on a lower indifference
curve than it was at B. The argument can of course be reversed,
letting the seller of Y advertise so as to make the public more
informed and leading it from some other point on the price line
(G for example) to B, where expected and actual satisfactions are
closer together.

It is submitted that the complexities confronting rational
choice at the mid-twentieth century make this more than just another empty box. Economic theory traditionally has assumed that
man either inherited or acquired through repeated experience the
ability to weigh rationally the relative satisfactions derived from
alternative baskets of consumer goods. In a world of poverty
where a large portion of income was parcelled out in daily purchases of food and clothing this assumption may have been valid;
if the grade of flour or meat purchased today did not live up to
expectations one could try a different grade tomorrow. The
household budget of our more "opulent society" is composed differently. Between 1930 and 1950 outlays on food and clothing increased from $29 billion to $96 billion, or by a little in excess of
threefold; outlays on various durable and semidurable household
furnishings and automobiles and accessories increased from $5
billion to nearly $30 billion, or by sixfold.[47] The cost of reducing

[46] Cf. Melvin Warren Reder, Studies in the Theory of Welfare Economics. Columbia University Press, New York. 1947. Pp. 72-73.
[47] United States Department of Commerce, Survey of Current Business. 1951 and
1956 National Income numbers.

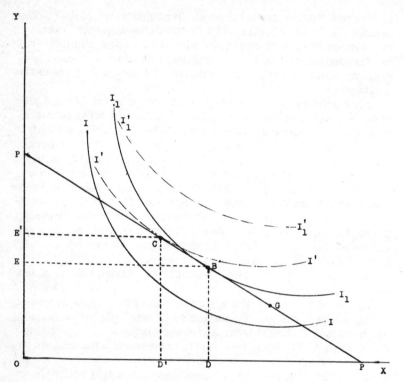

Fig. 5.2. Use of transformation curve to find the public's total satisfaction of a product.

imperfect buyer knowledge by repeated experimentation with such goods is obviously prohibitive, which incidentally may explain the emergence of consumer research institutions.

If, as Scitovsky asserts, imperfect consumers' knowledge is a source — by his estimate, the primary source — of market power,[48] it is then as appropriately a concern of public policy as merger, monopolization, price fixing and similar business practices which have generally been regarded as having a more direct bearing on the structure and performance of industry. This concern is most clearly expressed in Section 5 of the Federal Trade Commission Act, which prohibits unfair methods of competition, in the various labelling acts administered by the Federal Trade Commission, and in the general applicability of the antitrust laws to advertising media.

---

[48] Tibor Scitovsky, op. cit., p. 48.

Advertising, construed broadly enough to include all dissemination of information by sellers, conceivably could (1) increase consumer knowledge and lead the economy, through reducing the difference between expected and realized satisfaction, closer to the ideal output; (2) decrease consumer knowledge, with the opposite effect; or (3) leave the state of consumer knowledge unaffected. There is a strong presumption that misrepresentation and deceptive advertising make the state of knowledge less perfect. In doing so it reduces the probability that the output of the economy will be ideal, and for two reasons: It increases the difference between expected and realized satisfaction, and, by making knowledge less perfect, it creates a basis for greater monopoly power. Accordingly, provisions of the antitrust laws which outlaw misrepresentation and deceptive practices are as consistent with a policy objective of efficient resource allocation as those prohibiting the more commonplace forms of monopoly, and in recent years have been put to more frequent use. During 1957 the Federal Trade Commission issued 324 complaints and 213 cease and desist orders; 255 complaints and 180 orders were against deceptive practices.[49]

But advertising need not be deceptive in order to make buyer knowledge less perfect. Given a limitation on the capacity of an advertising medium, its occupancy by some large advertisers precludes competitors and potential competitors from occupying it on an equal basis. Such a constraint on the dissemination of information makes buyer knowledge less perfect than it otherwise would be. National network television, limited to three networks having a total of less than 75 prime nighttime viewing hours per week, is especially illustrative.[50] In 1955 the 25 largest users of network television accounted for 59 per cent of total network time sales.[51] The network facilities could not have accommodated 25 additional advertisers of equal size. Concentration of control in networking and in the use of network advertising — assuming it to be a superior medium for those who use it — contributes to concentration of control in industry generally. It also makes knowledge less perfect than it would be if there were no constraint on its dissemination. Hence, such concentration like deceptive advertising, is a proper concern of public policy.

---

[49] Federal Trade Commission, News Summary. January 16, 1958.

[50] See: Network Broadcasting. Report of the Committee on Interstate and Foreign Commerce, House Report 1297, 85th Cong. 2nd Sess. Washington, D. C. January, 1958. Chap. 4.

[51] Compiled from: Printers Ink Marketing Guide, August 24, 1956.

108   JESSE W. MARKHAM

GOALS FOR ECONOMIC ORGANIZATION AND ECONOMIC THEORY: SUMMARY

Classical economics provided a theoretical framework on which to construct policies designed to attain the goals of economic progress and efficient resource allocation. A re-examination of this relevant body of theory leads to the following observations which can be made with reasonable confidence:

1. Unless it can be shown that monopolistic organization is conducive to more rational consumer choice or to greater economies in the use of resources, it logically follows that an economy organized along competitive lines produces a national product superior to that produced under monopoly; i.e., competitive organization produces a more "ideal" output.

2. Conceivably, monopolistic organization can produce more efficiently than competitive organization under given technological conditions, and can generate a higher rate of innovation. It does not follow, even if monopolistic organization produces both of these favorable effects, that it better serves consumers' welfare than a competitively structured industrial organization; the outcome depends on the equilibrium output mix which would result if there were a monopolistic sector.

3. The form of market organization may possibly affect society's welfare by influencing the state of consumer knowledge. Under monopoly (oligopoly) the selection of channels and methods of communication between seller and buyer is subject to the discretion of the seller — the hand that coordinates market information is not "invisible." If firms with market power exploit the state of imperfect buyer knowledge they confront or make knowledge less perfect, they affect consumers' welfare adversely; if they select methods of communication which enable buyers to exercise more rational choice they affect it favorably. Since some firms will very likely profit from spreading knowledge and others from spreading ignorance, generalizations on the relationship between the profit maximizing incentives of firms with market power and the state of buyer knowledge are hazardous. All that can safely be said is that public constraints on the dissemination of false information and the monopolization of channels of information such as advertising media are in the public interest: they reduce the social costs of uninformed choice and tend to prevent the rise of monopoly power built entirely on imperfect buyer knowledge.

These observations do not establish a blueprint for the precise form of economic organization society should set as its goal, but they do establish a rational skepticism for monopolistic organization. The details must be shaped by facts, and the further usefulness of theory for purposes of establishing such a goal depends on the bases it provides for interpreting them. The facts, however, are not only to a large extent unknown, but are known to be infinite in number and subject to frequent change. Conflicting theories often can in some sense be empirically verified because all attempted verifications rest on limited facts. As George Gaylord Simpson has put it:[52]

Each student thus actually puts his theory into the data, and it is not surprising that each then gets his own theory out of these data when he is through.

The classical, Schumpeterian and "new competition" theories all look to how forms of economic organization serve consumer welfare; and although all three acknowledge the logical case for competitive market organization, each offers a factual case for differences in detail. Certain facts may document each case equally well.

The present posture of public policy — more specifically, antitrust policy — reflects in part the inconclusiveness of the facts on which these theories turn. It condemns the more flagrant forms of monopoly, virtually all collusive price fixing, certain specific actions which tend substantially to lessen competition, unfair methods of competition, especially misleading advertising, and treats agriculture as a special case. It has never contemplated the goal of approximate perfect competition, or even that which conforms to the less rigorous standards of workable competition.[53] But it is of some significance that in the broad sweep of antitrust policy the trend has been toward more severe circumscriptions of monopoly and unfair methods of competition, and this trend has developed concurrently with the development of a tremendous quantity of marketing facts. The drive toward more competitive resource allocation has even touched agriculture. If, as a logical proposition, the greatest reward of monopoly is, as Professor Hicks says, "a quiet life," then the most persuasive argument for laws preserving competition may be the assurance they give to the rest of society that it does not bear the costs of the monopolists' tranquility. The logic of economic theory

---

[52]George Gaylord Simpson, The Meaning of Evolution (Mentor Book edition). New American Library, New York. P. 37.
[53]Cf. United States v. Aluminum Company of America, 44 F. Supp. 97, 1942.

concerned with industrial progress and efficient resource allocation strongly suggests, although the facts do not in a scientific
sense prove, that this assurance should be at least as strong as
it is. In any case, neither theory nor the facts make a convincing
case that the assurance should be weaker, or that the goal of a
reasonably competitive economy which public policy presently
envisages should be less ambitious.

O. H. BROWNLEE

University of Minnesota

Discussion

EXCEPT INSOFAR as he considers competition a goal in itself,
Mr. Markham is concerned with means rather than ends. In particular, he takes as given objectives (1) efficient allocation of
a given bundle of resources and (2) efficient creation and exploitation of new technological information. He compares monopoly
and competition with respect to the extent that each environment
contributes to attainment of these objectives.

In evaluating the two types of organizations according to their
efficiencies in allocating a given bundle of resources, Mr. Markham employs as a point of departure a familiar theorem of static
welfare economics. This theorem states that if there are no external economics in production and consumption (i.e. if the level
of activity in one economic unit has no effect upon the technological relations in another and one person's consumption pattern is
not an argument in another person's utility function) and there
are no increasing returns to scale in production, then competitive
equilibrium yields the outcome that no one can be made better off
without making someone worse off. There is the possibility that
monopoly may be able to employ technologies that are not feasible for competitive units (i.e. there are marked economies of
scale). But Mr. Markham finds no evidence lending strong support to this possibility.

Although it is not relevant to Mr. Markham's argument, it
should be indicated that there is nothing sacred about achieving
an outcome such that no one can be made better off without making someone worse off. For example, that such a condition cannot be achieved with farm price supports doesn't convince farmers that such supports are bad. Perhaps of more relevance in
selling farmers on the desirability of a free market is the theorem that any of the many possible situations in which no one
could be made better off without making someone worse off could

be a point of competitive equilibrium. In particular, it would be possible to redistribute resources so that farmers could achieve their current incomes with a free market and nonfarmers would be better off than they could be with price supports.

Markham breaks some new ground in comparing the dynamics of competition and monopoly. He finds no evidence to support the contention that monopoly leads to more rapid discovery and innovation than does competition. I am not startled by this finding. Classical economic theory implies a greater adjustment to a given environmental change under competition than under monopoly and a correspondence between the amount of change and its speed.

A peripheral issue is the larger advertising expenditure associated with monopoly and the potential informational value of such advertising. Although one cannot deny that some advertising is informative, I believe that as a means of providing information, current advertising procedures are inefficient. One might compare the cost of the information provided by some of the consumer products testing agencies with the costs and information associated with the advertisements (for cigarettes and cosmetics, for example) to check the validity of this belief.

In his comparisons of competition and monopoly, Mr. Markham takes for granted the existence of a market to provide information to decision makers. Although I believe that the price mechanism is one of man's greatest inventions, and that its applications should be extended to areas in which it is not being used currently, there are cases in which competitive equilibrium could not be established or, if it could, would not yield the outcome that no one could be made better off without making someone worse off. These cases are those where there are increasing returns to scale or external economics in production or consumption. I will make some conjectures about organization for providing goods and services when the market cannot perform satisfactorily. These conjectures are related to Mr. Markham's findings.

The terms competition and monopoly may not be applicable to nonmarket situations. However, competition is essentially a highly decentralized form of organization in which many different independent units decide how to produce and how much to produce. Although monopoly may be decentralized with respect to decisions about how to produce (a cartel is an example), its decision with respect to how much to produce must be centralized. Consequently, we can consider competition and decentralization as virtually synonymous and monopoly and centralization as equivalent.

Because elementary education is a service such that one

person is willing to pay something in order that other persons' children receive it, we shouldn't organize its provision as we would that for wheat. However, we still have a choice as to whether the direction of such education is centralized or decentralized even though central governmental support is provided. At one extreme we could have the federal government specifying the curriculum, teaching methods, class sizes, etc.; at the other we could give grants to parents conditional upon these grants being spent to purchase education but let anyone who wanted to operate a school do so and sell the service. Some restrictions might be placed upon curriculum and teachers, but there could be considerable freedom with respect to how and what to teach. The organization would be decentralized rather than the highly centralized one at the other extreme.

Although we ought to make many more of our highways toll roads rather than freeways, much of our street and highway system can best provide services for which no direct charge can feasibly be levied. Revenues from taxes on motor fuels and from license fees will continue to be used to construct and maintain such facilities. However, there is some choice as to whether decisions with respect to how to build roads, where to locate them, etc., are made by a single agency or by the many state and local units, even though federal funds are provided.

Defense against military invasion for all of the citizens of a city can be provided as inexpensively as it could be if only one citizen were to be protected. Consequently, defense cannot feasibly be "sold" to individual citizens. But, again, we can have one or several defense agencies.

Just as competition appears to yield better results than monopoly in cases where a market is feasible, I would conjecture that decentralization generally will yield better results than centralization where markets cannot or should not be employed. A decentralized school system may contain some poor teachers and some useless courses. But it also offers opportunities for experimentation and innovations that are not characteristic of centralized systems. There is a low probability that most of the teachers will be incompetent and that much of the curriculum will be useless. Similarly, decentralization of the provision of highway services offers opportunities to experiment with new materials and new designs that otherwise might never be employed. Some of these experiments will be failures just as some competitive firms do not survive. But the long-run outcome probably will be better than that of no ventures and no failures.

This discussion has little relevance for agricultural policy. However, many of the schemes for solving the "farm problem"

— whatever it may be — are schemes which would keep farmers from competing with each other through taking away from them the freedom to make certain choices and substituting centralized decision making. Agricultural economists have shown such schemes to be inefficient in the sense that they violate the conditions for a static welfare maximum. Mr. Markham's evidence suggests that such schemes may also have serious long-run effects. A stagnant agriculture with all farmers poor farmers might be a result of highly centralized decision making.

Chapter 6

JOHN M. BREWSTER

U. S. Department of Agriculture

Society Values and Goals in Respect to Agriculture

THE CENTRAL FARM PROBLEM of our generation is excess productive capacity in agriculture which is reflected in price-depressing surpluses and the relatively low income position of agriculture. There are other farm problems, but most of them are rooted in this one. Therefore, it constitutes the orientation of this chapter.

The theme of this book, "Goals and Values in Agriculture," is most appropriate. For the heart of any serious social problem is a conflict of deep-seated value judgments concerning the kinds of people and forms of social organization that are most prized.[1] In such conflicts, choice of goals is inhibited by uncertainty as to what alternatives are possible and which ones are most desirable. Determinate goals arise as component judgments of traditional value systems become identified and reweighted in light of appraised alternatives to present ways of living and of making a living.

In line with this concept of goal formation, four premises provide the framework for handling the subject of this chapter. (1) Our large excess farm capacity is the product of our machine age. (2) This age, including modern scientific agriculture, is in great measure the outgrowth of America's premachine creeds of life that were so weighted as to be harmonized wonderfully well in our premachine economy of predominately family production units in both agriculture and industry. (3) The very technical advance generated by these creeds now throw them into conflict at many points, thereby creating serious policy problems in all major sectors of our society. (4) Technical advance has proceeded rapidly in both agriculture and industry since the Age of Jackson. But the impact of such advance on the premachine institutions

---

[1] "It is exactly this disagreement in value judgments that is the root cause of all social problems, both in the original definition of the condition as a problem and in subsequent efforts to solve it." R. C. Fuller and R. R. Meyers, Some Aspects of a Theory of Social Problems. American Sociological Review, 6 (1941): 27.

differs in each case. For up to now at least, the shift to machine methods remains as compatible with family production units in agriculture as do hand manipulations and animal power, whereas in industry the same shift has long since transmuted the older system of family units into modern corporate firms requiring perhaps hundreds of thousands of workers, disciplined and guided by a vast hierarchy of bosses, supervisors and managers.

Through these opposite impacts, should we not expect technological advance in agriculture and industry to have induced the farm and nonfarm sectors of society to give substantially different weights to the component value judgments of America's pre-machine creeds? If so, what is the nature of the cultural gap thus generated?

More importantly, new forms of economic organization have arisen in the nonfarm sectors in response to technical advance in industry. Could these have introduced impediments to resource movements that are the basic cause of agriculture's large excess capacity? In this indirect way, may not technical advance in industry be generating the same conflicts among America's pre-machine creeds within the farm sector of society that it has long since generated within the nonfarm sector? If so, may this not eventually induce farm people to reweigh these beliefs in a fashion similar to that long since found desirable by the nonfarm population?

Analysis of these issues leads to the conclusion that society has not determined what weights to give its older creeds so as to achieve desirable goals for agriculture. For there is no consensus of whether the impediments to the rate of outflow of resources needed to remove excess farm capacity lie in characteristics peculiar to farm people or in nonfarm market imperfections generated by technical advance in industry. This means that both the value aspects and the organizational aspects of the farm problem are like the sides of the same coin: each can be known or resolved only in light of the way in which the other is understood and resolved.

In developing the grounds for this conclusion we need to consider two preliminary questions: (1) What are the key value judgments that have been the chief guides to policy formation in America since early times? (2) What is the model of social organization that traditionally has been prized as the vehicle of their fulfillment? Although we have considered these questions to some extent elsewhere, they are indispensable here.

VALUE JUDGMENTS AS EXPRESSIONS OF THE
STATUS PRINCIPLE

This chapter is not concerned with values in general. Unless values are tied down to specific judgments of what is valuable and why, talk of values is pretty much up in the air. Our interests center in a few strategic judgments of value that have functioned as chief guides to policy formation in American life since early times.

Before identifying these judgments we should note that running through them all is the status principle which gives each of them tremendous strength and driving power.

As a possession, status is the standing — the dignity, the approbation, and esteem — that each human being covets for himself in the eyes of all observers, including himself. As a dominant drive of action, status is the aspiration of men for an ever higher standing and the fear of falling to a lower one than they currently enjoy. Among the characteristics of this aspiration that are of analytical importance,[2] the one most relevant here is the fact that its vital center is a love of merit and an aversion to demerit. This sense of merit and demerit is the experience of self-acceptance or self-rejection that arises from the conviction that one demonstrates or fails to demonstrate an equivalence between his capacities and the level of approbation and esteem he covets.

This means that the status striving cannot be equated with the mere thirst for popularity. To be sure, this is an important aspect of the status drive. As William James observed, "no more fiendish punishment could be devised...than that one should be turned loose in society and remain unnoticed by all members thereof. If no one turned round when we entered, answered when we spoke or minded what we did — a kind of impotent despair would ere long well up within us from which cruelest bodily torture would be a relief."[3] This, however, is only half the truth. An equally fiendish punishment is the feeling that one is so barren of meritorious capacities that he is unable to deserve the esteem of anyone. We are often popular with others but unacceptable to ourselves. Any attempt to equate status striving with thirst for popularity thus falls to the ground.

---

[2] These traits are more fully considered in the author's mimeographed paper, Value Judgments and the Problem of Excess Capacity in Agriculture. U. S. Farm Econ. Res. Div., ARS, USDA, Washington, D.C., May, 1960.
[3] William James, Principles of Psychology. Henry Holt and Company, New York. 1898. Vol. 1. Pp. 293-94.

Thus including a sense of merit and demerit, the status aspiration can be gratified neither by social esteem alone nor by self-esteem alone. The complete objective is twofold: To be the kind of person who deserves self-approbation, and also to belong to a social order that recognizes one's deserts. Every individual or group makes commitments of mind and conscience concerning which alternative ways of living and making a living are the proper ones for this purpose. These commitments are the value judgments that are a peoples' chief guides to policy formation, and in this way they shape its destiny.

AMERICA'S POLICY-GUIDING CREEDS

Early in American life, this status aspiration unfolded into at least four groups of value judgments that are relevant to our problem. These groups are called the work ethic, the democratic creed, the enterprise creed and the creed of self integrity.[4]

A. The Work Ethic

The work ethic centers in four component judgments.

(1) The first is called the work-imperative. Negatively expressed, this imperative is the judgment that one fails to deserve the esteem of self, family, country and even all men if he places love of backward or "easy" ways above love of excellence in any useful employment of his choice. Positively expressed, it is the judgment that the proper way to fulfill the status striving is to be a person who merits his own high esteem because of proficiency in his chosen field and therefore deserves a social order that prizes him for the same reason. With the so-called materialistic income incentive thus encompassed in the sense of merit, the drive that leads the farmer to adopt new cost-reducing and output-increasing technologies is obviously not merely a love of money but the aversion of mind and conscience to ways of life that deserve disesteem.

(2) The work-imperative includes the judgment that of many possible character types, the Self-Made-Man Ideal is the one most worthy of respect and emulation. For this imperative precludes any tie-up of status deserts with such personal traits as

---

[4]See pp. 11-33 of the citation in footnote 2 for a fuller discussion of these creeds than present space permits.

race or family pedigree which add nothing to one's proficiency in a given employment. In all considerations of merited advance, what counts are such things as initiative, diligence, and technical competence, which release one's potential into creative endeavor.

(3) At an early stage in American lore, the work ethic came to include the optimistic judgment that, in their creative potential, men and nations alike possess ample means of closing the gap between their present circumstances and their aspirations. According to this faith, human capacities are sufficient to improve the lot of the common man without limit. To believe less puts a ceiling on the American Dream and belittles the promise of American life. Thus the work-ethic is a wellspring of hope and confidence in a brighter future for all.

(4) Finally, in its judgment that proficiency in any employment of one's choice is the proper test of status deserts, the work-imperative obviously includes a unique concept of justice. This concept is expressed in the judgment that society owes to each man (a) the equivalent of his contributions and (b) also equal access to the necessary means of developing his creative potential to the fullest extent possible. The first of these is called commutative justice; the second is the justice of equal opportunity, sometimes called distributive justice.

There is no "natural" harmony between these. Meeting the first debt requires that society place no limit on inequalities of income that are out of line with equivalence of individual capabilities and contributions. At the same time, individual capabilities are themselves largely the function of goods and services that are within society's power to extend or withhold. Consequently, the justice of equal opportunity may require severe limitations on income inequalities that many regard as incompatible with equivalence between productive contributions and remunerations.

B. The Democratic Creed

The second key set of society values that has been in effect since early times are the two central judgments of the democratic creed: (a) All men are of equal worth and dignity, and (b) none, however wise or good, is good or wise enough to have dictatorial power over any other. These judgments include a positive concept of freedom which is expressed in the saying that all deserve an equal voice (or power) in shaping the rules which are deemed necessary for the sake of the general welfare. Thus, the democratic meaning of freedom has never been the mere absence of collective restraints on individual action. It has always meant

that men are free from arbitrary power when the views of each
have the same weight as those of any other in shaping the common rules that all must follow for the sake of the common good.

C. The Enterprise Creed

A third creed, indigenous to premachine America, is called
the enterprise creed. Its component values are expressed in
four important judgments. (1) The individual (or his immediate
family) is and ought to be responsible for his own economic security throughout life. Therefore, (2) a primary function of government is to prevent the imprudent from pressing either government or business into sharing the burden of their economic
security.

By equating the burden of economic security wholly with individual responsibility, this pair of judgments renders work ethic
beliefs the handmaiden of laissez faire attitudes. For it follows
from this equation that if the individual winds up saddled with the
hardships of insecurity, this is merely evidence of a misspent
life — habitual distaste for the work-imperative whose just deserts are privation. Thus government sins if it seeks to liberate
him from his hardships by either direction or indirection. A
typical expression of this habit of thought runs as follows:

The government has adopted the role of the "welfare state" and declared
its will to attain the "four freedoms," "full employment" and other gran-
diose objectives. This it proposes to do largely by redistributing the income of the people. By heavily progressive income taxation, it deprives
its successful citizens of their product and gives it to the less successful;
thus it penalizes industry, thrift, competence and efficiency and subsidizes
the idle, spendthrift, incompetent and inefficient. By despoiling the thrifty
it dries up the source of capital, reduces investment and creation of jobs,
slows down industrial progress, and prevents society from attaining its
highest level of consumption.[5]

The second pair of key judgments in the enterprise creed is
this: (3) Proprietors or their legal representatives deserve exclusive right to prescribe the rules under which their production
units shall operate; therefore (4) a prime function of government
is to prevent anyone, including the government itself, from en-
croaching upon the managerial power of proprietors to run their
businesses as they please.

---

[5]The American Individual Enterprise System, Its Nature, Evolution and Future.
McGraw-Hill Book Co., Inc., New York. 1946. Vol. II. P. 1019.

In contrast to the democratic creed, this pair of judgments includes a negative sense of freedom. To be free means to be left alone to run production units as one pleases, unmolested by collective constraints on the managerial power of proprietors. There is scarcely a greater source of mischief than this confusion of the negative meaning of freedom with the positive sense of freedom implicit in the democratic creed. This confusion drags virtually the whole American heritage under the skirts of the enterprise creed. In this way, this creed has been used over and over in efforts to block almost every piece of social legislation ever passed on the ground that it threatened our democratic way of life. A typical expression of this habit of thought runs thus:

It does not follow that because our difficulties are stupendous or because there are some souls timorous enough to doubt the validity and effectiveness of our ideals and our system, that we must turn to a State-controlled or State-directed economic system in order to cure our troubles. That is not liberalism; it is tyranny.[6]

Thus by confusing the sense of negative freedom implicit in enterprise beliefs with the sense of positive freedom implicit in democratic beliefs, and by equating the burden of economic security wholly with individual responsibility, our enterprise creed obviously makes democratic government the handmaiden of laissez faire sentiments and views; otherwise, it ceases to be democratic. Thus the creed tends to render us:

"... singularly unable to do well those things that cannot be done for profit and which depend upon the initiative — of the community working through the state." Thus we are hamstrung with the half-conscious assumption "that those things which can only be done effectively by the community are in some way on a lower level than those which are effectively done for profit by individuals and private groups."[7]

In generating this assumption, our enterprise creed is essentially the core of "the great American inhibition" that many analysts hold

... prevents us from ever doing enough toward education, toward making medical care available to all families without bankrupting them, toward

---

[6]Herbert Hoover, in acceptance of renomination, August 11, 1932. Campaign Speeches of 1932. New York. 1932. Pp. 8-9.

[7]John C. Bennett, How My Mind Has Changed. Christian Century, December 23, 1959. P. 1501. For an able economic analysis of the same point see John Kenneth Galbraith, The Affluent Society. Houghton Mifflin Company, Boston. 1958. Esp. pp. 132-38.

even such an obvious thing as the development of a reasonably efficient and well integrated system of transportation.[8]

D. The Creed of Self-Integrity

A final set of key values in our premachine heritage comprises the ethic of self-integrity. This ethic relates to the status deserts of dissenters. Its central judgment is that in case of conflict, both the individual and his group (or groups) are responsible for seeking new modes of thought and practice that will unify the hitherto conflicting views of each. In line with this judgment, (1) the community prizes its dissenting members as its agents for achieving new knowledge and practices that will enrich the life of all and (2) the dissenter in turn feels a strong obligation to identify himself with his own exceptional sentiments and views. In this spirit, both the individual and his group (or groups) take each other's role in order to find a way of composing their differences.

This ethic of self-integrity is best exemplified in research experience. Such experience involves a conflict — a tension — between the exceptional observations and thoughts of the individual thinker and some theory or concept believed true by his professional group. The very core of any genuine scientific problem is the fact that the individual has unique observations that cannot be explained as instance of a law (or laws) which others hold to be true. Thus he has an outlook on the universe which belongs to him alone — an outlook that runs counter to that of his community, say, with respect to how a certain disease spreads from person to person.[9] In all such conflicts, both the individual and his group (or groups), if committed to the ethic of self-integrity, share the common judgment that the highest responsibility of the individual is to follow the dictates of his own exceptional insights to the last ditch as a means of either being proved wrong or of discovering and presenting his community with solutions for its problems — with new truth, new art forms, new songs and new ways of relieving pain and achieving happiness in all walks of life.[10] This

---

[8]Bennett, pp. 1501-2. For a fuller treatment of this point, see Arthur M. Schlesinger, Jr., The Challenge of Abundance. The Reporter, May 3, 1956. Pp. 8-11.

[9]On the central position of the exceptional experience of the individual in research, see George H. Mead, Scientific Method and the Individual Thinker, in John Dewey et al., Creative Intelligence. Henry Holt and Company, New York. 1917. Esp. pp. 206-9.

[10]George H. Mead, Movements of Thought in the Nineteenth Century. University of Chicago Press, Chicago, Ill. Pp. 264-67, 360-62, 405-17. Also Paul Tillich, The Courage To Be. Yale University Press, New Haven. 1953. Pp. 104-5.

judgment binds them together with bonds of mutual respect despite their differences. This ethic bears good fruit. There is hardly an implement of modern life, a piece of art, or a law of science whose history does not run back to where it once had no other home than the strange idea of some dissenter.

THE MODEL OF SOCIAL ORGANIZATION TRADITIONALLY VIEWED AS FULFILLING OUR PREMACHINE CREEDS

The component judgment of the work ethic, the democratic creed, the enterprise creed and the creed of self-integrity — these are the deep-seated society values that have functioned as chief guides to hard decision making since early times in America. They are rural to the bone, yet they do not stop at the farm fence; they inhabit the mind and conscience of all America. No temples are built to them; nor are they put in shrines; neither are they chiseled in stone: theirs is a finer abode — millions of firesides throughout the length and breadth of the land.

But the fact remains that there is no natural harmony among these value systems. Except for the democratic creed and the ethic of self-integrity, the component judgments of any one creed cannot be derived from those of the other beliefs. In fact, they are shot through with incompatibilities. This is true of the democratic creed and the work ethic, for example. Men do not possess any specific meritorious capacity in equal degree; hence there is a sharp clash between the democratic belief that all deserve status of equal dignity and worth and the work ethic belief that they should be accorded differential status in line with their productive contributions, economic or otherwise. Again, a people may feel deeply committed to the work ethic judgments and yet completely reject those of the enterprise creed. Apparently, this is the case among the Soviets.[11] People may be so committed to the work ethic and so averse to the enterprise creed that they feel that for practical purposes the democratic creed should be laid on the shelf; at least, for the time being.

Because of these and other implicit incompatibilities, America's dominant creeds of life present us with difficult problems in social organization. The difficulty is rooted in two main facts. First, the human mind is incapable of blueprinting any conceivable

---

[11] For discussion of the Work-imperative in Communism, see Dorothy Thompson's column, Evening Star, Washington, D.C., October 17, 1957. Also pertinent are Kenneth S. Lynn's The Dream of Success: A Study of American Imagination. Pp. 67-97, Little Brown and Company, Boston, 1955, and Sydney Hook's Grim Report: Asia in Transition, New York Times Magazine, April 5, 1959.

social order that can rub out the implicit conflicts of these creeds. With great rigor and originality, reason can construct many alternative social orders — ideal systems of associated life. But these alternatives simply represent competing ways of living and of making a living. None can wipe out the implicit incompatibilities cited. This means that any given set of social rules or customs is possible only by virtue of a unique set of relative weights that we give our divergent creeds of life. Each change in these weights calls for a corresponding change in our ordering rules of life, and, in turn, change in our ordering rules is possible only if we give correspondingly different weights to the components of our creedal heritage. This means that the value aspect and the organizational aspect of any social (policy) problem are joined like Siamese twins. Neither can be resolved except as the other is resolved. Each side involves a knowledge problem. In organizational terms, this problem is a question of what alternatives to customary rules can be spelled out and their results quantified. In value terms, this problem is a question of what new weightings of competing creeds would be required by the alternatives to our customary ways.

This brings up the second difficulty: No amount of rigor in any conceptual system of rules and no amount of completeness in quantitative measurements can determine what uniform weights to give our competing judgments of what is desirable and why. For each individual or group is its own unique weighting mechanism. Thus theory and measurement can never specify what change in customary rules constitute the appropriate solution to any social problem. This is not the office of theory and measurement; their office is simply that of a tool to be used in analyzing the conditions that are generating present conflicts, and in quantifying the outcomes of alternatives that people (including analysts) might choose, giving new weights to their competing values in doing so. Because their office is thus instrumental, the ideal models of scientific theory and measurement are not to be equated with so-called normative systems of life and social organization. Such systems always rest on value biases which unless recognized lurk behind the mask of scientific objectivity.

Yet despite their implicit incompatibilities, the fact remains that in the premachine era, America's competing creeds of life were bound together with a unique system of weights in a new model of social organization that is commonly recognized as constituting one of the most unified belief systems in history.[12]

[12] See observations of Gunnar Myrdal, An American Dilemma, The Negro Problem and Modern Democracy. Harper and Brothers Publishers, New York and London. 1944. Pp. 1-6.

This model is called the Lockean model. It takes its name from
John Locke who, in his <u>Treatise of Civil Government</u>, first held
that the good world lies in a sharp division of society into a big
natural order, subject to no collective restraints on individual
action, and a tiny political sphere of popularly controlled government that keeps its hands off what Locke called the "State of Nature," which Adam Smith baptized in the new name of "natural
liberty," and which is today called the "free market." This
model obviously gives very heavy weights to the value judgments
of the enterprise creed, a fact never more accurately expressed
than by Jefferson in his famous maxim: "That government is
best which governs least." Cogent reasons for these heavy
weights lie in the historic events that entered the shaping of this
model and the sinking of its roots deeply into American life and
character. As modern social structures are a series of adjustments of this model and its uniquely weighted value judgments,
attention to its salient features and the great events that shaped
it provides pertinent data on why we think and divide as we do on
present issues, the current farm problem being only one of many.

However, as these are treated elsewhere,[13] we pass over
them here except for the observation that in no country have actual social structures so approximated the Lockean model as
those of premachine America. This is true because in that era
both the farm and nonfarm segments of our society were characterized by systems of predominantly family production units,
which is actually the kind of economic organization presupposed
by the Lockean premises.

DIVERGENT IMPACT OF TECHNICAL ADVANCE IN
AGRICULTURE ON PREMACHINE ECONOMY OF
PREDOMINATELY FAMILY PRODUCTION UNITS

With these observations in mind, we note the widely held view
that the various beliefs and values of people are largely a function of the social structures in which they live. In line with this
assumption should we not expect the influence of technical advance on the relatively heavy weights given the enterprise creed
in the past to differ for agriculture and industry? For its impacts on premachine institutions in each case are as opposite as
the poles because family production units are as characteristic
of present-day mechanized agriculture as in the premachine era,
whereas in industry they have long since passed into the realm of
memory.

---

[13] See pp. 34-47 of reference cited in footnote 2.

The reason lies in a fundamental difference in the nature of the Industrial Revolution in agriculture and in industry. This fact is evident from the vantage point of earlier times when farming and manufacturing were alike in respect to the sequence in which operations were carried on in productive units. Normally in both instances, they were done sequentially, one after another, usually by the same individual or family. Shift to machine methods quickly wiped out this age-old similarity. For, with minor exceptions of certain specialized poultry and livestock operations[14] the shift to machine agriculture leaves relatively undisturbed the sequential pattern of operations that has prevailed in farming since the domestication of plants and animals. In contrast, the same shift in industry transmutes this sequence into the modern simultaneous pattern of operations that is characteristic of the factory system. Thus in agriculture, the Industrial Revolution is merely a spectacular change in the gadgets with which operations are performed, whereas in industry it is a further revolution in the premachine order or sequence in which men use their implements. [15]

This second aspect of technical change is the one that demolishes the older order, as it multiplies the number of concurrent operations far beyond the number of workers in a family. Thus from the standpoint of sheer physical necessity, such advance has long since replaced the premachine system of family units with immensely larger ones, often requiring thousands of workers with different concurrent tasks that must be coordinated and guided by layer upon layer of supervisors and managers.

In contrast, technological advance in agriculture is mainly a spectacular change in the gadgets with which operations are performed. For this reason, machine methods and power, by and large, are as compatible as hand techniques with either family or larger-than-family units of production. Their compatibility with family units lies in the fact that, by and large, farm operations remain as widely separated by time intervals after mechanization as before; hence the number of things that can be done at the same time in farming is as close as ever to the number of workers in an ordinary family. But machine methods are equally compatible with larger-than-family units, as they introduce no

[14] For discussion of these exceptions see the author's paper, Technological Advance and the Future of the Family Farm, in proceedings issue, Jour. of Farm Econ. 15(5): 1606-7. December, 1958.
[15] As explained elsewhere, this fundamental difference between machine industry and agriculture stems from the contrasting nature of materials handled in each case (see John M. Brewster, The Machine Process in Agriculture and Industry. Jour. of Farm Econ., February, 1950. Pp. 70.)

new obstacle to expanding farm size beyond the capacity of an
ordinary family to do the work in any <u>particular</u> operation. Such
expansion simply involves multiplying the units of technology that
are already on well-organized family farms, as, in general, nothing about larger-than-family units of production in agriculture is
technologically unique. This means that now, as in the premachine era, virtually all economies of scale are realized well
within the size limits of family farms. Greater returns to management but not appreciably lower cost per unit of output may be
realized from larger-than-family farms.

As the acreage of land available for farming is now approximately fixed and as machine methods increase the area of land
one can cover per unit of time, marked growth of machine farming involves a sharp reduction in the total number of family farms
and farmworkers such as is now occurring.

Technological advance in agriculture thus has the singular
distinction of being mechanically progressive but socially conservative. It creates no new occupational class of people whose
new ways of living and of making a living force them to reweigh
America's premachine creeds of life in light of their new needs
of livelihood and sense of status deserts. Farm people may be
experiencing painful conflicts among their older creeds, but the
point here is that the generator of such conflicts lies outside
their own rapid technological advance.

REWEIGHTING PREMACHINE CREEDS IN RESPONSE TO
ORGANIZATIONAL NEEDS OF TECHNICAL ADVANCE
IN INDUSTRY

The reverse is true among nonfarm people, however, because
of thorough-going incompatibility of technological advance in industry with premachine institutions. The organizational aspect
of this conflict has found at least partial resolution in the rise of
modern organizations of business and labor and the value aspect
of the conflict has led to a sharp downward reweighting of the enterprise creed. This reweighting has increasingly liberated
democratic government of its former linkage to laissez faire attitudes, thus enabling it to become increasingly the handmaiden
of work ethic concepts of equity. Three observations bear out
this point.

(1) In separating the managerial and labor roles of family
production units into wide-flung bargaining classes, technological
advance in industry quickly generated a conflict between the older
enterprise beliefs that to proprietors (or their legal agents)

belongs the exclusive right (power) to run their business as they please, and the democratic creed that each deserves an equal voice in shaping the rules which all must observe for the sake of their collective welfare. For as the older identity of firms and households was destroyed it became evident to the new laboring classes that the freedom they most prized was liberation from the complete power of management over plant operations. To achieve this freedom, the so-called liberals sought a government that (a) would recognize that the power to shape the working rules of industry is in fact a joint power of all parties involved and (b) therefore a prime function of government is to protect the joint exercise of this power under legalized collective bargaining procedures.

The conservative classes that still held to the weights given the enterprise creed in the premachine era remained convinced that the world would fall apart if the positive meaning of freedom implicit in the democratic creed were made the organizing principle of industrial as well as political spheres of national life. As they were dedicated to the older laissez faire sentiments and views, their aim was to carry over into the Machine Age the older Lockean vision of the good world as one in which the chief end of government is to prevent anyone, including government itself, from interfering with the prerogatives of proprietors to run their businesses under whatever rules they see fit to prescribe. This was their summum bonum. To achieve it was the very essence of freedom.

Thus the very liberations deemed most precious by the so-called liberals were viewed as sure roads to serfdom by the so-called conservatives. This means that unless we pinpoint the specific maladies from which specific individuals or groups seek liberation, there is scarcely a whiff of wind between the teeth so devoid of meaning as the word "freedom." One man's freedom is the other man's tyranny, just as one man's orthodoxy is the other man's heresy. These conflicting views of freedom take the form of a power struggle wherein each participant seeks to persuade the public to reweigh its traditional values so as to make legitimate its own particular version of a free life by imposing corresponding restraints on its rivals. With the various collective bargaining acts since the 1930's, the so-called liberals succeeded in persuading society to give considerably more weight to the positive meaning of freedom in our democratic creed at the expense of its negative meaning in our enterprise creed.

(2) Similarly the shift to machine industry threw our enterprise creed and work ethic into sharp conflict with respect to the proper locus of responsibility for the individual's economic

security. In separating firms from households, this shift split
into separate classes the ownerships of labor services and the
implements of work. Under this condition, the individual may
possess even greater devotion to the work-imperative than before
and yet have less economic security than ever because his security now depends upon the way in which the management classes
and not himself invest and use his savings. Under this circumstance, the so-called liberals were quick to see the fallacy of
equating insecurity with the just deserts of one's habitual distaste for the work-imperative. Hence the new freedom they most
prized was liberation from the injustices of this error. To
achieve it, they sought a revised social order in which government, corporate management and the individual would shoulder
their fair share of collective responsibility for the latter's economic security.

Remaining dedicated to the premachine weighting of the enterprise creed, conservatives opposed any such social order,
saying that it would lessen the self-reliance and industry of the
rank and file. Not until the 1930's did the nation abandon their
persuasion; thereupon, it was found that public observance of
collective responsibility for individual security was in fact a
spur to greater productive effort and not a deterrent.[16]

(3) Still again, technological advance in industry brought to a
head the potential conflict between the work ethic concepts of
commutative and distributive justice. For, in splitting apart
firms and households, it removed the older limitation on size of
firms to the point at which families could supply most of their
labor and management. In this way, it led to such great income
inequalities that they were increasingly adjudged by so-called
liberals as incompatible with the work ethic judgment that society
owes to each an equal opportunity to the minimum income needed
to develop and use this productive potential to the fullest extent
possible. Thus the freedom the liberals most prized was liberation from the injustice of this inequality of opportunity. To
achieve it, they sought a remodeled society in which a chief end
of government is to establish and maintain greater equality of
opportunity by taxing the rich more heavily so as to make more
services available to all alike.

In contrast, by remaining dedicated to the premachine weights
of our central creeds, conservative classes by and large were
honestly convinced that the liberal proposals so violated our work
ethic concept of commutative justice that they would dry up the

---

[16]Galbraith, The Affluent Society. Pp. 112-18.

incentive to productive effort[17] by subsidizing "the idle, the
spendthrift incompetent and inefficient;" by "despoiling the
thrifty;" by slowing down new job-creating investments and thus
preventing "society from attaining its highest level of consumption."[18] The progressive rise of income taxes is only one of many
evidences that the work ethic concepts of commutative and distributive justice have been substantially reweighted in line with
liberal sentiment.

The foregoing types of drastic downward adjustments in the
weights formerly given the enterprise creed have enabled modern
industrial America to achieve new freedoms from all sorts of op-
pressions by placing collective restraints on individual action.
Through cultural influence, technological advance in industry has
done much to liberate democratic government from its older
linkage to laissez faire attitudes, thereby enabling free men to
use collective power increasingly as the servant of the equity
mandates of the work ethic.

IS TECHNOLOGICAL ADVANCE IN INDUSTRY INDUCING
VALUE PROBLEMS IN AGRICULTURAL SOCIETY
SIMILAR TO THOSE IT HAS INDUCED IN
NONFARM SOCIETY?

The question now arises as to whether technological advance
in industry is inducing value problems in our agricultural society
similar to those it has long since induced in our nonfarm society.
The issue turns on the answer finally given to two opposite theories concerning the essential cause of agriculture's large excess capacity. According to one theory, the cause lies in the
characteristics peculiar to farm people. This explanation may
be called the endodermal theory of the farm problem. The other
theory holds that the cause is the fact that new market structures
arising from technical advance in industry impede the amount of
outmigration of farm people that is needed to rid agriculture of
its burdensome excess capacity. This explanation may be called
the environmental theory of the farm problem.

Our concern here is not to prove which theory is false and
which is true, but to show that their value implications are as
opposite as the poles. To do this, we need to sketch the salient
features of each theory.

---

[17]Galbraith, The Affluent Society. Pp. 112-18. Said Samuel Insull, the great
utility magnate of the 1920's, "The greatest aid to the efficiency of labor is a long
line of men waiting at the gate." (Cited by Arthur M. Schlesinger, Jr., The Age of
Roosevelt. Houghton Mifflin Co., Boston. 1957. P. 120.)

[18]See reference cited in footnote 5.

The reasoning of the endodermal theory proceeds from the premise that the labor market behaves approximately in line with the competitive model. This means that if farm people themselves are responsive to their employment opportunities, then as surely as hens lay eggs and cows have calves, farm people with relatively low incomes, if given ample time, will shift into higher paying nonfarm employments until there is reached the combination of land, labor and capital under which comparable rates of return are realized from all similar resource uses in all sectors of the economy. However, during two decades of so-called boom economy, outfarm migration has not been anything like enough to do this; the lack is so great that agreement is general that the earnings gap between farm and nonfarm workers of comparable labor capacities is wider than can be explained by all factors consistent with perfectly functioning markets. Underemployment in agriculture is getting worse, not better.[19] This means that there are serious impediments to the rate of outfarm migration needed to rid agriculture of its large excess capacity.

Where do these impediments reside? According to the endodermal theory, they lodge in either of two characteristics of farm people or in both. One is their atypical values: they prize such experiences as country life, hunting, fishing, loafing and being self-bossed more highly than they do society's work ethic sense of obligation to improve their social and economic status by pulling up stakes and moving to higher paying employments assumed to be available elsewhere. The other impediment is alleged to be their lack of knowledge concerning their employment opportunities.

Assuming the correctness of this theory, the value aspect of the farm problem is clearly not a knowledge problem of what new weights we need to give our older creeds; it is merely a question of stirring up sufficient unction to enable us to observe the policy prescriptions of the competitive model. Assuming that society acted in strict consistency with its creedal heritage, this unction would take either of two forms, depending on whether the cause of excessive manpower in agriculture were held to arise from their atypical values of farm people or from lack of knowledge of their best employment opportunities.

(1) If emphasis is given to atypical values, it would take the form of pronouncements that society's creed of self-integrity

[19]Robert B. Glasgow and W. E. Hendrix, Measurements of Low Income in Agriculture as Problems of Underemployment and Economic Development. Paper presented in Economic Section of annual meeting of Allied Social Science Associations, Washington, D.C., December, 1959.

obliged it to respect farm people's judgment that a life of low income, combined with being one's own boss and the like, is more
worthy of esteem and emulation than a life that seeks ever higher
economic position by hopping from lower to higher paying employments like a bird from limb to limb. To be sure, our society
places high premium on superior proficiency in economic rather
than noneconomic employments. However, owing to the heavy
weight long given the creed of self-integrity, ours is also a society that feels a still higher obligation to respect honest dissent
from its own predominantly commercialized version of the work
ethic. This respect bids it honor the atypical values of farm
people instead of bothering them with programs designed to stir
up right motivations in them and reform their character so as
thereby to rid agriculture of its large excess capacity. Thus to
the extent that the large excess capacity of agriculture results
from atypical values of farm prople, it poses no public policy
problem except in great national emergencies when atypical
values must be sacrificed for the sake of national existence.

(2) The story differs, however, if main emphasis is given the
view that the underemployment of farm people is due to their
lack of knowledge of higher paying employment opportunities assumed to be available to them in the nonfarm economy. Under
this circumstance, the unction needed for removing agriculture's
excess capacity would take the form of pronouncements that the
weight which society has long given its work ethic sense of distributive justice obliges it to equalize the educational opportunities of farm people. Such programs might well proceed on three
fronts: (1) a widespread information service in rural areas concerning nonfarm employment opportunities, (2) an expanded labor
recruitment service for such opportunities and (3) grants of public funds.

But this blissful absence of hard-fisted value problems loses
validity if the environmental theory of the excess capacity of agriculture is accepted.[20] To develop this point, we need to note
that this environmental theory falls into two main parts. In the
first part, the logic proceeds from the fact that the assumption
that lack of knowledge of labor sellers about their employment
opportunities is the cause of their underemployment is incompatible with the assumption that the nonfarm market behaves in

[20] The substance of this and the next three paragraphs has been worked out in
detail by Wm. E. Hendrix, Income Improvement Prospect in Low-Income Areas, in
proceedings issue, Jour. of Farm Econ., December, 1959, pp. 1065-75, and Economics of Underemployment and Low Incomes, in proceedings of Economics and Rural
Sociology Section, Association of Southern Agricultural Workers, Birmingham, Ala.,
February 5, 1960.

approximate conformity with the competitive model with respect
to labor. For perfectly competitive conditions for profits and
survival would necessarily force nonfarm employers into competitive bidding and labor recruitment to the point at which they
equate marginal costs and returns for this activity as for their
other activities. In this way, they would extend to farm people as
well as to others the knowledge of higher paying nonfarm opportunities. But this is precisely what they do not do normally. This
means that we cannot say in one breath that the labor market behaves in conformity with the competitive model and in the next
breath that the cause of underemployment is the lack of knowledge of sellers of labor services concerning their employment
opportunities. Such ignorance is compatible only with imperfect
markets, not with the competitive model.

But why is agriculture saddled with a disproportionate share
of the nation's total underemployment? Why isn't underemployment spread proportionately among all sectors of the economy?

The environmental theory explains this by three characteristics of the farm economy. (1) Agriculture is the only major industry that conforms to the competitive model in both freedom of
entry and flexibility of labor earnings. Restrictions are seldom
placed on entry of qualified wage workers into farming. Although
much capital is needed to enter agriculture as an operator of a
highly productive farm, relatively little is needed to become an
operator of a low-producing farm.

(2) With respect to age, physical condition, education, ethnic
and geographic origins, and other factors, employers are enabled
to screen workers over and above actual job requirements. These
screening practices yield a large job-seeking advantage to nonfarm workers. For example, a relatively larger percentage of
underemployed farmworkers are above the age limit and below
the educational and physical standards used by many nonfarm
employers to screen job seekers beyond economically significant
job requirements. Again, when new jobs open, farm people are
more likely to be left out because of their greater distance from
the new job openings which makes it harder for them to be on the
spot when the openings occur.

(3) Finally, more than any other occupational group, agriculture is characterized by a combination of rapidly declining labor
needs and a natural labor increase that greatly exceeds the re-
placement needs created by deaths and retirements.

With these characteristics and with limited food and fiber
outlets, a perfectly competitive agriculture is joined to a larger
nonfarm economy that is normally characterized by less than full
employment and by imperfect labor markets that are generated

by technological advance in industry. Only under these conditions can its own rapid technological advance continually generate excess farm capacity, which is reflected in the fact that from 1949 to 1956 total farm output averaged 8 per cent more than consumption needs. [21]

If this environmental explanation of agriculture's excess capacity is correct, it follows that market imperfections generated by technological advance in industry is inducing the same value problems in the farm sector of the society that are similar to those it has long since induced in the nonfarm sector. Three observations bear out this point.

(1) Through its nonfarm market imperfections, society violates its own work ethic sense of both commutative and distributive justice with respect to agriculture. For in permitting these imperfections to impede an otherwise sufficient outflow of resources from agriculture, society puts farmers in a cost-price squeeze that so siphons off the benefits of their improved industry that they are the lowest paid of any major occupational group. Thus society violates its own work ethic sense of commutative justice with respect to farm people.

Nor is this all. Viewed in a time perspective, this underemployment of farm people lessens both their capacities and their incentives to invest in improving both their capital and their personal capacities. Thus in addition to being saddled with most of the economy's underemployment, farm people have been less able than nonfarm people to build up their productive potential. In this way, society's nonfarm market imperfections violate its work ethic sense of distributive justice with respect to farm people by withholding from them an equal opportunity to the minimum of goods and services necessary for developing their capacities to the fullest extent possible.

(2) If the only consequences of nonfarm market imperfections were the mere violations of society's deep-seated work ethic concept of commutative and distributive justice with respect to farm people, then unction could stir up remedial action almost automatically because everybody is for justice until faced with the question of whether it may not cost too much in terms of other values, such as the privilege to run one's business as one pleases. This is precisely the question that is raised if the cause of agriculture's excess capacity is the resistance of nonfarm market imperfections to enough outflow of farm resources to

---

[21] James T. Bonnen, American Agriculture in 1965, in Joint Committee Prints, 85th Congress, 1st Session, on Policy for Commercial Agriculture, table 1, p. 147, U. S. Govt. Printing Office, Washington, D.C., Nov. 22, 1957.

resolve the farm problem. Under this circumstance, remedy
might be found through a national policy of comprehensive supply
controls to limit aggregate farm output to aggregate demand at
stable prices. In principle, farmers tend to want such a program
to protect them against a market that denies them an equitable
share of the benefits of their technological advance. But they
also resist it in the belief that it is wrong to deny proprietors the
right to run their businesses as they please.

   At issue is not a question of the democratic freedom of each
to have an equal voice in laying down the rules which all must
observe for the sake of the general welfare; the issue is the kind
of malady from which the farmer most seeks liberation. Does he
most prize a democratic order that restrains him from farming
as he pleases in order to free him from being deprived of an
equitable share of the benefits of his increasingly superior industry? Or does he most want a democratic order that subjects
him to this injustice but leaves undisturbed his proprietary power
to farm as he pleases? Either choice is consistent with our
democratic creed. Thus, society's value problem with respect
to agriculture is strictly a clash between its deep-seated love of
commutative and distributive justice inherent in our work ethic,
and the equally deep-seated love of the sense of negative freedom
inherent in our enterprise creed.

   (3) As of now, society does not know what weights it should
assign to its older creeds in order to provide workable goals for
agriculture. It has only conflicting values. In line with the negative freedom implicit in its enterprise creed, it wants a world
that places no collective constraints on the customary privilege
of farmers to grow whatever and however much they please. In
line with its work ethic sense of justice, it also wants a world
that returns to farmers an equitable share of the benefits of their
cost-reducing and output-increasing technologies. Because of
these competing ends, society has no knowledge of what alternative to present marketing and production structures might fulfill
its work ethic concepts of justice through a minimum of collective constraints on the farmers to run their business as they
please. Neither does it have any clear idea of the extent to which
it might want to achieve a greater fulfillment of its work ethic
sense of equity at the cost of foregoing some prized negative
freedom of enterprisers to direct their businesses as they please.
Thus, in this instance, America has no clear knowledge of what it
most wants; neither the kind of people, the kinds of actions or the

forms of social organization it most prizes and aspires to achieve. [22]

Such conflicting values are the very heart of the knowledge problem that is the center of policy making, or the process of goal formation. For this reason, any serious social problem is ethical to the core; therefore, as Dewey aptly observed, "Anything that obscures the fundamentally moral nature of the social problem is harmful" as it "weakens personal responsibility for judgment and for action," and thus "helps create the attitudes that welcome and support the totalitarian state." [23]

(4) By throwing its older work ethic and enterprise creed into serious conflict with respect to our large excess farm capacity, nonfarm market imperfections thus generate a knowledge problem of determining both the most appropriate ends or goals of agriculture and also the most appropriate means of their achievement. "Ends" and "means" are thus equally indeterminate. For the means to any entertained goal are the other goals we would forego if we chose it. Through repeatedly taking one as tentatively chosen (given) and weighting it against the other, we finally reach a decision on appropriate ends and appropriate means simultaneously.

In the example under discussion, society's knowledge problem is that of reaching a decision as to how much less weight to give its enterprise creed than formerly so as to achieve greater fulfillment of its work ethic concepts of commutative and distributive justice by returning to agriculture a more equitable share in the benefits of its cost-reducing and output-increasing technologies. Conceivably, the latter may be accomplished through many alternative types of collective actions, all in line with the positive sense (meaning) of freedom implicit in our democratic creed. But how much will each alternative add to agriculture's share in the benefits of its cost-reducing and output-increasing methods, and how much more restraint will each alternative place on the older privilege of farmers to farm as they please? Without comparative knowledge of both types of consequences of each alternative, society does not have the data it needs in deciding which alternative is a desirable end. All it has to go on are rival judgments of value that cause dissension among people.

---

[22] The logic of this section is of the same form as that first originated by John Dewey in his analysis of the "moral situation." See John Dewey and James H. Tafts, Ethics. Henry Holt and Company, New York. 1908. Pp. 205-11, and revised edition, 1932, pp. 173-76. On this point also see observations of Gunnar Myrdal on the moral nature of any social problem in An American Dilemma. Harper and Brothers Publishers, New York. 1944. P. xlvii.

[23] John Dewey, Freedom and Culture. G. P. Putnam's Sons, New York. 1939. P. 172.

CONCLUSIONS

The foregoing analysis leads to three conclusions. (1) The first concerns the role of economic theory and measurement in the resolution of value problems, which we take to be the heart of all serious social problems. Clearly, society sorely needs a way of nailing down both the qualitative and quantitative results of alternatives that is wholly indifferent to the value biases of all individuals or groups. Economic theory is well suited to this need. For, at every step, it reasons from the premise that men seek to act in ways that will maximize their satisfactions irrespective of differences in particular value judgments that determine whether certain experiences are satisfactions or dissatisfactions for given individuals. Based on this premise, economic analysis is oriented to variations in the mere quantities of satisfactions, which in great measure are weighted and reflected in the relative prices that people are willing to pay for goods and services. It is not concerned with the value judgments that underlie these price-weighted quantities of satisfactions.

If, for example, the city of Las Vegas suddenly shifted from a gambling oasis to a resort for ministers, the change in the value judgments thus wrought would greatly increase the want-satisfying power of religious literature relative to slot machines in that area. But this fact would have no effect on the formulas involved in predicting the new price of such literature and slot machines; and in manipulating these formulas, it would be immaterial to the economist as an _analyst_, whether the way of life most prized by the people of Las Vegas was that of saints or gamblers.[24]

Because of this ethical neutrality, economic theory and measurement are admirable instruments for finding out the cost-price consequences that society would be likely to experience in using alternative ways of ridding agriculture of its burdensome excess capacity. Working in this way, economists can provide society with data it sorely needs in resolving its knowledge problem concerning which of many alternatives to present market structures systems will be most likely to fulfill its work ethic concepts of commutative and distributive justice for agriculture with the fewest possible constraints on the negative freedom that is implicit in our enterprise creed.

(2) But perhaps all this is premature. It is surely premature if it is presumed that we already know that the nonfarm market

[24] For excellent observations on the ethical neutrality of economic logic see Herbert Joseph Davenport, Economics of Enterprise. The Macmillan Company, New York. 1943. Pp. 126-27.

system behaves in approximate conformity with the competitive model. Under this circumstance, society's only value problem with respect to agriculture is that of enough unction to induce farmers and others to follow the policy prescriptions of the competitive model of economic theory. If the endodermal explanation of agriculture's large excess capacity should prove to be correct, we should expect the passing years to mark a sharply widening cultural gap between the farm and nonfarm sectors of society with respect to the relative weights that each gives to America's dominant creeds for the sake of making life as free and just as possible under modern conditions.

(3) Thus our final conclusion is that until consensus is achieved concerning the causes of agriculture's large excess capacity, both society in general and farmers in particular can have no clear knowledge of either the value aspect or the organizational aspect of the farm problem because, as explained, neither aspect can exist apart from the other. Until we can clarify the basic causes of the farm problem, we have no way of knowing, so far as the author can see, what are the actual value conflicts that we must face up to in dealing with it. To come to decisive grips with these causes is a tough job of analysis. But short of this, nothing definitive can be said on society's values with respect to workable goals for agriculture.

JOHN F. TIMMONS
Iowa State University

Discussion

DISCUSSANTS OF TECHNICAL WRITINGS have at least four alternatives open to them. The discussant may find himself in substantial agreement with all major ideas and use his alloted time to agree with the author. Second, he may be sufficiently uncertain of the precise meaning of the author's arguments that his time is spent in restating what the author was trying to say but didn't. Third, the discussant may have an article of his own on his mind and use the discussant role as an opportunity to unburden himself to a captive audience. Fourth, he may find himself in basic agreement with some of the author's ideas but in disagreement with others.

In reflecting upon my reactions to Dr. Brewster's excellent chapter, my discussion follows the last alternative with a touch of the second.

Dr. Brewster emphasizes the importance of goals as necessary foundations for the appraisal and development of farm policy. With this I agree. Conflicts among goals and conflicts between goals and implementing alternatives are stressed. Likewise, I agree with this point. The difficulty of "nailing down" qualitative and quantitative results of alternative policies in an objective manner is also emphasized. This point becomes obvious to students of farm policy.

The major contribution of Dr. Brewster's essay, as I view it, lies in his process of identification and development of four value concepts with their varied and conflicting interactions and with their reactions to exogenous stimuli such as technology.

Brewster introduces his four value concepts as the commitments of mind and conscience every individual or group of individuals makes in deciding upon one among alternative ways of living and making a living. Starting from a basic premise of human love for merit and aversion to demerit, Brewster unfolds this status aspiration into (1) the work ethic, (2) the democratic creed, (3) the enterprise creed and (4) the creed of self-integrity. Brewster points out inherent conflicts between these four values and the conflicts between these values in the minds of men and the results of means used by men to achieve these values.

Since these values originated in a premachine age of an overwhelmingly agrarian society, technological developments, and the social organizations they have engendered have had seemingly differential impacts upon farm and nonfarm groups. By and large farm people appear to have been able to accommodate technological developments within their historical set of values. In contrast, technology has necessitated the development of new social organizations among nonfarm people. These newer social organizations evolving from the nonfarm sector of society appear to come into conflict with the historical value-laden agrarian organizations.

At this point, I begin to question certain applications of Brewster's reasoning. While I agree with the initially differential impacts of mechanization upon farm and nonfarm sectors of our society, the extended impacts of mechanization disturb the historical values of the farm sector, too, and lead to new forms of social organization. For example, there are strains on rural values in the process of farm people shifting from underemployment on farms to nonfarm employment as well as strains on values in the urban areas where rural and urban people meet in a social as well as economic context. There are also greater strains on rural values as the farm sector strives to accommodate the greatly increased productivity of capital, land, and particularly labor resources in terms of the impact upon farm income.

The idea of receiving income from nonuse of 25 million acres in the soil bank may not be unlike the idea of unemployment compensation in terms of the work ethic or the enterprise creed. The pressure for higher price supports through organized efforts may not be unlike wage increases through the medium of labor unions. The use of income payments disguised as resource conservation investments may not be unlike featherbedding and work limitations practiced by urban workers in terms of the net effects upon Brewster's values.

The point I wish to make is that on the surface the effects of technology upon values and organizations of farm people appears less disturbing than upon nonfarm people. However, results of technology may be bearing down equally heavily upon farm people prompting them to alter their values in response to technology and its aftermath of productivity.

These impacts may be expected to present even greater stresses on rural values in the future. Until now, at least, agriculture has used almost exclusively the spending power of government to soften the impact of technology. On the other hand, urban sectors have used the police power extensively in a wide spectrum of adjustment from land uses to conditions of employment. As we regard the future, the acceptance and widespread application of the police power by urban people may bring about an extension of this power to farm areas as the two sectors jointly resolve the settlement of agricultural problems through legislation and other forms of group action in which preferences of both urban and farm people are registered as the solutions.

Until now, I have not questioned Brewster's four values as policy guiding creeds. However, I have not accepted the differential effects of technology upon these values in the farm and nonfarm sectors. Nor can I accept the idea that these values have altered materially the basic manner in which farm people as contrasted with urban people have endeavored to bring about adjustments in the machine age.

Now I would like to question the values Brewster sets forth as the commitments men live by and for. Suppose I were to suggest life, liberty and opportunity as the values underpinning our society. In penning the Declaration of Independence, Thomas Jefferson first stated life, liberty and property then replaced property with pursuit of happiness which may be translated into opportunity. The question arises whose life? whose liberty? whose happiness? The point is there are many kinds of values in our society depending upon where we attach ourselves to the means-ends continuum. I would be interested in learning whether Dr. Brewster's four values are ends-in-view used as means toward the

Jeffersonian values. Or are there other ends-in-view in between?

Suppose I were to suggest that people, both farm and nonfarm, could rally around the value of maximizing their net satisfactions or minimizing their net dissatisfactions. Suppose further that a productive norm could be derived from this supposition which would demonstrate how the maximization of net satisfaction could be achieved. In the process, a distributive norm might be stated which would tend to insure each resource contributor the value productivity of his resources used in the production mix. In this process, difficulties are experienced in articulating peoples' satisfactions and dissatisfactions. The identification and ordering of satisfactions and the means to achieve them becomes crucial, whose satisfactions? what order and what weight? The measurement problem most likely will be of ordinal rather than of cardinal nature. In the ordering process, the market most likely will be supplemented heavily with the ballot box and public reaction as preference indicators and the resolution process most likely will be a compromise based on acceptance and/or at least toleration.

The task of identifying and articulating values men live by and for is exceedingly difficult, and the added task of assigning weights of even an ordinal nature of values adds to the difficulty. Possibly this task might be viewed as an on-going process in which the basic values might be articulated in such terms of life, liberty and pursuit of happiness but in which the realizable ends-in-view change from time to time and from place to place and even from group to group.

Possibly Brewster's four values are relevant to this time and place as ends-in-view. However, other values might be equally relevant. I doubt that the Brewster values sufficiently articulate peoples' desires as a basis for developing and appraising policy alternatives. Even if they were sufficient in this respect, no weighting system is suggested for resolving inter-goal conflicts or a basis for compromise.

Values possess the important dual function in our society of helping define problems and of appraising remedial alternatives. In articulating and in appraising values competent of performing this dual function I suggest they meet the following conditions. First, the values be common to our society both rural and urban segments in the sense that people either accept or tolerate them. Thus values possess the basic glue that brings some degree of unity to our society and concomitantly prevents the society from falling apart. Second, the values be possible of achievement and not mere platitudes like life, liberty and pursuit of happiness which cannot be directly related to particular alternatives of action in resolving social conflicts. Third, the values could not be compromised in terms of more ultimate values since the values would in themselves be consistent with more ultimate values and sufficient to resolve conflicts at a particular time and place. This does not mean that conflicts in values might not arise. Nor does it mean that the resolution of these conflicts would result in the maximum achievement of a particular value. Rather, the resolution of value conflicts demands application of the principle of proportionality in which the maximization of all values held by different groups would be sought. This might involve achievement of a little less of one and a little more of another until an equimarginal point was reached which is characterized by compromise.

Brewster uses the terms goals, values, value judgment and creed almost interchangeably throughout his chapter. Possibly his argument would be clarified by sharper definitions of terms and strengthened by extended use of the means-ends continuum concept to which he alludes through mention of John Dewey. Also, the extension of the means-ends continuum of values into such ends-in-view of current programs as family farms, owner operatorship, parity, ever-normal grainary, world food, soil bank and resource conservation might aid in bringing his discussion into the arena of current policy discussion.

Turning to Brewster's conclusions, I am somewhat more apprehensive of the suitability of economic theory to the resolutions of value problems than he is. The identification and articulation of human values and their applications to the development and appraisal of implementing policies requires close collaboration of students from many disciplines. This, in turn, demands interdisciplinary studies planned and conducted jointly by students in psychology, anthropology, sociology, political science, ethic, jurisprudence, economics and other fields.

But as Dr. Brewster concludes, it is surely premature if it is presumed that we already know that the market system behaves in approximate conformity with the competitive model. Perhaps an entirely new model of human behavior is needed that will help extricate students from assumptions that must be relaxed severely to accommodate reality.

Brewster's final conclusion that until consensus is achieved concerning the causes of agriculture's large excess capacity, we have no clear understanding of either the value aspect or the organizational aspect of the farm problem seems reasonable since neither aspect exists apart from the other. Granted more study is needed on the causes of agriculture's present dilemma.

However, it remains doubtful that researchers have been completely successful in translating their findings into form which can be readily understood and utilized by other groups in our society more deeply involved in making and administering policies and programs than we are. In other words, we as scientists in particular fields probably know considerably more than we as a society utilize in our approaches to agriculture's problems. Thus, we face the two-fold challenge of putting together our knowledge from relevant disciplines in a form understandable by the public and in the process discover the areas of inquiry needed for enhancing our knowledge of values and means to attain them.

The research and educational challenge in the area of goals can most profitably be met through exchanges of views among the disciplines as is being experienced at this conference and through interdisciplinary studies jointly planned and jointly carried out. The goals we seek and use as criteria for appraising farm policies are not likely to be ultimate but instead evolving ends-in-view in the process of change but nevertheless consistent with American traditions of life, liberty and pursuit of happiness which are flexible enough to accommodate changes in keeping with changing needs.

Chapter 7

OLAF F. LARSON

Cornell University

Basic Goals and Values of Farm People

MY UNDERLYING ASSUMPTION is that the central rural-centered problem in American society is that of adjustment to the rapid cultural changes associated with the complex of impersonal social forces represented especially by science and technology.[1] The changes and adjustments are taking place in a society in which an achievement orientation, especially as indexed directly or indirectly by economic measures, has had particular importance for the individual. In economic terms the current consequence of the application of science and technology in agriculture — within the existing economic and social structure and accompanying value systems, and with the existing demand situation — is excess agricultural productive capacity in the United States. In more personal terms, too many people are working at producing food and fibre.

We are aware that the origin of the impersonal forces for current change is largely external to agriculture and the small community. We are aware that these forces have their impact upon the whole of American society, not just the agricultural part. Any student of American agriculture and rural life knows that the problems of adjustment to change are not being experienced for the first time in our society. But the rate of innovation — especially of the technological — has stepped up, and the capacity — or perhaps the inclination — of rural society to resist the external forces for change has been greatly reduced (for such reasons as commercialization, the minority role of the farm population nationally and within communities of residence, shifts in power and sanctions from the local community and from agricultural groups, and, perhaps, changes in values and goals).

The conclusion of economists that there is excess productive

---

[1] Other major forces for change are reviewed in Olaf F. Larson, Rural-Centered Problems of American Society, to be published in the Proceedings of the National Workshop for Extension Specialists in Rural Sociology, Community Development and Extension Studies, held August 28 - September 2, 1959.

capacity and too many workers in agriculture can be purely analytical. However, the policy implications of this conclusion immediately enter the area of values. Further, there is even a
challenge that the economists' conclusion really defines the most
important agricultural problem, if judged from the standpoint of
the long-run interests of society as a whole.[2] For example,
would the conclusion still hold in the event of a societal crisis
such as war?

In this paper, however, the economists' conclusions are accepted as providing the guide-line for discussion. Within this
framework, rejecting recommendations to lower productive capacity and to reduce the number of farm workers conflicts with a
certain set of values and goals commonly ascribed to American
farm people. Accepting the recommendations runs into conflict
with another set of values ascribed to the same people.

In this paper, we will concentrate on reviewing existing
knowledge of the values and goals actually held by farm people,
trying to emphasize the values and goals which facilitate or retard acceptance of the alternatives to economic adjustment in agriculture.

SOME PRELIMINARY OBSERVATIONS ON
DIFFICULTIES AND LIMITATIONS

One can readily concur that the value structure of a society
is of central concern and agree that the current problems of
American agriculture are related to value orientations. But the
field of values is beset with obstacles.

First of all is the matter of defining and conceptualizing. If
there is to be any communication in this area, it is necessary to
indicate the definitions being used and then immediately to acknowledge that there are ambiguities and alternatives.[3]

Values and ends or goals are closely related. For the purposes at hand, the sociological approach to values used by Robin
Williams in his book American Society is followed.[4] Here value

---

[2] See, for example, Charles P. Loomis' discussion of Earl O. Heady and Joseph
Ackerman, Farm Adjustment Problems: Their Cause and Nature and Their Impor-
tance to Sociologists, Rural Sociology in a Changing Economy. Published for the
North-Central Rural Sociology Committee by the University of Illinois College of
Agriculture, Urbana. November 13, 1958.

[3] Alternative approaches are reviewed by Clyde Kluckhohn and others, Values
and Value-Orientations in the Theory of Action, in Talcott Parsons and Edward A.
Shils (editors), Toward a General Theory of Action. Harvard University Press,
Cambridge. 1952. Pp. 388-433.

[4] Chapter 11, Value Orientations in American Society, in Robin M. Williams, Jr.,
American Society: A Sociological Interpretation. Alfred A. Knopf, New York. 1951.

is regarded as "any aspect of a situation, event or object that is invested with a <u>preferential interest</u> as being 'good,' 'bad,' 'desirable,' and the like."[5] Values thus are conceptions which influence "the selection from available modes, means, and ends of action."[6] Values are construed not as goals but as the criteria by which goals are chosen. Social values are those which are not only shared but regarded as matters of collective welfare by group consensus. Clusters of values around important concerns become value systems or value orientations. Vogt, with concrete illustrations from a dry-land farming community in New Mexico, indicates that the value orientations serve a selective function in giving direction to cultural processes, a regulatory function in defining limits of permissible behavior in a given role, and a goal-discriminating function for future action.[7] Concerning goals, others have pointed out that what is a goal in one situation operates as a means to a goal in another: i.e., "While income may be viewed as a means to other goals, it operates as a goal in many situations, as, for example, in changing occupations."[8]

Second, one is beset not only with the fact that values are of different orders — that there is some sort of hierarchy of dominance and intensity of values — but also with the fact that there is a situational aspect to values. It has been observed that individual and group crises and conflict situations throw values into relief; such situations may even bring out values otherwise latent which are actually more dominant than those ordinarily manifest. Merton suggests that it is often impossible at present to determine whether cultural values are or are not consistent in advance of the actual social situations in which the values are implicated.[9] Ramsey and associates at Cornell, attempting to relate value orientations to practice adoption by New York dairy farmers, concluded a need to deal with values in relation to specific situations, rather than with generalized societal values, if high correlations were to be obtained.[10] Too, one is plagued with the fact that American society "does not have a completely consistent and

---

[5] Ibid., p. 374.

[6] Kluckhohn, <u>op. cit.</u>, p. 395.

[7] Evon Z. Vogt, Modern Homesteaders: The Life of a Twentieth-Century Frontier Community. The Belknap Press of Harvard University Press, Cambridge. 1955. Pp. 4-7.

[8] Chapter 5, The Value System, in Lowry Nelson, Charles E. Ramsey, and Coolie Verner, Community Structure and Change. The Macmillan Company, New York. 1960.

[9] Robert K. Merton, Social Theory and Social Structure. Glencoe, The Free Press. 1957. Pp. 501-2.

[10] Charles E. Ramsey, Robert A. Polson, and George E. Spencer, Values and the Adoption of Practices. Rural Sociology, 24 (1, March, 1959): 35-47.

integrated value-structure."[11] Williams suggests that this is because of the division of labor, regional variations, culturally diverse groups, and proliferation of specialized institutions and organizations which tend to insulate differing values from one another.

Third, the methods for determining values and for measuring their distribution and intensity are poorly developed. What must be done is to make inferences about values from such evidence as choices observed or reported (as expenditures of money, time, and effort), directions of interest, emotional responses, and social sanctions employed. The study of values, as presently conceptualized, is a recent development. "There is little reliable data concerning the value system of American rural society in any previous period."[12] Inferences must be made from the evidence supplied by law, history, literature, philosophy, and religion.[13]

Fourth, there is currently a paucity of data, on a national or representative basis, to portray in any scientifically adequate way the values currently held by the farm people of the nation. One must depend upon limited data, scattered and not necessarily representative studies, and upon inferences from studies and data not directly concerned with values. Consequently, what can be said here is extremely general or is so specific to a situation as to raise a question about its generalizability. One accomplishment of this conference should be recognition of the meager empirical evidence for the topic under discussion.

SOME GENERALIZATIONS

Mindful of the obstacles and limitations, we proceed to venture some generalizations about the values (and inferentially the goals) currently held by farm people in the United States.

First, on the whole, farmers share the major value orientations, the countercurrents, and the contradictions which are found in American society. The evidence for this and the other generalizations will be developed subsequently. Presumably the goals are similarly shared although the expression of some goals is geared to the occupation of farming.

---

[11] Williams, op. cit., p. 386.

[12] Murray A. Straus, A Technique for Measuring Values in Rural Life, Washington Agr. Exp. Sta. Tech. Bul. 29, August, 1959.

[13] The author attempted to indicate the development of the major values held by American farmers in Olaf F. Larson, How Does Our Cultural Heritage Aid or Hinder Solutions to Rural Life Problems, Proceedings of the American Country Life Association. 1957. Pp. 11-19. The work of John M. Brewster, including his paper for this conference, is especially relevant.

Second, while some differences remain, farmers as an occupational group appear on the whole to be moving closer to, rather than further from, the central value orientations of American society.

Third, among farmers, just as among other occupational groups, there is a wide diversity in the extent of adherence and intensity of adherence to some of the most dominant value orientations, and probably even more diversity with respect to lesser values. There is diversity in the values stated or inferred and in the expression of values.

Fourth, the evidence of diversity increases as one examines value orientations more locally, more situationally, and in relation to specific variables. This diversity among farm people carries over into goals and means. Part of this diversity is associated with social organization and with cultural factors — for example, regional differences, differences among groups with given religious and cultural characteristics, etc. Other parts of the diversity may be due to the values which are "permitted" or "tolerated" by an individual's definition of the situation — a hill farm, middle age, a low educational level, and limited capital are not necessarily conducive to intense adherence to conventional expressions of personal achievement. Still other diversity may result from the set of circumstances whereby an individual is bypassed by the main currents of American life which transmit the major values and goals.

Fifth, while goals held by farm people are generally consistent with their values, the goals are not usually specifically or completely verbalized, nor is the means-end relation among goals clearly indicated. Unless they have thought in terms of goals, farmers are likely to express their ends in specific, short-run, predominantly farm-business-oriented terms. However, more specific attention given to goals results in the expression of more general, long-run ends with comparatively more emphasis given to noneconomic personal and family goals.

SOME EVIDENCE ON VALUES
AND GOALS OF FARM PEOPLE

In American society one would expect farmers to share in large measure in the value orientations of the larger society because of the pattern of historical development of the nation and because of the many factors which have favored a large and unhindered interchange of people and ideas between farm and nonfarm sectors. At the same time, there are reasons rooted in the

economic and social organization of rural life and in social history for expecting that between farmers and others there would
be some differences in value orientations and more differences in
the expression of specific goals and means in relation to values.

FARMER CONFORMITY WITH AND DEVIATION
FROM SOCIETAL VALUE ORIENTATIONS

At one time or another nearly every conceivable value or
trait has been imputed to American culture by observers.[14] Contemporary lists overlap but are not in complete agreement as to
the elements which constitute the core of American values, or
even as to the number of major values — 3, 7, 11, 15, 17, or some
other number.[15] Williams discusses 14 major value orientations
and one major countercurrent, all of which he is careful to say
represent tendencies only. A listing is a completely inadequate
way of presenting these orientations but will suffice to convey the
significance of some of them in relation to adjustment alternatives for farmers. For example, it seems reasonable to expect
support for economically rational measures from the values of:
(1) the stress upon personal achievement, especially secular occupational achievement, (2) efficiency and practicality, (3) a belief in progress which involves acceptance of change and the idea
that changes are in a definite direction and the direction is good,
(4) faith in science and the rational approach to problems, and
(5) approval of and seeking of a high level of material comfort.[16]
Adherence to these values would suggest a willingness to set
goals and adopt means suitable for movement toward agricultural
adjustment. Four other major values are in conflict among themselves as applied to agricultural adjustment; they are (1) approval
of the principle of equality of rights and opportunity, (2) freedom,
(3) democracy, and (4) a high value on the development of the individual personality. The value of external conformity and of the
stress on activity, work and being busy appear to be more

---

[14]Lee Coleman, What Is American? A Study of Alleged American Traits, Social
Forces, 19 (4, May, 1941): 492-99.

[15]Three lists of 7, 11 and 15 items are given in Alvin L. Bertrand and associates,
Rural Sociology: An Analysis of Contemporary Rural Life. McGraw-Hill Book Com-
pany, Inc., New York. 1958. Pp. 35-47. Another list of 17 values is given in J.
Gillin, National and Regional Cultural Values in the United States. Social Forces,
34 (2, December, 1955): 107-13. Also three major focal values for middle class
Americans are postulated by Cora DuBois, The Dominant Value Profile of American
Culture. American Anthropologist, 57 (6, December, 1955): Part 1, 1232-39.

[16]The relation of these to programs for low-income farmers is discussed in Olaf
F. Larson, Sociological Aspects of the Low-Income Farm Problem. Jour. of Farm
Econ., Proceedings Number, 37 (5, December, 1955): 1417-27.

secondary and situational in their relevance to the central problem, while the other values identified by Williams are even more
restricted in relevance.[17]

As far is is known to the writer, only one research study has
attempted to provide direct evidence on farmer adherence to this
set of generalized major value orientations. This is Ramsey's
study of a 10 per cent probability sample of dairy farmers in a
New York county in 1956, the county purposively selected because
census data indicated the presence of a relatively large percentage and number of lower-income farmers.[18] Carefully developed
and pretested scales were used to measure the five value orientations listed as of special significance for moving toward agricultural adjustment, plus conformity and individualism. Scales
were developed for five other values believed to be significant for
the purposes of the study. "Traditionalism" is the antithesis of
progress. "Familism" is opposed to individualism. "Farming as
a way of life," "belief in hard work," and "security" were also
included. Values were inferred from scaled responses given in
interviews to forced-choice questions which involved ranking
items.

Insofar as values were measured by the techniques used, it is
clear that these farmers ranged over the whole possible continuum with respect to their value orientations. A few were at the
extremes, representing strongly held values, but most were
somewhere in the middle of the range. They tended to be highest
on individualism and progress; they tended to be low on belief in
hard work, on farming as a way of life rather than as a means,
and somewhat low on achievement orientation as defined (choosing alternatives which result in a high status position, striving
for profit, etc.). On all other values, a middle range position is
most descriptive of the majority. (See Table 7.1)

Further, the correlations among the values were not high,
even where statistically significant (Table 7.2). Either the available instruments were not measuring values or the population
sampled does not hold highly consistent values when expressed in
a generalized and nonsituational context. Some relationships
were of the expected type, as the negative relation between traditionalism and farming as a way of life and achievement and
efficiency.

---

[17]These are: (1) a tendency to "see the world in moral terms," by which conduct
is judged, (2) humanitarianism, (3) nationalism and patriotism, and (4) the countercurrent, racism and group superiority.

[18]For a description of research procedures - including the development of value
scales and scores - and operating definitions of the values used, see Ramsey, Polson,
and Spencer, op. cit.

Table 7.1. Farmers Classified by Scale Scores for 12 Value-Orientations:
Cattaraugus County, New York, 1956

			Value			
Scale scores	Achievement	Efficiency and practicality	Progress	Faith in science	Material comfort	External conformity
			(per cent)			
0	3.7	0.0	0.0	0.0	2.6	0.5
1	16.8	1.1	0.0	2.1	7.9	3.2
2	20.5	4.2	2.1	8.4	13.2	14.7
3	24.2	21.6	6.3	17.4	19.5	19.9
4	18.9	26.3	20.0	16.3	19.6	15.8
5	3.7	16.8	20.5	18.0	16.8	19.5
6	1.1	12.1	20.6	12.1	8.9	10.0
7	0.0	4.7	15.8	8.9	2.1	5.8
8	---	1.1	4.7	2.6	0.5	1.1
9	---	---	1.1	0.5	---	0.0
10	---	---	---	0.0	---	0.0
No score	11.1	12.1	8.9	13.7	8.9	9.5
Total	100.0	100.0	100.0	100.0	100.0	100.0

Table 7.1. Continued

			Value			
Scale scores	Traditionalism	Farming as way of life	Belief in hard work	Individualism	Familism	Security
			(per cent)			
0	0.5	2.6	2.6	1.1	0.5	0.0
1	7.9	5.8	20.5	7.4	4.7	2.1
2	17.9	17.4	18.4	20.0	14.2	6.8
3	24.8	25.8	19.5	25.3	15.8	15.8
4	22.6	19.5	15.3	25.7	20.6	11.6
5	8.9	7.9	9.5	12.1	15.8	23.8
6	3.2	6.3	0.0	---	9.5	18.9
7	0.0	2.6	---	---	4.7	8.4
8	0.0	1.6	---	---	1.6	3.2
9	---	0.0	---	---	0.0	0.5
10	---	---	---	---	---	---
No score	14.2	10.5	14.2	8.4	12.6	8.9
Total	100.0	100.0	100.0	100.0	100.0	100.0

Note: 1. All percentages based upon 190 cases.
2. The higher the score, the more frequent the expression of adherence to the value.
3. The possible maximum scale scores range from 5 for individualism to 10 for faith in science and external conformity.

Table 7.2. Product-Moment Correlation Among Selected Value-Orientation Scales:
Cattaraugus County, New York, 1956

	Achieve-ment	Effi-ciency	Progress	Faith in science	Material comfort	Tradition-alism	Farming as way of life
Achievement	---	.12	.07	.19	.004	-.18	-.15
Efficiency	.12	---	.11	.09	.08	-.21	-.18
Progress	.07	.11	---	.06	-.16	.03	-.13
Faith in science	.19	.09	.06	---	-.03	-.58	.02
Material comfort	.004	.08	-.16	-.03	---	-.05	-.50
Traditionalism	-.18	-.21	.03	-.58	-.05	---	.005
Farming as way of life	-.15	-.18	-.13	.02	-.50	.005	---

Note: .12 or above significant at 5 per cent level.

In another New York study, a somewhat similar test was given to 240 junior and senior high school students in four rural areas in 1958.[19] Among the 12 value orientations measured were 7 comparable with the Ramsey study of farmers. These rural youth, a minority of them farm residents, also ranged over the whole continuum of scale scores. The boys tended to be highest on comfort and security, middle to high on achievement, low on familism, split high-low on both hard work and individualism, and divided about evenly on the continuum for conformity. On values measured because of their assumed significance for educational and occupational choice, the rural boys were low on service to society, work with people, and friendship; they were medium to high on creative work and evenly distributed on mental work.[20]

Information with value inferences on a national level is of-fered in a study made by Beers.[21] He took 47 national public opinion polls made between 1946 and 1950 for which results had been tabulated by occupational categories (including farmers). These were polls deliberately selected in the hope they would provide some evidence on comparative values of farmers and other occupational groups. Polls were grouped into five classifi-cations such as "economic action by government," "labor is-sues," etc.

This analysis clearly indicated that the general pattern of farmer opinion on nearly all questions was exactly like that of the

---

[19] For a description of procedures and definitions see Harry K. Schwarzweller, Value Orientations in Educational and Occupational Choices. Rural Sociology, 24 (3, September, 1959): 246-56. The results presented here are based on unpublished data obtained in connection with Schwarzweller's Ph.D. thesis, Value Orientations, Social Structure and Occupational Choice, Cornell University, 1958.

[20] Some of the twelve value-orientations were significantly related to sex. Boys tended to value achievement, security, material comfort, and creative work more than girls. Girls tended to value work with people and service to society more than boys.

[21] Howard W. Beers, Rural-Urban Differences: Some Evidences from Public Opinion Polls. Rural Sociology, 18 (1, March, 1953): 1-11

total population; in fact, the pro-percentages on four questions were identical for farmers and others and for eight questions farmers did not vary by more than 5 per cent from the total. On most of the issues, the bulk of the farmers and the general public were under overlapping distribution curves. At the same time, diversity remains. On 35 of the 47 polls, farmers were the occupational group representing the highest or lowest percentage of approval. Farmers were at one extreme or the other on six of the seven topics on economic action by government, on nine of the ten topics on labor issues, on seven of the eleven on international — especially U.S.-Russian — relations, on all eight of the topics on a variety of public questions (social legislation, universal military training, control of communism, special taxes, race relations, daylight saving time), and on five of the eleven topics of personal concern (importance of education, preferred types of employment, satisfaction with "lot in life"). Farmer differences with the general public were by far the greatest on three issues of self-interest (keeping price guarantees on farm crops, removal of taxes on oleomargarine, and daylight saving time). A followup of Beers' work, sorting by such variables as region, income, etc., and an up-dating would be of interest.

Behavioral evidence indicating that farmers tend to be guided in considerable degree by the same values and goals as their fellow Americans is provided by the net migration of an estimated 7,245,000 persons from farms in the nine years 1950-1959, by the decline in number of farms, by the increased percentage of the remaining farm operators employed at nonfarm jobs, and by the growing proportion of farm women in the labor force. Granting the importance of the "push" factors, these trends indicate that many farm people have values and goals conducive to economic adjustment.

Farmers Becoming More Like Other Americans in Values

With the overlap already existing between farmers and others, there is reason to believe that the gap is narrowing in ways reflective of values and important for goals. The farm family's gains in living facilities, the growing similarity of farm and nonfarm family living consumption patterns and homemaking practices,[22] the increased percentage in different age groups of farm

---

[22]Farm Family Spending in the United States: Some Changes as Indicated by Recent U. S. Department of Agriculture Expenditure Surveys. U.S.D.A., Agr. Info. Bul. No. 192, Washington, D.C. June, 1958.

children attending school, and the gains in school achievement by children of farm families are illustrations. Also, it is significant that regional differences among farm families are tending to even out some of these indicators.

Diversity Among Farmers Continues

On issues and programs with value aspects, it is certain that farmers are far from unanimous. On none of the 47 national polls analyzed by Beers were farmers unanimous; they approached unanimity on only four of the 47 — on items on which the general public was also quite one-sided (two questions involved labor and two U.S.-Russian relations).

Further light on diversity is provided by a study of the opinions of New York farmers on agricultural policies and programs which was made in 1951.[23] This was limited to operators deriving half or more of their income from farm operation. The study included 1500 farmers selected through an area probability sample. A high degree of approval was expressed for certain programs (research, extension, and technical assistance on conservation); a majority favored other programs (such as marketing orders for milk, surplus removal, and crop insurance). Opinions were strongly divided on three programs for which reaction was sought: production controls, price supports, and conservation payments. Cummings found that the responses for these three controversial programs could be scaled and four categories of farmers established:[24]

1. Disapproved all three programs — designated as "independence oriented" — 20.5 per cent of sample

2. Disapproved two but approved one program — 30 per cent of sample

3. Approved two but disapproved one program — 22.1 per cent of sample

4. Approved all three programs — designated as "security oriented" — 27.4 per cent of sample.

---

[23]The general findings are given in Edward O. Moe, New York Farmers' Opinions on Agricultural Programs. Cornell Ext. Bul. 864. November, 1952.

[24]Gordon J. Cummings, Values of Farmers with References to the Role of Government in Agriculture, paper presented at 1954 annual meeting of Rural Sociological Society; adapted from Ph.D. thesis, The Major Value Orientations of New York State Farmers with Reference to the Role of the Federal Government in Agriculture. Cornell University. 1954.

These opinion patterns were reflective of a fairly well integrated cluster of opinions related to the role of government and
agriculture. For example: "By contrasting percentages in the
two polar patterns, it was found that farmers who were said to be
predominantly security oriented were much more likely to endorse other agricultural programs and the expansion of agencies
than those said to be independence oriented. ... Those in the security oriented pattern were also much more likely to say that
the government was not spending enough money on farmers while
the independence oriented on the other hand were inclined to feel
that too much money was being spent on farmers. As to farmers'
share in the cost of farm programs, only 5 per cent in the security pattern said farmers themselves should pay more of the
cost compared to one-fourth of those with an independence orientation. Again, nearly one-fourth of the independents volunteered
the opinion that the (then) Production and Marketing Administration should be eliminated, while less than one-half of 1 per cent
in the security pattern expressed a similar opinion." However,
no significant relationship was found between these opinion patterns and receipt of conservation payments or participation in
price support programs.

Such evidence is in general accord with Paul Miller's contention that "The modern value orientation of rural people in the
United States is a condition of ambiguity." [25]

Situational and Local Aspects of Diversity in Values and Goals

Examples of the variations in the value hierarchy and in goals
which one finds from community to community are familiar and
numerous; variations within communities associated with variables sometimes unique to the community are also well established. Cases such as the Old Order Amish of Lancaster County,
Pennsylvania,[26] contrasted with the Spanish-Americans of El
Cerrito, New Mexico, may seem exceptions. However, the importance of value differences in the adjustment of nearby communities to similar problems has been stressed by the Harvard
study of the value systems of five groups in New Mexico. In one
of these — a small, dry-land, bean farming community — a strong

[25] Paul A. Miller, Social, Economic, and Political Values of Farm People, in
Problems and Policies of American Agriculture. Iowa State University Press, Ames.
1960. Pp. 80-96.
[26] The values of this and five other communities are summarized in Carl C.
Taylor and others, Rural Life in the United States. Alfred A. Knopf, New York.
1949. Pp. 504-7.

stress upon individualism appeared outstanding as the clue to understanding behavior, in contrast to stress upon cooperative community action in a second.[27] A recent study of an arid Great Plains community shows the chief community values to be endurance, ruggedness, independence, and success by hard work.[28] However, marked differences were found by three major farming types: cattle-cream, diversified, and cash wheat. For the cattle-cream group, this way of farming is something of a way of life. There was reported to be a contrast between the feeling of dignity of these farmers as independent proprietors and the meniality and subordination felt at other types of work. The "independence" theme persists in many of the local studies, as does evidence of a strong attachment to rural living.

Statement of Goals

From the viewpoint of adjustment to economic change, we can classify farmers into some major categories which are likely to persist. We might designate these as (1) adjustment oriented (gesellschaft oriented in sociological terms), (2) a group which is nonadjustment oriented because of traditional values (gemeinschaft oriented), and (3) a group which is nonadjustment oriented because self-definitions of the situation lead to a perception of being "stuck" in their situation.

Goals, goal priorities, and means appear to vary among these types. For all, the interrelationship of farm and family is typically important in goal setting.[29] Because of this, the goals expressed are strongly correlated with the stage of the family cycle.[30] At any stage, the statement of goals varies with the technique used to discover the goals held. Security and self-respect as goals show up directly or indirectly in many of the studies. Farm ownership as a goal or as a means ranks high. The studies give many indications that the occupation of farming is for many a goal in itself. Beyond these generalized conclusions, diversity appears.

[27]See Evon Z. Vogt and Thomas O'Dea, A Comparative Study of the Role of Values in Social Action in Two Southwestern Communities. American Sociological Review, 18 (6, December, 1953): 645-64; also Vogt's Modern Homesteaders.

[28]Based on preliminary and unpublished reports of the U.S. Public Health Service.

[29]This point has been developed in Earl O. Heady, W. B. Back, and G. A. Peterson, Interdependence Between the Farm Business and the Farm Household With Implications on Economic Efficiency, Res. Bul. 398. Agr. Exp. Sta., Iowa State University, Ames, Iowa. June, 1953.

[30]See, for example, Heady, Back, and Peterson, op. cit.; also Cleo Fitzsimmons and Emma G. Holmes, Factors Affecting Farm Family Goals, Res. Bul. No. 663. Purdue University Agr. Exp. Sta., Lafayette, Ind. July, 1958.

For example, a study of 70 farm families in an Indiana county found all wanting farm ownership and a high school education for the children. Variation, associated with stage in the family cycle, was found with respect to goals for the farm, family finance, indebtedness, health, housing, community participation, and recreation.[31] These families had some long-time goals but seemed to think principally in terms of short-time goals. Goals relating to debt, farm improvement, housing, and equipment were usually definite; other goals were less well defined.

In a New York county, when the county agricultural agent started to work with a group of farm families participating in the Farm and Home Management program, the goals stated were few, chiefly short-term and predominantly about the farm business.[32] Two years later the goals had increased in range, were more long-term and were stated predominantly about the family, the individual, and the community rather than about the farm business. The shift was toward the farm business as a means to achieving such goals as education for the children, leisure, comforts and conveniences of living, and good retirement.

The importance of the context in which an effort is made to determine farmer goals is brought out by two Wisconsin studies. In one, in which the focus was on values believed related to practice adoption, owning the farm free of debt, and providing a good education were ranked about equally high over three other alternatives given — having the farm well equipped, having modern conveniences in the home, and providing an opportunity for travel and recreation.[33] In the second study, where the focus was on decision making about several types of farming changes, "monetary returns" was given most frequently as a consideration in deciding whether to make a change (primary in two-fifths of all responses and secondary in one-fourth).[34] Here monetary returns was selected from four other alternatives including ease and convenience, care and quality, prestige, and relations with others.

[31] Fitzsimmons and Holmes, ibid.

[32] Ernest J. Cole, Determination and Clarification of Goals of Tompkins County, New York, Farm Families Through the Farm and Home Management Program. Master's thesis. Cornell University. September, 1959.

[33] Eugene A. Wilkening, Adoption of Improved Farm Practices as Related to Family Factors, Res. Bul. 183. University of Wisconsin Agr. Exp. Sta., Madison, Wisconsin. December, 1953.

[34] Eugene A. Wilkening and Donald Johnson, A Case Study in Decision-Making Among a Farm Owner Sample in Wisconsin, in The Research Clinic on Decision Making, Papers Read Before the Rural Sociological Society, August 25, 1958. State College of Washington, Pullman, Washington. January, 1959. Pp. 1-20.

CONCLUSION

In many respects, the evidence indicates diversity in values and goals held by farmers of the United States. Some of their values and goals are changing, as for example those concerned with work, comfort and leisure[35] and the means of achieving security. Further changes are in prospect. The New York study of independence- and security-oriented farmers found higher levels of education positively associated with an independence orientation toward the role of government in agriculture. It found professional agricultural workers — agricultural extension agents and vocational agricultural teachers — much more independence oriented than farmers as a group. These would appear to be forces operating in the direction of more independence in the future. At the same time, young farmers, regardless of education, tended to be security-oriented; thus we have a counterforce operating.

Diversity in values and goals is likely to persist, with the implication that there will continue to be conflicts among farmers with respect to agricultural policies and programs, just as there are conflicts among the major value orientations of American society.

Among farmers, some reduction in conflict might result from educational efforts consciously directed at assisting farmers in thinking through and identifying their values and goals. Such an effort would clearly aid individual farmers in arriving at a decision about their adjustment problems, as indicated by experience in the Farm and Home Management Program. However, only a part of the farm policy conflict is a matter of value conflict. Also involved is a matter of self-interest among competing groups and interests within agriculture (unless one wishes to define self-interest, in contrast with group interest, as a value conflict). These conflicts of interest among farmers are likely to be submerged only in times of overriding national crisis (assuming a continuation of the present pattern of social organization and relative importance of the several social systems).

---

[35] See M. E. John, The Impact of Technology on Rural Values, Jour. of Farm Econ., 15 (5, Proceedings Number, December, 1958): pp. 1636-42. Heady, Back, and Peterson (op. cit.) report that two-thirds of one group of 144 Iowa farmers studied had made investments in farm machinery and equipment in the past five years for reasons other than primarily to increase income.

ROY C. BUCK
Pennsylvania State University | *Discussion*

THE UNDERLYING THEME of Professor Larson's chapter suggests the presence of a deep-seated cultural lag in agriculture. There is a widely diffused and traditional orientation toward farming as an elemental feature of the society; a belief that people who work at food and fiber production are not only engaged in an economic enterprise but also are responding to a profound calling. The scientific and technological development of the last century has been unleashed upon agriculture in this value setting. The outcome has been a tremendous increase in productivity. Because of the sentiment and tradition associated with agriculture, not only on the part of farmers but by the nonfarm population as well, the agricultural industry has been slow to adjust in an economic sense to the means of increased production.

Professor Larson has said that there is an excess productive capacity and too many workers in agriculture. As he was quick to observe, this statement can very well be purely academic. For who is to take the risk of programming for the long run? War, drouth, population increases, and many other specters are held up in the face of those who say too many people are producing too much for the welfare of the industry. It is held that there is a greater uncertainty which needs to be covered. This is the uncertainty of the "very" long run.

On the other hand, it could well be that those who resist rather rigorous economic analyses of the farm problem are rationalizing vested interests, ego involvements, and commitments to a belief system which is so firmly entrenched that they are helpless in trying to understand an alternative position.

While Professor Larson does not explicitly suggest measures for solving the dilemma of the cultural lag suggested, he does point out that the value pattern of American society is of such variegated hue that there may be enough momentum gathered for a direct approach to a rational solution of the problem. It would seem that the basic conflict is between two equally cherished American values: the first is the belief in breaking production records and the second is the belief that America because of its heritage must maintain, practically at all costs, a significant share of its population on the land.

Professor Larson also points to another important dilemma, the family farm. He suggests that it may be wise in our educational and service efforts to separate agriculture as an industry

158

from the family for analytic and policy development. In some
quarters this would be heresy. There is no need to review why
this is true. While the writer must side with the idea that the
separation of the agricultural industry from the farm family
would no doubt generate many new avenues of thought, he is, as
he believes Professor Larson was, a little at a loss as to knowing what the wisest strategy would be for initiating such a change
in thinking. Here again we are faced with the inertia of tradition.

It would be incorrect to conclude that cultural lag defines the
whole problem with which Professor Larson is dealing. The evidence he cites from the review of research on farmers' attitudes,
values, and goals suggests that there is ambiguity, diversity, and
perhaps a kind of rootlessness. One can find support in the agricultural community for almost any value position. If one were to
drop the problem at this point, there is little to conclude other
than the farmer is fulfilling the image of the mid-twentieth century model of the common man. He seems to have his mind fixed
so he can change it. Or perhaps more accurately, there seems to
be no one value or goal motif which adequately describes the position of the American farmer.

While it was not Professor Larson's explicit responsibility to
go beyond a factual presentation of what we know about farmers'
goals and values, the writer wishes that he would have recognized
the significant role that agricultural and rural organizations play
in fixing the various points of view regarding agriculture and
rural life. One of the most significant changes that has taken
place in agriculture in the last 75 years has been the tremendous
increase in number and variety of organizations serving and
speaking for the agricultural industry. One can see at least two
levels at which the value problem can be studied. Professor
Larson has summarized what we know at the level of the individual farmer and his family. To date, we do not have an adequate
summary of the value positions taken by the various groups and
agencies affiliated with agriculture and rural life. In a sense this
second level may be more significant in that these groupings contribute a great deal to formulating the image of American rural
life to the general public.

Professor Larson points out a useful methodological suggestion near the end of his paper. He proposes that the group of
farmers who are nonadjustment oriented fall into two categories:
those who choose not to adjust and those who perceive themselves
as being stuck with no choice in the matter. We have been prone
to lump together those who appear to be holding back with regard
to practices and principles which lead to bettering economic and
social conditions. This suggestion of his would lead to many new

insights about change if research hypotheses were developed to pursue the idea. On the other hand, the writer believes that his adjustment oriented category could be broken down into at least two classes: those who adjust and don't worry about it and those who adjust in a context of anxiety. The underlying theme which seems to help in explaining what is behind Larson's classification is the concept of risk. The writer would like to make several general observations about risk as it would seem to be related to the problem of the agricultural industry and to the problem of goals and values among farm people.

Academically, risk has been the subject of economic and statistical interest. There are, however, other dimensions of the concept which would seem to have significance to the problem of farmers' goals and values. It is probably not an overstatement to assert that risk is one of the major problems shaping the value and belief systems of farmers. By risk is meant an awareness of uncertainty with regard to the outcome of a decision or system of decisions. Risk, as it relates to decision, functions within a larger context of uncertainty growing out of an inherent unknowability or less than perfect knowledge. The farmer and all of us, face life and life situations in uncertainty. A variety of alternative lines of action are open as possible answers to problem situations. Each one carries a specific uncertainty of outcome. Risk, then, is a property of the human situation. Man's problem is one of choosing among alternative lines of action in a situation of uncertainty wherein the maximum expected utility of the decision will be realized.[1]

Farmers and spokesmen for farmers have been diligent in educating the public, as well as each other, about the risk in the farming industry. One could very well develop at length an analysis and evaluation of ways in which risk has been defined and faced. Only an introduction to the problem will be attempted here.

Two knowledge themes have grown up around which people cluster and between which they vacillate in attempting to reduce risk. One emphasizes fate, divine revelation, magic, and tradition. Here farming is viewed as a "venture of faith" and that without divine intervention, luck, and continuation of the agricultural practices of "the fathers," the harvest is very likely to be skimpy. The other theme emphasizes reason, rationality, and science. Risk is a problem to be handled in the context of probability rather than faith. The history of the agricultural industry

---

[1] For an excellent discussion of uncertainty and risk, see Frank P. Knight, Risk, Uncertainty, and Profit. Houghton Mifflin and Company, New York. 1921.

would appear to be a study in the interaction between these two points of view. On occasion a "balance sheet" is drawn up and the conclusion is likely to be reached that the second emphasis is gaining in use as a referent for decision. This is the cause of worry in many quarters of society.

As Professor Larson noted, Robin Williams drew up such a summary recently in a discussion of American values. He developed the following propositions:

1. American culture is organized around the attempt at active mastery rather than passive acceptance.

2. American culture tends to be interested in the external world of things and events, rather than in the inner experience of meaning and affect. Its genius is manipulative rather than contemplative.

3. The world view of American culture tends to be open. It emphasizes change, flux, movement; its central personality types are adaptive, accessible, outgoing, and assimilative.

4. American culture places its primary faith in rationalism as opposed to traditionalism.

5. There is an emphasis on orderliness rather than unsystematic acceptance of transitory experience.

6. With conspicuous deviation, a main theme is universalistic rather than a particularistic ethic.

7. In interpersonal relations, the weight of the value system is on the side of "horizontal" rather than "vertical" emphases: equality rather than hierarchy.

8. Individual personality is emphasized rather than group identity and responsibility. [2]

Williams points out that adequate supporting evidence is not available for documenting all of these points. However, there would appear to be enough face validity in them to provide a useful basis for discussion of the problem before us in this session. The Williams summary suggests that the American value system is essentially secular in practice. There is diminishing evidence of the sacred theme embodying the motifs of revelation, mysticism, and tradition in the day-to-day life of American society.

If farmers' values are changing, there must be an intellectual point of origin and similarly an intellectual point of destination. The idea of a sacred-secular motif may be of some use in considering the nature of the change and its accompanying problems of adjustment. Let us see if the problem of risk in the

[2] Robin M. Williams, American Society. Alfred A. Knopf, New York. Pp. 441-42, and 372-441.

agricultural enterprise lends itself to an analysis in the context
of sacred-secular scheme.

Because agriculture was traditionally defined as a "venture of
faith" where the forces of nature worked relatively unmolested to
yield abundance or scarcity, there grew up over the years a very
real as well as imagined dependence upon nature on the part of
the farmer. The early solution to the problem was one of accepting a passive relationship with natural phenomena and to try to
accommodate to them. Reducing risk was by and large limited
to searching for means of tuning oneself to the rhythm of nature
and the imputed whims of the Almighty. Risk was inextricably
tied to fate. The human approach to reduce the negative consequences was to indirectly tackle the problem through the use of
religious ceremony, magical rites, and folk knowledge.

Until the fairly recent historical period, improved farming
practices were not likely to be direct attacks on the natural and
human phenomena giving rise to problems of production and the
market. An early example of the indirect attack was the incident
in which Israel was worshipping the golden calf. Here was an
early attempt at a grassland field day. More recently we experienced the rather active use of astrology as summarized in the
almanac in the decision making regarding planting, harvesting,
and livestock breeding.

As civilization advanced, new and better answers to the problem of risk were sought. The Protestant Reformation, together
with the Age of Enlightenment, gave birth to a new interpretation
of man's relationship with the ultimate. The worldly creation
was no longer seen as finished. Man was defined as a partner of
the Almighty in a continuing creative process. This new status
gave man a wholly new concept of his rights and obligations.

The invention of the scientific method and its accompanying
technology opened many lines of action leading to new approaches
to the reduction of risk in agriculture. The farmer's concept of
himself as an active partner in a continuing creative process in-
vaded the old idea of wrenching a living from what was believed
to be a finished and unalterable creation. With regard to the
physiological man, the new emphasis set the stage for the practice of preventive medicine. Socially, man was freed from the
bonds of family and the neighborhood to develop organizations for
pursuing special interests. Moral relativism began to replace a
strict and narrow code of rights and wrongs.

Society began to see the "practical value" of the scientific
method and its corollaries in other avenues of human endeavor.
Private and public resources were allocated for furthering the
search for truth in the empirical world. Educational philosophy

shifted to a pragmatic emphasis in which the motif was aggressive and problem solving rather than reflective and spiritual.
The educated man knew how to get things done. A great faith was
placed in the answer-giving power of science.

The land-grant college and the agricultural extension service
are two examples among a host of secular means developed to
help the farmer with his problems. Agencies such as these eat
away at the sacred knowledge theme. We see evidences of the
rational, calculating personality cropping up in agriculture here
and there, and we become uneasy about what we are doing. We
wonder if in the technological and scientific revolution in agriculture there has been erosion of beliefs, values, and perhaps
even practices that ought not to have happened. In our anxiety
we ask, "What hath man wrought?" Could it be that we want
to "eat our cake and have it too?" Indeed, the various agricultural agencies and organizations offer a rich area for studying
the value problem in agriculture.

What kind of a personality do we want in the American
farmer? How do we want him to relate himself to the problem of
uncertainty? Is it possible to have active sacred and secular
value orientations in the same skin without developing schizophrenic tendencies? When the farmer sees his alfalfa attacked
by spittle bug we want him to move quickly with the sprayer and
possibly check with the county agent for the latest insecticides.
Is it necessary for him to cover the sacred lines of action too?
It is fairly well documented that the probability of reducing the
bug menace with spray or dust is greater than with any sacred
line of action.

Because of the eclectic and pluralistic qualities of our culture
the question is one of the possibility of meaningful relationship
between the sacred and the secular in a time of increasing areas
of uncertainty carrying with them known probabilities or reasonable estimates. Man needs a set of guiding principles to help him
in this time of decreasing worldly ignorance. He needs a value
and belief system which will encompass the full meaning of partial knowledge. A new value theme needs to be developed which
will enjoin the sacred and the secular. The Protestant era prepared the climate for such a theme. The free enterprise system
and the every-man-a-king motifs have served us well over the
centuries, but they never came to terms with the story of man's
inevitable insufficiency and the need to mend the estrangement
with the Almighty. While the Protestant position freed man to go
ahead, it never clearly stipulated that going ahead did not mean
returning to the "old" law of God. Man's intellectual energies
have been divided between the search for the divine equilibrium
and the establishment of a worldly equilibrium.

Somehow there needs to be developed a point of view that what now appears to be secular can also have a profound sacred emphasis. A mythological statement portraying man as a partner in the continuing process of creation would indeed serve a useful purpose in these times.

In summary, then, we have attempted to sketch out a point of view regarding farmers' values and goals which choose risk as the central concept. We suggested that risk lends itself to analysis in the context of the sacred and the secular. It was pointed out that in this polarity there is the possibility of causing frustrations and inefficiencies both at the level of personality as well as in organizations. Finally, it was proposed that there needs to be a new mythological statement emphasizing the role of man as an extension of the Almighty in a continuing creation. While scientists and educators cannot deliberately create myths, they are efficient destroyers and reinforcers of them. We need to proceed with intelligence in our relationships with the agricultural labor force and its network of organized interests. We have value problems too!

GEOFFREY SHEPHERD

Iowa State University

Discussion

I AM DISCUSSING Mr. Larson's chapter under the slight handicap of not having seen it yet. Mr. Larson was not able to get his material in much ahead of time, for reasons beyond his control, and I had to leave town before it was presented. According to the title, however, Mr. Larson is to discuss the basic goals and values of farm people. On the rather hazardous assumption that any author ever discusses the subject assigned to him, I might proceed to discuss my projection of what Mr. Larson is going to say.

But rather than pile hazard upon hazard in this way, I shall perforce do with a clear conscience what some discussants do with no conscience at all — that is, pay no attention to the author's work, but instead write one of their own. Any relevance which my discussion bears to Mr. Larson's chapter, then, will indeed be purely accidental. But it does have direct relevance to the subject: basic goals and values in agricultural policy.

First, many scientists maintain that goals and values are not a proper subject for any scientific discussion. Science, they believe, can say nothing about values, and shouldn't, even if it could.

Economists, they say, can show on an objective basis, using marginal analysis, what is the optimum allocation of productive resources — that is, the allocation that will maximize the production of the goods and services demanded by consumers, with a given distribution of income. They can show the same thing concerning the distribution of an individual's income, given his wants for the different goods and services. But economists generally take the position that they cannot show on an objective basis what is the optimum distribution of income among the individuals in a society, nor what is the best structure of wants for any individual.

The reasons given for this position are two in number: (1) Appraising the distribution of income among individuals requires interpersonal comparisons of utility, which cannot be made objectively. (2) The structure of wants for any individual depends upon his value judgments, which lie outside the field of economics.

Here perhaps are the clearest and strongest statements of this position:

Economics is the science which studies human behavior as a relationship between ends and scarce means which have alternative uses.[1]

The economist is not concerned with ends as such. He is concerned with the way in which the attainment of ends is limited. The ends may be noble or they may be base.[2]

Economics cannot pronounce on the validity of ultimate judgments of value.[3]

Economics deals with ascertainable facts; ethics with valuations and obligations. The two fields of inquiry are not on the same plane of discourse.[4]

Many scientists in other fields hold similar views. "Scientific positivists" express their views somewhat as follows:

Scientific method reports what is, not what ought to be; it can discover social pressures, but not moral obligations; it verifies statements about the desired, and the most efficient means for securing it, not about the desirable in any further sense.[5]

[1] Lionel Robbins, The Nature and Significance of Economic Science. Macmillan, New York. 1940. P. 16.
[2] Ibid., p. 25.
[3] Ibid., p. 147.
[4] Ibid., p. 148.
[5] Arthur E. Murphy, The Uses of Reason. Macmillan, New York. 1943. P. 145.

Another view, of a similar general nature, is put in these terms:

> Reason...can tell us whether our estimates of value are logically consistent, and inform us concerning the causal means best suited to further the ends we have in view. The means are properly judged as good, however, only if the ends are good, and on this point "reason" has no jurisdiction, for "ultimate ends recommend themselves solely to the affections," or, as a more modern version of the same doctrine would say, to the primary "drives" which determine what the organism desires and on what conditions it can be satisfied. And since the means derive their goodness only from the end they serve, we can see why Hume should conclude that, in the field of morals, "reason is and ought to be the slave of the passions."[6]

Another statement agrees with this:

> Though knowledge is undeniably power, the moral ends for which that power is used cannot be determined by the science of human relations any more than they can be by natural science.[7]

And still another:

> The sense of value that is the basis of choice and freedom lies in a realm that science does not touch...freedom in its most essential sense is something of the spirit, and...this something of the spirit is beyond the realm of science.[8]

That is to say, according to the orthodox view: Science can appraise means, but not ends. It cannot make value judgments. For instance, it cannot objectively put a higher value on freedom than on security, or vice versa; that is up to the individual. Science cannot help us to make ethical judgments. Science can tell us how to get to where we want to go, but it cannot tell us whether we ought to want to go there in the first place. It cannot say: this is good, and that is bad. Science says: if you don't like spinach, that's all there is to it. De gustibus non disputandem est.

I think that this is a misconception, which arises from a faulty idea about what science can say about anything. With respect to means — and most scientists agree that scientists properly can appraise means — science can say that this means will be more

---

[6] Arthur E. Murphy, The Uses of Reason. Macmillan, New York. 1943. Pp. 97-98.
[7] Louis Ridenour, The Natural Sciences and Human Relations, Proceedings of the American Philosophical Society, 92(5): 354-55. Nov. 1948.
[8] A. H. Compton, Science and Human Freedom, Symposium on Human Freedoms. Coe College, Cedar Rapids, Iowa, 1952. Pp. 5, 10.

efficient than that one, but science properly cannot say that this means is <u>better</u> than that one. It may cost more, and the voters who are voting on the means may prefer to choose the means that costs the least rather than the means that is most efficient, because they value low cost more highly than they value efficiency.

Thus even in the case of means, science properly can only appraise in the sense that it can show the consequences of alternative means, not appraise in the sense that it can say that one means is better than another.

My point now is that science properly can appraise ends as well as means, in the same sense as it properly can appraise means. It can appraise ends and values in the sense of showing the consequences of alternative ends, the same as it can appraise means by showing the consequences of alternative means, leaving people free to choose among ends as among means, but free also from any attempt by scientists to say that they ought to choose one end rather than another, or that one end is better than another.

Thus if voters place a high value on security rather than progress, science cannot say that they should or should not do so, but only show the consequences of these values, leaving voters to alter their values or not as they wish, just as it leaves them free to alter their means. This conclusion is based on the anthropologists' conclusion that values and systems of ethics are not imposed upon us from on high but are built up from the ground up by men themselves.

MEANS AND ENDS

But now I come to my second main point, which is a very difficult one. This discussion, like most others in this field, runs in terms of means and ends and values which determine the ends we seek, and many of us refer to Dewey's formulation of the concepts in this field.

So it is a little disconcerting to find that Dewey himself urges us not to consider means as one thing and ends as another, but to consider them as correlative. The means cannot be appraised in abstraction from the end it seeks to attain.

The belief in fixed values has bred a division of ends into intrinsic and instrumental (or in current terminology, into ends and means) of those that are really worth while in themselves and those that are of importance only as means to intrinsic goods. Indeed, it is often thought to be the very beginning of wisdom, of moral discrimination, to make this distinction. Dialectically, the distinction is interesting and seems harmless. But carried into practice it has an import that is tragic.... No one can possibly estimate how much of the obnoxious materialism and brutality of our economic life is due to the fact that economic ends have been regarded as merely instrumental. When they are recognized to be as intrinsic and final in their place as any others, then it will be seen that they are capable of idealization, and that if life is to be worth while, they must acquire ideal and intrinsic value. Esthetic, religious and other "ideal" ends are now thin and meager or else idle and luxurious because of the separation from "instrumental" or economic ends. Only in connection with the latter can they be woven into the texture of daily life and made substantial and pervasive. The vanity and irresponsibility of values that are merely final and not also, in turn, means to the enrichment of other occupations of life ought to be obvious....

The other generic change lies in doing away once and for all with the traditional distinction between moral goods, like the virtues, and natural goods like health, economic security, and the like.... Inquiry and discovery take the same place in morals that they have come to occupy in sciences of nature. Validation and demonstration became experimental, a matter of consequences.[9]

Another comment is also illuminating:

The soundness of the principle that moral condemnation and approbation should be excluded from the operations of obtaining and weighing material data and from the operations by which conceptions for dealing with the data are instituted, is, however, often converted into the notion that all evaluations should be excluded. This conversion is, however, effected only through the intermediary of a thoroughly fallacious notion; the notion, namely, that the moral blames and approvals in question are evaluative and that they exhaust the field of evaluation. For they are not evaluative in any logical sense of evaluation. They are not even judgments in the logical sense of judgment. For they rest upon some preconception of ends that should or ought to be attained. This preconception excludes ends (consequences) from the field of inquiry and reduces inquiry at its very best to the truncated and distorted business of finding out means for realizing objectives already settled upon. Judgment which is actually judgment (that satisfies the logical conditions of judgment) institutes means — consequences (ends in strict conjugate relation to each other). Ends have to be adjudged (evaluated) on the basis of the available means by which they can be attained just as much as existential materials have to be adjudged (evaluated) with respect to their function as material means of effecting a resolved situation. For an end-in-view is itself a means, namely, a procedural means.[10]

It seems to me that these observations confirm my original point — that science can appraise ends as well as means. This point is further confirmed by the following observations of Dewey's:

[9] John Dewey, Reconstruction in Philosophy. Holt, New York. 1920. Pp. 166, 170, 171, 172, 174.
[10] John Dewey, The Theory of Inquiry. Holt & Company, New York. 1938. P. 496.

The "end" is merely a series of acts viewed at a remote stage; and a means is merely the series viewed at an earlier one.[11]

Means and ends are two names for the same reality.[12]

Men do not shoot because targets exist, but they set up targets in order that throwing and shooting may be more effective and significant.[13]

It seems to the writer that we have been muddling about in our thinking with reference to means and ends. Or it may be that what we need is merely a clarification of terms. In any case the need is urgent, and I hope that those who are competent in the fields of philosophy and ethics will perform this service for us. We need clear thinking about means and ends more than almost anything I know of in the field of philosophy, the more so because these concepts are used so much by economists who are trying to put their research on a solid philosophical basis.

SUMMARY

If the distinction between means and ends has any validity, there is nothing that is any more sacred or untouchable-by-science about ends than there is about means, nor about values than about any other preferences. In neither case can scientists properly say which ends or means are good or bad or ought to be accepted or rejected. In both cases, however, scientists can properly say what the consequences of alternative ends or means will be.

If scientists can show that the ends or means or values are harmless to the individual and to society — if for example an individual likes yellow better than blue — society does not need to say that they are good or bad for the individual or for society. But if scientists can show that the means or ends or values have harmful effects on the individual (such as opium) or on society (such as going through stop-lights) then society can say that they are bad, and enact legislation to curb them, and preachers can denounce them from their pulpits. But scientists as scientists cannot do this.

If, however, the distinction between means and ends is invalid, as Dewey says in the quotation above — and he ought to know; most people who talk about means and ends and values go back to Dewey — then the matter reduces to an identity, where whatever can be done about the one obviously can be done about the other, since they are the same thing.

[11] John Dewey, Human Nature and Conduct. The Modern Library, New York. 1930. P. 34.
[12] Ibid., p. 36.
[13] Ibid., p. 226.

Chapter 8

DALE E. HATHAWAY

Michigan State University

Policy Conflicts Relating to the Economic Organization of Agriculture[1]

U
NLIKE SOME EARLIER PERIODS, the major farm organizations have not presented a united front on major issues in agricultural price policy in recent years. Some of the differences in position on specific policy issues can be traced directly to the different beliefs and values held regarding the economic organization of American agriculture. Therefore, this paper attempts to trace some of the values expressed by spokesmen from these organizations, some of the beliefs apparently held by these groups, and the way in which these are associated with positions on farm policy relating to the present and future economic organization of agriculture.

No single paper can adequately cover all of the numerous issues involved in such policies. Therefore, the discussion is limited to certain elements of policy which are related to economic organization and which seem to be of key importance at the present time or likely to become so in the future. These are the family farm, the free market, vertical integration and the use of direct payments.

It is recognized that the leaders of farm organizations and the resolutions of farm organizations are not necessarily a perfect mirror of the beliefs and values of all farmer-members. Yet these positions must represent beliefs and values to which much of the farmer-membership ascribes (or does not strongly reject) or the organization either would be required to change the statements or lose membership. Moreover, in any case, these are the beliefs and values presented to the policy makers by representatives of farm organizations as representing farmers' opinions. Since policy makers do not have direct access to all farmers on every issue, these opinions carry weight in policy-making circles.

---

[1] The author received helpful comments from James Bonnen, Glenn Johnson, Alan Schmid, and Lawrence Witt.

SOME VALUES UNDERLYING POLICIES
RELATING TO ECONOMIC ORGANIZATION

A number of excellent papers have discussed some of the
values important to American agricultural policy, and this paper
will only attempt to trace those relevant to the specific issues
under discussion.

Certainly one of the basic values shared generally by American farmers is the democratic form of government. Brewster
suggests two value judgments are included in the democratic
creed: "(1) All men are of equal worth and dignity, and (2) none,
however wise or good, is wise enough to have dictatorial power
over another." [2]

A second, and closely related series of values relates to economic freedom. These values have been expressed in various
ways, but can be generally summed up as the position that proprietors should have the right to determine the rules (choice of
output, output levels and resource combinations) of their production units. The pervasiveness of this value in our society supports the drive for "right to work" laws as well as farmers' continued dislike of government interference in the operation of
individual farms. [3]

Another concept of substantial importance in agricultural
policy is that of "efficiency." Fortunately, those who include it
as a desirable value to be attained are not forced to define it, for
as economists know, this can be an extremely evasive term. The
simplest explanation for the high value placed upon efficiency
would be that it is merely a manifestation of our general desire
for a higher or improved standard of living. Thus, the resolutions of the American Farm Bureau state: "that efficiency of
production and maximum per capita production are primary elements in determining standards of living." [4]

While the desire for better living is indeed strong among
American farmers, this does not appear to be sufficient to explain the importance of this value in farm policy. It appears that
the concept of efficiency may also be related in the minds of
farmers to what Brewster has called the "work ethic." Thus, to
engage in honest toil is held to be good and desirable so that a
person who produces more or better products with a given
amount of effort is held in esteem. Therefore, to be a producer

---

[2] John M. Brewster, The Impact of Technical Advance and Migration on Agricultural Society and Policy. Jour. of Farm Econ., Dec., 1959. P. 1171.

[3] It can also be argued that both are the results of economic self-interest on the
part of those who oppose outside interference.

[4] Farm Bureau Policies for 1960. P. 6.

is considered desirable in our society and the man who doesn't produce something tangible is regarded less highly.

This suggests that efficiency becomes a value in and of itself, rather than just an instrumental means to achieve some higher value. The deep farmer aversion to the killing of little pigs under the first AAA and the somewhat lesser reaction to the Acreage Reserve Program appears to reflect something more than an all-inclusive concern for motherhood and an objection to money. If, however, farm people place a value on work and efficiency, the unfavorable reaction to these two programs becomes both consistent and understandable.[5]

Closely related to the value of production and efficiency is the judgment that men should receive just compensation for their contribution to society.[6] This is the concept of equity which runs through our agricultural policy and which underlies the concept of parity.

These values appear to play an important role in the policy issues relating to the economic organization of American agriculture. It is doubtful that there is great disagreement on policy issues involving these values.

SOME BELIEFS OF IMPORTANCE

One of the most important beliefs held by many farm people, and by many others including some of our greatest statesmen and philosophers, is that farm people are an important stabilizing force for a democratic form of government.[7] This belief does not extend to include all persons who till the soil, however, but generally includes only freeholders on units large enough to provide a decent income and small enough to be operated primarily by the farm family. Thus, we find among much of our farm population and many nonfarmers the belief that the family farm is a source of vitality to our democracy.

This belief would appear to hinge upon questions of fact, but apart from the study of two communities in California, little has been done to examine the basis for this belief.[8] Since, however,

---

[5] It is worth noting in this context that the Conservation Reserve Program which reduces production of crops in the name of another value — conservation — has survived and has won more general support.

[6] Brewster, op. cit., calls this commutative justice.

[7] See A. Whitney Griswold, Farming and Democracy. Yale Univ. Press, New Haven. 1952. Even Marx supported this by suggesting that farmers would have to be forceably separated from their desire for capitalistic democracy by the revolution of the workers.

[8] Quoted in the First Interim Report of the Subcommittee on Family Farms, U.S. Government Printing Office, Washington, D.C. March 31, 1956. P. 4ff.

it is something that may be of growing importance in future policy, it would appear to be a useful area of investigation for sociologists and political scientists.

Another group among both the farm and nonfarm population express the belief that the continued existence of democratic government rests upon the absence of government regulation of price levels for farm products. It is not uncommon to find the same individual expressing the value that both the family farm and "free" markets are necessary to the continued existence of our democratic form of government.

Another belief that is generally held by farm people is that the owner-operated farm represents the maximum achievement of individual freedom in modern industrial society. Even to the academic person (a traditional bastion of individual freedom) the proliferation of committees, foundations and projects may cause him to support the belief that farmers represent the largest remaining group with any hope of maintaining some freedom to run their affairs without outside dominance from some individual or another.

Another belief that is widely shared is that the owner-operated family farm is the most efficient form of organization for the production of farm products. This belief persists even though agricultural economists generally find approximately constant returns to scale beyond moderate size farms. This belief in the efficiency of the family farm may be due in part to the crucial role of individual management by an interested manager as an element determining the success or failure of a farm enterprise under the dynamic conditions of an uncertain market economy.

If one looks at the record of history to date, the evidence to support this belief appears strong. Those nations where farms are organized as family farms have clearly increased farm output more rapidly than have those under slavery, peasant and village systems, communal systems, and direct government operation. But, we hope at least, the record of history is not all written at this time. Recently we have observed increasing numbers of very large and apparently successful farms in the United States which are primarily dependent upon hired labor. Thus, there is increasing doubt as to whether the old belief continues to be valid.

A final belief or set of beliefs of importance to our discussion relates to the state of the market in our economic system. On one side there are farm people who believe that the market price is the best determinant of a person's contribution to society. These individuals generally hold that equity is achieved in the market and that interference with market forces, therefore, is unwise or unjust.

On the other side is a substantial group of farmers who believe that market power is distributed unequally between farmers
and nonfarmers, and that the greater market power of the nonfarm groups is used to the disadvantage of farm people. Such
persons hold that equity for farmers is rarely achieved in the
market because market power is so unequally distributed.

FARM POLICY IN THE CURRENT SETTING

One begins to understand the pervasiveness of the family
farm as a goal in American agricultural policy when one realizes
that up until very recently the family farm represented, in a single package, a method of achieving several of the values relating
to economic organization in American agriculture. This attitude
regarding the family farm is typified by the statement from the
legislative policies and programs of the National Grange for 1958
which said:

> The Grange farm policies and programs are predicated on the belief
> that family-type farms are the basis for the best and most efficient kind
> of rural America. They are a part of our heritage of equal opportunity,
> democratic society, individual respectability, and stable political order.[9]

The National Farmer's Union statement parallels this and
says:

> The Farmer's Union believes that, (1) Family farming (a) is the most
> efficient method of food and fiber production; (b) provides greatest pro-
> tection for the consumer since family farmers ask only to be allowed to
> earn parity of income with other groups; (c) is essential to a truly demo-
> cratic way of life. (2) The small business nature of farming is a strong
> bulwark against Communism or Fascism, but it leaves the family farmer
> without protection in the market place.[10]

A statement from the 1949 resolutions of the American Farm
Bureau Federation said this:

> Much of our leadership of state, business, school, and church comes
> from our farm homes. The future of our communities, our states, and
> the world depends upon how we train this potential leadership.[11]

Thus, we see until recently a widespread belief apparently
shared by all of the farm organizations that the family farm represented the most efficient method of organizing American

---

[9] P. 3.
[10] Farmer's Union Policy Leaflet No. 10, The Modern Family Farm, p. 3.
[11] P. 1.

agriculture, and moreover, that the family farm makes a significant contribution to political stability, economic freedom, and other values that farm people hold to be desirable.

As long as the belief was widespread that the family farm was the maximum way of attaining a bundle of values, one could expect that any major farm legislation would take the necessary steps to protect and encourage the family farm as the desired form of economic organization in agriculture. To the extent that other groups appeared to have economic power that was used to the disadvantage of the family farm, it generally has been considered desirable to offset this economic power either through increased bargaining power on the part of farmers, or through the use of government. Thus, farmer-cooperatives were given special status to achieve these ends, and direct aids of many kinds were inaugurated to help family farms. For many years there appeared to be no conflict between the policies that would promote the family farm and policies that would promote several other goals desired by American farm people.

As long as there were no apparent economic organizations in American agriculture more efficient than the typical family farm, there was no serious conflict between the goals of economic efficiency and the family farm. But in recent years, economic events have moved swiftly. We have seen increased numbers of large scale farms which appear profitable. In addition, one of the most widely discussed phenomenon in recent years is the spread of vertical integration. Vertical integration appears to result in substantially lower production costs for certain farm commodities. It does, however, have many features which alter substantially the relationships considered to be part of the traditional family farm.

Among other things, vertical integration often removes a major portion of the management decisions from the hands of the operator. Some state that with vertical integration the farm operator becomes a specialized supplier of labor and certain capital. Often the integrator makes the major decisions as to the type of technology to be employed, the timing of production and marketing and the method by which the products are handled in the production and marketing processes. The removal of these traditional management decisions from the individual farm operator seems to be a departure from the ideals of freedom of individual management visualized in the family farm.

To the extent that vertical integration actually results in lower cost and more efficient production of farm commodities, there is sown the seeds of a basic conflict between greater efficiency in the farm economy and the maintenance of the other

176   DALE E. HATHAWAY

values achieved by the family farm. This conflict was recognized
by the Grange in its 1958 statement which said:

> The Grange recognizes the trend toward centralization of control or
> vertical integration in connection with the production, processing, and
> distribution of a number of agricultural commodities. This gives those in
> control added economic and competitive strength. There may also be
> greater over-all efficiency in such integrated handling of commodities.
> However, if the capital and management for production, marketing,
> and other farm services are provided by off-the-farm business interests,
> these interests will ultimately control the agricultural economy for the
> commodities involved.... We believe that unless farmers do this, the
> direction and control of agriculture will be lost to business or govern-
> ment. [12]

The National Farmer's Union also has taken a position that
vertical integration of American agriculture controlled by nonfarm businesses is a serious threat to the many traditions to
which the family farm contributes. Therefore, unless farmers
themselves can control vertical integration, it represents a serious threat to the various values that the Farmer's Union believe are achieved by the maintenance of family farms. The
American Farm Bureau Federation also suggests that vertical
integration represents a threat to individual freedom and management.

Another policy area over which there is a great deal of conflict relates to the use of certain types of production payments.
This conflict also seems closely related to the desired type of
economic organization in American agriculture. The position
taken by the Farmer's Union and Grange has been that the use of
production payments would be desirable under certain circumstances as a method of maintaining the family farm in American
agriculture. On the other hand, the American Farm Bureau Federation has taken a vigorous and specific stand against the use of
production payments as a method of carrying out agricultural
programs. The Farm Bureau statement says:

> Payment limitations, such as have been applied to other government
> programs including the agricultural conservation payments program, soil
> bank, and commodity loans, would place a ceiling on opportunity and level
> individual farm incomes downward. Inevitably, farm income would be
> distributed on the basis of the politics of equal shares instead of by the
> market on the basis of each individual's economic contribution to so-
> ciety. [13]

The Farm Bureau statement also says: "Ultimately, the payment approach also would be a trap for consumers, since it

---

[12] P. 10.
[13] Op. cit., p. 10.

would encourage inefficiency and thereby result in high real food and fiber cost."[14]

Thus, the Farm Bureau position toward the use of this particular method of implementing farm programs seems to rest largely on the feeling that production payments would be distributed in a way that would reduce efficiency in American agriculture. This feeling would appear to rest upon the assumption that there are economies of scale in agriculture, and upon the value judgment that the market is the most valid determinate of what a man's contribution to society is worth.

On the other side, the National Farmer's Union has held the position that whenever the other programs fail to produce the desired income levels for family-size farms, that the difference be made up by some kind of income deficiency payment. They, however, would limit these payments to family-sized farms and not pay them to larger than family-sized units. Thus, it appears that one of the differences in a major policy issue depends fairly heavily upon differences of opinion regarding (1) the importance of allowing or encouraging large-scale production because of the gains in efficiency, versus (2) the importance of maintenance of a maximum number of somewhat smaller sized units, which are generally termed as family-sized farms.

A third closely related issue is that of the limitation of payments to individual producers under any programs. Recently there have been limitations on the size of payments under the soil-bank programs and limits to price support loans that would be allowed an individual farm operator.

The American Farm Bureau Federation has opposed the placing of any maximums upon the receipt of aid under the various farm programs, either in total or on individual farms. They say:

> A ceiling on individual loans does not remove the basic causes of high program costs. More significantly, it tends to reduce the size of farm units and thus to lower production efficiency.[15]

Thus, implicit in the Farm Bureau statement on both the use of direct payments and the placing of limitations upon the size of loans or other kinds of aid to individual farms under government programs, is the belief that there are substantial and significant economies of scale in our agricultural economy. On the other hand, both the Grange and the National Farmer's Union have supported the limitation of size of payments and/or size of price support loans to individual farmers. They suggest that the

---

[14] Ibid.
[15] Ibid., p. 11.

large-scale units are not more efficient than are the typical well-managed family farms. In addition, they suggest the subsidization of the large-scale units will increase the difficulties for the family farms, which ought to be preserved because they contribute to the attainment of other values in our society.

The final, and perhaps greatest issue dividing the farm organizations at the present time relates to their belief as to the relative market power of farmers in the market. Presumably, if everyone believed that the competitive economic model was not only desirable as a social norm, but also existed in reality in our modern economic society, they might consider that the incomes generated by the market were an accurate measure of the individual's contribution to society. There is, however, apparently no general agreement among the organizations as to whether or not market power is distributed equally or unequally between farm and nonfarm people.

The Grange statement says:

The Grange believes that farmers are entitled to bargaining power comparable to that enjoyed by labor and business. Farmers are both.

Through legislation, government has helped develop the bargaining power of organized labor. Other federal laws often enable business to regulate and control production and marketing of its products and services.[16]

This statement carries the suggestion that farmers need stronger bargaining power and if it cannot be achieved otherwise, it would be desirable for government to help farmers achieve and maintain this bargaining power which could be used to enhance their income position.

The National Farmer's Union statement relating to the relative bargaining power of other groups in the society strongly parallels that of the Grange. They say:

Businessmen utilizing their rights under the Fourteenth Amendment have organized great corporations with limited liability which gives them enormous power in the market place. Members of labor unions have brought about the passage of laws which protect them in their collective bargaining rights. Minimum wages and maximum hours legislation and workmen's compensation laws also were enacted to protect the working people. Unlike businessmen and labor, farmers have not yet been extended the legal authorization and facilities to exercise similar bargaining power. Farmers today find themselves somewhat in the position of labor and business a hundred years ago.[17]

---

[16] 1960 Summary of Legislative Policies and Programs of the National Grange. P. 9.

[17] National Farmer's Union Official Program for 1960. Pp. 10-11.

It appears then that much of the difference between the farm organizations rests on the evaluation of their leadership and/or their membership as to the relative bargaining power of other major groups in our society vis-a-vis those of farm people. The Farm Bureau position would appear to be that farmers would receive a just compensation in the market place if it were not for the encouragement of excessive supplies by the price support program. On the other hand, two of the major farm organizations appear to represent members who feel very strongly that the farmer's bargaining power in the market place is such that, without some redress of the difference in power via the use of government action, farmers will not receive an equitable income through the market place.

Inconsistencies would appear in both positions. The Grange and Farmer's Union express concern over the loss of freedom of individual management involved in vertical integration, but are apparently willing to accept a similar restriction by government to gain increased bargaining power. Conversely, the Farm Bureau voices strong opposition to any reduction of freedom of management under government programs to gain bargaining power, but expresses no major concern over the potential loss of management control via vertical integration.

SOME FACTS THAT ARE NEEDED TO RESOLVE CURRENT CONFLICTS IN AGRICULTURAL POLICY

Some of the major issues in farm policy at the present time would appear to hinge around the question of the effects of various governmental and private arrangements to improve income levels in agriculture upon the efficiency with which resources in agriculture are used and upon encouraging or retarding changes in methods of economic organization in agriculture. Does the addition of price stabilizing programs remove the main competitive advantage enjoyed by the family farm? Do certain programs tend to limit farm size below that which would require the fewest resources to produce our food and fiber? What exactly are the management controls exercised under vertical integration? To what extent do the forms of economic organization in the nonfarm economy give nonfarm groups economic power which is used to the disadvantage of farmers? These are questions of fact about which current opinion varies substantially. An improvement in agreement about facts in this area will narrow the policy conflicts but not remove them.

180   DALE E. HATHAWAY

THE POSSIBLE RESOLUTION OF VALUE CONFLICTS

At the present time economic forces and events do not appear promising for a painless resolution of the value conflicts relating to the economic organization of American agriculture. If economists could provide calm assurance that an unregulated (by government or by integrators) farm output would produce equitable farm incomes at approximately the level enjoyed by the nonfarm economy and without a further diminution of the number of family farms, all would be well.

Unfortunately, quite the opposite appears to be the case. Increasingly, informed opinion is growing that the free market will produce incomes even lower than present levels. Moreover, the minimum resource bundle necessary to organize an efficient production unit in agriculture with present technology nearly precludes farm family accumulations of this size in a single operator's lifetime. Thus, the obtaining of outside capital through vertical integration or through corporate organization separating ownership and management become alternative methods of organizing farms. These alternatives, which might achieve the values of efficiency and free maikets, would mean the abandonment of the social values believed to be achieved by the family farm or would require their attainment via other means.

On the other hand, abandonment of the value of individual freedom and free markets via the creation of an agricultural public utility will not automatically mean the achievement of the social values that are held to be served by the family farm. There are many reasons for the spread of vertical integration beyond the desire for price stability and the unequal bargaining power of nonfarm marketing agencies. These reasons and the steadily increasing capital requirements in agriculture, may mean the traditional family farm will recede in favor of other types of organization.

This unpleasant dilemma means that the task of the social scientist in farm policy is important. Farm people and policy makers must clearly recognize the value conflicts that they face. The social scientist has a major responsibility to identify these conflicts. Moreover, there should be an exploration of the other goals which farm people might pursue to achieve the values that are held regarding democracy, freedom and efficiency. Ours has not traditionally been a society of static social institutions in the past, nor should we insist that it must be in the future. However, some of our most cherished values are in conflict and existing goals seem incapable of providing a solution. Therefore, investigations as to acceptable methods of social adjustment need to proceed rapidly.

WALTER W. WILCOX

Library of Congress

Discussion

I AM IN AGREEMENT with all major points made by Professor Hathaway in his informative chapter. My discussion is in the nature of a supplement to it.

The major part of his chapter is taken up with a discussion of the differences in the positions of the three general farm organizations relative to the family farm, the free market, vertical integration and the use of direct payments. In a section near the end, Professor Hathaway raises a number of factual questions relating to these issues.

He says, "An improvement in agreement about facts in this area will narrow the policy conflicts but not remove them." I am in full agreement with this statement. If we could get a substantial body of agreed economic facts in these areas I doubt that the remaining conflicts in policies would be very significant.

Thus far in discussing goals and values we have failed to focus on the extent to which group conflicts within our society and within agriculture are based on beliefs without foundation in fact. As I watch the legislative process work from day to day I am chagrined at the great variance between what the opposing groups are saying to each other and the relevant facts.

I hope before this book ends we will have a great deal of discussion about the nature of research and educational programs which would rapidly increase the body of agreed relevant facts in the farm policy area.

We should recognize that for purposes of self-survival and growth, competing organizations of farmers magnify rather than minimize their differences. Except for differences in the geographic distribution in membership, differences in the commodities produced, and differences in the scale of operations of their members, policy differences on the four issues listed by Hathaway would be nominal if the relevant economic facts were understood by farm leaders. One hears repeatedly that we cannot make progress in adopting more desirable farm policies because of conflicts in goals and values among farm and nonfarm groups. In my opinion, a more accurate statement would be that because of mistaken beliefs about the nature of the economic consequences of alternative policies, groups fail to discover their common interests. Most of the group conflicts as we know them today in the farm policy field are the result of mistaken beliefs regarding the effects of existing policies and expected effects of

182 DALE E. HATHAWAY

alternative policies. And we should ask ourselves: Why is this situation so prevalent today?

Why is such a small part of the research and educational resources in agricultural economics devoted to obtaining a better understanding of these policy issues? Why do our brightest graduate students work on the more concrete but less important problems of firm and industry efficiency under static conditions of equilibrium?

Why do our extension services so largely engage in a conspiracy of silence in these areas?

Professor Maddox was correct in calling our attention to the persistence of conflicts of economic interests among groups in our society. Fuller information would not eliminate economic interest conflicts. Dairymen within and outside fluid milk marketing order areas would continue to have conflicts of interest. Northeastern poultrymen and dairymen would continue to have conflicts of interest with the midwestern feed grain producers. Individuals and corporations with money invested in large farming enterprises would continue to have conflicts of interest with family farmers.

But if the magnitude of the conflict of economic interest in any particular policy proposal can be quantified, even roughly, the policy formation and legislative processes can achieve a reasonably equitable compromise or settlement.

...it is the ethical outlook — of the legislators, of special interest groups and basically of the citizens — that plays the major role in determining political action in regard to economic problems.... Sharp conflicts of interest are encountered in relation to most social and economic problems.... In a society as large as ours, however, the groups immediately helped or harmed may be only a small part of the total economy. The decision may lie with the disinterested.... Many of those not vitally affected by the measure act largely on the basis of equity or other ethical considerations.[1]

It is not necessary that there be full agreement on all facts relating to specific alternatives for this process to work satisfactorily. Nor is it necessary that all professional agricultural economists be in agreement with respect to a particular issue. If social action is to be purposive and intelligent relative to the issues involved, however, the relevant facts must be isolated and agreed to by a majority of those participating in the settlement of the interest conflict.

It is useful, next, to distinguish between economic interest

---
[1] Walter W. Wilcox, Social Responsibility in Farm Leadership. Harper & Brothers, New York. 1956. P. 4.

and noneconomic beliefs and valuations. Individuals and groups differ with respect to the importance they attach to specific noneconomic beliefs and valuations such as the valuation of freedom in the enterprise creed sense. In this area economists can contribute to minimizing group conflicts by analyzing the extent to which the economic interest goals conflict with noneconomic beliefs and valuations. The conflict between higher farm income goals and producers' freedom under specific policy proposals can be analyzed in a meaningful way by competent professional agricultural economists.

As the writer sees it the agricultural economist has an opportunity to make a far greater contribution in the area of farm policy goals in the next few years than in most other areas.

First, through research and educational programs he can and should throw more light on which economic beliefs are based on fact and which are mistaken.

Second, he can and should help groups discover their common interests and quantify to the extent possible the magnitude of their conflicts of interest in specific policy proposals.

Third, he can and should analyze the nature of and the extent of the competition and conflict between groups' economic goals and their noneconomic valuations in order that they can more intelligently reweight their valuations and arrive at a consensus with respect to a policy or policies which minimize their conflicts and maximize their aspirations.

Chapter 9

DONALD R. KALDOR
Iowa State University

HOWARD H. HINES
Iowa State University

Goal Conflicts
in Agriculture[1]

P RECEDING CHAPTERS have discussed in detail the values
of American society in general and of farm people in the
United States in particular and have identified a number of
goals of farm people. Our assignment is to analyze the goal conflicts of agriculture, particularly those arising between farm and
nonfarm people and between groups within the farm sector. In
accordance with the book title, the discussion will focus on goal
conflicts in relation to agricultural policy.

Divergent views on agricultural policy are common. The
current situation is characterized by sharp disagreements among
farmers and between farm and nonfarm people. These disagreements reflect a mixture of (1) goal conflicts and (2) interpersonal
differences over questions of (a) fact and (b) analysis. Differences in analysis arise when one of the parties to a dispute fails
to follow the rules of logic. Differences in information or the
failure to accept a common set of rules of evidence can lead to
different beliefs about the facts. Disagreements involving questions of analysis and facts can be reduced by more and better information and higher standards of scholarship. This is the basic
function of research and education in agricultural policy. Even
with the best possible information and the highest standards of
scholarship, however, some disagreements over farm policy will
remain. These disagreements will center around the problem of
goals and values.

[1] It was originally planned to have a sociologist, Ward W. Bauder, collaborate
with the present authors. After a series of discussions it became clear that an integration of sociological and economic approaches to the subject would indeed be useful, but that it could not be accomplished by us, certainly not in the time at our
disposal. The present paper has been much improved by Bauder's suggestions, but
not to the point where he should be held responsible for any of the views expressed.

MEANING OF GOAL CONFLICT

The meaning of "goal conflict" which appears to be most useful for the present purpose emphasizes the nature of the substitution relationship in the production of goal attainment. For a conflict to exist between goals, this substitution relationship must be of a special kind; namely, a higher level of attainment of one or more goals must involve a lower level of attainment of other goals.

According to this view, goal conflicts arise because of a scarcity of means to achieve ends.[2] Interunit conflict — and this chapter is concerned almost exclusively with conflicts between, rather than within, decision-making units — may arise if people want the same things; it may also arise if they want different things, if what they want requires the same scarce means. A world in which there was no scarcity of means, either because wants were very meager or because the power to satisfy wants was abundant, would be a world without goal conflicts.[3]

The basic restraints on goal attainment by individual decision-making units may be classified into the following two broad categories: (1) the limited total supply of means and the "state of technology" determining the transformation of means into goal attainment and (2) the claims of other decision-making units on the limited total supply. The first is bound up with the physical environment and its characteristics, whereas the second is related to the social environment, particularly the arrangements for the ownership and control of the supply of scarce means and the distribution of the fruits of their use.

There is a third restraint, perhaps less basic than the other two, but still of great importance. It is the skill with which the scarce supply of means is utilized in goal attainment. This also is related to the social environment, especially its arrangements for the administration of scarce means.

An individual decision-making unit may increase its goal attainment via two main routes: (1) by increasing total goal

---

[2] T. N. Carver, Essays in Social Justice, Harvard University Press, Cambridge, Mass. 1915.

[3] In his discussion paper, Cochrane appears to accept our definition of a goal conflict, but apparently disagrees with the idea that goal conflicts arise because of a scarcity of means to achieve ends. However, if one accepts the proposition that a goal conflict exists when a higher level of attainment of one or more goals involves a lower level of attainment of other goals, it must follow as a matter of principle that there must be some increase in total goal attainment power which would permit a higher level of attainment of all those goals that are in conflict. Consequently, a scarcity of goal attainment power (means to achieve ends) must exist if such goal conflicts exist.

attainment power and (2) by obtaining a larger share of the existing goal attainment power. The critical problems of goal conflict involve the latter. As long as individual decision-making units enhance their goal attainment by the first route, there is no necessary sacrifice of goal attainment for other decision-making units. However, when goal attainment is increased via the second route, one or more decision-making units must forego some of their goal attainment. A goal conflict then arises.

Public policies in the United States have been concerned both with increasing total goal attainment power and changing the distribution of the existing goal attainment power among decision-making units. While policy goals are seldom unambiguous, they presumably describe the characteristics of a preferred social situation. Typically, they are intermediate ends in a vast and complex system of means-end relationships extending from ultimate means on the one hand to ultimate ends on the other. Thus, they are instrumental goals — means for achieving more ultimate ends — in contrast to primary goals — those ends desired for their own sake.

Even in the zone of intermediate ends, however, there is a hierarchy of goal levels. A goal at one level becomes the means for achieving other goals at higher levels. So what is a means and what is an end for policy-making purposes depends on the level at which goals are identified. The choice of goal levels in the formulation of public policy has a bearing on the problem of interunit goal conflict, as will become evident at a later point.

The analysis of goal conflicts of agriculture requires two critical kinds of information: (1) knowledge of the goal structures of farm and nonfarm people and (2) knowledge of the relevant goal substitution relationships. Existing knowledge about the first is exceedingly small. While more seems to be known about the second, at least for certain types of goals, even here the information is largely qualitative. If, in what follows, some types of goal conflicts are discussed more fully than others, this simply reflects the available information, and does not indicate a judgment that these are the most important ones.

"Values are not the concrete goals of action, but rather the criteria by which goals are chosen." Values have an ordering function with regard to behavior. As Robin Williams puts it, "They are modes of organizing conduct, principles that guide human action."[4]

This scheme, we should emphasize, represents a rational,

---

[4] Robin M. Williams, Jr., American Society. Knopf, New York. 1951.

objective analysis of goal conflicts – as they might be seen by an
outside observer but are rarely seen by actual participants.
Among the latter, the situation is likely to be quite cloudy. Probably not all goals will be explicit; some may be implicit, or inarticulate, "felt" rather than "stated."

GOAL CONFLICTS BETWEEN FARM AND NONFARM SECTORS

Farm people share the major values of society as a whole.
Likewise, farmers hold many goals in common with other sectors
of American society, especially the more generalized, higher-
level goals. This area of agreement has grown as farming has
adopted business methods of thought and as rural families have
been reached by the same mass communications as urban families.

The general goal of equality has social, political and economic
dimensions. The economic dimension has dominated agricultural
policy in the United States for many years. To most farm people,
the phrase "equality for agriculture" means primarily economic
equality. This dimension frequently has been viewed as either an
ingredient in social equality or as the essential means of achieving
it. In recent times, political equality has not been a major issue
of agricultural policy. Political inequality, however, has played
an important role in the effort of agriculture to achieve economic
equality.

The goal of economic equality for agriculture has been expressed in a number of ways, including (1) a "fair" share of the
national income, (2) equal per capita income and (3) comparable
returns for labor and capital in farming. Not all expressions of
economic equality have operational significance. They give
widely different results in terms of income levels and the distribution of income within agriculture. It is obvious that economic
equality means different things to different people.

The way in which the goal is defined will affect the nature and
intensity of the resulting goal conflicts. Space does not allow us
to discuss all of these variants. So, for the purpose at hand,
economic equality will be defined as a situation in which real income earning opportunities for labor and capital in farming are
on a par with those in other sectors of the economy. This definition does not imply that all farm families would earn incomes in
excess of some minimum welfare standard. It simply means that
the terms on which income is earned in farming would be the
same as in other industries. If this goal were achieved, income
opportunities in farming would be as good as in other industries,

but all industries would have some poor people because all industries have some people whose resources are too few or too poor in quality to earn satisfactory incomes. This problem, however, is not specific to any one industry.

An income goal conflict between farm and nonfarm people may arise whenever public efforts to increase the incomes of farm people result in the transfer of income from nonfarm people to farm people. The transfer may occur via the market place or the taxing and spending power of government. Every such transfer does not necessarily involve a conflict of goals, however. This will depend, among other things, on the goal structure of nonfarm people, the conditions under which the transfer occurs and the amount of the transfer.

If other things are equal, nonfarm people undoubtedly prefer low food prices to high food prices. When low food prices are the result of an excess supply of farm products, the real income gain of nonfarm people is obtained in large measure at the expense of farm people. Consumers are able to buy food at prices below long-run opportunity costs of production. Their gain is reflected in a disparity in returns to resources in farming and low incomes of farm families.

Undoubtedly, some nonfarm people would be happy with this situation. They would not look with favor on public efforts to achieve economic equality for agriculture if these increased food prices. For others, however, the interest in cheap food under these circumstances may conflict with their interest in distributive justice. Many nonfarm people apparently recognize that the social goal of economic equality applies to farm people as well as themselves. Thus, their interest in cheap food may be tempered by their interest in economic equality. Evidently, this has been one of the considerations behind urban support for government programs in agriculture. Still, it is unlikely that they want to pay more for food than is consistent with equal income opportunities for farm people.

While many urban people have supported government expenditures to raise the incomes of farm people, they probably prefer programs that would provide economic equality for agriculture consistent with minimum food prices at the lowest possible expenditure of public funds. Yet as the Brannan Plan made clear, there are conflicts involving economic equality for agriculture, cheap food and low government expenditures for farm programs among urban groups. In general, it appears that the higher income groups have been more concerned about government expenditures and less concerned about food prices than lower income groups.

Because alternative farm programs can have different effects on the incomes of nonfarm people, the intensity of the farm-nonfarm conflict involving income goals may vary with the type of program. Of two programs equally effective in achieving economic equality for agriculture and equally acceptable on other grounds, the one that produces the smallest adverse effect on nonfarm incomes would create the least amount of farm-nonfarm conflict.

In relation to income goals, programs that achieve equal income earning opportunities for farm people by raising the economic productivity of their resources are likely to make for less farm-nonfarm conflict than programs that raise incomes by excessive stock accumulation, diversions to lower valued uses and/or underemployment of resources. By raising the economic productivity of resources less of the income increase experienced by farm people is reflected in an income decrease in the nonfarm sector. National income increases at the same time the incomes of farm people are raised. Even when the economic productivity of farm resources is increased, there is likely to be some redistribution of national income in favor of farm people. However, this is likely to be much smaller than when farm family incomes are raised by other methods. When national income is increased, there will be some distributions of this income that actually could make everybody better off.

Comparatively few farm programs, however, have been designed to increase farm family incomes by facilitating adjustments in resource use that would raise economic productivity. In part, the Farm and Home Development program has done this, as also has the Rural Development Program and the Extension Service. This, however, has been a minor fraction of the total public effort to deal with the income problems of agriculture.

Most of the effort has focused on raising farm prices. The price support and production control programs have been accompanied by a significant amount of economic waste. Farm products have been diverted from higher valued uses to lower valued uses, and some resources have been unemployed. The excessive accumulation of stocks has diverted an inordinate amount of resources into storage facilities. And there probably has been some effect on the transfer of farm resources to more productive nonfarm employment, although this may not be large.

Typically, these programs have transferred income from nonfarm consumers and taxpayers to farm people. In the process, there has been some reduction of the national income, so that the farm income effect has been less than the decline in the incomes of nonfarm people. In other words, nonfarm people would have

had larger real incomes if the farm income effect had been induced by a simple redistribution of money income between farm
and nonfarm people. While these programs have raised the income of farm families, they have not eliminated the disparities
in income-earning opportunities in agriculture. And they have
been unnecessarily costly in the sense that the income gains to
agriculture have not been achieved with a minimum income loss
to the rest of society.

The specific methods employed in past efforts to achieve
economic equality for agriculture reflect the influence of various
nonincome restraints. Other goals have conditioned the choice of
programs to achieve economic equality, including goals relating
to family farming, farm population and entrepreneurial freedom
and responsibilities in agriculture. While a few nonfarm groups
have expressed a position, there is little real evidence that the
majority of nonfarm people have been particularly concerned
about these goals one way or the other.

Many farm people apparently want income equality for agriculture without inducing significant changes in the organizational
structure of the industry. A few have even expressed the view
that organizational trends should be halted and satisfactory incomes should be provided for the existing number of farm families. In general, there has been strong rural opposition to program proposals that would facilitate the movement of resources
from farm to nonfarm employments, even though average income
earning opportunities off farms are admittedly higher than on
farms. Likewise, there has been strong opposition to proposals
that would facilitate the reorganization of the industry into fewer
and larger farms.

Unquestionably, there are important nonincome amenities
associated with farming, at least for many people. There is the
opportunity to be one's own boss, to make managerial decisions,
to live close to nature away from the traffic and congestion of the
large city and so forth. Quite naturally, a person enjoying these
amenities would prefer to go on enjoying them and still earn as
large an income as he would if he gave them up and accepted a
nonfarm job. Many more people would want to farm today if they
could have these things and at the same time have an income
equal to what they earn in their present jobs.

Under present and prospective technological and market conditions, the farm industry cannot support the existing quantity of
resources at return levels that compare favorably with those in
the nonfarm economy. If economic equality is to be achieved with
the existing organizational structure, nonfarm people will have to
be willing to forego a large amount of income. Is the nonfarm

sector likely to pay this cost? Are the benefits to nonfarm people sufficient to make this sacrifice worthwhile?

Unquestionably, there are some benefits to nonfarm people from the existing organizational structure in the farm industry. In the short run, the pressure on public and private facilities in urban areas would be greater. Some nonfarm people might find more intense competition for nonfarm jobs. In view of reapportionment problems, few urban people are likely to accept the argument that the best safeguard to our democratic way of life is a large farm population living on small farms. Strong opposition to policy measures that would reduce farm population has been voiced by business groups in small towns that are largely dependent on the surrounding farming community for income generation. These groups undoubtedly benefit from the existing organizational structure.

Yet, it is extremely unlikely that these benefits would be sufficient in the minds of most nonfarm people to offset the cost of providing economic equality for farm people within the existing organizational structure of agriculture. The interests of a majority of nonfarm people appear to lie in programs that would achieve economic equality for agriculture by raising the economic productivity of farm family resources and ease the adjustment burdens which these would entail.

The problem of income inequality in agriculture has a large part of its roots in the rapid advance of farm technology. The biggest beneficiary of these improvements has been the nonfarm population. Agriculture, however, has not been able to fully digest these technological changes. This has meant lower incomes for farm families and a smaller total national income than would otherwise be the case. Although there is reason why farm people might oppose the introduction of better production methods, they are today strong supporters of the use of public funds for agricultural research. Undoubtedly, this support has been based mainly on observation of the income effects on the individual producers, particularly the early adopters.[5] The interest of farm people in technical progress in agriculture in the years ahead might diminish as they learn more about the income effects on the industry. Should this happen, farm and nonfarm people might be at odds over the rate of improvement in farm technology, farm people favoring a slower rate and nonfarm people favoring a faster rate.

---

[5] Other considerations are the increase in leisure which new techniques permit and the reduction in individual uncertainty about disease, pests and weather problems.

Farm Pressure Groups

The major farm organizations represent attempts to move in the direction of organizational equality between farm and nonfarm people. They are a part of the farmers' movement which, like the labor movement, originated in a felt need for relief from maladjustment. Unfortunately, the farmers' movement is often associated with its occasional violent acts of rebellion and radical legislative proposals rather than with its expression of a significant historic development growing out of deep and persistent maladjustments between the economic enterprise of agriculture and the social status of rural people on one hand, and the economic enterprise and social status of urban people on the other.[6]

Although there have been others, the major objectives of farmers' organizations have been and remain adjustments in the market and price system by alteration of the organizational structure of the system or the farmers' relations to it. Efforts to achieve these objectives have followed two principal channels. One has brought extensions of farmer control over the system through cooperatives, and the other has attempted to change it by means of governmental regulation. The latter has placed farm organizations in the role of pressure groups, active in lobbying in state legislatures and Congress.

The oft-repeated criticism that agriculture is a house divided stems largely from regional and commodity differences in policy goals, but there are also other basic differences. A recent analysis of policy statements of the three groups suggests that in their positions on international affairs as well as on domestic issues, the Farmers' Union is the least conservative, the Farm Bureau the most conservative, and the Grange is intermediate.[7]

Because of the declining proportion of population in agriculture, farmer organizations represent a smaller and smaller minority. This influences their mode of operation and consequently their policy position. They are no longer in a position to take the bold action of the Nonpartisan League, since in all but the most rural states farmers would be hard pressed to obtain a majority of the popular vote. Instead, they take what advantage can be had from the outmoded apportionment situation in the states and the still strong position of the agricultural bloc in Congress. They may begin to trade favors with other lobby

---

[6] Carl C. Taylor, Rural Life in the United States. Knopf, New York. 1955.

[7] Wayne C. Rohrer, Conservatism-liberalism and the farm organizations. Rural Soc., 22:163-66. 1957.

groups in obtaining their desired goals, but so far, for the most part, farmers' organizations have avoided "deals" in their lobbying activities and depended on general appeals to the rural-based values of society and the good fortune of disproportionate representation.

CONFLICTS INVOLVING AGRICULTURAL SUPPLIERS, PROCESSORS, AND MARKETERS

Let us turn from farm organizations and agriculture as a collectivity to consider the individual farm firm. Small, with creditors but no stockholders, with few workers and fewer employees, the farm firm is simple or even primitive compared with typical firms in the corporate sector and especially its "Big 200." The farm business is intertwined with the farm family, and as we know, income goals have conflicted with family-held traditional values such as avoidance of change. But these differences are disappearing — in part because the sales efforts of agricultural supplier firms and sometimes of marketing and processing firms have helped to strengthen the profit goal and in particular to develop favorable attitudes toward changes necessarily associated with rational production planning. (Salesmanship and advertising are, after all, effective and socially approved methods of bringing about changes in goals and values in our society.)

Unlike the large corporation, therefore, the typical farm firm conducts its business affairs with little need to worry about social responsibilities or business "philosophy."[8] Honesty and other common ethics guide farmers without having to assume sophisticated forms. The farm's simple internal structure creates no problems of management hierarchy or stockholder and employee relations. Its small size and lack of market power free it from concern for sales strategies and price policies: it is a "price taker." A suitable "corporate image" is wanted neither to defend the long-run political position of the firm by means of public relations nor to assuage the psychological conflicts of its manager.[9] Not Red Roof Farm but Jersey Standard seeks to operate "in such a way as to maintain an equitable and working balance among the claims of the various directly interested groups — stockholders,

---

[8] Edward S. Mason (ed.) The Corporation in Modern Society. Harvard University Press, Cambridge, Mass. 1959.
[9] Francis X. Sutton, et al., The American Business Creed. Harvard University Press, Cambridge, Mass. 1956.

employees, customers, and the public at large."[10] The agricultural firm can carry on its daily business affairs unencumbered by policy pronouncements, creeds, and images. Problems of this kind appear only when agriculture as a whole ventures into public policy.

Although as a rule the farm firm is small and simple, it is not isolated or autonomous. It sells food and fiber not to consuming households, but to a series of marketing and processing firms. It produces not by merely combining ordinary labor with the original productive powers of the soil but by using so many purchased inputs that modern farms might properly be called processing firms rather than "primary producers." Exactly as parts makers stand behind automobile assembly lines, manufacturers and sellers of machinery, fertilizers, formula feeds, motor fuel and electricity and other agricultural inputs assist the modern farmer.[11]

The existence and secular growth of agricultural input industries complicate the farm management function, of course, but they do not seem to generate major conflicts in the area of goals and values so long as our focus is on the individual farm business. True, the objective of the fertilizer salesman is to maximize his own and his company's returns, which may lead him to push his farmer customers into purchases of uneconomic amounts and qualities of fertilizer.[12] Overextension of credit may also result from its use as a form of price competition (or as a device for product differentiation), and obviously prices themselves will also be points of controversy.

If, however, we take the point of view of agriculture as an industry, instead of that of one of its member firms, the picture changes. A "composition effect" appears. The use of purchased inputs has been a principal reason for the growing output of

---

[10] Mason, op. cit., p. 60.

[11] A special income concept has even been developed to take account of this situation. "Farm gross national product represents the portion of gross national product originating on the farm. It is a value-added concept and is obtained by subtracting from the total value of farm output the value of (intermediate) materials used up in the production process, such as fertilizer, purchased feed, and motor fuel. It measures production occurring on farms without duplication and is 'gross' only in the sense that depreciation and other capital consumption allowances are not deducted." U.S. Department of Commerce, Note on farm gross national product, Survey of Current Business, 38(Oct., 1958):11-14.

[12] Jesse W. Markham, The Fertilizer Industry. The Vanderbilt University Press, Nashville, Tennessee, 1958. For a contrary view, see Zvi Griliches, Are farmers irrational? Jour. Polit. Econ., 68:68-71, 1960. Also see: "...Reply" by Markham, "Rejoinder" by Griliches, and "Positive policy in the fertilizer industry," by Vernon W. Ruttan, 68:630-34. 1960.

agriculture as well as (in connection with growing use of capital in general) a means of substituting for labor in producing each particular level of output. Together with the well-known secular behavior of demand for agricultural products and the immobility of labor, these developments have created the "agricultural adjustment problem." At this point the nature of the controversy will depend upon the kind of public policy proposed as a solution. Policies which would raise the qualities or lower the prices of farm inputs would not necessarily improve the income position of farmers as a whole, though they might help quick-adapting individuals, at least for a time.[13]

Much the same convergence and divergence of goals appears when we examine the farm and farming in relation to marketing and processing firms. Once again we notice that these firms have been active in helping to develop a rational, or "commercial" point of view among farmers. A well-known example is in dairy farming, where improvement of product quality on the farms by careful management and by rapid adoption of improved practices has long been fostered by dairy plants. Meat packer efforts on behalf of the "meat type" hog is another current example. As for quantity of product, we can be sure that at any moment of time a marketing or processing firm's profits would be improved if it could increase the volume of its business.[14] Where the effort to do this takes the form of raising the public's aggregate demand for food and fiber, for example by advertising or product quality control or the development of new product forms, farmers will ordinarily approve. (We recognize but do not discuss the issues involved in making a social evaluation of demand-creation activities.) On the other hand, this same objective of volume sales may breed a conflict in the public policy area, where processors

---

[13] This, however, does not necessarily condemn such policies as proscription of monopolistic practices, facilitation of entry of new firms into agricultural input industries and others likely to have these effects. Consumer welfare and in general the proper allocation of resources in the economy will also have to be considered.

[14] Thus, President Porter Jarvis of Swift & Company writes, in his company's 1958 Year Book, "Federally inspected beef production in 1958 was down 7.2 per cent from the same period in 1957. Pork was down 2 per cent, veal 24.5 per cent and lamb 6.5 per cent. Industry efforts to utilize current capacities more fully intensified the bidding for reduced livestock marketings. As a result, livestock prices were high relative to selling prices of meat. This situation, together with the general upward trend of marketing costs, produced almost continuous pressure on profit margins. Results in beef, veal, lamb and pork divisions were unsatisfactory." Among retail food marketers, the same point is operative. See B. R. Holdren, The Structure of a Retail Market and the Market Behavior of Retail Units. Prentice-Hall, Inc., Englewood, N.J. 1960.

will oppose policies that might restrict farm output.[15] This is one reason why, on the whole, one would expect processors and marketers to resist public policies that might raise farm prices; another is that the public criticizes food processors and sellers for their prices rather than for their margins.[16]

In our present assignment, we are not asked to consider all aspects of the structure and performance of agricultural marketing and processing businesses but only the effects of these on farmers, directly or indirectly. Increasing the degree of competition among bakers might give consumers better and cheaper bread without significantly bringing higher prices to the wheat farmer. At any rate, this kind of result is a possibility; one is not justified in assuming without proof that farm incomes would necessarily rise after this kind of trust busting. On the other hand, one can imagine changes in industry structures that might not reduce consumer prices but might redistribute the proceeds from marketer to farmer. Of course, both consumer and farmer might gain at the expense of the disestablished monopolist, and if this result could be reliably predicted we could be sure that proposals for this kind of market reform would attract strong political support. In short, according to the forms they take, antitrust and other trade regulation in this area will involve different kinds of conflict and consonance among goals.

Broader social consent for antimonopoly policy will usually also occur if the proposed measures for alleviating monopoly are consistent with widely accepted goals, such as those of maintaining or creating a competitive economy. Proscription of unfair and restrictive practices and perhaps even trust busting by dissolution of firms should be preferable for this reason to more narrowly conceived devices of countervailing power such as establishment of countermonopolies. If public policy does not come forward with these remedies, however, farmers may want to solve the problem by setting up their own marketing and supplying

---

[15] As for the input suppliers, we note that under the title, "The doctrine of inefficiency," the National Plant Food Institute expresses shock at proposals "suggesting that fertilizer and pesticide factories be closed down — a type of Soil Bank for the farm chemical industry." "Obviously, we would have less total output if farmers were less efficient — but only at the cost of food shortages, and much higher food prices for consumers. Official figures indicate, for instance, that during the past 10 years improved efficiency by American farmers saved consumers at least $70 billion on their food expenditures." Plant Food Rev., 6:3, Spring, 1960.

[16] "Although packers conducting legal operations were squeezed between higher prices for their raw material and ceiling prices on meat, to the point where the government had to pay them heavy subsidies during World War II, they drew at least as much public denunciation as cattle ranchers and hog raisers who were really profiting." Simon N. Whitney, Antitrust Policies: American Experience in Twenty Industries, The Twentieth Century Fund, New York. 1958. Vol. I, p. 87.

firms, as indeed they have often done already. The NFO experiments with bargaining associations are obviously intended for
this purpose, although their success is bound to be limited unless
they can obtain and maintain a much greater dominance of the
total supply than they have yet been able to do. Cooperatives also
have been used for this purpose. Farm Bureau-sponsored businesses are well-known examples. The latter, by the way, may
generate goal and value conflicts within the sponsoring organization, between members whose principal reason for associating
with the organization is the "business" objective of buying eco-
nomical fertilizer or insurance and those who conceive it as
essentially an agency for political action.

GOAL CONFLICTS WITHIN THE FARM SECTOR

Most of the important farm policy goal conflicts within the
farm sector appear to center around the distribution of farm income, the organization of the industry, regional economic development and entrepreneurial freedom and responsibility. These
conflicts are reflected in the policy positions of the general farm
organizations, commodity groups and individual farm leaders.
At times they have caused serious cleavages within the ranks of
particular organizations. In part, they account for the current
inability of agriculture to present a united front on legislative
matters in the Congress.
    The conflicts arising over income goals are closely bound up
with the economic interdependence of the farm industry. Agriculture is highly competitive. There is competition among producers of the same product, among producers of related products
and among producers in different geographic areas. Because
opportunities for product substitution in production and consumption are widespread, economic developments impinging on one
important product or area are quickly transmitted to other products or areas. As a result, efforts of one group to better its
income position can have adverse effects on the incomes of other
groups within the industry.
    Some of the more serious goal conflicts within commodity
groups have involved partially differentiated products or shifts in
geographical specialization with attendant effects on the distribution of commodity income. While most producers probably have
been concerned about changes in their competitive position irrespective of the cause, program-induced shifts have usually generated more vigorous opposition than those prompted by "natural"
economic developments.

In wheat, producers of hard red spring and durum have been
at odds with producers of other wheats over quota allocations.
Spring wheat producers have argued that the surplus problem is
not in hard spring or durum but in other wheats. Therefore, they
should not be required to share the same adjustment burden by
having to reduce their production in line with that of other wheat
producers. Undoubtedly, there is an element of truth in their
argument about the relative size of the surplus in hard red spring
and durum. The stockpile of wheat is made up almost exclusively
of wheats other than hard red spring and durum. This is a result
of the way price support differentials have been set. Other wheats
have been overpriced relative to hard red spring and durum.
While this might suggest that price support differentials and quota
allocations need some adjustment, there can be little doubt that
the wheat surplus problem includes spring wheat. This would
become apparent rather quickly under free market conditions.
Substitution opportunities among the classes of wheat are sufficient to induce large spill-over effects when prices of nonspring
wheats get far out of line with the prices of hard red spring.

In dairying, producers manufacturing milk in the Midwest
have objected to restrictions on the flow and utilization of fluid
milk in Eastern milk markets. Their point is that producers in
the East have been sheltered from midwestern competition under
marketing orders and unduly strict sanitation requirements. By
restricting fluid milk use under classified pricing schemes, additional milk has been diverted into manufacturing uses. This,
they argue, has depressed prices and incomes of dairy producers
in the Midwest.

The shifting location of cotton production, induced by advances
in technology and irrigation development, has prompted a policy
goal conflict between producers in the irrigated areas of the
West and those in the Old South. Producers in the irrigated areas
have objected to production controls and the size of their allotments. They believe their production has been unduly restricted
in relation to that of the older producing areas. Apparently, many
producers in the newer areas consider their competitive position
strong enough to meet both domestic and foreign competition, and
therefore, they favor a return to free market pricing.

In recent years, some of the sharpest conflicts within the
farm sector have been between wheat and cotton producers on the
one hand and feed-livestock farmers on the other. The surplus
problem in wheat and cotton came to a head in 1953 when supplies
reached marketing quota levels as set forth in the Agricultural
Adjustment Act of 1938, as amended. Under the impact of the
quota programs, the area in wheat and cotton declined by more

than 28 million acres between 1953 and 1955. Producers of wheat and cotton were free to shift their resources to other crops, and for the most part this is what they did. Upwards of two-thirds of the land taken out of wheat and cotton went into grain sorghums, oats and barley — grains that compete directly with corn in livestock production. While these programs took some of the pressure off wheat and cotton, much of it was transferred to the feed-livestock economy. This contributed to the build-up in feed grain stocks, lower prices for feed and livestock products and reduced incomes for feed-livestock farmers.

The control programs, including the Soil Bank, have not eliminated the excess supply problem in either feed grains or wheat. Feed-livestock farmers fear that additional efforts to solve the wheat problem will bring increased pressure on an already serious feed grain situation. The opportunity of wheat and cotton farmers to divert resources to other crops under the quota programs meant a smaller cut-back in income for them but at the expense of other producers. Feed-livestock farmers are afraid this might happen again. The opportunities to substitute wheat for feed grains in livestock production are much greater than the opportunities to substitute feed grains for wheat in the human diet. Thus feed-livestock producers probably have more reason for concern over the solution to the wheat problem than wheat producers have over the solution to the feed grain problem.

A growing number of producers in both groups seem to recognize that both problems stem from the same basic cause — an excess supply of resources in the farm industry. Yet, there appear to be strong pressures within each to minimize its own adjustment burden, notwithstanding what this may do to the adjustment problems of other groups. Beggar-my-neighbor methods are still popular among groups in and out of agriculture.

Feed-livestock producers have some conflicts within their own ranks. Some of the important feed deficit areas have typically favored low feed grain prices, whereas feed surplus areas have generally favored high prices. It is probably more than coincidental that many dairy and poultry producers in the Northeast have looked with approval on administration efforts to reduce price supports. To the dairy producers of this area, cheap feed coupled with milk marketing orders may appear to be the solution to their economic problem. To most of the livestock farmers of the Midwest, cheap feed ultimately means cheap livestock and lower incomes for them.

The drift toward a feed-livestock economy in the South and the rapid expansion of cattle feeding on the West Coast are causing concern to midwestern feed-livestock farmers. There

are people in the Corn Belt who believe the developments in the
South were prompted in large part by the corn acreage allotment
program. However, the proposition that the corn program pushed
corn production out of the Corn Belt is not supported by the facts.[17]
Aside from some push from the cotton program, these developments appear to be mostly the result of normal economic forces.
Nevertheless, midwestern producers are not likely to be strong
supporters of any program that will strengthen the competitive
position of other areas.

One of the more interesting goal conflicts within the farm
sector involves the use of product advertising and promotion.
For example, a successful program to advertise and promote the
use of pork will have the effect of increasing the demand, so that
more will be consumed at any given price. Given the nature of
the substitution elasticities, this is likely to mean a decline in the
demand for such closely competitive products as beef and poultry.
In the short run, the incomes of hog producers may rise, whereas
the incomes of beef and poultry producers may fall. Extending
the program to cover all meat may diminish but is not likely to
eliminate the problem of goal conflict within the industry.

RESOLVING GOAL CONFLICTS IN AGRICULTURE POLICY

According to the assignments, this chapter is supposed to say
something about the resolution of goal conflicts in agricultural
policy. Basically, this is a political problem and properly falls
in the field of political science. It should be analyzed by a political scientist (or by a politician!). A couple of economists are not
likely to have anything significant to say about this kind of problem. We shall, therefore, limit ourselves to but a few comments.[18]

One approach to the general problem of goal conflicts is to
minimize their intensity. This implies reducing the degree of
scarcity of means to achieve ends either by decreasing the variety
and intensity of men's desires or by increasing total goal attainment power. For centuries, Western civilization has been mainly
preoccupied with increasing goal attainment power. The Western

---

[17]Geoffrey Shepherd and Kurt Ullrich, Our corn-hog-cattle belt.   Iowa Farm
Sci., 14(Feb., 1960):5-6.

[18]The particular problem of concern here is that of selecting from among conflicting goals. For example, if Smith's and Jones' claims for more income are in
conflict, whose claim should be satisfied? The solution to this problem involves a
value judgment. Our view is that such value judgments are an essential ingredient
of social action, but the disciplines of economics and sociology do not provide any
basis for making such judgments.

concept of freedom has given free reign to men's desires subject only to the proviso that there be no significant injury to other people. This basic value largely precludes the possibility of lessening goal conflicts by reducing the variety and intensity of man's wants. This leaves the possibility of increasing goal attainment power.

This problem has two important facets: (1) expanding the supply of basic means and (2) doing a better job of utilizing existing means in achieving ends. Aside from the possibility of gifts, the first calls for investment in people, research in the physical and biological sciences, natural resources and plant and equipment. The second also requires investment, particularly in activities and institutions relating to the administration of resources. For example, it calls for investment in research in the social sciences.

The second has particular relevance to the problem of reducing goal conflicts in agricultural policy. The intensity of these conflicts can be lessened by designing more efficient programs. As mentioned earlier, if two programs are equally effective in achieving the goal of income equality for agriculture and equally acceptable on other grounds, the one that achieves this goal with the smallest sacrifice of other goals, including the goals of nonfarm people, will be the most efficient. Minimizing goal conflicts implies exploiting all opportunities to reduce the sacrifice imposed on one group in achieving the goals of another group. While this is a sound principle and has some application to the existing agricultural policy situation, the main difficulties in designing more efficient programs to achieve economic equality for agriculture grow out of nonincome restraints relating to other goals held by farm people.

It seems reasonably clear that achieving economic equality for agriculture via programs that raise the economic productivity of resources owned by farm families will minimize the cost to nonfarm people. However, this would mean a major reorganization of the farm industry, including fewer and larger farms and a smaller farm population. As long as farm people strongly desire something approaching the existing organizational structure in agriculture, there are few important opportunities to reduce the intensity of this goal conflict. But the urbanization of rural America is proceeding at a rapid clip. In the process, the relative importance which farm people attach to the existing organizational structure appears to be diminishing. So the time may not be far off when programs to raise the economic productivity of farm family resources will find much wider acceptance among farm people.

Perhaps the greatest potential for lessening the intensity of goal conflicts between farm and nonfarm sectors is in an increase in the unity of diversity — an increase in the incidence of overlapping identities and multigroup memberships between farm and nonfarm groups. However, this is likely to be accompanied by some intensification of the goal conflicts within agriculture, probably along the lines of labor-management conflicts in the nonfarm economy.

Our democratic political system is the main instrument for resolving goal conflicts in agricultural policy. In theory, the majority principle operating under the rule of one-man-one-vote is the basic tenet of this system. The aggregation of individual interests occurs by a process of free discussion, voting and the delegation of power. It is a system that requires a high level of knowledge on the part of its citizens for efficient operation.

In practice, the procedures for determining representation and the allocation of decision-making power and other factors have given the system certain biases. In agricultural policy matters, there has been an agricultural bias. Even the agricultural bias has been biased. At times, some geographical areas, farm commodities and farm income groups have been favored over others. What can or should be done about this problem, we leave to others.

It should be pointed out, however, that the changing structure of agricultural organization is also changing the political influence of agriculture. The decline in farm population as measured by the census will cost the predominately farm states a number of congressional seats in the near future. As this continues, the political power of agriculture is almost certain to diminish. And this is likely to mean that the interests of nonfarm people will be more fully reflected in the farm programs of the future.

University of Minnesota

Discussion

THE AUTHORS of this paper begin with the proposition that a goal conflict exists when "... a higher level of attainment of one or more goals must involve a lower level of attainment of other goals." With this proposition one cannot quarrel. But then they borrow a proposition from economics, and proceed to argue that "... goal conflicts arise because of a scarcity of means to achieve ends." They are very sure of this position for they take an even more positive stand a few lines later as follows: "A world in which there was no scarcity of means, either because wants were very meager or because the power to satisfy wants was abundant, would be a world without goal conflicts."

Now this writer believes that this proposition holds true for the world of economic goals, or real goods goals. But it is totally meaningless for another world of goals — ideological goals. Men have been killing one another for centuries because one man held a goal regarding the true road to heaven different from that of another man. More means or fewer means has no meaning for this conflict of goals. The beginning of this paper treating with goal conflicts reminds me of Neville Chamberlain and his bourgeois goals going to deal with Adolph Hitler and his Wagnerian goals; Chamberlain's rational utilitarianism caused him to miss the whole point of the conflict. So in the case of this paper — the limited structure of the paper forces it to miss and/or treat with little perception many goal conflicts.

The authors recognize at one point in their paper that goals are the overt manifestation of subjective valuations. They say, "Values have an ordering function with regard to behavior." And this is true; man's valuation of things guides and directs his behavior toward those things — sets his goals. But man can and does value things other than worldly goods or real income. Some men, for example, value the superiority of the white man over the black more than they do high incomes or even life itself. Still other men value more highly the running of a four-minute mile, or expressing their inner thoughts in art, or walking down a nature trail more than they do holding a steady job. And still others value rural living, the ideal of the family farm and the instinct for workmanship more highly than they do a highly commercial life leading to higher incomes.

Now the point of all this is that the goal conflict arising out of the situation wherein some men hold the goal of the superiority of the white man over the black and other men hold the goal of equality of treatment for men of every color, will not be resolved, or minimized, by increasing the "total goal attainment power" (i.e., increasing the means to achieve ends). There is no such thing as total goal attainment power in the kind of world under consideration here; the very concept renders impossible effective thought and action relative to this conflict. This conflict will be resolved, or minimized, only as the subjective valuations on which the goals are based are changed over time by such things as war, where the value systems of certain of the protagonists are destroyed, or miscegenation, where the black and white characteristics are lost, or scientific development and education, where new information is brought to bear on the problem, or the rise of a new philosophy carrying with it a new and different system of values.

Let us consider another case — the case of the goal conflict within the same farm people and among different farm people arising out of two goals held in some degree by all farm people: the goal of the good life associated with rural living in a social organization of many small free-holders or family farms, and the goal of the good life associated with rising real incomes. It is perfectly clear that the latter goal among all farm people is advanced, or rendered more achievable, by making more abundant the means of achievement (i.e., productive resources). But achieving the goal of rising real incomes through the vehicles of farm technological advance and capital formation has reduced the number of free-holders in the past 20 years, gives promise of reducing the number still more in the 1960's, and will in my opinion ultimately destroy that ideal, and eliminate that type of producer in our society. Now this writer submits: (1) that the growth of goal attainment power in the form of more productive farm resources has not resolved, or minimized, the goal conflict under consideration — on the contrary it has intensified it, and (2) there is no such thing as total goal attainment power applicable to both of these goals. This idea of total goal attainment power leads us astray rather than aids us in this analysis of goal conflicts.

Goal conflicts will be understood, with perhaps increased potentialities for resolving them, only as the value systems of the men and women involved are understood — only as the nature and structure of human valuations, the processes of change in the ordering of valuations and the conversion of subjective valuations to observable social goals are understood.

The dim outlines of an analytical model for considering goal conflicts emerges from the paper by Kaldor and Hines. That model assumes the following form: on the farm side of society we have two prominent goals that are well recognized — (1) the drive for equality of incomes and (2) the maintenance of the family farm and the traditional values of a rural society; on the urban side two goals, as they relate to agriculture, may be identified — (1) the goal of low food prices as a means to increased real incomes and (2) the goal of distributive justice for farm people. This model is not explicitly stated or recognized, but it threads through much of the discussion. And it seems to me that if the authors had used their time, first, to sharpen and expand this analytical model, second, to develop the changes in goal priorities that have occurred over time, and third, to have used it to analyze the goal conflicts resulting from different courses of action in agriculture, we would be further along the road to understanding the potentials for action in agriculture than we are now. How would the authors have gone about this — you ask? The formulation and refinement of the model would follow a process similar to that employed in the formulation of econometric models — the building of the model would be dependent first upon the authors' knowledge of the subject area under consideration, second upon their ability to state the variables involved with precision, and third upon their artistry in relating the variables in the model in a representative fashion. Such a model would, of course, be qualitative in nature, but it would serve to organize and focus the discussion of goal conflicts in agriculture in the same way that the demand and supply cross does economic behavior.

Changes in the ordering of goals over time would need to be studied in terms of changes in human valuations over time. And there is little likelihood that this could be done in a direct fashion, such as through interviewing and surveying. An indirect approach would probably be required in which changes in valuations, hence goals, were deduced from the changing content of farm magazines and newspapers, from changes in the resolutions and actions of farm interest groups, and from studies of changed activities of farm people (e.g., educational behavior, political behavior). And a similar indirect approach would be required on the nonfarm side. But from these behavioral results, as they have changed over time, we should be able to piece together and construct the changing ordering pattern of relevant goals over time.

In terms of the crude model formulated by him from the Kaldor and Hines chapter, this writer would hypothesize that an historical analysis would indicate that the priority of the rural-living, small free-holder goal would have declined relative to the income equality goal over the past 30 years, and on the nonfarm side, the distributive justice goal for farm people would have declined in priority relative to the cheap food goal over the same period. In other words, the present writer hypothesizes that the increased tendency toward commercialization, the increased emphasis on material well being and the greater social mobility would have worked to downgrade the goal of the traditional rural life on the one hand, and the goal of distributive justice for farm people among urbanites on the other.

Whether the above goals are stated with sufficient precision to be useful and whether the above hypotheses regarding their ordering are in fact true will be ascertained only after some good research that clearly does not exist now. But assuming that the goals are usefully formulated and that the hypotheses are true, then some reasonably firm policy conclusions flow from them. The pursuit of programs designed to achieve the income equality goal, but which require important changes in the organization of resources and in the institutions of rural-living, are likely to give rise to less intense goal conflicts within agriculture now than 30 years ago, the state of the income disparity being equal. On the other hand, with the lower ordering of the distributive justice goal for farm producers among urban people, the sympathic interest of urban people in the income equality goal of farm people will have been lost to an important degree. Thus, programs designed to achieve the income equality goal for farmers, which must operate to raise food prices to consumers, run squarely against the now higher priority goal of cheap food among urban people. Consequently, we would expect to find a more intense goal conflict between farm and nonfarm people arising out of policy efforts to increase farm prices and incomes. The economic struggle between farm and nonfarm people is now more naked than it once was. The rural-life tradition is less of a restraining influence over the drive for increased incomes among farm people than it once was, and the distributive justice goal for farmers among urban people is less of a restraining influence over the drive for low-priced food. Thus, the struggle over distributive shares is sharpened and intensified — the rural-urban goal conflict is intensified.

This, the writer believes, is the state of affairs as of the 1960's whether the foregoing analysis is correct or not. But the point of this discussion is not to score a point — it is to indicate the direction in which goal conflicts may be analyzed.

In the latter part of their paper, the authors make a series of statements that are particularly annoying to me. Regarding the resolution of goal conflicts they have this to say, "Basically this is a political problem and properly falls in the field of political science. It should be analyzed by a political scientist (or by a politician!). A couple of economists are not likely to have anything significant to say about this kind of problem."

The above statements might be acceptable coming from an economic theorist (even this the writer doesn't really believe), but it is certainly not acceptable from men who do research and teaching in agricultural policy. In the first place it should be recognized that politicians and political scientists often do not give us any formal help in this area of the resolution of goal conflicts: the politicians because they are practitioners not students, and the political scientists because they tend to be concerned with institutions and political operations rather than the structure of social action.

Finally, as everyone involved with determining goals and values knows full well, agricultural economists have taken over the field of agricultural policy. They teach policy; they do research in policy; they give speeches on policy and they hold conferences on policy. And they are fast learning the connection between valuation problems and policy issues. Now are we going to turn around and say that we cannot make a contribution to the resolution of goal conflicts in agricultural policy (i.e., make a contribution to the taking of effective action in problematic situations involving goal conflicts)? This writer says no. As a very minimum, we must be prepared to explore and discuss the conditions under which, and the means by which, resolution may be achieved. And in some situations we must be prepared to undertake the maximum — that is, be prepared to put our heads on the block and say — "this is the way." If we can't do this, then we should turn in our agricultural policy badges.

WILLARD F. MUELLER
University of Wisconsin

Discussion

THE AUTHORS have done a very nice job of discussing some of the goal conflicts (1) between the farm and nonfarm sectors, (2) between farmers and the marketers of farm inputs and outputs and (3) within the farm sector itself.

FARM-NONFARM CONFLICTS

The authors interpret the conflict between the goals of farm and nonfarm people as centering largely around the desire by farmers for income equality and of nonfarmers' conflicting goals concerning low food prices, distributive justice, and the adverse effects of farm programs on nonfarm incomes. They point out that "if other things are equal, nonfarm people undoubtedly prefer low food prices to high food prices. When low prices are the result of an excess of supply of farm products, the real income gain of nonfarm people is obtained in large measure at the expense of farm people.... However, the interest in cheap food under these circumstances may conflict with their [nonfarmers'] interest in distributive justice."

Similarly, other things equal, the farm program that "produces the smallest adverse effect on nonfarm incomes would create the least amount of farm-nonfarm conflict."

The authors go on in this vein explaining how, ceteris paribus, other aspects of alternative farm programs may influence the intensity of the conflict between farm and nonfarm people. This writer finds little in this discussion with which he disagrees. His chief comment is that they have not included what he believes to be a very major source of the objection of many nonfarm people to most price support and other farm programs aimed at achieving the goal of distributive justice.

The writer would venture the hypothesis that the primary hostility toward farm programs stems from the fact that ours is largely an economy of privately-organized economic power. Most nonfarm industries are able to take care of their own "adjustment" problems without significant direct government aid, with only a relatively few exceptions such as "cheap" imports. The reader unquestionably can think of other exceptions to this generalization. However, most of these exceptions also are under actual or threatened attack, and are defended much as are agricultural programs — on grounds of being special and temporary cases. But significantly, most American business and labor interests have as an ultimate objective the achievement of private economic power with a minimum of direct government intervention to achieve or maintain it.

The American public really complains very little about industries which are able to adjust capacity nicely to shifts in demand, thereby generating price stability and preventing disastrous consequences on profits. The writer contends that most Americans not only consider this normal industrial behavior but sound and desirable economic behavior as well. As long as prices and profits are generated in a free (and by free most Americans mean free from government intervention) market, consumers complain little about the level of prices and profits. Because Americans still hold this view about what constitutes the normal way of determining prices and returns, they feel it is economically abnormal to have government take a hand in generating the level of prices, incomes and profits. This is why we usually defend — or apologize for — such intervention in agriculture and elsewhere in the economy by insisting that it is really only temporary and due to abnormal economic conditions.

As long as most nonfarm people have such a conception of the way our system should operate, there will be continuing hostility toward programs aimed at improving farm incomes by procedures foreign to the way most of the rest of our economy handles its "adjustment" problems. Simply put, it is not the high food prices that are the main concern of nonfarmers, but the "abnormal" way in which they are generated; and it is not simply a matter of conflict between consumers' interests in cheap food and distributive justice, but a basic hostility toward the procedures used to bring about such distributive justice. Let's face it! Apparently most of the American public and certainly the controlling public press (including most farm journals) believe that there is something basically un-American about most of the means used since the Thirties to bring about distributive justice for agriculture. And, conceivably, as more sectors of our economy increase their market power through private means, and this includes labor, hostility toward government-buttressed power may actually increase.

If the preceding characterization is correct, perhaps the only way to lessen this source of farm and nonfarm conflict is the development of farm programs which emulate the procedures of other parts of the economy. This, of course, calls for lessening direct government intervention, especially in terms of large expenditures for supporting farm prices. Programs which the writer envisions as creating the least conflict are those aimed at providing a legal framework within which farmers assume the bulk of the administrative and other costs. The actual programs created within this framework could conceivably vary considerably, and of course, many would probably not achieve much for farmers.

CONFLICTS INVOLVING AGRICULTURAL SUPPLIERS, PROCESSORS AND MARKETERS

The writer especially likes the introductory discussion to this chapter. It sets out concisely the way in which the unique market structure of agriculture determines the farm firm's conduct. As the authors put it, "Its small size and lack of market power free it from concern for sales strategies and price policies: it is a 'price taker.' A suitable 'corporate image' is wanted neither to defend the long-run political position of the firm by means of public relations nor to assuage the psychological conflicts of its manager .... The agricultural firm can carry on its daily business affairs unencumbered by policy pronouncements, creeds and images. Problems of this kind appear only when agriculture as a whole ventures into public policy."

It is, of course, this characteristic of the market structure of farming which causes farmers to look upon one another as neighbors rather than rivals.

But the market structure of allied supply and marketing industries may induce actual or imagined conflicts between farmers and these allied industries. Included among the authors' examples of supplier-farmer or farmer-processor relations which may result in conflicts are the following: (1) the efforts of the fertilizer salesman to push farmer customers into purchases of uneconomic amounts and qualities of fertilizer, (2) the desire of processors for increased volumes of farm products and (3) the interest of farmers for greater competition in processing industries.

The writer takes only two exceptions to the authors' treatment of this area of conflicts.

First, they say categorically, "As for quantity of product, we can be sure that at any moment of time marketing and processing industry profits would be improved if they could increase the volume of their business."

This is a conclusion about which we cannot be sure without analysis of the market structure and demand elasticities of the industry about which we are speaking. For example, fruit processors who give their blessing to diverting or destroying a large part of the peach crop in years of large supplies do so because this improves their profits, not just those of farmers. Hence, we cannot say categorically that farmers and processors always will be in conflict with respect to the appropriate size of marketings, and hence over programs designed to control the volume of marketings.

Another point on which the writer disagrees with the authors is their conclusion with respect to the kinds of remedy to monopoly in the food processing industry which is most acceptable to the public. They contend that "Usually, wider social consent for antimonopoly policy will also occur if the proposed measures for alleviating monopoly are consistent with widely accepted goals, such as maintaining or creating a competitive economy. Proscription of unfair and restrictive practices, and perhaps even trust busting by dissolution of firms, should be preferable for this reason to narrowly conceived devices of countervailing power such as establishment of countermonopolies."

The writer questions whether the public seriously prefers government proscription of unfair trade practices and trust busting to the attempted development of countervailing power by the parties most immediately affected by market power. He has the feeling that the authors are expressing the values of liberal economists (and perhaps sociologists) rather than interpreting the values of the American public. I think that one of the chief reasons Galbraith's countervailing power concept is much more acceptable to the lay public than to most economists is that it runs counter to the welfare concepts of economists but is consistent with the views of many Americans as to the appropriate way to handle the monopoly problem in our economy. The widespread support given to agricultural cooperatives as a way to solve farmers' market problems illustrates vividly that this approach is considered entirely legitimate within our system. And, significantly, cooperatives are most often justified on grounds of helping farmers establish countervailing power.

CONFLICTS WITHIN THE FARM SECTOR

In their discussion of goal conflicts within the farm sector the authors assert that most of the important conflicts "appear to center around the distribution of farm income, the organization of the industry, regional economic development and entrepreneurial freedom and responsibility." They then go on to cite many well-known examples of this including the conflicts between producers of hard red spring wheat and durum wheat, midwestern manufactured milk producers and eastern fluid milk producers, wheat and cotton producers and feed-livestock farmers, and between producers sponsoring advertising programs of substitute products. Significantly, all of these conflicts have economic origins; they do not result from different noneconomic goals or value systems. The writer does not criticize this characterization of the origins of the main conflicts within the farm sector, and admits to being of an economic deterministic persuasion himself.[1]

But if these conflicts are mainly economic in origin, is it not likely that they can be analyzed most appropriately within an economic framework? If so, economists should have considerably more to contribute to analysis of such goal conflicts than the authors seem to be willing to concede.

As an illustration of his point, the writer thinks that cartel theory and experience provides a very useful frame of reference for analysis of conflicts related to governmentally authorized and enforced supply control programs in agriculture. Using such a framework we can pinpoint the main economic sources of conflict among farmers in an industry contemplating this particular type of program. Very briefly, on the basis of theory supported by industrial experience, cartels are likely to be encouraged and operate successfully and stably when an industry is relatively depressed, its demand is very inelastic, firm numbers are small,

---

[1]Of course, the writer is not implying that the authors of this paper believe that all conflicts among farmers have economic origins.

entry is difficult, production costs are similar, product differentiation is slight and economic incentives of participants are similar. In other words, the degree of conflict among farmers is a function of these economic variables; as you change one, the degree of conflict changes. One important variable is the extent to which incomes are depressed at any given time. This explains why, when times are really bad, this variable offsets many other sources of conflict. But with the return of prosperity this variable becomes less important and the original cartel arrangement may become unacceptable to many participants.

Another crucial variable in the case of supply control programs is the extent of differences in the production costs of various groups of producers. Although a governmentally authorized and enforced cartel may control firm output and entry, cost differences among farmers may be so different that many farmers may be unwilling to accept a supply control program now, although many have relatively low incomes. First, the largest, most efficient producers have sufficiently lower costs so that they do quite well at a time smaller firms are doing very poorly. Hence, cost differences among producers are so great that the kind of program which is good enough for low-cost producers is not good enough for high-cost producers. And the kind of programs which are necessary to get prices high enough for small producers may require such strict production control and permit such slow expansion of individual farms that even many small producers would object because they would be prevented from expanding rapidly to larger size.

Analysis of this and other variables suggested by cartel theory helps in understanding the severity of conflicts arising from alternative programs. Also by analyzing the way in which various variables are likely to change in the future, e.g., smaller (or greater) differences in the costs of various farmers, economists should be able to predict whether the intensity of conflicts within the farm sector is likely to lessen or increase. The writer suspects that such a purely economic analysis would indicate a more favorable atmosphere for supply control programs in some farm products in the future than exists today.

These comments have not been intended as a criticism of the authors' treatment of goal conflicts. Rather, the writer is merely suggesting an alternative framework which recognizes explicitly the economic origins of many goal conflicts within agriculture.

Chapter 10

ROSS B. TALBOT

Iowa State University

Trends in the Political Position of the American Farmer: A View Based on the Looking Glass of Foreign Observers

A MERICAN POLITICS, like all forms of public activity in the United States, is always in the process of becoming. The pull of change is constantly being exerted on the rock of stability. The pressure relaxes and intensifies; the direction is varying and often uncertain; the primary causes are perplexing and undetermined, although, at least to some degree, man-made and man-guided. So it has been, at least, as one views the historical trends in the political situation of the American farmer. He has been caught in the semifinal, or probably the final, stage of W. W. Rostow's cycle.[1] America has, in a somewhat unsteady fashion, been constantly moving toward the status of an urban-industrial nation. The farmer has utilized the technological and materialistic advances, but he has rather consistently fought against the changes in political power which were almost surely to follow the shifts in economic and social power. The political lag in the United States may be viewed as a portion of the overall cultural lag, although it can be studied as a separate phenomenon and partially accounted for through the unique and oft-times perverse processes of our political system.

After the first reapportionment of the United States House of Representatives, 101 of the 106 representatives were elected by farmers and planters.[2] By 1957, Vice President Nixon is alleged to have remarked that only 100 of a then House membership of 435 were "directly affected" by the farm vote.[3] As the 1960 census reports for the states continued to dribble in, a tentative conclusion appeared to be that the migration from rural areas is even more substantial than predicted. According to the 1959

---

[1] W. W. Rostow, The Stages of Economic Growth. Cambridge University Press, Cambridge. 1960.

[2] A. N. Holcombe, Our More Perfect Union. Harvard University Press, Boston. 1950. P. 53.

[3] Des Moines Register. September 20, 1957.

213

calculations of the United States Department of Agriculture, the number of commercial farms will have declined from the then estimated 3.1 million to 2 million by 1975. Thus the continuing conflict between majority rule and the protection of minorities will increasingly involve rural America.

One way to view the political struggles of the American farmer is to reflect on the writings of foreign observers of the American scene. To reconstruct the trends of political power in this manner is somewhat hazardous because the farmer was not the central focus in the studies of Tocqueville, Bryce, Ostrogorski, Brogan, Laski or Beloff. Only if we view Graham Hutton as a political observer do we find a person who was closely interested in the farmer. However, this approach does seem to have some real merit. At any one time, the farmer has only been a part of the total political context. Within this limited role, these observers have been rather consistently perceptive in their portrayals of him.

DEMOCRACY IN AMERICA[4]

By the time Tocqueville came to America, we had concluded what might be termed a peaceful political revolution. Power had passed from the remarkable and aristocratic Federalists, to the more democratic but quality-conscious Jeffersonians, and on to the more egalitarian Jacksonians. Within this changing environment Tocqueville looked, studied and wrote. His now famous doctrine of the tyranny of the majority was a prediction on his part, not an analysis of an immediate condition: a forewarning to Europe of the oncoming of democracy because of the almost, but not quite, inexorable course of events.

Tocqueville was not a particularly acute observer of agrarian life either in France or the United States.[5] But his observations of the American scene led him to conclude that "... the doctrine of the sovereignty of the people came out of the townships and took possession of the states."[6] He was obviously impressed by the New England town meeting and considered this institution to be one of the principal causal factors in the growth of a democratic America. On first reading one might receive the

---

[4]Alexis De Tocqueville, Democracy in America. Phillips Bradley (ed.). Alfred A. Knopf, Inc., New York. 1945. (Vols. I and II.)

[5]George Wilson Pierson, Tocqueville in America. Abridged by Dudley C. Lunt from Tocqueville and Beaumont in America (Anchor A 189). Doubleday and Co., Inc., New York. 1959. Pp. 446-47.

[6]De Tocqueville, op. cit., Vol. I, p. 56; also p. 65.

impression that Tocqueville had a strong tinge of agricultural fundamentalism in his personality make-up. His admiration for Thomas Jefferson lends additional credence to the idea. However, at this point Tocqueville seems more moved by fear than love. He definitely feared the growth of cities;[7] he loved what we might term a natural, although not necessarily a landed, aristocracy.

Consistency is not Tocqueville's principal virtue, although this difficulty seems to arise in part because of his inability to distinguish clearly between short-run and long-run trends. At one point, he remarks that "in America land is cheap and anyone may easily become a landowner"; at another time, he states: "Agriculture is . . . only suited for those who already have great superfluous wealth or to those whose penury bids them seek only a bare subsistence."[8]

His first comment seems accurate for much of 19th century America; the latter statement points to the trend in farming in the latter half of the 20th century. The political implications of these two views of American farming are now becoming manifest in the American political scene. Entry of new farmers into commercial farming is becoming increasingly a matter of inheritance or marriage. The movement up the agricultural ladder from subsistence farming, or hired worker, to the status of commercial farmer is constantly more difficult and improbable.

One of Tocqueville's signal contributions was his discussion of "political associations"; that is, what we would today call pressure groups or, more objectively, interest groups. He recorded their activity, in a general fashion, and outlined the causes for their existence and the means by which they were institutionalized. He noted the paradox, and one so evident in rural America, between the drive for individual freedom and the desire to combine in order to achieve the benefits of the various forms of material power.[9] Perhaps one of his most prescient insights was his prediction that these associations would become, in limited form, a new aristocracy: "Private citizens, by combining together, may constitute bodies of great wealth, influence, and strength, corresponding to the persons of an aristocracy."[10] Is this not what is happening in modern America — rural and urban?

Tocqueville does believe that the idea of equality "suggests"

[7]Ibid., Vol. I, p. 129.
[8]Ibid., Vol. II, pp. 186 and 154, respectively.
[9]Ibid., Vol. I, Chap. XII. Political Associations in the United States. Pp. 191-99.
[10]Ibid., Vol. II, p. 324.

to Americans "the idea of the indefinite perfectibility of man."[11] Such an idea had a firm hold on the farm organizations and certain farmer-oriented political parties of the last century. Modern farm groups, and particularly the largest — the American Farm Bureau Federation — have neglected if not forsaken this conception of man's nature. The notable exception to this observation is, as usual, the National Farmers Union (formally, The Farmers Educational and Co-operative Union of America).

One might suggest that it is within this issue of the nature of man that we find a primary cause for the present conflicts between the farm organizations: the Farm Bureau leadership believes in social Darwinism — the farmers who are "fit" are those who will survive. The Farmers Union leadership and perhaps to a lesser extent that of the Grange, are the egalitarians — "as the twig is bent so the tree inclines." Some portion of the present alliances of political interests can be accounted for through an understanding of these respective beliefs regarding man's nature.

THE AMERICAN COMMONWEALTH[12]

Lord Bryce was certainly no stranger to the United States. He traveled here in 1870, 1881 and 1883-84. From 1907-13, he was the British Ambassador to the United States. It was in 1888 that his two-volume study — The American Commonwealth — first appeared in the British bookstores. So there is something like a fifty-year gap between Tocqueville and Bryce. When the latter's first study of the United States was published, the Civil War was still strongly evident in American politics. The party system had gone through a unique metamorphosis. Southern slavocracy had become the guiding element in the Democratic party just prior to the Civil War and was now attempting to revive its shattered power. Lincoln and the Civil War had led the American farmer into the Republican bulwark.

Within the executive branch, Jacksonian emphasis on presidential supremacy had been discarded. The Democratic party was returning to the Jeffersonian idea of legislative supremacy, with one major alteration in that the power of decision-making over substantive policies was moving into the rooms of the

---

[11]Ibid., Vol. III, First Book, Chap. VIII. How Equality Suggests to the Americans the Idea of the Indefinite Perfectibility of Man. Pp. 33-35.

[12]James Bryce, The American Commonwealth. 2 Vols.; used herein were Vol. I. Macmillan and Co., New York. 1895; and Vol. II. Macmillan and Co., New York. Revised edition, 1910.

standing committees. This trend was weakening the efficacy of the party caucus. The Republican party, at least under the aegis of Lincoln, had grasped the idea that the president was the American tribune, our form of the elective kingship. However, by the time Bryce began to prospect American political institutions, we were imbedded in a period of "Congressional Government." The presidency was in a state of quietude and subordination, if not frustration, from which it was not to emerge until the days of the first Roosevelt.[13]

Lord Bryce was an advocate of what might be termed the "look-see" approach to the study of social and political phenomena. He became much more closely acquainted with the American character than did Tocqueville and perhaps as much as five-sixths of his exposition was based on personal conversations.[14] He found the American farmer to be "a keener and more enterprising man than in Europe," an "honest, kindly sort of man, hospitable, religious, practical." But the farmer was also "naturally a grumbler, as are his brethren everywhere" and inclined to "lending too ready an ear to politicians who promise him redress by measures possibly unjust and usually unwise."[15]

Bryce believed that "a sort of natural selection carries the more ambitious and eager spirits into the towns, for the native American dislikes the monotony and isolation of a farm life with its slender prospect of wealth."[16] The political implications of this necessary isolationism are found in his comment: "A farmer of western New York may go through a long life without knowing how his representative behaves at Albany."[17] But Bryce was heartened in being able to conclude that "of the tendency to aggregation [of wealth] there are happily few signs so far as relates to agriculture."[18]

It is perhaps one of the ironies of American history that the American farmer had the least political power when he had the most numerical strength. There are rather evident reasons for this situation, among the more important being that the farmer

---

[13] The generalizations about the course of American political parties are based largely on W. E. Binkley, American Political Parties — Their Natural History. Alfred A. Knopf, Inc., New York. 1943 and 1958 editions; his President and Congress. Alfred A. Knopf, Inc., New York. 1947; and Holcombe, op. cit.
[14] James Bryce, The American Commonwealth. Edited and abridged by Louis Hacker. G. P. Putnam's Sons, New York. 1959. Vol. I, p. xl.
[15] Bryce (1910 edition), op. cit., Vol. II, pp. 298-99.
[16] Ibid., Vol. II, p. 300.
[17] Ibid., Vol. II, p. 240.
[18] Ibid., Vol. II, pp. 918-19.

wanted to be "let alone." [19] He sought the freedom to work out his own destiny with the federal government helping out in terms of low tariffs and cheap land. Beginning at about the Bryce period, there was a willingness to permit the formation of land-grant colleges and experiment stations so that he, the farmer, could "make two blades of grass grow where one grew before."

However, Bryce does seem to be deficient in his failure to note the evidences of agrarian discontent. Low farm prices, along with the "vicious" practices of the railroads and "Wall Street," were stirring the farmers into organizational protest and political action. The rise and decline of the Grange, Greenback Party, Grand Alliance and the like might have been observed by Bryce, but he makes little note of them. The farmer was just beginning to understand and practice, and doing neither at all effectively, that policy is made through institutions that are based on organized power.

One of Bryce's major contributions was his observation and analysis of the American lobby.[20] But it is indicative of the farmer's weakly-organized position that Bryce does not even comment on the existence of the farm lobby, at least not at the Washington level. He does observe, as did Woodrow Wilson in his Congressional Government (1888), that the policy-making process in Congress is "really a plan for legislating by a number of commissions,"[21] that is, by standing committees. However, the powerful House and Senate Agriculture Committees were just beginning to take important and aggressive steps in the development of national farm legislation. As an addendum to this point, there is evidence that these committees are now declining in authority.

DEMOCRACY AND THE ORGANIZATION OF POLITICAL PARTIES [22]

In the critical days of 1960 when we are encircled by Sputniks and depressed by the ominous rumblings that have followed the fall of the U-2, it may be prudent to take only quick note of the views of a Russian, M. I. Ostrogorski. His study of the American party system was published just after the turn of the 20th century

---

[19] Earle D. Ross, The Civil War Agricultural New Deal. Social Forces. 15(1, October, 1936): 97-104.

[20] Bryce (1910 edition), Vol. I, Chap. XVI, The Lobby. Pp. 677-82.

[21] Ibid., Vol. I, p. 172.

[22] M. Ostrogorski, Democracy and the Organization of Political Parties. Vol. II. The Macmillan Co., New York. 1902; and Democracy and the Party System in the United States. The Macmillan Co., New York. 1926.

and in it he deplored the three evils, as he viewed them, of Democracy, Party and Plutocracy.

His general hypothesis might be stated as follows: The United States Constitution was an excellent and remarkable document, but the wisdom of its framers has been controverted through the growth of extra-constitutional devices. The "multitude" (Democracy) had forced into positions of almost absolute power the "caucus-controlled" parties that were largely the instruments of the Plutocracy, which controlled the party organizations through bribery and other forms of corruption.

Such a capsuled synopsis hardly does justice to Ostrogorski's detailed analysis, but it does enable one to make a few general comments about his thesis as it pertains to trends in the political position of the American farmer. Ostrogorski was not opposed to political parties, in fact he accepted the necessity of parties in a democratic political system, but he did deprecate their permanence. Political parties, he thought, should be organized around issues at each election and then dissolve once the election had been held — just as Madison had erroneously predicted, in Federalist 10, would happen.

However, these party organizations became entrenched in Congress, as well as in the state legislatures, and came to constitute a sort of iron oligarchy. Lobbyists, "the agents of the corporations,"[23] were influential in imposing their privileged point of view on the legislators and thereby on legislation. The rigid discipline of the caucus prevented the elected politicians from being concerned with the "general interest" and placed them in the position of doing nothing. Or, a more likely possibility was, he thought, that the legislators would be involved in the self-perpetuating practice of "sending to their farmer-constituents packets of seeds (distributed at national expense), by providing their 'workers' with offices, and by appropriating in cash as much as possible for their districts."[24] Perhaps his most famous remark concerning the House of Representatives was that "every interest is represented in it except the general interest."[25]

Unfortunately, for our purposes at least, Ostrogorski had little to say directly about the American farmer. He did observe that "the farmers' movement created a hotbed of social discontent in the West, which became a permanent menace to the political stability embodied in the traditional parties"[26] — an insight

---

[23] Ibid., 1926 edition, p. 291.
[24] Ibid., 1926 edition, p. 373.
[25] Ibid., 1902 edition, p. 698.
[26] Ibid., 1902 edition, p. 441.

which, in the more accurate idiom of his day than ours, probably
puts "the cart before the horse."

Ostrogorski developed a theory of weak political parties which
would still prove attractive to the present-day Farm Bureau and,
to a lesser extent, the Grange. But his emphasis on the need for
proportional representation and the possibility of having the "interests" represented in the Senate — although they would be in a
subordinate position and called Associate Senators — strike one
as rather impossible proposals for our times, considering the
almost endless proliferation of interest groups.

GOVERNMENT OF THE PEOPLE AND POLITICS IN AMERICA[27]

Certainly one of the most insightful foreign observers of the
United States today is Denis W. Brogan. Of his several books,
the two that are directly pertinent to our subject were published
in 1933 and 1954. In terms of both time period and point of view,
we may classify the first period as pre-New Deal and the second
as post-New Deal.

Much had happened in farm politics between Bryce and the
first study of American politics and government by Brogan. The
farmer had passed through the halcyon days of 1909-14 and,
income-wise, the prosperity of World War I; then into the trough
of despair and bankruptcy as he suffered the early and sharp impact of the Great Depression. Just prior to this period, the
National Farmers Union was founded, had enjoyed the dizzy prosperity of numbers, but emerged with little in the way of substantive policy. By 1927 the Farmers Union was rather completely
reorganized and its immediate center of activity was shifted to
the Great Plains area. A local "farm bureau" had been sponsored
by the Binghamton, N. Y., Chamber of Commerce and was to be
fostered in other areas by the Federal Extension Service and its
growing local officialdom called county agents. The Farm Bloc
had been organized in Congress during the early 1920's, perhaps
due to Farm Bureau efforts, and had achieved some success,
although it had been thwarted in its efforts to convince President
Coolidge of the value of McNary-Haugenism.

In 1933, Brogan was clearly pessimistic of America's future
and rather subtly antagonistic toward the American farmer. He

[27]D. W. Brogan, Government of the People. Harper and Brothers, New York.
1933; Politics in America. Harper and Brothers, New York. 1954; and Preface,
1943 edition of Government of the People. Harper and Brothers, New York. 1943.

believed that the Supreme Court's use of its assumed power of
judicial review was harmful to democracy and the national interest. Both political parties were, in his view, coalitions of
sectional interests and had little to offer in the way of programmatic reforms. He did not foresee, at least not as clearly as
A. N. Holcombe, that the rise of the American city was about to
make its march apparent within American politics.

Whatever the facts, the fiction of American politics is still that everything
must be done to foster 'a bold peasantry, a country's pride.' To incline
the balance in favor of the country and to look to the farmer for the
American answer to social and political problems was the official creed. [28]

Brogan's contention that the American farmer was primarily
interested in tariffs and prohibition seems rather hyperbolic,[29]
but his chapter entitled "Country Versus City" is still very worthwhile reading. In it he describes, as well as has any political
scientist, the constitutional, political and social causes for the
farm-small town overrepresentation in Congress and the state
legislatures.[30] Brogan believed there was little indication "that
the rural American, no matter how disillusioned he may be as to
the results of prohibition, will lightly let go his political power or
abandon his watch over his erring city brother."[31] Later, with
perhaps some sense of wry satisfaction, he prophesied that "once
the tide [of political change] is obviously on the turn, the politicians will turn on their recent [rural] allies with ferocity."[32]
Such an occurrence seems just barely possible, considering the
nature of American politics, but the prediction should be one,
today, that would give the farmer and his organizations cause for
reflection and judicious concern — as no doubt it has.
    The period of the 1930's was the most brilliant decade in
American agricultural history, at least in terms of action if not
accomplishment. Never, perhaps, were social, economic and
political conditions more favorable for a "New Deal." Relief and
welfare measures were mandatory and forthcoming; credit facilities were created or expanded; price support programs became

[28]Ibid., Government of the People, p. 101.
[29]A few years before, however, André Siegfried had observed: "The low-selling
price (of farm products) was not due to favorable output, but rather to the effect of
world prices on a partially export industry. As a result the farmers no longer believe in free trade, but wish to serve a protected home market and to dispose of their
surplus by dumping." André Siegfried, America Comes of Age. Harcourt, Brace and
Co., New York. 1927. P. 187.
[30]Brogan, Government of the People, op. cit., Part III, Chaps. 1 and 2.
[31]Ibid., p. 114.
[32]Ibid., p. 115.

the hinge-pin of farm policy; the existing emphasis on the research and educational function was intensified and enlarged; soil
conservation activities were initiated on a nation-wide scale; and
crop insurance was experimented with. In all of this eruption of
subsidy and turmoil, the trends in the political position of the
farmer were rather shadowy and obscure. Seemingly, all segments of the American society were participants in the Great
Crusade (or Grand Barbecue, if you wish). The farm organizations maintained a fairly constant coalition of purpose and strategy, except for their evaluation and support of the Farm Security
Administration.

It was probably a combination of conflicting ideologies, per-
sonalities and interests that brought about the existing schism
within the farm organizations. Ideologically, the Farm Bureau
could just barely tolerate the Farm Security Administration (FSA)
in the early depression years and thereafter the question came to
be as to just when the FSA must go, which it did by 1946. In the
area of price support legislation, there was a fair amount of organizational unity even through the Agricultural Act of 1948. The
election of President Truman that year divided the farm groups
into rigid or flexible price supporters and, soon, into opposing
camps in regard to the Brannan proposals. Since that time it has
been somewhat of a novelty to find the farm organizations to be
in any particular agreement over farm policy matters. More explicitly, the gap constantly widened as the emphasis on ideology
increased and the search for the farmer's interest became more
neglected.

In his 1954 study — Politics in America — Brogan was obviously a happier man. The New Deal was to his ideological tastes.
The American political system, despite its cumbersome deficiencies, had come through the storms of depression and war. He
viewed our political parties as chaotic and would have approved
of much more highly centralized, class-structured, programmatic parties than we now have, but there was more hope than
despair over our predicament.[33]

Brogan was still just as disturbed by agricultural fundamentalism as he had been in his earlier work. "The farmers are
[still] sacred" and, in some indignation, he quotes Frederick the
Great's remark about Empress Maria Theresa, regarding the
partition of Poland — "she wept and took." And, writes Brogan,

---

[33] For reasons that are not at all clear, Brogan takes a more pragmatic approach
toward American political parties in his 1943 preface to Government of the People
than he does in Politics in America (1954). Note pp. viii and xiv.

"so does the American farmer."[34] However, he has become more perceptive in his observations of pressure group politics. He notes, although in no detail, that the American farmers have a diversity of interests within their own industry, that these interests are not likely to be class-based but are primarily commodity-based, and that because of this diffusion of power within agriculture, as elsewhere in the American economy, "members of Congress have acquired a good deal of sceptical skill in dealing with the claims of pressure groups."[35]

Brogan's own value system disturbs, in some instances, the incisiveness of his diagnosis. When he states that "no victory of the economic underdogs fighting as a class party is possible unless farmers and workers are allied,"[36] he misses the trend in American farming. For better or worse, the American commercial farmer is becoming increasingly business-oriented and at least mildly antagonistic toward organized labor, with the exception again of the leadership of the National Farmers Union, and an unknown portion of its membership and that of the other major farm organizations.

MIDWEST AT NOON [37]

Graham Hutton is clearly impressed with the qualities of character which he claims to have discovered in the midwestern farmer. His impressions, however, are not directly related to political trends, perhaps because of his assignment with the British Information Office. Nevertheless, a couple of his insights might be considered quickly. "Midwest farmers," he writes, "and many other farmers, still expect to end on a cross between two city slickers, an American on one side and a foreigner on the other."[38] To be facetious we often tend to exaggerate and distort. The rural, Protestant, midwestern American has been forced to stretch his vistas beyond such a narrow parochialism.

---

[34] Brogan, Politics in America. Pp. 357 and 361, respectively. There is neither the space nor the need to recount all of the major pieces of New Deal farm legislation. A lively and accurate portrayal of the early years of that period, and its effects on farm policy, is found in Arthur Schlesinger, Jr.'s two volumes (thus far) — The Crisis of the Old Order. Houghton, Mifflin Co., Boston. 1957; and The Coming of the New Deal. Houghton, Mifflin Co., Boston. 1959.

[35] Ibid., p. 356.

[36] Ibid., p. 72. Brogan can just barely tolerate the materialistic tendencies in the farmers' political attitudes and actions — "When the American farmer is prosperous enough to ride to the polls, he votes Republican." (1943 Preface, op. cit., p. xi.)

[37] Graham Hutton, Midwest at Noon. University of Chicago Press, Chicago. 1945.

[38] Ibid., p. 55.

In another vein, Hutton discusses the individualism of the American farmers in contrast to their "genius for organization and association to further their common interests."[39] It is at this point that the American farmer is going to have to act even more effectively if he is to counteract the loss of his political power. One can well agree with Hutton that the modern farm organization is almost infinitely more efficient than were its predecessors. But the emphasis has been on supplying producer and consumer services — gasoline, insurance, feed, fertilizer, farm equipment and the like. The central issue now is: Will the farmer so discipline himself that he will be able to control sufficiently the production of his varied commodities?

To some extent at least, James Harrington was accurate in his diagnosis: Political power follows economic power. Although the rural areas have some built-in political advantages in the protection of their declining numerical strength, efforts are under way to counteract their diminution in political power by an improvement in organized economic strength. The Farmers Union wants to acquire this economic bargaining power through the means of national legislation; the Farm Bureau wants to employ its own national and state organizations to do the job. It would appear that in the first instance, the political power is not sufficient; that in the latter, there is neither the organizational will nor the group discipline that would be necessary to accomplish the objective.

THE AMERICAN DEMOCRACY[40]

Harold Laski brought to the American scene his own pair of ideological glasses. He had taught at Harvard and later at several other of our colleges and universities, had traveled widely throughout the United States, and had known many of the "greats" in American political life. But his portrayal of the United States was in terms of 1933 and not 1948, when his magnum opus on America was published. He wrote of "the immense horde, perhaps as many as five millions, of migratory workers and their families who today haunt the highways of America," believed that "the fate of the family-sized farm is not less grim," and apparently convinced himself of "the reality of an American peonage."[41]

Laski had a constant desire to reform America in light of his own ideal images. In some real sense, as Alfred Cobban has

---

[39] Ibid., p. 78.
[40] Harold Laski, The American Democracy. The Viking Press, New York. 1948.
[41] Ibid., pp. 487, 489, 242, respectively.

indicated, this was Laski's strongest quality. He was a political scientist-philosopher with a mission. This unity of direction, when fused with the intellectual abilities which were his, gave him a wide, if not a notably sympathetic, audience.

But Laski's ideology often did not fit in with the real America. That is, he was excellent at justifying his own preferences but often inaccurate in stating conditions. Strongly committed to the need for a farmer-laborer alliance[42] in order — from his view-point — that we might have a potent liberal-socialistic, central-ized party to combat the powerful and omnipresent, if not fascis-tic, business interests, Laski was not able to step back and view the American farm economy with any remarkable degree of ob-jectivity. What he wrote about in 1948 might have been politically possible in 1933, but not a decade and a half later. The American conscience should be disturbed about the conditions of our mi-grant workers, both domestic and foreign, but their miserable social and economic conditions are becoming less significant in American farming, if for no other reason than that they (the mi-grant workers) are less in demand and fewer in numbers. Their political power is weak and inarticulate.

Laski was probably correct in his diagnosis that there was an increased spread in the class structure within American agricul-ture. The social-economic-political gap between the haves and have-nots might well be a cause for legitimate concern. Even when concerned, however, a democratic course of action does not present itself to us either as clearly or as neatly as it did to Laski.

THE AMERICAN FEDERAL GOVERNMENT[43]

Max Beloff's analysis of the American political system is probably the most balanced and judicious study of our political institutions that we have had from a foreign student. Urbane, in-cisive and knowledgeable, he writes in a style which is meagre in quantity but persuasive in quality.

Mostly by indirection does Beloff concern himself with farm politics. His over-all thesis would appear to be that our political institutions are not geared to the role we must play in the modern world. Our diffusions of power have been protectors of human liberty. But we now live in a domestic society in which the

---

[42] For example, ibid., pp. 238-39.
[43] Max Beloff, The American Federal Government. Oxford University Press, New York. 1959.

demands on government are beyond what our present political institutions are able to supply, and in a world society wherein our
power position is waning because of an inability to provide a
concerted and dynamic sense of direction in our relations with
friend, neutral and antagonist.

Although he never quite says so, Beloff indicates that the position of the American farmer is one important manifestation of
our increasing difficulties. "The older agrarian America is still
present over enough of the country to make the pro-agrarian bias
of some American political institutions something with which the
American statesman must always reckon." Again, "the Department of Agriculture comes to be the spearhead of the farmers —
and its head is likely to prove a major political liability if he
rejects the role."[44]

In the area of foreign policy, Beloff notes that the shift in agriculture to a form of "dumping program" — albeit a program
with some genuine benefit to the national interest — brought with
it a shift of control over the agricultural attachés from the Department of State to the more amenable, at least from the farm
organization's outlook, Department of Agriculture.

Although Beloff does not make this exact analogy, it does
seem to be of some importance to note the impact of our federal
system of government on the structure and process of farm organizations — which are also federations, if not confederations.
That is, one of the realities of farm politics is for the national
organization to be pushing and pulling in one direction, the state
organization in another. This condition is particularly evident,
at times, within the AFBF in their relations with certain state
organizations, although it is not unknown in the other farm groups.

Without rancor, but with sympathetic understanding, Beloff
points to what might be termed the "external" American dilemma.
Thrust into a position of leadership within the free world, har-
assed by the strategy and the increasing power of the Communist
world, we continue to be uncertain and timid in our endeavors to
modify our free institutions in such a manner that we will be able,
through the long pull, to be both free and secure.

FUTURE TRENDS — SHORT AND LONG RUN

What are the future trends in the political position of the
American farmer? Any sensible estimate seems to depend on
the assumptions set forth regarding the central issue of war and

---

[44] Ibid., pp. 13 and 88, respectively.

peace: Herein we will assume that there will be no major shifts
in the existing and tenuous balance of power between ourselves
and the Communist nations; the cold war will continue, or be
slightly accelerated.

In the short run — say, perhaps, within the present decade —
there is considerable evidence that the farmer's political power
will not seriously deteriorate. He is overrepresented in a considerable number of the state legislatures, and these institutions
still have potency in terms of taxes, appropriations, economic
regulations and reapportionment — among the more important reserved and concurrent powers which they still exercise. Charles
Hardin has clearly outlined the rural advantages in the halls of
Congress: overrepresentation in the House and, in terms of the
principle of majority rule, in the Senate as well; control over the
powerful Committees on Agriculture (and Forestry, in the Senate)
and the subcommittees on agricultural appropriations; protection
in the form of undisciplined parties from the harassing cross fire
that might strike agriculture if our congressional policy committees could truly direct party policy; maintenance of the status quo
because of the unity of intent between certain congressional committees, special interest groups, and rather semiautonomous administrative units within the Department of Agriculture; and assistance from the realization that the farm vote, though dwindling,
might still be a crucial vote in a presidential and, especially, a
congressional election.[45]

The "farm vote" of then Senator Kennedy shows how the
farmer receives additional and substantial reconsideration when
a politician moves from the nonfarm sanctuary of a highly urban-
ized state and strives for our highest political office.

James Burns points out that during Kennedy's last three years
in the House his vote was "often" to cut the appropriations of the
Departments of Agriculture and Interior, and that in doing so he
departed from Democratic party policy.[46] Kennedy did give a
"distinctly favorable nod toward the controversial Brannan plan,"[47]
but the compensatory payment features of that plan would have
been of some economic assistance to the urban low-middle and
low income groups. At the 1956 Democratic convention, it was
apparent that the midwestern and Great Plains delegations were
"sticking solidly with Kefauver," partly because Kennedy had
voted against rigid, 90 per cent farm price supports.[48]

---

[45] Charles M. Hardin, Farm Political Power and the U. S. Governmental Crisis.
Jour. of Farm Econ., 15(5, Dec., 1958): 1646-59.

[46] James M. Burns, John Kennedy, Harcourt, Brace and Co., New York, 1959, pp.
88 and 91. The years were 1950-52.

[47] Ibid., p. 125.

[48] Ibid., p. 189.

As has so often and necessarily happened in American politics, a presidential candidate must attempt to accommodate the
wider and more diverse interests of a national constituency in a
considerably different manner than was done when he represented
a local or state area. Former Senator Kennedy has, we may assume, learned this lesson well. The Congressional Quarterly
made a comparison of the farm vote of senators Humphrey and
Kennedy.[49] The results were as follows:

Year	In Agreement (per cent of total votes)
1953	0.0
1954	36.7
1955	20.0
1956	51.4
1957	70.0
1958	90.9
1959	95.2

The political cynic might speculate that it would soon be necessary for Senator Humphrey to prove that his "liberal" position
on farm policy was as advanced as that of his opponent's. The
point is, however, that the diminishing farm vote is still sought
after in the clash of the presidential electoral process.

Holbert Carroll's study brings forth excellent evidence to
show that the farm groups and the farmer-oriented congressional
committees on agriculture have directed American foreign policy
into channels which are of primary advantage to the farmer. He
points out several instances in which the international aspects of
American foreign policy have been distinctly subordinated to the
domestic interests of the American farmer.[50]

Foreign observers still stress the ideological potency of agricultural fundamentalism in American politics. Daniel Bell contends that the American belief in the sanctity of property rights
has enhanced the farmer's power and lessened that of organized
labor.[51]

But there is considerable data of a damaging nature on the
other side of the ledger. There have been quite distinct, but still
largely unorganized, rumblings of discontent with current farm

---

[49] Congressional Quarterly Weekly Report, week ending March 25, 1960, Vol.
XVIII, No. 13, pp. 472-73.
[50] Holbert N. Carroll, The House of Representatives and Foreign Affairs. University of Pittsburgh Press, Pittsburgh, 1958; for examples, pp. 34, 48, 55-56, 63, 125,
and 274.
[51] Daniel Bell, The End of Ideology. The Free Press, Glencoe, 1960. P. 194.

policy. The urban housewife is becoming more articulate and
any fresh talk of higher price supports or "bread taxes" can and
has brought down a wrath of letters on the representatives of the
urban constituents. Costs of the present farm programs are extensive, even though the farm organizations and certain members
of Congress have plausibly contended that the allocation of costs
is unfair to the farmer.

The Bureau of the Census has estimated that reapportionment
in the House of Representatives, based on the 1960 census returns, will bring nearly a 10 per cent change in the present allocation of House seats — there will be approximately 20 gains and
20 losses. Although these changes will not occur until 1963, and
the rural-small town control over most of the state legislatures
will not have been relinquished by that time, it would still seem
almost certain that the farm vote in the House will be further de-
preciated.

The urb-suburbanization of the United States has weakened
noticeably the vigor of the belief in the family farm. Empirical
evidence on this point is still sketchy and inchoate, but random
conversations in a few metropolitan areas lead this writer to the
conclusion that it is later than the farmer thinks.

The ideological split between the Farm Bureau and the Farmers Union-Grange-commodity interests alliance (a group of allies
with something quite less than a unified position on matters of
strategy and goals) has weakened the farmer's political posture.
If continued, it will further the likelihood that the urban areas
will be the progenitors of farm policy in the future. This division
can probably be healed only by a new and less ideologically oriented farm leadership, which is practically to say that in the
short run it cannot be mitigated.

The farmer himself is entwined in his own enigma. He would
like a higher income from the products he sells but a decrease in
price of the things he must buy. Overproduction and inelastic
demand curves do not cause him to control carefully his own production plans. Politicians are fearful of taking the control or the
free market route because, among other reasons, they are afraid
that either approach will affect them adversely in the rural-small
town ballot boxes.

W. R. Parks recently pointed out that the economists themselves have, to a degree, frustrated both the politicians and the
farmers.[52] Their analytical tools and largely inarticulate major

[52]W. Robert Parks, The Political Acceptability of Suggestions for Land Adjustment. In Dynamics of Land Use: Needed Adjustment. Iowa State University Press,
Ames, Iowa. 1961.

premises have brought forth a medley of proposals which have added to the environment of uncertainty and discontent.

CONCLUSION

Some of our finest studies of American political institutions have resulted from the efforts of the foreign observers that we have discussed herein. As political anthropologists, they seem to have outstanding qualities in terms of the clarity, depth and scope of their presentations. We might hope for somewhat more specialization; not an inquiry into endless detail, but rather a more thorough analysis of some of the "functional" politics of the American economy.

If the invitation could be issued in the form of an agenda of suggested areas for study, it might be outlined about as follows. First, will future trends in farm politics see an increasing emphasis placed on the growth of economic power with less and less reliance, for reasons already enumerated, on the actions of Congress? Why the intensity of the ideological divisions within American agriculture at just the time a few social scientists are writing about the decline, if not the end, of ideology? Is this phenomenon only an outgrowth of the intense desires of certain farm leaders, or do significant ideological schisms exist within rural America?

The proliferation of commodity organizations could be a third area for fruitful study. Does not their increasing and persistent presence indicate the competitiveness within American agriculture, the materialistic goals and pragmatic methods of the farmer and his distrust of the major general farm organizations?

The fourth item on the agenda might be concerned with the growth of vertical integration and contract farming. Will the farmer become more and more the handmaiden of the business organizations? In essence, this issue centers around the question as to the future of the farm cooperative. If the farmer is to achieve the type of bargaining power which will place him in a truly countervailing position with business and organized labor, it would appear that his fate rests with his cooperatives.[53]

It might also be enlightening to study the changing policies of the farm press. For many years, the more liberal elements in American politics have contended that this was a "kept" press;

---

[53] An excellent presentation of this point of view is found in the annual address of George B. Blair, president, National Council of Farmer Cooperatives. 1960 Blue Book, Official Yearbook of the National Council of Farmer Cooperatives. Pp. 1-7.

that it represented business interests who were the actual power
behind our farm policy. But the casualty rate of the farm newspapers and periodicals has been considerable. Have the remain-
der begun to adopt a more flexible point of view in matters involving farm policy and political strategy?

Next, the price support, P.L. 480, cotton subsidy and other
such programs have made certain business interests an integral
part of our farm policy. Those who have storage warehouses,
trucking firms, shipping lines, along with others who want to obtain certain metals and minerals through barter have become
very active political participants. To what extent are these business interests behind U.S. farm policy?

Lastly, the foreign observers should take a long look at their
picture of the modern meaning of agricultural fundamentalism.
Their stereotype of the way the farmer views his role in American life is becoming more and more inaccurate. Will the dominant picture come to be "the farmer in a business suit," or the
farmer in a pair of union-made overalls?

The political position of rural America will continue to deteriorate; rural Americans will continue to seek ways to slow down
the pace.

DON F. HADWIGER
Southwest Missouri State College | *Discussion*

MOST POLITICAL SCIENTISTS would affirm, the writer thinks,
that the foreign observers cited by Professor Talbot have made
significant contributions to our literature on American government. Graduate and even undergraduate students in political
science have been obliged to become familiar with the works of
these men, with the exception perhaps of Max Beloff and Graham
Hutton. The commentaries by Tocqueville and Bryce have pointed
up the changes occurring in United States society and politics between the 1830's and the turn of the century. Ostrogorski's book
is basic reading for those who seek an understanding of the
American party system and, to a lesser extent, Laski's observations on the American presidency are thought to be valuable.
Brogan can be offered as a lesson in style for political scientists
and others.

The writer would question, however, whether we could learn
much from the works discussed here about trends in agricultural
politics which will be important during the 1960's. Professor

Talbot in fact found little in his citations which was useful in his concluding section, and it seems to this writer that this should have been expected, for two reasons. In the first place, as Professor Talbot pointed out, all but one of these men were interested in the broad picture of American government and politics, in which context agriculture received scant attention. According to the testimony here, for example, Bryce was presumably not much interested in — if in fact he even knew of — the discontent among farmers in the Plains, the South and the Midwest. He apparently made no mention of the farmer organizations which had already secured the passage of unique and highly significant state and national legislation and which, shortly after his book was published, put together the most impressive third party in our nation's history. Surely a man so inattentive to the politics of agriculture during his own time could contribute little to the present subject. In fact, one gains the impression from Professor Talbot's discourse that the occasional comments by these men upon agriculture were more often than not misleading or erroneous.

If our primary interest here is in current trends, and trends which might be significant in the future, rather than trends occurring in the past, then the writer would offer a second reason for seeking evidence elsewhere than in the writings of these men: their observations on agriculture have been outdated by the impact of relatively recent events in this field. This is especially true with reference to Tocqueville and Bryce, who had no inkling of the automobile, the tractor, the college of agriculture and the REA. Therefore it seems to this writer extravagent to promote, as a commentary on farmers in the 1960's, a remark made by Tocqueville in 1835 — a remark, incidentally, in which he employed the present tense verb. It is true that the other men wrote during the present century, but even their most recent commentary fails to take note of the shifts in farm politics which occurred in the late 1940's, of which some American analysts were aware. Nor is it likely that they could have predicted the events of the 1950's, when the impact of the explosion of productivity was not fully taken into account even by those who conducted our great farm policy debates.

It might be suggested, in short, that if we are to look abroad for a better understanding of current and future trends in agricultural position, we should seek an observer who has given major attention to this problem, and who is well-informed about the present situation. We might turn, for example, to the London Economist.

The writer intends to proceed a little differently than he did from this point in the discussion which he prepared for the conference, and he would like briefly to explain the reason for this. Professor Talbot very kindly sent the paper to me about a month before the conference, and after reading it over, the writer sincerely felt that there are trends in agricultural position which were not within the scope of the paper, and that note should be taken of these trends at this conference; the discussion during the past two days has convinced the writer that this is so. The writer originally planned to make reference to the evidence of other trends in a series of questions, hoping in this way to avoid giving the impression that he was presenting an independent paper, although his questions were pretty obviously leading questions. But since attention has been drawn, repeatedly, to the crime of straying from the main paper, the writer knows now that he would be convicted despite his precautions. So the writer means to make a clean breast of it, bad conscience or no conscience, and in the time available, to follow up his leading questions with less restraint.

One occurrence in agricultural politics during the past ten years has been the development of partisanship in the consideration of agricultural policy. In the House vote on the 1959 wheat bill, 60 per cent of the urban Democrats, according to the Congressional Quarterly, voted in favor of the bill, despite the efforts which had been made to marshall consumer opinion against it. The bill was opposed by 100 per cent of the urban Republicans.[1] May we consider this to be one indication that the day has passed when congressmen from the rural areas could hope, like Ostrogorski, that after the elections the parties would silently steal away?

If bipartisanship is of declining utility, what might be done to cement coalitions along party lines within the Congress? There is ample basis for continued cooperation between the Farm Bureau and some business and professional groups, which McCune has revealed. Is it realistic to expect that this assemblage will meet opposition from an enduring farm-labor coalition? It is true that many farmers do not like unions — some national farm magazines would in fact give the impression that farmers view unions as the cause of all their troubles. Yet 23 per cent of the farmers in the Wisconsin Agriculturalist poll had carried union cards,[2] and surveys by Wallaces Farmer, Iowa State University,[3]

---

[1] Congressional Quarterly Weekly Report. June 26, 1959. P. 851.
[2] Wisconsin Agriculturalist, April 19, 1958. P. 18.
[3] As reported in Wallaces Farmer, January 17, 1959, a survey conducted by Iowa State University in 1958 revealed that 51 per cent of the Iowa farmers interviewed were "very anxious" to see industry move into their town, and another 40 per cent thought it "would be all right."

Lubell,[4] and others have indicated that many farmers are becoming more sympathetic toward the desires of the urban worker. Democratic congressmen and senators from mixed constituencies outside the South have obviously found it possible — and presumably quite expedient — to be completely receptive to the demands of both groups.

Can the urban Democrat reciprocate by supporting legislation which would raise farm income? He hears from the consumer, of course, but one may speculate that Senator Clark of Pennsylvania reflected, before voting in support of the 1959 wheat bill, that he might receive more help on the things in which he was interested from senators Humphrey, McCarthy, Douglas, Hartke, Hart, McNamara, Morse, Neuberger, Proxmire, Church, McGee, Carroll, Young of Ohio (and who knows who may be there next year from Kansas, South Dakota, Iowa and Nebraska) than he might have obtained from senators Bricker, Thye, Potter, Ferguson, Cordon, Welker and other Republicans.

A study of the apparent decline in bipartisanship will lead, the writer thinks, to the discovery of some trends in regional position within the Congress, especially with reference to the South and Midwest. The Southerners have provided most of the Democratic component for the bipartisan coalition which formerly dominated the farm policy process in Congress. Fifteen of the 22 Democrats on the House Agriculture Committee are still from what might appropriately be called Southern constituencies, although five of the eleven Democrats on the Senate Agriculture Committee are now from the Midwest. The group making up the other important part of the bipartisan farm policy team were rural Plains and Midwestern Republicans, whose numbers have dwindled somewhat during the past eight years. In seeking basic causes for the decline in congressional bipartisanship, one finds much to indicate that cooperation between representatives of the South and Midwest is becoming increasingly difficult, at least with reference to agriculture. In the realm of agriculture, Southern areas are increasingly aspiring to competition with the Midwest in the production of corn, meat and dairy and poultry products. As a result Midwesterners might be as enthusiastic as Southerners would be unenthusiastic about a quota system which would prevent rapid expansion of the area in which these commodities are produced. Southerners are also trying with some success to lure midwestern industry, which reminds one of the fact that the politics of one area is increasingly union-oriented, while the other continues to resist unionization. There is the old

[4] Samuel Lubell, Revolt of the Moderates. Harper and Brothers, New York. 1956. P. 174.

but rejoined debate over the place of the Negro, which bursts out whenever representatives of the national Democratic party come together. The civil rights question has forced the South into a fairly conservative position on other issues, such as education and housing measures, which are increasingly championed by midwestern Democrats.

In the search for trends in agricultural position we might pose another set of questions relative to the ascendancy of the presidency within our national political system. Recent events which have heightened the crisis in world affairs make it unlikely that the next president will share President Eisenhower's modest concept of the role of the executive branch. It seems to the writer that there is a crisis also with reference to policy dealing with certain agricultural commodities, especially wheat. Over the past eight years the expression "freedom for farmers" has apparently involved, at least in part, the freedom of farm spokesmen to hassle interminably over matters which, from the point of view of the State Department, the taxpayer and perhaps also the farmer himself, need to be resolved. Has the time about come when some decisions will have to be imposed upon the clashing ideological and economic interests of which agriculture is presently composed? In the field of agriculture, too, there is a complexity which has, the writer thinks, been recognized in recent legislative proposals which would provide the executive branch with a variety of tools for dealing with the farm problem, and which would permit the president a good deal of discretion in the use of these tools.

To the extent that the executive branch does undertake, and is permitted, a dominant role in the initiation and development of farm policy, and to the extent that farm policy does become a partisan matter it becomes most relevant to ask what influence farmers can bring to bear in statewide elections and on the process of choosing presidents. The number of farmers is relatively small, and will of course diminish, but there exists abundant evidence in surveys and election returns, corroborated by the testimony of numerous politicians, that the farm vote has been pivotal in recent elections within some states outside the South, due to the fact that this vote is extremely volatile.

Illustrative of the volatility of the farm vote is the spectacular shift which occurred in the Wisconsin farm vote for senator between 1952 and 1958: while there was only a 4 per cent change in the Democratic majority in the three highly populated counties (which produced 35 per cent of the vote in 1958), the total state vote switched from 54 per cent Republican to 57 per cent Democratic.

After comparing the voting behavior of Wisconsin population groups through four elections, Leon Epstein concluded that "the

lavish attention which politicians of both parties give to farmers
and farm issues," was due to "the demonstrated capacity of Wisconsin farmers for wholesale switching of party allegiance."[5]
That farmers in some other states similarly possess this capacity
has been indicated in studies by Michigan's Survey Research Center,[6] by V. O. Key,[7] and by Wallaces Farmer.[8]

What has been the effect of the farm vote since 1952 upon party
fortunes? Of the 26 districts held by Republicans in 1952 in which
the 1950 population was classified as 65 per cent or more rural,
ten of these are now Democratic, or to put it another way, the Democrats have increased their representation in such districts outside
the South by 100 per cent. It is also worth noting that in these 26
districts the average percentage of votes cast for Republican candidates declined by 5 per cent as between 1952 and 1954, by 2 per
cent as between the 1954 and 1956 elections, and by 4 per cent in
1958, for a decline in average percentage as between 1952 and
1958 from 63 per cent to 52 per cent.

Other evidence of the impact of the farm vote is perhaps to be
found in the fact that after the 1958 elections 11 of the 14 states
participating in the Midwest Democratic conference had Democratic
governors, in the fact that Republicans lost control of the lower
house of the state legislatures in eight of the 17 states outside the
South in which 1950 populations were 22 per cent or more rural,
and in the other 9 states the Republican legislative majority was
trimmed.

As to the potential effect of the farm vote in presidential contests, it had, the writer submits, a considerable impact on precon-
vention politics within the Democratic party in 1960. With respect
to the importance of the farm vote in a national campaign it can be
noted that a pre-election survey conducted in 1956 by the New York
Times indicated that the farm issue appeared pre-eminent in a
number of states. A Wallaces Farmer poll following that election
revealed that it did have an impact in that state, although foreign
policy was, as one should expect, the major issue.

In summary, there is evidence of at least four trends affecting
agriculture position — the movement of farm policy into the partisan arena, the growing need for strong leadership from the executive branch on agriculture policy, the widening incompatibility of
the South and Midwest, and the increased power of the farm vote
in elections.

[5] Leon Epstein, Size of Place and the Division of the Two-Party Vote in Wisconsin. Western Political Quarterly, 9(March, 1956).
[6] Angus Campbell and Homer C. Cooper, Survey Research Center, Group Difference in Attitudes.
[7] V. O. Key, Jr., Politics, Parties, and Pressure Groups, Fourth Edition. Thomas
Y. Crowell Co., New York. 1958. P. 581.
[8] Wallaces Farmer. August 1, 1959. P. 46.

Chapter 11

C. E. BISHOP

North Carolina State College

K. L. BACHMAN

U. S. Department of Agriculture

Structure of Agriculture[1]

T HE AUTHORS WERE REQUESTED to discuss the structure of agriculture that would prevail if agriculture were organized in a way consistent with society's values for and goals of economic organization and to point out the degree of change in the present structure that would be required and the implications for agriculture in terms of technology and factor prices. We have taken the term "structure of agriculture" to refer to the pattern of asset control and the framework of decision making in the industry. Structure, therefore, is concerned with the number, size and location of agricultural plants, the pattern of ownership and management "binding these plants together into firms, the interfirm arrangements of a formal or informal nature that influence firm actions and the governmental lines of authority at state and/or federal levels that may modify firm decisions."[2] Structure is determined partly by our values, which may also be altered by changes in structure. Conflicts also may develop and persist between values and economic forces. In such instances, society often takes action to reconcile these conflicts.

In developing this paper, the authors found it necessary to anticipate the contents of Dr. Brewster's paper, "Society's Values and Goals in Respect to Agriculture," Professor Hathaway's paper, "Goals of Agriculture for Economic Organization," and the paper presented by Professor Kaldor and associates, "Goal Conflicts of Agriculture." As a basis for the development of this assignment, therefore, the authors found it necessary to first briefly state their own beliefs with respect to the beliefs and values of society that relate to the structure of agriculture.

---

[1] Q. W. Lindsey, J. G. Maddox, N. C. State College, H. L. Stewart and J. M. Brewster, Farm Economics Research Division, Agr. Res. Ser., made helpful suggestions in preparing this paper.

[2] Essentially this same definition was developed by R. A. King, "The Design and Use of Synthetic Models in Guiding Changes in Market Structure," a paper presented to the Southern Association of Southern Agricultural Workers, Birmingham, Ala., February, 1960.

BELIEFS AND VALUES HELD BY
FARMERS AND FARM SPOKESMEN

We shall focus attention on four beliefs and values which are especially pertinent to the structure of agriculture and to the role that farmers play in the economy. Foremost is the widely shared judgment of farmers and farm spokesmen that American agriculture should be structured by family farms. A family farm is commonly described as one on which most of the managerial and labor activities are combined in the same family. Farm spokesmen especially are inclined to believe that farming should be organized as small independent proprietorships embodying the management and labor functions in the family that operates the farm business.

The philosophical ideas on which the family farm is rooted assumes also that such an organization either is or can be developed into a unit that will employ the family labor efficiently and that will yield returns for farm resources that are high enough to enable farm families to enjoy levels of living equal to those enjoyed by other families in society.

Emphasis on the family farm is deeply embedded in our heritage. From the beginning and extending throughout the settlement of the new world, there were no serious institutional barriers to combining into one person or family the managerial and labor roles that were segregated into lord and servant in the older European civilization. John Adams and Thomas Jefferson[3] argued that the inherent right of the colonists to govern themselves had its close counterpart in the claim of every colonist to possess land in his own right. Their arguments proceeded from the political philosophies of the 17th and 18th centuries, which proclaimed property, together with life and liberty, the foundations of a good society. A good society, therefore, was regarded as one in which land ownership was widely distributed and in which the land was owned in limited quantity with the farm family living on the land it farmed. In this setting, each individual was presumed to develop in line with his own capabilities. Thus the good society would be achieved.

There was faith in the market to provide farmers with a fair return. Earnings were determined largely by individual efforts. The family farm, therefore, was considered as providing a

[3]R. Freund, John Adams and Thomas Jefferson on the Nature of Landholding in America. Journal of Land Economics, May, 1948, p. 107.

motivation for increased productivity and as a means of assuring the individual the fruits of his own labor.[4]

An agriculture of predominately family farms has been a dominant goal in public policy concerning the structure of agriculture in the United States. Especially significant was the Homestead Act passed in 1862, which gave land to families who agreed to settle the land for specified periods of time. This act reflected the faith that a farm family owning the land it farmed could dig its living out of the soil. Farming was viewed in a subsistence orientation. The vast technological changes that occurred during the last century were not expected. There was little or no concern over the possibility that the rate of growth in the supply of farm products might exceed the rate of growth in demand.

In 1916, the Federal Land Bank system was established to encourage the development of family farms and farm ownership in the United States. In the early 1930's, the Resettlement Administration sought to relocate families in areas that were redeveloped and were to be operated on a family farm basis. The Farm Security Administration also came into being in an effort to perpetuate these goals by assisting farmers and individuals who wish to farm with their capital and credit problems. Each of these acts has affected the distribution of land holdings and the structure of American agriculture.

The family farm is an ideal that is not shared by many other countries nor is it universal among our own farmers. Certainly, the family farm structure was not characteristic of much of the cotton and tobacco areas of the South or of farms in the West and Southwest. In both the far West and the Coastal Plain of the Southeast, farms using many hired laborers are prevalent. In the West, the farm workers are paid cash. In the South, they are paid in kind. The family farm in the United States really developed its stronghold in the New England and midwestern states. The kind of agriculture that developed in the South and far West conflicted with some of the principles on which the family farm philosophy was based — that all individuals had the greatest opportunity to come into their own when they possessed rights in land and had the freedom to use it in accordance with their opportunities.

A second and related major value of many farmers and farm spokesmen is that farm families should own as well as manage

---

[4]For a statement of these and related philosophical principles in American agriculture, see J. M. Brewster, Impact of Technical Advance and Migration, Proceedings Issue, Jour. of Farm Econ., December, 1959.

and till their farms. This value implies that farming should be reserved for farmers. It arises partly because society respects sole ownership of individual proprietorships. An individual who is in debt is expected to work and save in an attempt to achieve the status of full and complete ownership. When management and ownership are combined in the same person, the owner is entitled to gains and losses arising from good management. One receives the fruits of his own endeavors. Again, this value reflects the faith that the market will return appropriate rewards for productive efforts.

This desire for full ownership and the struggle for it by farm operators contrasts sharply with goals now commonly accepted in nonfarm businesses. In nonfarm business, multiple ownership and perpetual indebtedness are accepted as a general rule and separation of management, labor and ownership is typical.

A third widely held value is that efficiency is desirable and that each entrepreneur should be permitted freedom of management to decrease costs whenever he finds the opportunity to do so. This view is related also to one of the concepts underlying the family farm: through family farm ownership individuals have the opportunity to gain from increased productivity and frugality and would therefore seek the most efficient methods of production. It was thought that when entrepreneurial freedom was permitted, the competitive system insured efficiency. This freedom of management value often takes the expression that farm production should be free from regulation by other sectors of the economy and free also from public regulation. It implies the belief that the conditions of perfect competition are reasonably well approximated in agricultural markets. But there is now greater doubt that the perfect competition model is descriptive of agricultural market conditions. Consequently, somewhat less emphasis is now placed upon independence in management by farmers.

Another value which in the past had a great deal of support among farmers and farm families and which probably has substantially less support now is that farming is a preferred or superior occupation and that there should be free entry into farming. That is, farmers have held the view that if their sons like farming they should be encouraged to go into it regardless of abilities or financial position. This view is based partly upon the traditional faith of farmers that they can close the gap between their circumstances and their aspirations by obtaining title to land and working hard. Also, farming was supposed to have social and cultural advantages; tilling the soil was regarded as a superior occupation. This value is related to the value of entrepreneurial freedom. The development of the frontier with its appeal to farm families and the challenge and dreams of independence associated with it fostered the view that farming is a superior occupation.

The values, both present and past, held by farmers and farm spokesmen have been important in influencing the structure of agriculture. They have affected the pattern of ownership of agricultural assets, the interrelations among firms and the ability of farmers to control decisions with respect to agriculture. As economic forces have altered the conditions confronting farmers, it has become clear that conflicts in values with respect to the best structure of agriculture exist. These conflicts are deep seated. The forces giving rise to these conflicts need to be analyzed and their effects determined if farmers are to be in position to make rational choices among policy alternatives available to them. But this analysis must also consider the somewhat different prevalent beliefs in other parts of our society.

BELIEFS OF URBAN PEOPLE IN REGARD TO FARMERS

Most urban people believe that food should be both abundant and low priced and that supplies should be dependable. There is much public support for this goal of abundant food. The separation of urban people from the source of supply of their food has no doubt encouraged the prevalence of this belief. It has been a factor, for example, in the willingness to promote and subsidize development of additional land resources, even when the supply of farm products increases at a greater rate than demand for these products.

A related value held by many nonfarm people is that farming should be free and competitive. This no doubt reflects a public image that competition and freedom are generally desirable and that agriculture represents an industry ideally suited to the workings of competition. Further, a structure involving both free competition and subsidization of resource development assures the public of plentiful food at low prices.

The nonfarm public tends to regard the farmer as a special kind of individual, a hard-working, frugal person who possesses different standards with respect to clothing, education and consumption patterns than his urban counterparts. Therefore, living costs are presumed to be lower on farms than in urban areas. The farmer's production of food presumably insures against real want.

Farm families, however, are no longer satisfied with consumption patterns differing from those of urban residents, and relatively little food is now used on the farms where grown. But farm families now want essentially the same consumption pattern as urban families and if farm families are to enjoy this consumption pattern, their incomes will need to support it. They are not willing to be viewed as second-class citizens. Changes in the structure of agriculture may be required, however, for farm families to obtain incomes that will be on a par with incomes of comparable nonfarm families.

STRUCTURAL CHANGES RELATED TO
BELIEFS AND VALUES

Economic forces are continually changing. Changes in these forces dictate changes in the structure of business. There are three sets of forces which we believe have especially important effects upon the structure of agriculture and which we shall discuss in the rest of this paper. They are: (1) changing technology and increasing capital requirements in agricultural production, (2) specialization of function in production and (3) industrial development of rural areas and decentralization of industry.

Technological Developments and Increasing
Capital Requirements

Changes in technology and mechanization of agricultural production provide opportunities for increased efficiency in production and reduced cost. Also, these changes usually involve increases in the scale of the farm business.

The technological revolution in agriculture is rapidly transforming it into one of the higher capital-using industries. The recent changes in production per man-hour serve as an index of this change in technology and the substitution of capital for labor. Production per man-hour has increased 90 per cent in the last 10 years, or 6 per cent per year.[5] This is from 2 to 3 times the increase per year in nonfarm output per worker.

This increase in production per worker has had and will continue to have a tremendous effect on farm size and capital requirements. In the 15 years from 1940 to 1954, the number of farms with volume of sales of more than $10,000 almost doubled.

---

[5]U.S. Agr. Res. Ser., Farm Economics Research Division, Changes in Farm Production and Efficiency. U.S.D.A., Stat. Bul. 233. Revised September, 1959.

The number of commercial farms with sales of less than $5,000 was cut in half.[6]

Sales per commercial farm averaged about $7,600 in 1954. The average investment amounted to about $34,000. Recent projections of numbers of commercial farms, output and capital requirements would indicate a volume of sales of about $17,000 and investments of about $70,000 per commercial farm in 1975 at 1954 prices.[7] At 1960 prices the investment would total nearly $90,000.

These projections do not necessarily conflict with the family farm as a goal since they meet the condition that labor be supplied by the individual farm family. Available evidence indicates that such changes in size of farm can easily be made within the framework of a family farm structure of agriculture.

Past changes in scale and efficiency in farming have occurred without any increase in the use of hired labor. Farms operated by family labor have maintained their dominant position in United States agriculture. The tendency for the size of farm to continue to rely primarily on the labor of the farm family is explained partly by the willingness of farm families to accept lower earnings on labor and capital than the earnings received in other sectors of the economy where larger businesses prevail.[8] Adjustments in the levels of farm and nonfarm earnings obviously represent a long-term rather than a short-term prospect. However, such a rise in the rates of return in farming to levels comparable to those in other sectors might in turn provide a more direct test of the prevalent and comforting hypothesis that almost regardless of type of farming, there are no significant economies of scale in agriculture beyond the size limits of family farms.

As scale is increased, further conflict seems likely between changes in technology and the value that the farm should be owner operated. This conflict stems from increases in capital requirements and the narrowing of the profit margin resulting from the expansion in production.

The increased amount of capital needed in farming is causing farmers to reassess their ideas in regard to getting started in farming and in regard to farm ownership. The tendency for the supply of farm products to outrun demand has made it difficult

---

[6] J. V. McElveen, Family Farms in a Changing Economy. U.S.D.A., Agr. Info. Bul. 171. March, 1957.

[7] K. L. Bachman, Prospective Changes in the Structure of Farming, presented at the 36th Annual National Agricultural Outlook Conference, November 18, 1958, Washington, D. C.

[8] See G. L. Johnson and Joel Smith, "Social Costs of Agricultural Adjustments," in Problems and Policies of American Agriculture. Iowa State University Press, Ames. 1959. P. 261.

for farmers to accumulate sufficient capital to bring about adjustment needs as rapidly as technological advances make new adjustments possible and profitable. Hence, farmers are turning more to outside financing for farm adjustments. This development is in conflict with the goal of full ownership.

In the past, agriculture has financed most of its growth in capital from savings. From the standpoint of agriculture as a whole, Tostlebe estimated that during the 1940-49 period, 90 per cent of the new capital came from savings of farmers.[9] There appears to be good reason to believe that this pattern is changing. In the future more capital from nonfarm sources and larger capital loans would appear likely.

There appears also to be general agreement that the larger capital loans will require more emphasis by farmers and lenders on the total credit needs of the farm and the likely effects on income. This will probably mean that educational, loan and service agencies will need to work more closely with farmers in developing sound business plans.

Continued expansion in scale thus may also conflict with the basic idea in the family farm that the management and labor function should reside in the same person. This is particularly true of the prevalent belief that the farmer should have complete freedom in management. As scale increases, eventually a point may be reached at which the farm business enterprise, like many nonfarm businesses, may find it profitable to develop some specialization in the management, labor and capital functions.

The increased capital requirements and the associated technological developments place a premium on sound management decisions in agriculture. As a result, commercial banks and other credit agencies are turning to more direct participation in the farm planning and in the major management decisions of the farm operator. Public credit agencies were developed to perpetuate freedom in management as well as encourage ownership of the land. Since the 1930's, however, the Farmers Home Administration has required farm plans as a basis for its loans.

Other public credit agencies also are becoming increasingly aware of management requirements for profitable operations. They are giving less attention to security and more attention to the purposes of the loans and to economic prospects for repayment. These developments represent a shift away from complete freedom of management by the farmer who obtains credit.

On the other hand, farmers' beliefs have probably encouraged

[9] A. S. Tostlebe, Capital in Agriculture. Princeton University Press, Princeton, N. J. 1957. P. 19.

the development of some types of credit. For example, the use
of land purchase contracts has grown rapidly in recent years as
an instrument for obtaining outside capital with minimum down-
payments. Land purchase contracts differ from mortgage financing chiefly because the title remains with the seller until all
or a specified percentage of the total payment has been made.
Such arrangements are consistent with farmers' beliefs in the
desirability of ownership, freedom in management and faith in
their ability to close the gap between their present situation and
their aspirations. Purchase by land contract, however, usually
entails greater risk for the farmer buyer than does conventional
financing. Many students of agricultural financing believe that
credit systems in agriculture should encourage wider sharing of
the substantial risks involved in modern farming.

The growth in capital requirements is making it difficult for
new farmers to go into farming in the framework of historical
values held by farmers. It is no longer sufficient to dole out or
otherwise make available small parcels of land and instill in
people the hope of being able to close the income gap by going
into the farming business, as was formerly considered to be the
American ideal. The high instability in agricultural earnings
makes it virtually impossible for such farmers to obtain a line
of credit consistent with the needs of modern agriculture. Certainly, if vertical integration continues to increase or if there is
a shift to perpetual financing of farms, American farmers must
be prepared to give way on their views with respect to management rights as the sole prerogative of the farm operator and also
with respect to the desirability of combining all management and
capital functions in the same individual.

Growing Specialization in Farming

Traditionally, agriculture in the United States has been an
industry in which individual units commonly carry on several
enterprises. But a definite trend toward product specialization
has occurred in recent years. The number of major enterprises
per farm dropped about a fourth from 1940 to 1954. With the development of specialized machinery and equipment, many farmers
have found it profitable to specialize in the commercial production of a relatively few enterprises to better utilize the large
capital investments needed. Specialization in dairy and poultry
farming, for example, is increasing significantly.

Even more important has been the growing specialization of
farmers in certain phases of farm production. Specialized

nonfarm industries produce inputs for farmers or furnish marketing and processing services formerly carried out on the farm. Most dramatic has been the growth of large-scale industries to produce inputs for farm use. Farming can now be called a "nonfarm input industry." More than half the inputs used in agriculture come from nonfarm sources and the percentage has increased sharply. The proportion of total inputs represented by nonfarm inputs has increased from about a third in 1940 to more than half in 1958. These nonfarm inputs include machinery, fertilizer, pesticides, gasoline, feed additives and other services now produced in the nonfarm sector. They have substantially replaced farm land and farm labor in the production process.

Economic forces leading to specialization of function in production require coordination in decisions and are in conflict with independence of decision making. This conflict has become especially apparent in the case of contract farming in which decisions are made at some central point to apply throughout the entire system of production and marketing. Specialization and integration do not necessarily conflict with the aspects of the family farm pertaining to labor. In most instances, the work is still performed by the farm family. The conflict with the concept of the family farm stems from a reduction in the range of decisions left to the discretion of the farmer.

This value that the management function should be vested in the farm family is in large part peculiar to agriculture. As a society, we do not concern ourselves with the fact that an individual or family operating a gasoline station, for example, often has much of the management function performed by an integrated parent company, even though much of the capital also is supplied by this company.

Specialization of farmers in production is consistent with the value held by farmers that only farmers should farm. Farmers themselves, however, are not consistent on this point in that their values permit expansion in activities by farmers, taking over certain nonfarm functions through the formation of cooperatives, yet they are concerned when nonfarm firms make inroads into agricultural production. Many farm leaders, for example, believe that it is desirable for farm people to form cooperatives and to perform marketing and processing functions normally performed by nonfarm firms. The same spokesmen, however, are often greatly concerned when nonfarm firms begin moving into the production of farm products. Only in part does this inconsistency in outlook seem to be tied into specific bargaining problems of farmers.

Currently important is the conflict between independence of

management and the feeling of many farmers and farm spokesmen that higher farm incomes are needed. Specialization of
farmers in the production function has made the farmer's income
more dependent on prices. Price decreases associated with the
rate of expansion in the production of farm products together with
rising costs for increased quantities of nonfarm inputs has conflicted with the belief of farm people that the market will provide
satisfactory incomes. Regulation of farm production, on the other
hand, conflicts with the value of urban residents that food should
be low in price and abundant. Regulation also conflicts with freedom of entry and with the value held by farmers that efficiency
should be encouraged and that the techniques of production that
promise lowest cost should be adopted.

Freedom of entry is a cherished ideal of many people. But
freedom of entry is the effective regulator of profits in a competitive economy. If returns on resources are desired that are
larger than would prevail under conditions of freedom of entry,
producers must decide whether they prefer freedom of entry or
higher returns.

Industrial Development

A third force that is altering the structure of agriculture is
industrial development in rural areas and the decentralization of
American industry. Industrial development brings with it opportunities for higher incomes, especially higher returns for labor
services. In many instances, business developments in rural
areas are shattering the farmer's view of farming as the best of
all possible ways of life. As local industrialization develops,
farm families see people with higher levels of living and higher
incomes. They soon learn that it is possible to achieve these
incomes and levels of living.

Faced with the growing complexities of farm management,
increased capital requirements in farming and alternative opportunities in nonfarm employment, many farm people are turning to
nonfarm occupations. Part-time farming is increasing; many
farmers are holding land in the hope of gaining from increased
land values in the future or as a means of obtaining some measure of security against industrial recessions.

The earnings from nonfarm uses of capital also are becoming
increasingly important not only to part-time farmers but also to
operators of larger commercial farms (Table 11.1). Annual average income from nonfarm investments totaled more than $1,000
for operators of class I farms and nearly $400 for operators of

class II farms. Somewhat similar results are shown in a recent study of farmers in western Oklahoma. In this area, nonfarm assets averaged nearly $10,000 per farm, with several groups having nonfarm assets averaging $15,000 to $20,000.[10] Experience with nonfarm investments would seem likely to lead farmers to expect somewhat similar returns from farm investments.

Table 11.1. Average Off-Farm Income of Farm Operator, Specified Sources, 1955*

Class and type of farm	Income of farm operator			
	Nonfarm business †	Interest, dividends, trust funds, and royalties	Rental of nonfarm real estate	Total specified items
	Dollars	Dollars	Dollars	Dollars
Class I	532	407	68	1,007
Class II	154	181	29	364
Class III	96	160	45	301
Class IV	158	84	27	269
Class V	200	47	30	277
Class VI	80	11	11	102
Part-time	403	28	72	503
Residential	272	74	30	376

*Farmers' Expenditures, Cooperative Survey USDA-U.S. Dept. Commerce, Dec., 1956. Vol. III, Pt. 2, 1954 Census of Agriculture, p. 50.
†Net income.

Bellerby emphasizes the beliefs of U.S. farmers that agriculture is a preferred occupation in explaining the long-term unfavorable farm-nonfarm income relations in the United States. In this connection, he states: "Farming [in the U.S.] has developed largely on a family basis with hired labor as a comparatively small part of the land force; except in respect to acreage the production unit has therefore been small. Subsistence farming involving varying degrees of selfsupply has traditionally given rise to the assumption that a farmer can attain a greater degree of independence and insurance than is attainable in other occupations."[11]

There is reason, however, to believe that these assumptions may be changing. In considerable part, this change is related to

---

[10] L. J. Connor, W. F. Lagrone and W. B. Back, Farm and Nonfarm Income of Farm Families in Western Oklahoma, 1956. Okla. State Univ. Bul. B-552. March, 1960. Oklahoma State University and ARS, USDA cooperating.

[11] J. R. Bellerby, Agriculture and Industry Relative Income. Macmillan & Co., New York. 1956. P. 292.

industrialization in rural areas. The challenge in agriculture in
this context is to create opportunities for adjustment within agriculture that will enable those who wish to continue in farming to
earn returns on their resources equal to the returns received for
comparable resources in other uses and to create channels for
migration of people from farms and into nonfarm employment
who prefer to migrate at prevailing relative wages. In many instances, nonfarm capital has moved into agriculture with the hope
of obtaining capital gains from increased land values. This has
been especially true near industrial centers. There is strong
evidence that the rapid rise in land values that has occurred over
the last 30 years may have run its course. In the late fifties increases in land values have slowed perceptibly; sales records
indicate decreases in average real estate values have occurred
in the Corn Belt and Lake states. Probably, there will be less
gain in the immediate future from increased land values in predominantly rural areas. Also, we may find in the future that
farm people will be less willing to accept a low return for their
labor and capital used in farming in the hope of reaping windfall
gains from land ownership.

CONCLUSIONS

     The values held by farm and nonfarm people affect the struc-
ture of United States agriculture. They also affect the views of
various segments of our society in regard to the role of the
farmer in our economic system. Economic forces change over
time, however, and when these forces are superimposed upon
values, conflict develops between these forces and values with
respect to how agriculture should be structured. Conditions
created result in a change in values or impediments to the fulfillment of economic goals. Changing economic forces are now
causing farmers and society in general to make some difficult
choices between deep-seated values with respect to the structure
of agriculture and the levels of income of farm families.
     For many decades, farm people have been willing to accept
substandard rates of return for labor and management, partly in
the hope of reaping windfall gains from increased land values.
Conditions now seem to be changing. Agriculture has found it
difficult to obtain the price stability needed to plan profitable and
efficient production. The emphasis on agricultural adjustment
has been to decrease cost by adopting improved technology. This
has led to greatly expanded agricultural production and to changes
in optimum size of farm firms. These changes have been so

large that we are forced to rethink the beliefs involved in the
family farm full ownership and management freedom. In the past,
for example, the family farm was defined in terms of the management and the family labor force. The alterations in the structure
of American agriculture that have occurred recently and are now
occurring make it difficult to maintain freedom of entry into agriculture and to retain entrepreneurial independence of farmers
without decreasing the incomes of farm families. It is likely,
therefore, that in the future family-operated farms will have
more of the management functions performed by off-farm sources.
Farmers in turn will need to reassess their beliefs and to develop
a more consistent course of action in guiding the forms taken by
the adjustments.

JAMES T. BONNEN
Michigan State University

Discussion

LET'S BEGIN by pointing out a few problems that have given rise
to considerable confusion in the discussion of agriculture's policy
problems. The first of these concerns the very nature of conflict
in human society. Why do so many social scientists insist on believing that it is possible and desirable to attain a human state in
which contentment and peace is universal? If that wondrous body
of human experience, the humanities, tells us anything about the
nature of man, conflict is an inevitable concomitant of human existence. The best we can ever hope for is some acceptable balance between conflicting forces in nature and in human society.
Indeed, it is to be doubted that man could ever be happy in a universally placid environment. Is it not true that when things get
"too quiet" we find distractions and recreations which inject ex-
citement, danger or uncertainty into our lives? The fact that we
are eternally fated to live with some degree of conflict suggests
the usefulness of a threshold concept for differentiating in policy
analysis between acceptable and unacceptable levels of conflict.
But then, what is conflict? Or what even is a "value conflict"? We must yet define consciously and adequately one of the
central comcepts about which we have been conversing for three
days. The writer submits that the meaning is not self-evident
and that the term has been used here in quite a number of different ways. Let the writer list some of these different usages. (1)
There is the case of conflict where specific values or goals of the
parties to conflict are <u>completely inconsistent</u> and goal attainment

by one party prevents absolutely the attainment by another of some specific goal. (2) There is the case of <u>competing</u> values and goals under conditions of approximate equality of power. In this case it is to the advantage of all parties involved to do some <u>trading</u> of goal attainment much as commodities are traded in a market characterized by free competition. (3) There is also another case of <u>competing</u> values and goals where substantial difference in power exists between the parties involved. In this case the differential power positions focus in a <u>bargaining</u> process which normally results in the gain or goal attainment being distributed in some manner related to the distribution of power among the parties to the bargaining process. (4) There is the case of <u>irrationality</u> (inconsistency of action) due to semantic difficulties or to communication inefficiencies. This usage of conflict does not involve values except as they may be related to the semantic difficulties. This usage can be applied to individuals or group behavior. (5) There is also another case of <u>irrationality</u> as an explanation of conflict which is limited primarily to the behavior of individuals. This is the explanation of apparent irrational conduct and conflict derived from Freudian analysis of frustration and from abnormal psychology.

Before we spend much more time conversing with each other about values and conflict in agricultural policy, agricultural economists, the writer thinks, would do well to pursue philosophic value theory further than they have and also to investigate the considerable body of literature on conflict that now exists.

A second difficulty commonly encountered in policy discussions is the frequent lack of historical perspective and understanding among those in agriculture who are concerned with the present policy difficulties. This has led to some very widely held beliefs about facts in agriculture that are contrary to actual objective fact.

Perhaps the best example of this in agriculture is to be found in the beliefs concerning the role of private enterprise and government in the early as well as later economic development of this country. There is no denying the importance of freedom and private initiative in our nation's growth, but the federal and state governments have made huge public investments in the development of this country. Yet this is conveniently forgotten or denied by some social scientists as well as farm leaders and others in attempts to promote private enterprise as an important social goal in formulating agricultural policy. They do a disservice to their own cause.

What are the facts? Early governmental expenditures were made to develop transportation systems and to protect the settlers from Indian attacks. First, canals and later roads such as the Wilderness Road and the Cumberland Road were built to the West. River transportation was improved. "Land-grant railroads" were flung across the continent in good part with public capital. Later both mainline highway and secondary roads were built. Various forms of public aid were and still are extended to irrigation, drainage and rural electrification projects. In recent decades the United States has undertaken major resource development projects such as the TVA and the Missouri Valley Authority. Most of this development has been created with or "triggered" by federal and state resource investments — and agriculture and private enterprise have thereby profited greatly. Other, even more direct, examples of government investment in agriculture abound: Rural Free Delivery of mail, farm-to-market roads, conservation payment programs, and the federal farm credit system including the Federal Land Banks, the Production Credit Associations, the Intermediate Credit Banks and the Farmers Home Administration — all examples of agencies set up to facilitate the flow of capital into agriculture. The development of human resources also has long been a concern of this society. Many states early founded public universities. The land-grant college system was begun under the Morrill Act of 1862 which made large grants of federal land to states for the establishment and support of land grant colleges. At every turn in our history, federal and state governments have fostered development through protective legislation, public investment and subsidy. Indeed, the first Act of the First Congress of the United States, after enacting a system for the administration of oaths, was the passage of a bill designed by Alexander Hamilton to protect and subsidize infant industries through tariff regulations.

In analyzing or discussing policy conflicts in agriculture, it seems to me to be most important to distinguish carefully between beliefs about facts and beliefs about normative matters or values. Many of our present difficulties both in policy analysis and in policy actions result not so much from the existence of conflicting values held, but from the confusing of facts with values (i.e. the tendency to believe what is, is what ought to be) and the failure to hold accurate beliefs about the facts of our past history and present situation.

There is a third difficulty which commonly confounds policy discussions today. In handling values and beliefs there is a ready tendency to lump these into farm-held values and beliefs and urban-held values and beliefs. This assumes a homogeneity within urban culture and within rural culture which simply does not exist. While quite a few values are held in common over many social sectors of the United States, great diversity characterizes both urban and rural culture. There are probably greater differences in beliefs and values between the Southern Appalachian farmer and an Iowa commercial farmer than there are between the same Iowa commercial farmer and a Chicago businessman. We would be well advised in our analyses to handle values and beliefs in terms of more specific socio-economic groupings than simply urban or rural people. Bishop and Bachman recognize this necessity of greater differentiation when discussing farm-held values but seem not to recognize it when treating nonfarm values and beliefs.

To turn more to the specifics of Bishop and Bachman's paper, the writer would first point to their definition of structure. This definition is derived in most part from market structure theory and is limited in meaningfulness to economic variables. It does seem to me that in discussing problems as broad and as complex as the relationship between values and goals and the structure of agriculture that something more inclusive than simply an economic definition is probably necessary. At least the writer is made uneasy by a definition which is designed to be related to values and goals but which among other things leaves outside its scope relevant social groupings.

In discussing industrial development and its effects on agriculture the authors seem to attribute the melding of urban and rural cultures in this country to industrial development. This, if it is their intent, seems to me to be a substantial oversimplification. One can point to too many rural communities today which have experienced rather thorough integration with urban culture and have come into contact with little or no direct industrial development. Surely the extension of urban culture and the erosion of rural institutions have resulted in major part from the extension of modern communication and transport systems into rural areas. To see this, one need only to reflect momentarily upon such innovations as rural electrification, Rural Free Delivery, the telephone, radio and television, the automobile, the all-weather farm-to-market road and other aids to physical movement.

In discussing the beliefs and values held by farmers and farm spokesmen, the authors mention the value of freedom. They discuss freedom in terms of management and indicate that as a value this means that "farm production should be free from regulation by other sectors of the economy and free also from public regulation." Much confusion has resulted in public discussions of the value of freedom in farm policy. It is a concept with which philosophers have difficulty. Social scientists would be advised to exercise great care in its use. Rarely these days is the term freedom qualified in its use in agricultural policy. It is thus often used or thought of as absulute freedom. This conception of freedom has done and is still doing much mischief in agricultural policy, for in any practical sense, for man, no such thing as absolute freedom exists. Rather there is only some relative degree of freedom as one has greater or lesser ranges of choice between alternatives in the pursuit of some set of goals. The search for absolute freedom tends to produce great saints such as St. Francis of Assisi, and great sinners such as the Marquis de Sade. While those hot in the pursuit of absolute freedom are quite conspicuous in agriculture these days, one finds strangely little evidence amongst us of saintliness.

GLENN L. JOHNSON
Michigan State University

Discussion

THE ORIGINAL OUTLINE of this discussion of goals and values in American agriculture gave Bishop and Bachman the task of describing the "structure of agriculture if made consistent with society values for and goals of economic organization; degree of change from present and implications for agriculture in the light of modern technology and factor prices; and comparisons with other economic sectors if they were modified accordingly."

It is not surprising that our authors found it difficult to fulfill this assignment. They were not furnished a statement of "society values for and goals of economic organization" and this conference has not yet agreed on such a statement. Indeed, one participant has referred to such statements as unattainable Holy Grails. The writer is not going to waste much discussion time (which is a scarce resource at this conference) placing blame on anyone for this situation.

Instead, the writer will demonstrate that we are not in possession of a generally acceptable procedure for developing and using value concepts in the solution of policy problems and then present a hypothesis about the nature of our deficiency which suggests some remedial measures.

THE DEMONSTRATION

The lack of a generally accepted philosophic position for

developing and using value statements will be demonstrated mainly with quotes from papers presented at this conference.

For instance, differences among the value and goal statements presented by Markham, Brewster, Timmons, Larson, Hathaway and by Bishop and Bachman are, in themselves, evidence that we do not have a generally accepted method of developing and using normative concepts for solving policy problems.

There is also absence of agreement on how normative concepts enter into the definitions of problems. Bishop and Bachman, for instance, conceive of problems as differences between concepts of "what ought to be" and "what is" as they write, "Economic forces change over time . . . and when these forces are superimposed upon values, conflict between these forces and values . . . develops."[1] By contrast, Brewster regards "the heart of any serious social problem to be a conflict of deep seated value judgments."[2] Wilcox took a third position and argued that our serious policy problems can be solved with answers to questions of fact.

Turning from use to development of normative concepts, we find Brewster and Foote at nearly opposite poles. Brewster writes, "no amount of rigor in any conceptual system of rules and no amount of completeness in quantitative measurement can determine what uniform weights to give to our competing judgments of value . . . . The ideal models of scientific theory and measurement are not to be equated with so-called normative systems of life and social organization." By contrast Foote discussed the operation of a maternity hospital as an example "of how values and goals and social action can be conceived scientifically." Foote must note with some satisfaction that Brewster does discuss values with some rigor and that he does assign weights to value judgments. Shepard's comments served to underscore our lack of agreement. So does Shannon's statement that "the role of the scientist is one of describing cost and consequences rather than specifying goals."[3]

In 1956, Heady wrote, "Some few workers, perhaps, feel their directive is to change values . . . . This approach is for ministers and boy scout leaders not economists."[4] Recently he wrote, "In

[1] C. E. Bishop and K. L. Bachman, Structure of Agriculture. This book. P. 249.

[2] John M. Brewster, Society Values and Goals in Respect to Agriculture. This book. P. 114.

[3] L. W. Shannon, Goals and Values in Agricultural Policy and Acceptable Rates of Change. This book. P. 274.

[4] Earl O. Heady, Basic logic in farm and home planning. Jour. of Farm Econ., 38 (1956): 808.

case of true education, the problem is to provide information, knowledge and principles which allow the individual to form his own values."[5] Another sentence implied that providing information, knowledge and principles does not mold individual values in the sense of having predictable and, hence, controlled effects on them. We read Heady and Burchinal's remarks about "a problem of determining what mix or combination of goals is optimum, desirable or acceptable."[6] Still later we heard "this conference has as one objective an explicit examination of value-goal patterns as they impede or facilitate . . . developments designed to bring incomes in agriculture to levels comparable with nonfarm activity or to adjust resource use in the directions indicated by the pull of the market."[7] What, we may ask, if some values do impede? Who changes them? Boy scout leaders? Or economists using "information, knowledge and principles?" Or, perhaps ministers? Fortunately, Heady is slowly overcoming a restrictive position in philosophic value theory and the philosophy of science. Incidentally, I can point out somewhat similar though less pronounced inconsistencies in the writings of Glenn Johnson.[8]

The disagreement between Foote and Greene on the possible existence of a public interest represented another lack of agreement on normative matters at this conference.

Cochrane's normativistic attack on the Kaldor and Hines modern welfarism further illustrates our lack of agreement. The Kaldor group envisions value conflicts as the problem of allocation among competing ends[9] while Cochrane envisions them as problems of determining ends!

In 1958, Ken Parsons launched an attack against the position of J. D. Black and Heady which is also the Kaldor and Hines position.[10] At this conference, Heady and Burchinal bowed to this

---

[5]Earl O. Heady, How Much Should We Allocate to Education? Farm Policy Forum, 12(2, 1959-60): 26.
[6]Earl O. Heady and Lee Burchinal, The Concern With Goals and Values in Agriculture. This book. P. 5.
[7]Ibid., P. 12.
[8]Glenn L. Johnson, Burley Tobacco Control Programs, 1933-50. Ky. Agr. Exp. Sta. Bul. 580. February, 1942. P. 88; _____ and Harry M. Young, What About the Burley Tobacco Control Program? Ky. Agr. Ext. Service Circ. 516. 1953. Pp. 25-26; L. A. Bradford and Glenn L. Johnson, Farm Management Analysis. John Wiley & Sons. 1953. Pp. 350ff. and p. 429; _____ and Joel Smith, Social Costs of Agricultural Adjustment . . . , Problems and Policies of American Agriculture, Iowa State Univ. Press, Ames. 1959. P. 250; _____, Value Problems in Farm Management, Jour. of Agr. Econ., 9 (June, 1960): 1f; and _____ and L. K. Zerby, Values in the Solution of Credit Problems. TVA Symposium on credit. (Spring, 1960).
[9]Don Kaldor and Howard Hines, Goal Conflicts in Agriculture. This book. Discussion by W. G. Cochrane.
[10]Kenneth Parsons, The Value Problem in Agricultural Policy, Agricultural Adjustment Problems in a Growing Economy. Iowa State University Press, Ames. 1956. P. 295f.

attack and recognized John Dewey's means-end continuum[11] though
not to the exclusion of the position presented by Kaldor and Hines.
Thus, Heady and Burchinal demonstrated within the confines of
one chapter that they do not have a consistent position. At least
they argued simultaneously that (1) the values of means and ends
are interdependent,[12] (2) ends should be maximized[13] but (3) values
should not be imposed on others.[14] If the values of means depend
on the values of ends and we should maximize ends, then it seems
fair to ask how we avoid imposing values for means?[15]

Time does not permit further exploration of the conflicting
positions presented at the conference with respect to the development and use of value concepts.

A HYPOTHESIS AND SOME SUGGESTIONS

The writer has a hypothesis to present which deals with this
failure of the discipline to secure a generally acceptable means
of developing and using value statements in solving policy problems. He hypothesizes that our inability to work effectively in
this area stems in part from our various commitments (often as
a result of accidents in our personal educational histories) to
special positions in the philosophy of science and philosophic
value theory. He hypothesizes, further, that our commitments
to these special positions prevent us from utilizing the contributions which other positions have to make to the solution of special
problems. Consequently, the writer would hypothesize that a
fuller understanding of these positions and of the interrelationships among them might free us of some intellectual schackles
thereby increasing our productivity.

If it were not for two considerations, the writer would advocate that we ignore all positions in philosophic value theory and
the philosophy of science and proceed on a "common sense" basis
to solve problems. The two deterring considerations are (1) the
subtle nature of our commitments to restrictive positions and (2)
the strong possibility that our common sense can be made more

---

[11] Heady, Burchinal, op. cit., p. 4.
[12] Ibid.
[13] Ibid., p. 5.
[14] Ibid., p. 2.
[15] This should not be construed as complete acceptance of the Parsons point of
view on the part of the discussant who is convinced that Parsons (and Dewey earlier)
regards the values of ends and means to be interdependent because he fails to recognize "an identification problem," and does not fully appreciate the role of opportunity
costs in determining value. See G. L. Johnson, Value in Farm Management. Jour.
of Agr. Econ., 9 (June, 1960): 8ff.

effective with contributions from unknown positions. We have to understand our positions in order to change them by either contraction or expansion. These two considerations seem to condemn us to examine and study alternative approaches within the philosophy of science and within philosophic value theory. The writer regrets that this book has not included more chapters which would be helpful in this respect.

In making this study and examination of alternative positions in the philosophy of science and philosophic value theory, the writer would suggest that we follow the advice of John Wisdom, Trinity College, Cambridge, who advocates[16] that we divide all statements about how to develop and use value concepts into two groups (1) those which are simple and easily understood and (2) those which are complex, strange and hard to understand.

The simple, easily understood statements can be divided into the helpful which we can retain and the useless which we can reject.

The strange complex difficult statements create trouble. For one thing complexity is easily confused with profundity. Further, meaningless statements and portions of statements may be confused with meaningful ones and followed at the expense of undue restriction on our activity. A possible procedure seems to be that of examining the meaning and usefulness of such statements in developing and using value concepts for solving individual problems. This procedure permits full utilization of common sense but not at the expense of ignoring important restrictions and contributions which may be contained in strange, complex and difficult statements on how to develop and use normative concepts.

Perhaps it would be helpful to try to indicate what this approach might lead us to do.[17] The writer expects that it would

---

[16] These suggestions were made to the discussant by Professor Wisdom during a period of sabbatical leave study at Cambridge University. They are contained in a manuscript entitled Paradox and Obsession: Freedom and Order, which was loaned to the discussant. Professor Wisdom anticipated possible publication by Blackwells. Other results of the discussant's sabbatical leave study are presented in Value Problems in Farm Management. Jour. of Agr. Econ., 9 (June, 1960): 1ff. Also see footnote 4 in this discussion.

[17] For a more detailed exposition of this approach see G. L. Johnson and L. K. Zerby, Values in the Solution of Farm Credit Problems. TVA Symposium on credit, Knoxville, Tenn. (Spring, 1960). The source of some of the ideas presented in this reference and in the above footnoted paragraph include: Kurt Baier, The Moral Point of View: a rational basis of ethics. Cornell University Press. 1958; Abraham Edel, Ethical Judgement, the Use of Science in Ethics. The Free Press, Glencoe, Ill. 1955; Paul Edwards, The Logic of Moral Discourse. The Free Press, Glencoe, Ill. 1955; E. H. Madden, The Structure of Scientific Thought. Houghton Mifflin Co., Boston. 1960; and S. E. Toulmin, An Examination of the Place of Reason in Ethics. Cambridge Univ. Press. 1950.

cause us to distinguish less sharply between techniques for developing and using factual beliefs, on one hand, and normative beliefs, on the other. Further, he imagines that we would tend to regard both as about equally realistic or unrealistic and that we would regard both as essential in defining and solving many problems. Also, we might even regard it our duty to help develop both types of beliefs. And, because errors in forming both factual and normative beliefs can lead to wrong actions, we would be expected to be about equally sensitive concerning our responsibilities for such errors. We might even become as sensitive about imposing false factual concepts as about imposing normative concepts on others. We would probably insist that our concepts be internally consistent as well as consistent with our experiences and observations. Experience with values as well as the physical world would be considered but not to the exclusion of other possible sources of normative concepts. Father O'Rouke would probably be less critical of us. Failure of a solution to produce anticipated results might cause us to search for the factual and/or normative concepts responsible for this failure that we might correct it.

Many will reject these suggestions as to what this nonrestrictive approach might lead us to do. Many of the objections will arise because the approach ignores restrictions contained in what the objector believes is the proper approach to science or the study of values. Such objections would substantiate the writer's basic hypothesis if ignoring the restrictions were to lead to increased ability to develop and use normative concepts in solving policy problems.

In closing, the writer would like to observe that some of the most intense discussion has dealt with the problem of developing and using normative concepts. If the contributors had concentrated on this problem rather than assuming that we have agreement on how to develop and use normative concepts, Bishop and Bachman might have been spared the difficult assignment of describing the structure of agriculture if organized according to a vaguely known set of "society values and goals for economic organization."

Goals and Values in Agricultural Policy and Acceptable Rates of Change

THE INCREASE IN AGRICULTURAL PRODUCTION

INCREASING AGRICULTURAL PRODUCTIVITY in the United States since the early 1900's is part of a world-wide change in agricultural productivity. The United States is among the leaders in increasing productivity per capita per acre of cultivatable land. We reap the benefits of increased productivity but must also struggle with some of the problems attendant to high productivity.

Regional and Temporal Variations in Food Production

High Productivity Does Not Solve All Problems

Before launching into a detailed discussion of optimum or desirable rates of change in the transition from rural to urban it might be well to examine change in agricultural productivity and some of its pertinent correlates. Examination of various indexes of food production on an international basis indicates that although world production has been increasing in recent years, there are important variations on a regional basis. Regional variation in food production is a part of the problem and to some extent a solution to the problem for efficient surplus producers. The desirability and feasibility of extensive interregional shifts of surplus produce is the subject of considerable controversy.

As an example of recent changes in world food production, using 1934-38 as a base of 100, United Nations' data show an

---

[1]Although only one author's name appears on this paper it was written in consultation with Professor Raymond J. Penn, Department of Agricultural Economics, University of Wisconsin.

increase to 107 for the period 1948-51, 112 for 1951-52, 117 for
1952-53, 120 for 1953-54 and 120 for 1954-55.[2]

North America Leads in Increasing Food Production

During the same period North American food production increased about 50 per cent, twice as much as European food production. Food production in the Far East, excluding the Chinese
mainland, increased about 10 per cent. These figures do not
really become meaningful unless the increase in population in
these areas is taken into consideration. Since gross productivity
is not our chief concern we must turn to changes in per capita
food production. It has not been increasing at such a pace; the
rapid growth of world population does much to negate the general
increase in productivity.

With 1934-38 as a base of 100, United Nations' data show a
per capita world food production index of 95 for the period 1948-
51, 97 for 1951-52, 100 for 1952-53, 102 for 1953-54 and 101 for
1954-55.[3]

During the same period North American per capita food production increased around 20 per cent. Food production per capita
decreased 15 per cent in the Far East, about 5 per cent in Latin
America and around 10 per cent in Oceania. No area other than
North America experienced an increase of around more than 10
per cent during this period.

The Relationship of Population Growth to Increased
Food Production

Although world population has been increasing during the past
few years at the rate of 1 1/2 per cent per annum and food production has been increasing at about 2 1/2 per cent per annum,
the great variation in growth and production rates from country
to country means that population will press against available food
supply to an increasing extent in some areas.[4] Just how much
surplus in one area may be used to alleviate shortages in another
area is controversial.[5] Although the basic problem with which we

---

[2]Report on the World Social Situation. United Nations, New York. 1957. Table 1,
Index Numbers of Total Food Production, p. 50.

[3]Ibid., Table 2, Index Numbers of Per Capita Food Production, p. 50.

[4]Ibid., p. 57.

[5]See, for example, Helen C. Farnsworth, Imbalance in the World Wheat Economy.
The Journal of Political Economy, 66 (1, February, 1958): 1-23.

are concerned is sometimes defined as overproduction, what we probably need is an effort to increase agricultural production in all parts of the world. The rapidly growing underdeveloped areas are in most urgent need of higher food production.

If a particular crop is taken into consideration such as corn, the variation in yield per acre around 1950 ran from 45 to 50 bushels in top corn-producing states in the United States to less than 10 bushels per acre in many African political entities. Some of the latter are self-governing countries; others are nonself-governing dependencies, but all are relatively underdeveloped.

Cultural Variation and Food Production

Cultural variations in farming practices have been emphasized in regional differences in yields and in changes in yield over time. Marvin P. Miracle has pointed out that while production methods do vary in detail in non-European farming in Africa, they have the following general characteristics:

(1) hoe culture predominates, and machinery is infrequently employed; (2) usually little care is given to the preparation of a seedbed; (3) clean cultivation is rarely attained, either because maize is grown with other crops or because the farmer is unable to keep up with the growth of weeds; (4) improved seed is not typically used; (5) fertilizers are not commonly applied except, perhaps, on small plots around the dwelling where maize may be grown as a garden crop; (6) maize may receive some irrigation, along rivers especially, but irrigated maize is a small fraction of the total; (7) crop rotation is essentially a question of crop sequences during the three or four years that land is under cultivation and (8) maize may be grown at any time in the sequence, but is most often first and seldom last.[6]

The increase in agricultural productivity over time is even more striking if a longer trend is taken. Farm production per acre has moved upward fairly steadily since 1919 with the exception of the Great Depression period. Farm production per animal unit has moved upward at even a greater rate during this period. Output per man-hour gradually increased during the period from 1910 to about 1935 and then at a very rapid rate until the present. The latter period was one in which output per man-hour of farm labor more than doubled.[7]

---

[6] Marvin P. Miracle, Maize in Tropical African Agriculture. Tropical Agriculture, 35 (January, 1958): 5.
[7] See Olin T. Mouzon, International Resources and National Policy. Harper and Bros., New York. 1959. Chap. 3, pp. 31-74, for an excellent presentation of U.S.D.A. and other data on farm production.

THE SHIFT FROM RURAL TO URBAN

The Movement of Population from Agricultural Production to Industrial Production

Push and Pull in Rural-Urban Migration

One of the consequences of increased agricultural productivity per capita has been a movement of the population from rural to urban areas. The need for fewer and fewer persons on the farm has resulted in a general decline in the relative cost of food and has freed millions of farm workers for more productive activities in industry, commerce and service. This movement from the farm to the city has not been entirely a push from the farm due to desperation, i.e., declining need for labor in order to satisfy production demands, but has in addition been a consequence of pull from what is conceived by some to be the very attractive city. It is unfortunate that some descriptions of what has been transpiring on a world, national and relatively local level have been influenced by the value position of the writer. Objective discussion of change has often been replaced by nostalgic references to a way of life that probably never existed.

The past 50 years have seen phenomenal change in the proportion of the population residing in urban areas.[8] The extent of this change is shown in Table 12.1.

Table 12.1. Urban Population of the World, Per Cent of Increase in Urban Population of the World and Per Cent of Increase in Total World Population: 1800-1950*

| Years | Population Living in Localities of 20,000 Inhabitants or More | | Total World Population |
	Per cent of world population	Per cent increase over previous period	Per cent increase over previous period
1800	2.4		
1850	4.3	132.3	29.2
1900	9.2	193.5	37.2
1950	20.9	239.6	49.3

*United Nations, *op. cit.*, Tables 1 and 2, p. 114.

[8]See Rose Hum Lee, The City. J. B. Lippincott Co., Chicago. 1955. Chapters 3-6. This text is unusual in its approach to urbanism and urbanization in that it places considerable emphasis on the international transformation from rural to urban.

The Consequences of Leaving the Farm for Those Who Leave

The transformation from rural to urban living has proceeded at an even more rapid pace in the United States. Within the United States it has varied from region to region.[9] This is a cause for some concern to many people, not the least of whom are the agricultural economists and sociologists.[10] Before we become too concerned about the move from the farm we ought to at least obtain some idea of the outcome — what are the persons who have moved doing for a living? How are they making out in their new environment?[11] Has the transition from rural to urban been more beneficial than harmful for the majority? Have they raised their level of living?[12] By 1956 the farm population of the United States was only about 13 per cent.[13] The transition from rural to urban is shown in Table 12.2.

[9] For a breakdown by geographical regions and a brief discussion of migration see Donald J. Bogue, Residential Mobility and Migration of Workers, in William Haberer, Frederick H. Harbison, Lawrence R. Klein, Gladys L. Palmer (eds.), Manpower in the United States. Harper & Bros., New York. 1954. Pp. 143-53. For detailed statistics see U.S.D.A., Farm Population: Estimates for 1955-1959. Agricultural Marketing Service, Washington, D.C. 1960.

[10] For a very carefully prepared analysis of changing patterns of agricultural production in the United States see: U.S.D.A., Family Farms in a Changing Economy. Agricultural Information Bulletin No. 171. U.S. Government Printing Office, Washington, D.C. 1957. P. 94.

[11] Extensive studies have not been made of the adjustment of persons moving from farms in recent years. Several studies have been made of particular groups but they do not enable us to answer the larger question. William H. Metzler, Socioeconomic Aspects of Manpower Adjustments: Low-Income Rural Areas. Rural Sociology, 24 (3, September, 1959): 226-35, stated in reference to migrants from rural to urban areas in West Virginia, "The habits and values of these people are a strong handicap in their adjustment to the responsibilities of urban life." Andrew W. Baird and Wilfred C. Bailey in Farmers Moving Out of Agriculture, (Mississippi State University Agricultural Experiment Station Bulletin 568, October, 1958) found that income went up for those who left farming in Mississippi. Howard W. Beers and Catherine Heflin in Rural People in the City (Kentucky Agricultural Experiment Station Bulletin 478, July, 1945) found that farm migrants to Lexington differed from those who had been reared in urban places in terms of ecological distribution, income and occupation.

[12] Baird and Bailey, op. cit., p. 5. Annual income: still farming = $541; left farming = $679. Also see Alvin L. Bertrand and Harold W. Osborne, Rural Industrialization in a Louisiana Community. Louisiana State University and Agricultural and Mechanical College Agricultural Bulletin No. 524. June, 1959. Pp. 30-32. Level of living increased for plant employees to a greater extent (110 per cent) than open-country respondents (75 per cent) between 1950 and 1957.

[13] Douglas G. Marshall, Wisconsin's Population: Changes and Prospects. Wisconsin Agricultural Experiment Station Bulletin 194. February, 1956. P. 4.

Table 12.2. Workers in Farm Occupations and Persons
in Urban Areas in the United States*

Year	Per Cent of All Workers in Farm Occupations	Per Cent of Population in Urban Areas
1820	71.8	7.2
1840	68.6	10.8
1860	58.9	19.8
1880	49.4	28.2
1900	37.5	39.7
1920	27.0	51.2
1940	17.1	56.5
1950	11.6	64.0 (59.4)**
1958	7.9†	

*U.S. Bureau of the Census, Statistical Abstracts of the
United States, 1953. U.S. Government Printing Office,
Washington, D.C., 1953. P. 184.
†Bureau of the Census, Annual Report on the Labor Force
— 1958, Current Population Reports. U.S. Government
Printing Office, Washington, D.C., 1959. P. 7.
**Old urban definition.

Changing Characteristics of the Production Unit

Farm Size and Way of Life

At the same time that farmers are leaving their farms, those
remaining in agriculture are increasing the size of their operation so that production is not reduced by any amount proportional
to the loss of producers. The average farm in Wisconsin, for example, increased from 113 acres in 1925 to 147 acres in 1954.[14]
What are the correlates of this change? Is one way of life being
replaced by another? About 75 per cent of Wisconsin's farms
were between 30 and 220 acres in 1954 and family operated.[15]
Has one way of life already replaced another as the media of
mass communication make it possible to share another way of
life without residential propinquity?[16] The latter position is a

---

[14] Marshall, op. cit., p. 34.
[15] Marshall, op. cit., p. 35.
[16] See C. C. Taylor, et al., Rural Life in the United States. Knopf, New York.
1949. Pp. 522-33. Taylor lists 14 trends of change in agriculture: 1) the lessening
of rural isolation; 2) commercialization of agriculture; 3) change from hoe farming
to mechanized farming; 4) change from folk beliefs and practices to the use of science; 5) shifting of processes from farms to factories; 6) loss of folk arts and skills;
7) increase in part-time farming; 8) decreasing proportion of population in rural
areas and on farms; 9) decline in agricultural ladder; 10) decline in the status of
hired farm labor; 11) rising levels and standards of living; 12) decreasing rural-
urban difference; 13) changing methods of obtaining security and 14) steady decline
in primary types of association.

popular one among sociologists.[17] The sociologist would hypothesize that television and Life magazine, for example, have brought
a different way of living further and further from the city, and
that change has been particularly rapid in recent years as a consequence. Not only are we interested in movement from farms
and its consequences, but even more specifically, the consequences of a rapid loss of farm population. This leads us into the
major concern of the paper, what is an acceptable rate of change
from rural to urban?

The Consequences for Existing Rural Institutions

Does movement away from the farm result in a rising per
capita cost of institutions and inferior institutional services in
rural areas? Is this in itself a cause for concern about movement from rural to urban areas at too rapid a pace? What are
the consequences of this movement in terms of level of living for
those remaining on farms? It is difficult to secure a direct answer to some of the questions that are raised in this paper. It is
necessary in seeking an answer to substitute data that point toward an answer rather than data that provide a definitive answer.[18]

Does the movement of people away from farms change the
composition of the farming population? Are the more or less
able persons drawn away by opportunities in the city?[19] What
are the consequences of this in terms of the dependency load
carried by the rural population? It is here that we can bring in

---

[17]See Evelyn M. Duvall and Annabelle B. Motz, Are Country Girls So Different?
Rural Sociology, 10 (September, 1945): 263-74; Howard W. Beers, Rural-Urban Differences: Some Evidence from Public Opinion Polls. Rural Sociology, 18 (March,
1953): 1-11; Otis Dudley Duncan, Gradients of Urban Influence on the Rural Population. Midwest Sociologist, 18 (Winter, 1956): 27-30.
[18]Marshall, op. cit., p. 39. Although the plight of the farmer is of much concern,
farm operator level of living has risen from 106 and 107 in 1930 and 1940 to 149 in
1950 and 155 in 1954.
[19]See C. T. Pihlblad and C. L. Gregory, Selective Aspects of Migration. American Sociological Review, 19 (June, 1954): 313-24. Persons migrating from rural to
urban areas average higher on I.Q. tests than those remaining. Also see Frederick
C. Fliegel, Aspirations of Low-Income Farmers and Their Performance and Potential for Change. Rural Sociology, 24 (3, September, 1959): 205-14. Migrants and
non-migrants varied in level of aspiration. Farm operators who were low in aspiration were favorably oriented toward farming. They tended to plan to stay in farming.
The study was conducted in Fayette County, Pennsylvania, June 1957.

an interesting parallel with migration from the farm and village in underdeveloped areas, but without the same consequences.[20]

The Most Desirable Cultural Milieu

Measuring Goodness of Milieu

Although rural-urban migration has been thought of in terms of a push from rural to urban areas in recent years, with the implicit notion that something very fine was being left, out of necessity, it is also possible to think in terms of the limited cultural opportunities in rural areas, limited medical facilities, limited recreational facilities, etc. The question of whether rural farm, rural nonfarm or urban life is best is not easily settled. How do we measure goodness of milieu? Thorndike and others have constructed scales that measure differences in milieu and have found that there is little correlation between size and goodness in cities.[21] Other studies have contrasted rural life with urban life.[22]

No Monopoly on Goodness for Rural Areas

The basic proposition for consideration is that farming is a way of life endowed with intrinsic good for the whole society. The

---

[20] One concern over the migration of the indigenous inhabitants of underdeveloped areas to mines and industry was the composition of the migrants. Since the younger and healthier young men in the village were drawn off out of proportion to their numbers and agriculture was not mechanized their loss tended to have direct consequences on the amount of food raised in the village. The dependency load of the village was increased, and nothing was done to increase the productivity of those remaining. Persons remaining on farms have had no difficulty in producing sufficient food for the needs of the country in the United States.

[21] E. L. Thorndike, Your City. Harcourt, Brace and Co., New York. 1939. Thorndike studies 310 cities in the United States. Three hundred items were measured in each and 37 were selected as being items characteristic of the goodness of cities. These were items on health, education, recreation, social and economic status, creature comfort and miscellaneous items. Good traits were associated with each other. There was little correlation between size and goodness scores but a city of 50,000 or more offered more specialized opportunities. Also see Paul B. Gillen, The Distribution of Occupations as a City Yardstick. Kings Crown Press, Columbia University, New York. 1951. P. 42. Gillen shows that occupational index based on the proportion of the population of a city employed in various activities from professional to labor does not vary with city size. In fact the greatest variability is within the smallest size category of cities.

[22] These questions are discussed at some length in T. Lynn Smith et al., Social Problems. Thomas Y. Cromwell, New York. 1955. Chap. 7, Rural Problems. Smith presents data from the United States Bureau of Agricultural Economics on ten different levels of living items. The more rural the county the poorer the showing that the county made. Figure 7.4, on page 191 is particularly pertinent in reference to the push vs. pull hypothesis of motivation to migrate.

question seems to be whether or not people are being pushed off the farms more rapidly than they would like to leave and that something precious is being lost as a consequence. Is something equally good being developed in the city in time to replace the valued cultural milieu of rural areas? Has the family farm been more than a means of making a living? Does rapid movement away from the family farm destroy a social situation that promoted thrift, patriotism, neighborliness, honesty, morality and respect for the law? Although the urbanization hypothesis of deviant behavior is widely accepted, it is an oversimplification of the process whereby deviant behavior develops. This is not the place for a detailed evaluation of the various competing explanations of deviant behavior but it must be noted that virtues alone are not generated on the farm any more than are vices the sole product of the city.

Are youth already defining the city as a more attractive place as a consequence of their contact with both rural and urban life styles?[23] Statistics indicate that fewer farms are operated by young farmers than formerly. Farm boys are now working off the farm part of the time; others are working off the farm as a regular means of livelihood, although perhaps continuing to live on the farm.[24]

We have previously made the point that man is not an economic man pure and simple, but there are values other than economic ones. Nevertheless, when discussing desirable rates of change we must remember that the change from country to the city and an industrial commercial life has already resulted in a higher level of living for the population in the United States. It is difficult to quarrel with change that results in a higher level of living, particularly when it cannot be demonstrated that undesirable costs and consequences necessarily follow.[25]

[23] Marshall, op. cit., p. 38. In 1920 over 25 per cent of the farms in Wisconsin were operated by men under 35 years of age, but by 1950 only 19 per cent were operated by men of this age category.

[24] Marshall, op. cit., p. 40. In 1930 slightly more than 8 per cent of the farm operators in Wisconsin were working off the farm but by 1954 20 per cent were working off the farm for 100 days or more per year. For a description of part-time farming in the United States and in Wisconsin see Glenn V. Fuguitt, What the Census Tells Us About Part-Time Farming in Wisconsin. Department of Rural Sociology, College of Agriculture, University of Wisconsin, Madison. 1959.

[25] Marshall, op. cit., pp. 43-45. The level of living of Wisconsin farmers has improved; the desire for improvement is probably a consequence of increased contacts between rural and urban dwellers. Also see Colin Clark, Conditions of Economic Progress. Macmillan, New York. 1952. Clark argues that economic efficiency and per capita income of a nation increase as the proportion of the working population in primary (agricultural) production decreases, and as the proportion of its workers in tertiary occupations (trade, the services and administrative jobs) increases. Clark found that the proportion of the gainfully employed in secondary industries (manufac-

URBANIZATION AND ITS RELATION
TO INDUSTRIALIZATION

International Nature of the Transition
to an Urban, Industrial Life

Urbanization More Rapid than Industrialization in Underdeveloped Areas

What we observe in the United States is an advanced stage of the change throughout the world to an industrial civilization with increasingly larger aggregates of people engaged in scientifically organized operations yielding a high degree of efficiency in production.[26] Table 12.3 shows the relationship of per cent of economically active males to per cent of population in cities and socio-economic development scores in various areas of the world.

Capital equipment, science and better organization replace manpower. The depopulation of rural areas is a sign of modernization according to Davis.[27]

Urbanization of U.S. and Other Developed Areas More Closely Related to Industrialization

But what if urbanization occurs more rapidly than industrialization? What are the consequences of urbanization proceeding at such a rate that employment is not immediately available? It is believed that urbanization is proceeding at too rapid a rate in some underdeveloped areas at present. When urbanization and industrialization in underdeveloped areas today are compared

turing) appears in the more advanced countries to rise to a point where its maximum level is reached and then recedes. It was about 26.4 per cent in the United States in 1920 and was in 1952 25.8 per cent. Also see Paul J. Jehlik and Ray E. Wakeley, Population Change and Net Migration in the North Central States, 1940-50. Iowa Agricultural Experiment Station Research Bulletin 430. July, 1955. P. 512: "Along with the reduction in number of farms and farm families, the decrease in rural population through migration, the increase in farm mechanization, the improvement of farm management practices, the increase in farm production and the market decrease in the use of hired labor, a substantial increase in average farm operator level of living took place in the North Central states."

[26] See James S. Slotkin, From Field to Factory. The Free Press, Glencoe, and the Research Center in Economic Development and Cultural Change, The University of Chicago. 1960. P. 156. This volume deals with the process of industrialization in underdeveloped and advanced areas, drawing a parallel between what might seem to be widely divergent situations but in which certain processes are in operation.

[27] Kingsley Davis and H. H. Golden, Urbanization and the Development of Pre-Industrial Areas. Economic Development and Cultural Change, 3 (October, 1954): 6-24.

Table 12.3. Per Cent of Economically Active Males Engaged in Agriculture,
Per Cent of Population in Cities and Development Scores by Continents

Areas	Economically Active Males Engaged in Agriculture*		Population in Cities*		Development Scores[†]	
	Per Cent	Rank	Per Cent	Rank	Per Cent	Rank
World	60		13			
North America	17	1	29	2	33.99	1
Oceania	35	2	41	1	30.06	3
Europe	38	3	21	3	31.62	2
U.S.S.R.	54	4	18	4-1/2	30.00	4
South America	62	5	18	4-1/2	24.28	5
Central America and Caribbean	69	6	12	6	23.65	6
Asia	70	7	8	7	20.36	7
Africa	78	8	6	8	19.03	8

*The data for males in agriculture and population in cities were taken from: Kingsley Davis and Hilda Hertz Golden, Urbanization and the Development of Pre-Industrial Areas. Economic Development and Cultural Change, 3 (October, 1954): 6-24.
[†]Lyle W. Shannon, Underdeveloped Areas. Harper and Bros., New York. P. 447. The scale score of each continent is determined by the scale score of each country within the continent, weighted by its population. There were 17 items in the scale. The items were indexes of production and indexes based on end-product data for around 1950. United Nations sources were used for the data. The scale is described in Chapter XIII of the volume.

with urbanization and industrialization in the United States at an earlier period, it appears that industrialization and urbanization in the United States were more highly correlated than they are in underdeveloped areas today.

Social Problems Attendant to Urbanization and Industrialization

Rapid Change Renders Traditional Controls Ineffective

The problems induced by urbanization that outstrips industrialization or other urban employment opportunities have been dealt with by sociologists and economists.[28] The breakdown of social controls, the absence of housing, inadequate water supplies, sanitary facilities, fire protection, police protection and other services have been described in connection with rapid urbanization in the United States and in underdeveloped areas.

[28] Report on the World Social Situation, op. cit., Chapters VII and VIII, pp. 111-92; G. A. Theodorson, Acceptance of Industrialization and its Attendant Consequences for Social Patterns of Non-Western Societies. American Sociological Review, 8 (No. 5, October, 1953): 477-84; Bert F. Hoselitz, The City, the Factory, and Economic Growth. American Economic Review, 45 (No. 2, May, 1955): 166-84; and C. Bauer, The Pattern of Urban and Economic Development; Social Implications. Annals of the American Academy of Political and Social Science, 305 (May, 1956): 60-69; Kingsley Davis and Ana Casis, Urbanization in Latin America. The Milbank Memorial Fund

The increase in deviant behavior, perceived to be attendant to rapid urbanization, and at least in part a real increase as a consequence of ineffectiveness of traditional social behavior, has been studied in the United States, Europe and now in underdeveloped areas. Urbanization outstripping industrialization simply transfers rural poverty to urban areas, it is said. Are the consequences of even this undesirable? Kingsley Davis doubts it.[29] It may even stimulate economic growth since the accumulation of people in the city represents a potential setting for industry. Davis argues that overurbanization has its limits and that movement to the city will fall off when opportunity is not present. On the other hand, the presence of large numbers of people who have not been integrated into the economic institution may be a stimulus to revolution and a new social system that it is believed will provide opportunity. Unfortunately it may not. There is great doubt as to whether there is any easy, painless course to economic development.

The question to which we return is whether or not people are leaving farms at a rate more rapid than they can be readily accommodated in the city. What is a desirable rate of change in terms of the acceptability of in-migrants into the urban economy? What are the crucial variables in determining rate of acceptance?

The Effect of Rapid Urbanization on the Labor Market

In underdeveloped areas the change from rural to urban took place at an exceedingly slow rate for many years — now the rate

(Footnote [28] continued)

Quarterly, 24 (April, 1946): 186-207. Several excerpts from Table II, Report on the World Social Situation, op. cit., p. 127, are shown below:

Urbanization and Structure of Employment

Country and Year	Per Cent of Population Living in Cities of 20,000 or More	Per Cent of Active Labor Force Employed in Manufacturing	Per Cent Active Labor Force in Agriculture
Egypt (1947)	29.1	5.5	62.8
Mexico (1950)	24.0	8.4	60.9
France (1946)	31.4	18.9	38.0
Sweden (1950)	34.5	28.7	20.5
United States (1950)	42.8	26.3	12.5

[29] Davis and Golden, op. cit., pp. 6-24.

has rapidly increased so that the most fantastic examples of urban growth are to be found in underdeveloped areas rather than in developed countries like the United States. This transformation from rural to urban occurred at a steadier rate and over a longer span of years in the developed countries.[30] The urban labor market in the United States, although it has had surpluses at times, has never been glutted with hoards of untrained industrial job seekers as in some underdeveloped areas.[31] The availability of employment opportunities for in-migrant laborers is without doubt a large factor in determining their acceptance. This is not to say that economic opportunity disposes of adjustment problems but that a needed group of in-migrant workers is more acceptable than a group who will become dependent due to their lack of employment.

The Problem of Value Assimilation Among In-migrant Labor

The degree to which in-migrant laborers are accepted on the urban scene is also determined to a considerable extent by their assimilation or failure to assimilate the dominant values of the urban society. Perhaps more crucial than assimilation of values, but usually following value assimilation, is observable behavior that is taken as evidence of value assimilation. Unlike in-migrant workers in underdeveloped countries, those in a developed country such as the United States probably have somewhat more stable and longer range goals. Their goals are less of a target nature than are the goals of new arrivals in underdeveloped areas.[32] Target buying has, of course, always been something of a problem among in-migrant laborers from the viewpoint of middle-class persons whose values culminate in a quite different rank-ordering of expenditures. The social worker has viewed lower-class spending in much the same way and has

[30] For a recent text dealing quite extensively with world urbanism see Nels Anderson, The Urban Community: A World Perspective. Henry Holt and Co., New York. 1959.

[31] See M. B. Deshmukh, Study of Floating Migration, Delhi. In: The Social Implications of Industrialization and Urbanization. UNESCO Research Center, Calcutta. 1956. P. 150.

[32] See E. E. Hoyt, Want Development in Underdeveloped Areas. The Journal of Political Economy, 59 (No. 3, June, 1951): 194-202; S. D. Neumark, Some Economic Development Problems of African Agriculture. Journal of Farm Economics, 41 (No. 1, February, 1959): 43-50; A. Curle, Incentives to Work. Human Relations, 2 (No. 1, 1949): 41-47; E. E. Hoyt, The Needs of East African Workers. Human Organization, 11 (No. 2, Summer, 1952): 27-28; E. E. Hoyt, The Impact of a Money Economy on Consumption Patterns. Annals of the American Academy of Political and Social Science, 305 (May, 1956): 12-22.

been critical of the in-migrant laborer who purchases television and a car before properly feeding and clothing his children. This is a pattern of buying that we have encountered in an on-going study of value assimilation among in-migrant Mexican-American workers in two communities presently being studied with the support of the National Institutes of Mental Health and the Urban Research Committee of the University of Wisconsin. The problem of value assimilation and behavioral change constitutes a major part of our concern over the adjustment of the rural dweller, or the in-migrant worker who has moved to the city.

The Transitory Nature of Urban Problems

It is frequently contended that the individualism of the former rural dweller makes it difficult for him to adjust to the city, that industrialization is a dehumanizing process that robs him of his individualism. While this is true in some respects, freedoms are acquired that he has never before known. Some of the so-called dehumanizing of the industrial society is probably not a necessary characteristic of it but only a transitory characteristic of some specific institution that has not yet completed its development in the urban setting.[33]

The basic problem of change from rural to urban, from farm to factory, has been presented with a brief discussion of some of the costs and consequences. What we observe in the United States is part of a greater long-term cycle that will eventually culminate in world urbanism. Even those who remain in the production of foodstuffs will maximize their return with the products of an industrial order based on scientific research.

DETERMINING THE DESIRABLE RATE OF CHANGE

Gains and Losses as a Consequence of Change

What Problems Do We Desire to Avoid in the Host Community?

Here we are concerned with what is the desirable or optimum rate of change. How fast should the transition take place?

---

[33] Yale Brozen, Technological Change, Ideology and Productivity. Political Science Quarterly, 70 (No. 4, December, 1955): 522-42. Brozen deals with overspecialization, centralization and loss of initiative and efficiency in some industrial organizations.

Although some of the consequences of rapid urbanization have been described, we have not specified which consequences should be avoided. The role of the scientist is one of describing costs and consequences rather than specifying goals. Therefore, it is more appropriate that mention be made of a number of consider- ations that may be important to the public and their policy makers in determining what is an acceptable rate of change.

Taking the role of the citizen, are we concerned about the consequences of a rapid influx of untrained rustics? If so, are we willing to train persons now in the category of inefficient farm producers so that they will become desirable additions to the urban labor force? This assumes that inefficient farm producers are trainable, and it may well be an incorrect assumption in some cases. The rate and extent to which people may be trained be- comes a factor in deciding what is a desirable rate of change.

Are we concerned about the number who can be housed in ex- isting facilities and for which fire, sewer, water, telephone and other services and facilities are available? Is pressure on ex- isting facilities desirable as a stimulus to enlargement, modern- ization and expansion of industrial and service activities? If this is the case, some short-run dislocation may have long-run con- sequences of a great value. The ability of a community to expand services and facilities is tied in with the question of capital sup- ply, and this may become a determinant of desirable rate of change.

Are we concerned about the number of in-migrants for whom immediate employment will be available, considering the rate of investment in new productive facilities in the United States? Is population concentration sufficient stimulus to the investment of unproductive capital in such ways that the level of living will rise? If so, a certain amount of unemployment may not be too serious a problem in the long run.

What Do We Desire to Avoid Losing as a Consequence of Rural Depopulation?

What effect does rapid urbanization have on the rural commu- nity? Does the declining farm population mean a rising per capita cost of basic institutional services in rural areas so that a bad situation becomes worse? While it might seem that rural areas educate children for a lifetime of gainful labor in the city with nothing received in return, leaving the farm to become a producer of finished goods and consumer of farm products may just about balance out the relationship. How much worse off would the farm community be if the out-migrant stayed to share farm income? [34] Whatever the effects of depopulation, the question is one of which alternative has the fewest undesirable consequences, as the public defines them.

Do we believe that rural life is an important source of the virtues in our society? Is there evidence that the culture of our society, or at least some aspect of it is preserved in a rural setting to a greater extent than in the urban setting? Do we accept differential rates of official delinquency, crime and other forms of deviant behavior as evidence of the superiority of rural life from some viewpoints? [35]

What is to be Gained as a Consequence of the Rural-Urban Transformation?

How important is it that modern medicine be made available to everyone, and how soon do we wish to accomplish this goal? One study has shown that only 1 per cent of the children in large metropolitan counties do not have medical services in elementary schools, 6 per cent in lesser metropolitan counties, 32 per cent in counties adjacent to metropolitan counties, 36 per cent in isolated semi-rural counties, and 61 per cent in isolated rural counties. [36]

If this contrast in availability of medical services is not considered appropriate, any one of many other sets of data are available to show differences in medical care on a basis of the proximity of an area to an urban center. To make a really stark contrast in terms of the healthfulness of people in an urban industrial society, as contrasted to rural subsistence society, we have only to turn to underdeveloped areas.

In a study of labor productivity in the Belgian Congo the physical condition of workers from the Mayumbe, Tshuapa and Middle Kwilu districts was described as follows upon their arrival from tribal areas: [37]

[34] This problem is presented in some detail in John F. Cuber, Robert A. Harper and William F. Kenkel, Problems of American Society: Values in Conflict. Henry Holt and Co., New York. 1956. Chapter 18.

[35] For a discussion of this point see: Marshall B. Clinard, The Sociology of Deviant Behavior. Rinehart and Co., New York. 1957. Chapter 3; Clinard, The Process of Urbanization and Criminal Behavior. American Journal of Sociology, 48 (September, 1942): 202-13; Arnold Rose, Theory and Methods in the Social Sciences. University of Minnesota Press, Minneapolis. 1954. Pp. 25-49.

[36] Annual Report, Federal Security Agency, Office of Education, 1949, p. 33, quoted in William E. Cole, Urban Society. Houghton Mifflin Co., Boston. 1958. Pp. 103-21.

[37] P. de Briey, The Productivity of African Labour. International Labour Review, 72 (Nos. 2-3, August-September, 1955): 6-7.

1. they all suffer from parasitic worms of the intestines
2. some suffer from parasitic worms of the blood
3. all have malaria
4. all have incipient yaws, for which they have received little or no treatment
5. most have or have had gonorrhoea
6. many have syphilis
7. some of these conditions reduce their haemoglobin level, which in many cases is as low as 65 per cent, a red blood count of 3 to 3-1/2 million.

Moreover, it was stated that this picture is generally true for all of Africa, although the specific diseases vary.

The contrast between rural and urban in terms of mortality has always favored rural areas in the United States due to the prevalence of communicable diseases and the problem of water supply and sanitation. In more recent years public health measures and the development of specialized medicine in urban areas have resulted in a rapid decrease in death rates in urban areas. Urban death rates in urban industrial states are now lower than rural death rates in the same area.[38]

Goals and Values as Determinants
of the Desirable Rate of Change

When is the Existing Social Structure Disrupted by In-migration?

How important is the problem of value assimilation? We have stated that the community may define unassimilated migrants as a problem because their behavior conflicts with middle-class norms in the larger society. The problem of assimilating midwestern commercial farmers is probably small in comparison to that of assimilating subsistence farmers because urban, industrial values are more readily acceptable to the former than the latter. The midwestern commercial farmer has become urban in his outlook in many respects, in contrast to the subsistence farmer found in mountainous or semi-mountainous states and the northern cutover areas. The values of the subsistence farmer stress getting along, making do with what you have, as contrasted with managerial skill, emphasis on production and a higher level of aspiration. William H. Metzler has contrasted the values of the subsistence and commercial farmers in some

---

[38] Dorothy G. Wiehl, Mortality and Socio-Environmental Factors. The Milbank Memorial Fund Quarterly, 26 (October, 1948): 335-65.

detail and concludes that the habits and values of subsistence
farmers are a great handicap in their adjustment to urban life.[39]
Unfortunately, there is no standard by which we can judge the
rate at which communities can accept in-migrant workers in reference to the various criteria mentioned. It is the same with migrants and their families in urban areas in underdeveloped countries. A few in-migrants or gradual in-migration does little to
upset the existing social structure; rapid in-migration of large
numbers of persons creates problems, particularly when employment is scarce and community facilities are strained. No one
has determined how much in-migration can be accepted without
some disruption of established relationships, of existing ways of
dealing with human adjustment problems, or of the traditional
status structure of the community. Most sociologists will agree
that gradual in-migration presents no problem, but at what point
and at what rate does the changing proportion of in-migrants
make for what kinds of problems? We cannot yet do more than
speculate about this.

The Necessity of Specifying Goals

If our single goal is to stimulate change, then a high rate of
in-migration to urban areas is desirable. If we, i.e., the public
and its policy makers, believe that cities are already beset with
problems and desire to hold new problems to a minimum, then a
low rate of in-migration would be the safest course. A desirable
rate of change cannot be specified without knowledge of the goals
towards which we are struggling.

This is just as pertinent in the transformation of the world's
economy from a rural subsistence type to an urban industrial and
commercial type as it is in the changing economy of the United
States. On the international level there are political considerations as well as strictly humanitarian considerations. The same
is true for the present farm problem of the United States.

The question of whose welfare we are trying to maximize, if
anyone's, is important in consideration of a desirable rate of
change. Is our goal to bring surplus rural dwellers into urban
areas as rapidly as possible on the assumption that this will maximize their welfare? If so, how do we avoid such an undesirable

---

[39] William H. Metzler, Socio-economic Aspects of Manpower Adjustments: Low-
Income Rural Areas. Rural Sociology, 24 (No. 3, September, 1959): 226-35. Also
see Basil G. Zimmer, Participation of Migrants in Urban Structures. American
Sociological Review, 20 (April, 1955): 218-24.

reaction in the host community that acceptance and assimilation of the in-migrants will be difficult? If we are primarily interested in the welfare of city dwellers, then we must ask which alternative will be most expensive for them in various kinds of costs. Would they rather take care of the surplus farm population in the country through some form of subsidy, or would they rather bear the cost through increased institutional expenditures in urban communities where the new worker may not make an immediate contribution to the economy?

Is there such a thing as the general welfare, or are there only subcategories of general welfare with various groups jostling for position in order to maximize their own gain, their proportion of the fruits of production?

Perhaps nothing should be done. There is some evidence to indicate that those farmers who are economically motivated are already looking to nonfarm employment for better opportunities.[40]

The question of timing must be considered when attempting to determine what is the optimum or desirable rate of change. How urgent is the need for bringing a group into the commercial, industrial economy? What will be the consequences of gradually integrating people into the economy as contrasted to action designed to facilitate immediate movement from one sector of the economy to another?

The Weight of Values in Determining Policy

What kinds of costs, social or economic, are we willing to pay, and what kinds of costs do we wish to avoid in the process of transforming the national and world economy?

Although we have mentioned human values previously in this paper, we have not emphasized the fact that human values may be one of the most crucial determinants of what is a desirable or optimum rate of change. It may well be that the family farm as a value, as an end and a means, will hold people on the farm past the time that such activities can be justified from an economic standpoint. The desirable rate of change may be that rate which is acceptable to both the farm population and to the larger population.

It may well be that a rate of change dictated by economic considerations alone is too rapid and that change must come more slowly. Perhaps the most economic rate is not the desirable rate to even urban dwellers.

---

[40] Fliegel, op. cit., pp. 205-14.

If means and ends are not differentiated in rural areas, and we seem to have such a situation, a certain proportion of rural dwellers have no intention of moving to the village or the city. Their daily labors are an end in themselves as well as a means. An optimum or desirable rate of change is no change at all from their viewpoint.

There are, of course, regional variations in farming and in the attitude of farmers toward their activities.

When considering what is a desirable rate of change we must balance the social and economic costs of changing against the social and economic costs of not changing. Since costs are determined by values and values vary from group to group, it is not possible to talk of what is a desirable rate of change unless we are told which group is assessing the desirability of a particular rate of change.

If the rate of change is to be controlled, that in itself is a cost of change, for it implies that direct or indirect restraints or incentives will be employed.

CONCLUSION

The Desirable Rate of Change Is the Acceptable Rate of Change

The Desirability of a Grass-Roots Approach

It could be concluded that the desirable rate of change is one that is acceptable to people directly affected — in other words, the decision to leave rural life, to be consistent with values held by many persons in our culture, should be made by the farmer and should be one that he makes with the idea of maximizing his level of living, rather than in response to coercion.

This is not to say that change cannot be speeded up by pertinent action, but simply that coercive economic or political action is not the answer. Much the same can be said in reference to underdeveloped areas. The difference is that coercion does not seem consistent with the value system within which American farmers operate, and it is difficult to control their behavior in this fashion. On the other hand, there are social systems in other cultural and subcultural areas of the world where independence of action has not been such an important part of the value system and where a certain amount of coercion may be effective. Knowledge of the culture is crucial, and it is probably true that our technical assistance programs have had some failures because we had little or no knowledge of what approach would be consistent with the culture in which it was desired to bring about certain changes.

Misuse of the Concept of Cultural Relativity

It should be noted that the concept of cultural relativity has come in for a considerable amount of misuse by those who accept cultural differences as almost insurmountable obstacles to change. It is one thing to be aware of cultural differences and the necessity of taking them into consideration in planning for change, but it is quite another thing to accept cultural differences as barriers to action.[41] Differences in subcultural groups and differences in goals and values on a rural-urban basis make for difficulties in implementing change but do not preclude efforts along these lines. The important thing is to have an awareness of cultural differences, differences in goals and values, at the time that change is being planned.

Pulling vs. Pushing from Rural to Urban

Making a Move from the Farm Attractive

Since the entire problem of change, as framed herein, is related to a decline in farm income or a desire for greater income on the part of persons in the agricultural sector of the economy, the possibility of increasing income through nonfarm activities might be a way of accelerating change. In this case, new horizons, or ways of reaching the goal of a higher income, are presented to the farmer so that he will be pulled from the farm at a rate acceptable to him rather than pushed at a rate that makes him resentful.

In areas where farm activities have for a considerable period of time been supplemented by nonfarm activities, the first step has been taken and change can proceed at a more rapid rate without various types of dislocation.

---

[41] This point has been developed more fully by Chester L. Hunt, Cultural Barriers to Point Four. The Antioch Review, 14 (Summer, 1954): 159-67; and Frank E. Hartung, Cultural Relativity and Moral Judgments. Philosophy of Science, 21 (No. 2): 118-26. Paris. 1954.

Defining Industrial Employment as Attractive

The same may be said for underdeveloped areas. Change will come about more rapidly when the indigenous inhabitants have come to define the fruits of industrial work as highly desirable. This means that unless motivations are entirely target in nature the framework of mind conducive to urban or industrial employment is present when desires expand. When a higher level of living is demanded by either rural dwellers in the United States or the indigenous inhabitants of underdeveloped areas, they will take such action as appears to lead them toward the higher level of living as long as they are not required to engage in behavior that is inconsistent with values that are of even more importance to them than their level of living.

A desirable rate of change in the United States, taking democratic values into consideration, is one that derives from the attraction of the city rather than from a coercive push away from what is still valued.

This paper has suggested a wide variety of factors that must be taken into consideration in determining what is a desirable rate of change from rural to urban.

The economist and sociologist cannot tell you exactly what rate of change is desirable without a catalog of national values and the costs and consequences of trying to maximize them for each of various subcategories of the population.

BIBLIOGRAPHY

Bulletins

BAIRD, A. W. and BAILEY, W. C. Farmers Moving Out of Agriculture. Miss. Agr. Exp. Sta. Bul. 568, Oct., 1958.

BEERS, H. W. and HEFLIN, C. Rural People in the City. Ky. Agr. Exp. Sta. Bul. 478, July, 1945.

BERTRAND, A. L. and OSBORNE, H. W. Rural Industrialization in a Louisiana Community. La. Agr. Exp. Sta. Bul. 524, June, 1959.

FUGUITT, G. V. What the Census Tells Us About Part-time Farming in Wisconsin. Dept. of Rural Soc., Col. of Agr., Madison, 1959.

JEHLIK, P. J. and WAKELEY, R. E. Population Change and Net Migration in the North Central States, 1940-50. Iowa Agr. Exp. Sta. Res. Bul. 430, July, 1955.

MARSHALL, D. G. Wisconsin's Population: Changes and Prospects. Wis. Agr. Exp. Sta. Bul. 194, Feb., 1956.

U. S. BUREAU OF THE CENSUS. Annual Report on the Labor Force — 1958, Current Population Reports. U. S. Govt. Printing Office, Washington, 1959.

U. S. DEPT. OF AGRICULTURE. Farm Population: Estimates for 1955-59. Agr. Mktg. Ser., Washington, 1960.

——. Family Farms in a Changing Economy. Agr. Info. Bul. No. 171, U. S. Govt. Printing Office, Washington, 1957.

Books

ANDERSON, N. The Urban Community: A World Perspective. Henry Holt and Co., New York, 1959.

BOGUE, D. J. Residential Mobility and Migration of Workers. Chap. XI, Manpower in the United States. W. Haberer, F. H. Harbison, L. R. Klein, G. L. Palmer (ed.). Harper & Bros., New York, 1954.

CLARK, C. Conditions of Economic Progress. The Macmillan Co., New York, 1952.

COLE, W. E. Urban Society. Houghton Mifflin Co., Boston, 1958.

CUBER, J. F., HARPER, R. A., and KENKEL, W. F. Problems of American Society: Values in Conflict. Henry Holt and Co., New York, 1956.

DESHMUKH, M. B. Study of Floating Migration, Delhi. In: The Social Implications of Industrialization and Urbanization. Calcutta, UNESCO Research Center, 1956.

GILLEN, P. B. The Distribution of Occupations as a City Yardstick. Kings Crown Press, New York, Columbia University, 1951.

LEE, R. H. The City. J. B. Lippincott Co., Chicago, 1955.

MOUZON, O. T. International Resources and National Policy. Harper & Bros., New York, 1959.

SHANNON, L. W. Underdeveloped Areas. Harper & Bros., New York, 1957.

SLOTKIN, J. S. From Field to Factory. The Free Press and the Research Center in Economic Development and Cultural Change, the University of Chicago, Glencoe, 1960.

SMITH, T. L. AND ASSOCIATES. Social Problems. Thomas Y. Crowell, New York, 1955.

TAYLOR, C. C. et al. Rural Life in the United States. Knopf, New York, 1949.

THORNDIKE, E. L. Your City. Harcourt, Brace and Co., New
    York, 1939.
UNITED NATIONS. Report on the World Social Situation. United
    Nations, New York, 1957.
U.S. BUREAU OF THE CENSUS. Statistical Abstracts of the
    United States; 1953. U.S. Govt. Printing Office, Washington,
    1953.

Journals

BAUER, C. The pattern of urban and economic development:
    social implications. Annals of the American Academy of Po-
    litical and Social Science. 305:60-69. 1956.
BEERS, H. W. Rural-urban differences: some evidence from
    public opinion polls. Rural Sociology. 18:1-11. 1953.
BROZEN, Y. Technological change, ideology and productivity.
    Political Science Quarterly. 30:522-42. 1955.
CURLE, A. Incentives to work. Human Relations. 2:41-47.
    1949.
DAVIS, K. and GOLDEN, H. H. Urbanization and the develop-
    ment of pre-industrial areas. Economic Development and
    Cultural Change. 3:6-26. 1954.
—— and CASIS, A. Urbanization in Latin America. The Milbank
    Memorial Fund Quarterly. 24:186-207. 1946.
DE BRIEY, P. The productivity of African labour. International
    Labour Review. 72:6-7. 1949.
DUNCAN, O. D. Gradients of urban influence on the rural popu-
    lation. Midwest Sociologist. 18:27-30. 1956.
DUVALL, E. M. and MOTZ, A. B. Are country girls so differ-
    ent? Rural Sociology. 10:263-74. 1945.
FARNSWORTH, H. C. Imbalance in the world wheat economy.
    The Journal of Political Economy. 66:1-23. 1958.
FLIEGEL, F. C. Aspirations of low-income farmers and their
    performance and potential for change. Rural Sociology. 24:
    205-14. 1959.
HARTUNG, F. E. Cultural relativity and moral judgments.
    Philosophy of Science. 21:118-26. 1954.
HOSELITZ, B. F. The city, the factory, and economic growth.
    American Economic Review. 45:116-84. 1955.
HOYT, E. E. The needs of east African workers. Human Or-
    ganization. 11:27-28. 1952.
——. Want development in underdeveloped areas. The Journal of
    Political Economy. 59:194-202. 1951.

284   LYLE W. SHANNON

HOYT, E. E. The impact of a money economy on consumption patterns. Annals of the American Academy of Political and Social Sciences. 305:12-22. 1956.

HUNT, C. L. Cultural barriers to Point Four. The Antioch Review. 14:159-67. 1954.

METZLER, W. H. Socio-economic aspects of manpower adjustments: low-income rural areas. Rural Sociology. 24:226-35. 1959.

MIRACLE, M. P. Maize in tropical African agriculture. Tropical Agriculture. 35:5. 1958.

NEUMARK, S. D. Some economic development problems of African agriculture. Journal of Farm Economics. 41:43-50. 1959.

PIHLBLAD, C. T. and GREGORY, C. L. Selective aspects of migration. American Sociological Review. 19:313-24. 1954.

THEODORSON, G. A. Acceptance of industrialization and its attendant consequences for social patterns of non-western societies. American Sociological Review. 8:477-84. 1953.

WIEHL, D. G. Mortality and socio-environmental factors. The Milbank Memorial Fund Quarterly. 26:335-65. 1948.

ZIMMER, B. G. Participation of migrants in urban structures. American Sociological Review. 20:218-24. 1955.

GEORGE K. BRINEGAR

University of Connecticut

Discussion

THE MAJOR PROBLEM that had to be faced by Shannon in his chapter, and by the writer as a discussant, was that of figuring out how to talk sense about acceptable rates of change. It is, of course, impossible to talk about a rate of change, period. We can only talk about rates of change in something — economic growth, productivity, employment, defined values and other specifics. Shannon solved this problem, and appropriately, for purposes of his present chapter, by centering attention on increasing agricultural productivity, and the effects of migration from rural to urban areas. He concludes by stating:

"The economist and sociologist cannot tell you exactly what rate of change is desirable without a catalog of national values and the costs and consequences of trying to maximize them for each of various subcategories of the population."

This writer's criticism of this chapter, and he assumes the major function of a discussant is to criticize, is not of what Shannon has said but of what he has left unsaid. More specifically, his chapter offers little help to persons interested in coming up with guess-estimates of whether current rates of change in agricultural productivity are too high or too low. The writer had hoped to get a picture of Shannon's answer, with its rationale rather than only a rationale which suggests it would be nice if we knew everything.

The writer therefore proposes to attempt to get hold of this problem of evaluating the appropriateness of the present rate of increase in agricultural productivity by centering attention first on the notion of progress and second on the notion of balance among various rates of change.

THE NOTION OF PROGRESS

The notion of progress is fairly new in the history of thought and perhaps not as widely assumed to be a meaningful concept — certainly not as an inevitable trend — as in the past. Be this as it may, we must act as if we knew the answers to the problems centering around this notion of progress. Our alternatives in the final analysis are to assume that (1) progress exists or it does not, and (2) if it does exist we can identify it and affect its rate or we can't, and (3) lastly if it exists it is either good or bad. While we can not answer these questions a criterion is available for choosing which answer to assume as correct. Choice among possible answers can be made on the basis of asking what the costs are of making a mistake in picking an answer to assume as correct. The logic of choice in this type of situation is to trace out the secondary effects of choice among answers, first on the assumption the right answer was selected and second, on the assumption the wrong answer was selected. Without presenting the details of this procedure, I simply state that the answer flowing from this process is to act as if progress is possible, that it can be identified and its rate affected, and that it is good.

If it is granted that it makes sense to act as if progress is good and can be speeded by our behavior we must face the problem of what to do. This we do by looking at the problem of balance.

THE NOTION OF BALANCE AMONG RATES OF CHANGE

The notion of balance in rates of change can serve a useful role in the identification and selection of alternatives. In fact, it can be argued that the only thing wrong with progress is that it is uneven in the sense that one rate of change outruns another or to say the same thing in other words, that one rate of change lags behind another.

The major emphasis of most papers on the subject of progress or on its components such as productivity, etc., is on the relationships of one set of changes or rates of change with another. Thus, such questions arise as to whether agricultural productivity is increasing at too fast a rate compared with the demand for food, the outward mobility of rural people, the ability of the nonfarm community to accommodate the recent arrivals, the ability of the rural community from which they left to adjust. This type of balance can be looked upon as if one rate of change is too great or as if another rate of change is too low – in fact, these are the same problem.

Given the observation that one rate of change is too high – compared with others – we have the choices of speeding other rates of change or of slowing the rate of change that was found to be too fast. How is choice made? If the only problem of concern was that of balance the choice would be made on the basis of which in some sense was the least difficult. However, if we have decided to act as if progress is both possible and good the first choice is to·speed the lagging rates of change. To go further with the problem of making choices to speed or to retard rates of change in order to obtain balance it will be helpful to turn to specifics. Let us use productivity in agriculture.

We shall assume that the rate of increase in productivity in agriculture has outrun many of the other components that fit together in determining the extent to which balance exists. Before asking which of these components should be altered it will be useful to first ask why productivity in agriculture has been increasing as fast as it has.

The major causal factor bringing about increases in the productivity of agriculture appears to be the accumulation and application of knowledge. Thus, the cause of the agricultural productivity problem is in terms of most peoples' values, an end, as well as a means, to increases in efficiency and higher levels of living. To get at the cause of the high rate of increase in productivity in agriculture would require that the rate of knowledge accumulation be slowed and/or that people be prevented from using existing knowledge. The extent to which the accumulation of knowledge can be slowed as a means of decreasing the rate of increase in productivity is nominal for short time periods of 20 to 30 years. A moratorium on new knowledge accumulation would be unlikely to produce any significant effects on agricultural surplus in this generation — if existing knowledge were applied, productivity in agriculture would still continue to increase for many years. The second choice is to make it impossible for people to apply existing knowledge and to thus slow down the rate or even to reverse the trend in agricultural productivity. A number of techniques are possible, though none seem to be especially happy choices. For example, a major depression would aid greatly, a tight rationing of any or several inputs such as land, fertilizer, seed or labor would help as would a halving or more of output prices. Since these alternatives used singly leave much to be desired, it is appropriate to look at other possible choices.

A second group of choices is encompassed in the rates of change that are too slow in relation to the rate of increase in productivity in agriculture. These may be grouped, as is customary by economists, into items affecting supply or inputs and demand or outputs. On the demand side there exists the whole array of measures that could be adopted to increase the demand for food, which, while not without some hope, especially in the foreign trade area, do not seem to offer more than modest contributions to bringing about a balance between productivity increases in agriculture and the other relevant components. On the supply or input side, an array of techniques are also available that can be used in bringing about balance, though again there are no simple ways to manipulate the rate of change of a single variable to bring about, in an acceptable way, an appropriate balance. In sorting out these alternatives, however, we find that a speeding of a number of existing rates of change would contribute to bringing about the desired over-all balance.

In the so-called second group of changes that might be introduced to bring about balance with the level and rate of change in agricultural productivity it becomes possible to look for small changes at the margin, as well as for "major" reforms. An inspection process of this sort is eclectic in the sense that any changes that may aid in the catching up process — with the rate of increase in the productivity of agriculture — become possibilities worth examination. Moreover, such an investigation might reveal that the cause of the imbalance — too high a rate of increase in agricultural productivity — should be speeded. For example, suppose the costs of producing food and fiber were to be reduced another 25 or 50 per cent in the next few years; this might be the answer to how the United States might become a major supplier of food to the rest of the world.

THE AVOIDANCE OF MAJOR VALUE CONFLICTS

When the observation of an "excessive" rate of change in productivity is put in its proper place by concentrating on the complementary rates of change that are lagging, the possibility of
avoiding major value conflicts and of muddling through is enor-
mously increased for several reasons. First, the number of variables with which appropriate balances can be reached are usually great, and they can usually be used in combination. By the
manipulation of several variables by small amounts, rather than
concentrating on a single variable, the impacts of the adjustment
process are diffused. Moreover, since different people have different values the complete adjustment may be brought about
through a series of acts in no way inconsistent with the values of
the specific people directly involved. Further, the value conflicts
in agriculture, in general, do not appear to be moral absolutes
but rather centered on notions of equity, fair play, etc. — thus, the
quantitative aspects are of great importance.

Let us pause for a moment and ask how well does existing
agricultural policy square with bringing about the adjustments
needed in relation to the existing rate of increase in agricultural
productivity. The quick answer is, probably, better than one
would think at first blush. The extent to which appropriate adjustments have been made in terms of labor mobility, etc., are
impressive as Shannon has so well pointed out in his paper. That
the investment of capital in people is becoming recognized more
widely as a central problem is encouraging. The great variation
in our agricultural programs, with all their contradictions, is
encouraging in that, at worst, only a number of little mistakes
are being made. The extent of excessive production in agriculture is small — some 8 per cent — in comparison with other sectors of the economy when account is taken of excess capacity.

The above is not intended to argue this is the best of all
worlds. On the contrary, we are failing to bring about the many
possible and desirable "little" adjustments that are needed if we
are to catch up with the output of knowledge that has been bringing about the rapid rates of increase in agricultural productivity.
The costs of not catching up are lost alternatives, not retrogres-
sion, which means the direction of change is correct — we just
are not moving fast enough in exploiting the opportunities for
change we see about us. This in a large measure comes from
confusing the things that can be treated as variables with the
things to be treated as constants. Thus, we should take off our
blinders.

SUMMARY

If the notion is accepted that it is desirable to decide to act as if progress is good and that it can be speeded by the use of our heads, the observation of a rate of change that is too high points to the problem of finding ways of speeding complementary rates of change in order, so to speak, to catch up. If it is found that a catching up is impossible one may be forced to conclude that the excessive rate of change disturbing the balance must be slowed, though such a conclusion, if correct, is highly unlikely.

If we look at agriculture in the United States today, does it make more sense to conclude that the rate of increase in productivity should be slowed or that other rates of change should be increased or is it possible that increasing the productivity in agriculture will open up new opportunities? The writer's own judgment is that the things that need to be changed are the lagging rates of change as well as to increase the rate of change in productivity in agriculture. If this diagnosis is correct, the future is in the hands of the groups that assume the diagnosis is correct. If the diagnosis is incorrect, there is no hope for the future anyway, and little is lost.

Let me recognize that my conclusions flow from value judgments as well as what have been presumed to be the facts.

CONCLUSIONS

My conclusions, or were they my initial starting points, concern two matters: (1) how to think about rates of change, and (2) a guess-estimate of the appropriateness of the rate of increase in productivity in agriculture.

In thinking about rates of change of the type under examination here, the writer thinks we need to focus on how little we need to know to make our behavior more effective rather than how much would we like to know to make sure we are correct. Put in other words the best we can do is to try to learn to live with our ignorance rather than to eliminate it. If we are willing to take as given the notion that knowledge in the sciences is good we must accept the by-products of this knowledge — increase in productivity. It then follows that changes will occur which will upset past balances. Thus we have the opportunity to look for methods to speed up the lagging rates of change and in the interval to take measures that will shift the impact of imbalance among various groups in such ways as seem expedient and reasonable.

On a guess-estimate of the facts, I reach the conclusion that

the rate of increase in productivity in agriculture is not to be deplored or slowed but rather that major efforts should be made to
speed lagging rates of change, to increase the productivity of
agriculture and to adopt measures that will redistribute among
people the gains and losses that result from increases in productivity, etc.

   This writer is not impressed with the fact that we don't know
exactly what to do or how to do it. He is impressed with the fact
that people seem to be able to deal effectively with specific acute
problems when they are willing to meet them head on. The alternative of caution in a competitive world has no survival value.
This is not to argue that this new experiment of people, to use
their heads and live by reason, will be successful — at this point
in history all peoples are committed to the notion, and the only
variable is in the degree to which people attempt to speed the
rate of progress in all of its components, one of which is productivity in agriculture. Let's get on with the experiment of knowledge accumulation and its application and see how it turns out —
every new page of this history seems more exciting.

   These conclusions that I reach, and I'm sure you will agree,
were necessarily developed on the basis of little knowledge.

Chapter 13

LAUREN SOTH

Des Moines Register and Tribune

Acceptable
Farm Policies

T HE TITLE GIVEN ME for this chapter leads to the question, "Acceptable to whom?" Farmers? Consumers? Processors? Retailers? Exporters? Importers? Our partners and allies in other countries? All these "publics" or "interests," as well as others that might be listed, are concerned with the national farm policies of the United States. Each interest group in some measure sets a limit on public policy affecting agriculture.

A farm policy that required public ownership of packing plants clearly would be out of the question in America. But on a more subtle level, any policy affecting the supply of livestock must reckon with the interest of the meat packing industry.

Developing farm policies broadly acceptable to every group from the large meat packing firms to the farm organizations which want to establish tight control over farm production is a towering political task. But it is the method of democratic government to try to reconcile the conflicting interests. An acceptable policy probably will not really please anyone; it will be the least common denominator — the solution tolerable to all. Such a policy must avoid the extremes. It represents compromise. It is the "art of the possible."

In examining what farm policies are acceptable, or possible, in the United States in the 1960's, it will be useful to look first at the nonfarm interests which have a voice in policy. What are the limits on farm policies established by interest groups outside agriculture?

I

Farm people and their leaders are inclined to think of the nonfarm interest in agricultural policy as primarily a concern about food prices. They believe the resistance to policies which would raise farm income stems from this consumer interest. They think of opposition to government price supports, production controls and subsidies as a <u>consumer</u> opposition. There is much evidence to support this view.

But the author doesn't believe it is <u>entirely</u> realistic, for two reasons: One, the American consumer as such has little voice in politics. Economic pressure groups with weight are almost exclusively producer oriented.

Two, the nonfarm public in this country has grown so rich that food has become of secondary importance in most household budgets. (Food is still the largest single item in the average budget. The author uses "secondary" here in the psychological sense.) The margin of average family purchasing power above basic food necessities has widened rapidly since the 1940's. Demand for food has become less elastic. The public has become so accustomed to plenty of food that it no longer is so greatly concerned about the matter of cost. One hears complaints about the prices of food, of course, but those the author hears are rather mild. The attacks on government farm programs in recent years which have tried to appeal to this consumer interest have not roused the citizens to revolt.

There are some indications that in the postwar recession periods consumer demand for food was maintained or even increased slightly. People seem to have reacted to the mild unemployment by reducing installment buying for consumer durables but not by cutting food spending — perhaps even splurging on steak to ease the pain of not getting a car or refrigerator. Food has attained a new status in the United States economy — former "luxury" foods are now "necessities," and variations in consumer spending for food have been reduced. Because of his affluence in food, the consumer does not think of food as a vital issue of public policy.

If there is any pressure group in America that represents people as consumers, it is organized labor. Union leaders make very little noise about food prices, and when they do it is the processor or the distributor who gets the blame, seldom the farmer. The high cost of living <u>in general</u> serves as a labor union target — but not often the cost of food. This may be partly a feeling of sympathy for the farmer as a low income earner and partly the desire of labor leaders to build a farmer-labor front in politics. But the author thinks the main reason is the simple one that most wage earners just aren't greatly excited about the cost of food.

Many labor union leaders even have supported farm policies which would mean higher food costs in the market place or in taxes. They could not do this if labor union members were complaining about the grocery bills and about the rich farmers getting subsidies. Labor union leaders put their main emphasis on wages, hours, working conditions. When they complain about the high cost of living, their solution to the problem usually is higher wages, not lower prices. They do not pay much attention to the outgo side of the family budget, especially not in the case of food. One only needs compare the political pressure applied by the labor leaders on the medical cost problem with the pressure they apply on farm policy to appreciate the point that food costs are not a large political issue.

Food costs may have been a big issue in the Great Depression when the action programs to raise farm income began. Henry A. Wallace and the farm organization leaders of that day were worried about consumer reaction, and they really feared that the "farm monoply" being created might be abused to the detriment of the consumer. These statesmanlike reservations led to the Consumers Counsel set up in the Agricultural Adjustment Administration. But a guardian of the consumer interest proved largely unneeded. The food consumer has done exceedingly well under the farm programs.

So this author's conclusion is that opposition to farm policies to raise farm income does not derive mainly from outraged consumers. Judging by the record, this writer believes farm policies which raised food prices above the level of recent years would be acceptable to consumers. In other words, consumer resistance is not likely to be a major hindrance to the adoption or carrying out of policies to limit market supplies of farm products, or raise price supports, or increase taxes for farm subsidy payments.

II

This is not to say, however, that urban congressmen will not oppose such farm income support policies. This author is merely arguing that this opposition comes from something besides a surge of feeling about high food costs. What does it come from then?

It comes, the author believes, mainly from business interests and from the nonfarm public as a whole on ideological grounds. Farm programs of the federal government have been under attack from the beginning as socialistic, as setting a pattern for intervention in business, and as therefore intolerable to the business community. The National Association of Manufacturers and the

U.S. Chamber of Commerce repeatedly issue statements condemning the farm programs as unwarranted government meddling in the economy. They advocate policies of "freedom for farmers." But it isn't the freedom of decision making for farmers which concerns them so much as the implications of such programs for other types of business.

Business groups often are able to overlook their moral objections to subsidies and government intervention in business if the intervention is beneficial to them. They are inconsistent in approving tariffs, fair trade price laws, and the like, while indignantly opposing similar programs for farmers. They are also inconsistent at times in failing to mark the difference in management between industries of a few large firms and the farm industry with $4\frac{1}{2}$ million units. The planning and discipline over supply which can be obtained privately by oligopolistic industries require government action in the case of farming.

Despite these inconsistencies, it is well to recognize that the ideological objections to government farm programs are powerful. The theory about free enterprise and free markets has powerful appeal in United States politics, whether the facts fit the theory or not. Farm policy planners must recognize that there are definite limits to government management of agriculture which will be tolerable to business leaders. These leaders have great political influence directly, and in addition they have a great indirect influence through some farm organizations.

Associated with this attitude about free enterprise is the view that price-setting or market controls are wrong if done by government but right if done by private business. Presumably, it would be approved doctrine for the Swine Growers Association to set quotas on hog marketings for farmers, but it would be unacceptable if the government did the same thing.

Most social scientists probably would argue that if monopolies are to be created in agriculture, with power to control output and set prices, then these monopolies must be governmental, so that the people can maintain a checkrein on them. However, the political climate in which farm policy is made seems more agreeable to private farm monopoly.

III

So far the author has considered acceptability of farm policies to nonagricultural groups from the standpoint of food prices and from the standpoint of general business ideology. On the first point, the author's conclusion is that it is not a big factor

in itself. On the second, his conclusion is that it is a very large
factor.

A third factor affecting public acceptance of farm policies is
the relationship of those policies to the general prosperity. One
of the big selling points for farm income support programs always has been that high farm income is essential to national
prosperity. At times, this argument has been ludicrous — for example, the old "seven to one ratio" slogan. Each dollar of gross
farm income was supposed to generate seven dollars of national
income. So high price supports for agriculture were promoted on
the basis of increasing national income.

The author hasn't heard anyone making that kind of argument
lately. The ratio would have to be changed to about ten to one instead of seven to one, and it is becoming wider year by year.
The rise in national prosperity in recent years while agriculture
has been suffering a decline makes it more difficult to put over
the story that depressions are "farm led and farm fed." Nevertheless, a farm policy, to be acceptable to nonfarmers, ought to
be defendable as not causing trouble elsewhere in the economy.

A good example right now is the soil bank. By various calculations, one can show that 60 to 80 million acres of cropland
ought to be removed from production. And from the agricultural
economic viewpoint, a great deal of it ought to come out of specific areas. The cities and towns in these areas, however, have
a natural reluctance to being put out of business. So it simply
isn't feasible, either for political reasons or economic reasons,
to remove land from production in such sweeping fashion. The
gains to agriculture as a whole have to be balanced against
losses to the areas affected and the social costs of a massive adjustment in institutional overhead. There has to be some compromise between retiring land which is least efficient in crop
production and preventing wholesale business disaster to certain
areas.

From the point of view of many farm related businesses —
those supplying production goods and services to farmers as well
as those buying, handling or transporting farm products — volume
of farm production is more important than the level of net income
to the farm producer. In other words, the great bulk of so-called
"agri-business" is not primarily interested in a high level of net
farm income but in a high level of production of agricultural
products.

This creates a natural area of contention in agricultural
policy. Farm policies that are the best from the standpoint of
raising farm income quite often will not be acceptable to agri-
business. Farmers should not expect that national farm policy

can be based entirely on their interests. Neither can the farm
related businesses expect that policy should be adapted entirely
to their interests.

IV

In the last eight years, the influence of farm related businesses on agricultural policy has been relatively stronger than at
any time in my experience. Agricultural policy has tended to
swing away from emphasis on raising the net income of farmers
and toward maintaining a large volume of production.

This is not entirely because of the change in 1953 to a political administration with a more conservative economic policy. It
is partly because a majority of the agricultural community
wanted such a change. The largest farm organization, many
farm commodity organizations and other groups, including probably a large proportion of the members of the Farm Economics
Association, favored a trend away from crop acreage control.
They also favored lower price supports and were opposed to direct subsidy payments from the federal government.

Of course these groups didn't consciously favor lower farm
income. They thought low price supports and full production
would bring higher income. Or at least they thought the "freedom
for farmers" they were advocating was worth some minor losses
in income for a while.

It has always been something of a mystery to this author why
the voluntary acreage allotments or even the marketing quotas
were deemed to be such onerous controls. These restraints are
modest indeed compared with those that exist in almost every
trade or business. Yet the emotionalism about farm controls has
been so intense that half the people of this country probably still
think farmers are supervised by federal marshals whenever they
do their spring planting.

This raving about controls is still going on — and some farm
organization leaders are doing a great deal of it. They say that
farmers don't have freedom of choice, that crop production is
frozen into uneconomic patterns geographically because allotments prevent change. There is some truth in this "freezing of
crop patterns," but it has been vastly exaggerated in the telling.
Many of us in the Farm Economics Association have been guilty
of emphasizing the inefficiencies of crop acreage allotments on
an historical base to the degree that we have overlooked the inefficiencies of overproduction and low net farm incomes.

The point being made is that acceptability of farm policies

among farm groups, as well as among city groups, often turns on ideology and opinions about what is morally right or wrong – instead of on practical considerations. Furthermore, acceptability depends on the state of knowledge about the problem to be met. Fifteen years ago, or even 10 years ago, agricultural leaders and farm economists did not really grasp the significance of the sharp upturn in production and in productivity of agriculture. Neither, the author thinks, did many see what rising national affluence was doing to the demand for food. The war and the postwar years with large exports to Europe tended to hide the true situation. In recent years, however, a growing awareness of the overproduction problem has crept over the farm community.

What was unacceptable 10 years ago is becoming more and more acceptable as time goes on. A few years ago a statement by a prominent agricultural leader that congress would not pass, farmers would not accept and the U.S.D.A. could not administer controls that would really work, seemed fairly reasonable. Now, after several years of lower farm prices and incomes, farmers appear to be more willing to accept some forms of regulation in production and marketing. Acceptability of controls depends on how bad the income pinch is.

The Iowa Opinion Poll conducted by The Des Moines Register in early April of 1960 indicated that about two-thirds of Iowa farm people favor some kind of discipline over farm production in return for price support protection. In this poll, only 18 per cent of the people interviewed were in favor of abandoning government price supports and crop controls and going to a free market. About 18 per cent had no opinion. The remaining 64 per cent were in favor of crop acreage allotments or something stronger in the way of production control. About 12 per cent were in favor of production control with grain quotas in bushels.[1]

These results are significant in light of the fact that the Farm Bureau, which opposes production control, is so dominant in Iowa, with more than 100,000 members. After two years of freedom from acreage allotments on corn, Iowa farmers want to return to the allotment plan.

It is significant, also, that the Illinois Agricultural Association approved a resolution calling for compulsory crop acreage retirement, and the Iowa Farm Bureau suggested the possibility of requiring participation in the soil bank as a condition for receiving price support benefits.

---

[1] Polls conducted by Wallaces Farmer have shown about the same distribution of opinion.

Again, acceptability of farm programs depends on the seriousness of the economic plight which the programs are designed to correct. It is foolish to be dogmatic about what farm people will or will not accept. Many of us who have been associated with farming and farm people take as a matter of faith that farm people are more independent, more resentful of government regulation than other people. Despite the fact that this idea is imbedded deeply in our folklore — and one must recognize that folklore itself has a bearing on attitudes — it is doubtful that the difference between farm and city people in attitude toward regulations is very great. It seems to the author that farmers will accept order and discipline readily enough if they are convinced they will be helped by doing so. We must not generalize too sweepingly from the cases like that of Stanley Yankus, the Michigan farmer who went to Australia because he couldn't bear the wheat quota regulations.

Remember that substantial majorities of farmers have voted for crop marketing quotas in cotton, tobacco and wheat year after year. The rejection of corn acreage allotments here in the Farm Bureau-dominated Corn Belt was a special situation. Corn allotments obviously had not been successful: cross compliance on other feed crops was not applied, and farmers were promised at the time of the vote that corn price support would continue at about the same level if they voted to throw out the allotments. So it seems to me that was hardly a test of farmers' objections to controls.

One cannot be dogmatic about what farmers will accept in the way of national farm policies. Some farm groups favor government action more than others; it is a gross error to talk about "farm opinion" as though it were a solid, identifiable reality.

Still, I shall indulge in one bit of dogmatism about farm attitudes. Farmers will not accept a national policy of laissez faire. They do not want free markets and no controls, no matter what some farm leaders say. By every test that can be applied, the conclusion is that most farmers will choose government subsidy or government regulation rather than completely free competition when the chips are down.

This is only to say that there are limits to the power of the "freedom from control" ideology.

V

In conclusion, the bounds of acceptability of national farm policies are wider than many politicians assume but are still fairly narrow. Consumers are not up in arms about the cost of food and would not rebel at some increases, in the author's judgment. The chief barrier to changes or innovations in farm policy is the ideological barrier — both in the body politic as a whole and in the farm community itself.

This ideological barrier is elastic. Under present circumstances, radical changes in farm policies are not likely to be acceptable. But if farm income continues to decline, farm people will become more willing to accept production restrictions. In wartime or depression, some policies are acceptable which would not be in other times. For example, subsidy payments to livestock producers were quite acceptable during the war. But there does not seem to be much chance that such a program could gain backing now — even from farmers themselves. The same is true of a large-scale food stamp program. It would be acceptable under some circumstances but not when the general prosperity is high. In the author's view, direct payments, as a method of sustaining farm income and of stabilizing such cyclical enterprises as livestock, would be preferable to government purchases of commodities on such a large scale as in the 1950's. Also, food stamps are superior to direct relief handouts as a method of providing food for low income families. But one must recognize that these two programs have been saddled with a "socialistic" label and are just not politically digestible now.

Radical changes in the relationship between government and private industry are always unlikely in this country. Even in the early 1930's, though there was much radical talk and despair was widespread, no majority could be mustered for drastic alteration of the system — such as nationalization of principal industries. The New Deal was essentially a propping up operation, with some reform, to be sure, but it was not the revolution which hard-shell opponents of F. D. R. tried to make it out to be.

Judging from our national history, one would expect that alterations in farm policy will be halfway steps, with no neat cure-alls likely. John D. Black once took me to task gently for saying that "we will continue to muddle along by compromise, experimentation and half measures — this is the way of democracy and it is the best way." Black accused me of a counsel of despair. He was more hopeful than I that a nice, round package of farm legislation could be written which would meet the problems of agriculture. But in laying out his specifications, it seemed to me he was actually engaging in "compromise, experimentation and half measures." And he later conceded as much to me.

At any rate, I still believe that this principle of moderation and compromise is the key principle in making farm policy

acceptable in this country. And I don't think this is a counsel of
despair. It provides some assurance that our mistakes — and
they will be made — will be little ones.

SAMUEL LUBELL

Columbia University

Discussion

AMONG THE LIST of conference participants I recognize the
names of only two newspapermen, Lauren Soth and this author's.

A newspaperman always feels flattered when experts — professors and government officials — ask him to talk before them.
In this case, though, my left eyebrow is raised just a bit.

The program has been arranged so that Soth and this writer
are paired off, with Lubell commenting on Soth's paper, so that
we can have our own private little battle.

I am not suggesting this was the purpose of having this author's talk follow Soth's. Maybe it was just a coincidence.

Several of the speakers at earlier sessions have made the
statement that the heart of the nation's dilemma, over agricultural policy, is a deep-seated conflict in value judgments. This,
of course, is the theme of this conference. The emphasis
troubles the writer.

In the philosophic sense one can argue, of course, that virtually everything people do or do not do involves a value judgment.
Also there is no question that agricultural problems are complicated by some conflicts of values and goals.

Still, this writer believes the farm crisis is essentially a
crisis of technology out of control.

The heart of the problem is less a clash of values than that
we simply do not know _how_ to bring production and demand into
balance.

The pace of technological improvement in agriculture is too
rapid, and the potential for further productivity increases is too
rich to be overcome by any policy of adjustment that anyone has
so far proposed.

That statement is made, perhaps the writer should stress, not
as a farm expert which he is not. Still he has been systematically interviewing farmers for more than ten years. To be able
to ask these farmers sensible questions he has had to talk to
many farm experts and do much reading — too much reading — on
agricultural developments.

Every year that this writer goes out into the farm belt, he

comes back feeling that the problem of balancing agricultural supply and demand has become less manageable than it was the year before. We seem to be slipping further and further behind the technological eight-ball.

Or perhaps the writer should say, if he can be permitted to scramble his metaphors, we appear to have learned how to make two eight-balls grow where only one grew before.

Examine, if you will, the varied adjustment approaches that are advanced and ask yourself whether any would achieve balance with technology.

The free market? Changes in prices do cause farmers to shift some of their resources from one type of agricultural production to another. But the evidence is overwhelming that the price mechanism by itself cannot be used to reduce total agricultural productivity.

In recent years many farmers the writer has interviewed have complained "some farmers around here have had to quit." Always the writer asks, "What happened to the land that the farmer had to give up?"

Always the reply comes back that the land was taken over by a more efficient farmer who probably is producing more on the same land.

What of the migration of farm population to the cities and towns? This movement has been impressively large in recent years. But if anything it has only spurred the greater use of farm machinery and other crop stimulants.

What of controls on production as a solution to the farming problem?

Certainly these can be made more restrictive and more effective. But neither the farmers, nor the politicians nor the consuming public has pushed for really effective controls. In part this represents a conflict with the traditional beliefs in so-called free enterprise, but I doubt that ideology is the main source of farmer resistance to government controls.

In my own surveys the writer has found that the main divider between farmers who want production controls, and those who oppose them, is how farmers calculate their chances of riding out the adjustments that might be forced by declining farm prices.

Nearly all farmers think that there are too many farmers in the country and that some farmers are going to be squeezed out. If a farmer thinks he can survive the "shake-out," possibly because he is clear of debt or because he is a better farmer, he tends to say, "I'll take a chance on a free market for a couple of years anyway."

In contrast, if a farmer feels uncertain about his ability to ride out a decline in farm prices he tends to favor production controls.

Right now there are more farmers on this uncertain side than there are willing to gamble on a free market.

However the farmers who prefer government intervention to a free market want these production controls to be only partially effective. They want enough slippage in the system of controls to avoid too drastic an adjustment. Also whatever program is set up, the farmers try with might and main, with fertilizer and machinery, to beat the program.

The farmer's resistance, in short, is not based on "values" but on calculation. It is not primarily a problem of his allegiance to some principle, but that he has calculated that either truly effective controls or a free market would be too disruptive on his own farm.

Another suggestion that has been gaining support among some farm experts is the idea of solving the farm surplus problem by getting rid of the marginal and submarginal farmers.

This notion is, the writer suspects, largely a statistical mirage. Some nimble-machined statisticians have figured that the excess production on the market roughly equals the farm output contributed by the smallest, most marginal producers. The statisticians seem to have reasoned that if the production of the marginal farmers can be erased away, the production figures can be brought into balance with demand.

But this is like telling a man to cut down his weight by amputating an arm or a leg.

Last year this writer worked with the Iowa Extension Service and the Des Moines Register-Tribune on a state-wide survey of farmer reaction to the so-called Conservation Reserve. We found that it was easy enough for the government to rent the poorest lands or farms which were being operated by older, sickly people who were looking for some means of cutting down on their work load.

By increasing the rate of payment, it was also clear, more productive land could be taken out of production. But long before 60 or 80 million productive acres could be retired, you would precipitate a major social and economic crisis. Not only would communities be threatened with being put out of business but tenants everywhere would be threatened. Thousands of tenants would be displaced as farms were placed into the reserve and the bargaining position of other tenants would be weakened.

After our Iowa survey, this writer wrote a series of articles that appeared in newspapers around the country. From a dozen states he got letters from city people asking how they could put

the farm they owned and which was now run by a tenant, into the
reserve. Some of these letter writers were widows; others were
managers of estates or had inherited a family property or had
bought farms as a hedge against inflation. These letter-writers
were attracted by the prospect of being freed of the chores of
getting along with a tenant and of converting their land acreage
into the equivalent of a government bond, which paid a fixed return each year.

Nor does it seem likely that the so-called marginal farmer
will be lured out of farming by the expansion of nearby industrial
job opportunities. The more likely result – at least this is what
is found as one travels among farmers – is the intensification of
part-time farming, with the farmer using his job in the factory or
town as a means of holding onto his land.

Here, we do come into a real conflict of values. Many
farmers do not feel that dollar efficiency is the most important
value in life.

In Lucas County the writer remembers stopping at one farm
which was on a slope. The road into it was eroded and rutted. A
1952 Dodge car stood outside the farmhouse which was unpainted
and weather-beaten.

The farmer living there had put his land into the conservation
reserve and gone to work for a neighbor to make enough money
to finish paying for his land.

The writer decided to put the issue to him bluntly. "Some
people say that farmers like you, on such small acreages, ought
to quit farming. Why don't you?" he asked.

This farmer didn't get angry. He replied quietly, "Nothing
would make me quit farming. I like it as a way of living."

"What if the government gave you training for a new job?"
was the next question.

"I'm too old for that," he replied.

He then went on to say, "We don't expect much out of our
farm. I used to work up in Story County and made a lot more
money up there than I do down here. But people around here are
much more friendly. They're not in such a hurry. They don't
work so hard. They stop and talk more."

At that point his wife, who was cooking dinner on the stove,
broke in, "Up in Story County people have dollar signs in their
eyes. Down here they don't."

In rich, fertile Story County this family had felt itself a mis-
fit. In Lucas County the soil was poorer and more eroded – but
still more friendly.

Again, Professor Duncan was with the writer when we talked
to a highly intelligent farmwife on another small, hilly farm in
Wayne County.

"We like a farm as a place to bring up children," she explained. "My father doesn't understand that. When he visits us he
keeps asking how can we try to farm down here. To him farming
is a business. He owns nearly a section of land in Greene County.
He has four tractors and every other kind of machine you can
think of. But I can remember how he worked us kids when we
were young to get that machinery."

When the writer asked her, "What would it take to get you to
quit farming?" she replied, "I don't think you could get us to
quit."

Her husband works off the farm in Des Moines and uses the
car all day. This farm wife, if she has to go anywhere during the
day, either hitchhikes or rides the tractor.

Why didn't they buy another car?

She laughed and replied, "All the money around here is too
busy. None of it is ever idle."

There are many persons who do not believe that money is the
dominant value in farm life. They will not be drawn off the land
easily. It is also anything but honest thinking to put the blame on
them for our farm surpluses and not on the major producers.

Curiously, the automobile has given many of these people the
technological means by which they can stay on their land and supplement their limited farm earnings with an off-farm job.

To sum up so far, conflicts over values and goals are important, but even if these conflicts could be reconciled — and many
cannot be — they would not yield us a solution of the farm problem.

It is the extent of the adjustment that would be required to
balance production and demand — not ideological conflict — that is
the crux of the farm policy dilemma the nation faces.

Put another way there is no solution to the farm problem.

We would be wise, in fact, to drop the word "solution" from
our thinking, to revise our dictionaries and label the word "obsolete." It is self-deceiving to talk as if the goal of agricultural
policy can be some program which will enable us to feel the
problem is taken care of and can be forgotten.

To most of the problems that vex our society there are no
solutions. There is only an unending search for a higher percentage of satisfaction from the alternatives we can pursue.

This appears also to be Lauren Soth's view. On this point we
two newspapermen are in accord, that "the only alterations in
farm policy" we can expect will be "halfway steps, with no neat
cure-alls."

As Soth emphasizes the key word is "acceptable." The problem is to formulate policies which will be acceptable to many

varied groups and interests. What is acceptable will have to be determined by moderation and compromise — plus some cash.

How does one go about searching for this highest common denominator of acceptability?

One possible approach that the writer would like to propose is to deal with the problem as an exercise in collective bargaining between the farmer and his legislative representatives on one side, and the representatives of the consuming public on the other.

Of course, some collective bargaining now goes on through the agricultural committees of the Senate and House. But the process is considerably obscured by the fact that these committees generally present their demands in terms of detailed changes in technical formulas, in such things as price supports, minimum acreage allotments and so on.

Open collective bargaining might make clear the real nature of our agricultural problem to both the farmers and the public.

What could come out of such an approach?

There seem to be five possible reforms in our thinking:

1. A recognition by the nonfarming public that farm surpluses are a valuable asset to our society, vital insurance against drouth and crop failure at home and famine abroad.
2. A recognition by the farmer that a dollar ceiling has to be put on what this insurance is worth — a fixed limit to the cost of the whole farm program.
3. A general recognition by both farmers and the nonfarming public that an effective halt has to be called to inflation.
4. A general recognition that whatever farm program is adopted must be effectively policed so the government gets what it pays for.

   This would require an end to using lax administration of the farm program as a means of buying votes.

5. Agreement on a new, more realistic definition of who is a farmer.

Five years ago, in a book on world trade, the present writer wrote:

Currently the tendency is to think of our surpluses as costly liabilities. But two world wars and the whole course of the postwar period have shown that the free world's strongest single asset is the ability of the American economy to generate sizable surpluses of every kind, from food and machinery to medicine and clothing.

When famine threatened India and Pakistan, we were able to send these countries shiploads of wheat, without taking a slice of bread from an American consumer. Should Asia's "rice bowl" fall into Communist hands, it would be our surplus stocks that other Asiatic countries would have to look to for the food which would keep them free.

Although the heads of many foreign governments do not seem to realize it, our productive resources are the cushion which permits them to sleep in political stability and freedom.

It was encouraging that both Vice President Richard Nixon

and his self-appointed chief prodder, Nelson Rockefeller, endorsed the idea of a stockpile of some farm products as a reserve
against drouth and famine.

Such a reserve should be created and an orderly, less expensive storage program set up to see that wheat, corn and other
commodities do not rot and spoil; also to see that the government
gets full value for every storage dollar paid out.

In exchange for recognition of the fact that surpluses are an
asset, the public is entitled to an effective limit on the cost of the
farm program.

The cost of such a program is expressed, of course, in two
ways, food prices and the subsidy coming out of the treasury.

In his paper, Lauren Soth dismisses resistance by the consumer as a factor of major importance in determining farm policy.

This author's own interviewing indicates a considerable concern over high food prices among consumers, particularly among
worker families.

The rise in food prices in recent years has also had some
upsetting effects on the rest of the economy.

Many families have told the author that two to three years
ago they had to increase their weekly allowances for food. The
increase generally was on the order of a jump from $25 to $30 a
week. This increase forced many families to curtail their buying
of other things. This was particularly true during the recession,
and it has remained true, since then, in areas where workers
have not been able to get overtime.

Resentment against the rise of price in groceries is also the
factor cited most often by workers in justifying their demands
for wage increases.

The fact that union leaders, as Lauren Soth points out, "make
very little noise about food prices," is only evidence of the widening gulf that has been developing between union leaders and
their members. Most union members would prefer wage and
price stability to further inflationary rises in food prices and
higher wages.

What might be more to Soth's point would be to ask why, when
the prices received by the farmer do decline, aren't the benefits
passed on to the consumer?

The second cost effect of the farm program is on the general
budget.

The several billions of dollars that are going into farm-price
supports and storage costs represent that many billions which
could be diverted to expanded defense, or to some other worthwhile purpose.

Now this writer happens to believe that federal taxes are too low in relation to our need. It is sometimes said that federal taxes take one day's pay of every week's earnings.

Is it too much to ask every family head to contribute 52 days of service during the year to the defense of his country?

It is also unfortunate that the Defense Department, by tolerating so much waste, makes it difficult for people to do their patriotic duty.

Nor is the farmer standing alone in the subsidy line. He has a lot of company in the people who are getting some form of government subsidy.

Still, we appear to have reached the point where whatever goes out of the budget for one purpose conflicts with spending for other needs.

A farmer once interviewed in Boone County suggested a possible way of dealing with this problem. He thought Congress should put a limit on what the total cost of the agricultural subsidy should run — so much and no more.

Once the total cost had been determined, the farmers and their representatives could fight it out among themselves as to how they could live within it.

I'm not sure this is a practical suggestion but it has the merit of dramatizing one need — of an upward limit to what the agricultural program can cost the taxpayer.

On the farmer's side, his representatives should be seeking alliance with those other elements in the economy who are opposed to a policy of continuous inflation. Repeatedly farmers have told me, "The prices we're getting are all right if the cost of what we buy didn't keep going up."

Currently the main squeeze on the farmer is not coming from a decline in farm prices. The squeeze is being exerted through rising costs. This squeeze, in turn, presses the farmer to take advantage of every manageable technological advance to increase his own productivity.

On this score some shift may be needed in the orientation of both the farmers and farm experts. Farmers, of course, have long been educated to the fact that they suffer from a basic organizational disadvantage, in adjusting their production to changing market demands.

Many of the papers that have been read at this conference have concentrated on this conflict of economic organization between different segments of the economy, of how difficult it is for the farmer to hold up his prices by curtailing production as industry can, or by withholding his labor from the market as a trade union can.

But perhaps more attention should be devoted to the cost side

of the squeeze, to what it is that operated to make continued inflation the policy of the administrations elected in 1952 and 1956
in Washington.

The author suspects that the economists are devoting too
much time and energy to comparisons of industrial and agricultural organization and not enough attention to the implications of
the management of our economy from Washington.

A fourth reform that is needed is a stiffer administration of
whatever program is adopted so that the government gets full
performance for what it pays for.

One is shocked by the number of farmers who tell one that
they put land into the soil bank which never was planted to any
crop.

Others have said, "The government is a sucker to pay me for
doing something which the farmers intended to do anyway."

No government should make a fool of itself with its own citizens. Many so-called conservation practices need overhauling to
conserve respect for the government.

Part of the trouble, of course, is that some farm programs
have been put into effect primarily to buy votes. This was true
of the soil bank program that was rushed into operation during
the 1956 presidential campaign. As this writer wrote at the time,
most farmers looked on the soil bank as a "vote buying farce."

One Minnesota farmer the writer recalls referred to the land
he had put into the soil bank as "Benson's acres."

When asked what he meant by that he replied, "We call them
Benson's acres if they're acres we put into the soil bank that
wouldn't have produced anything anyway."

Another blow to the morality of the farm program was Secretary Benson's decision to extend price guarantees to corn producers who had not signed up for acreage reductions. The corn
farmer who had signed up felt Benson's action was immoral.

The farmers, the government and the nation — all will be
better off if each farm program is regarded as a contract which
requires farmers to measure up to the exact performance for
which they are being paid.

As the farm programs have been drawn up and administered
they have been an invitation to abuse.

Finally, surveys by the author among farmers make him feel
one other thing is needed — a clearer definition of just who is a
farmer, and just who is entitled to farm income payments, subsidies and other advantages of a farm program.

During the recent primary contest in Wisconsin, for example,
the author stopped at one farmhouse before which three automobiles were parked. The farmer living there protested bitterly,

"You can't make a living farming anymore." When asked about the three cars parked outside, he explained that both he and his two sons had full-time jobs off the farm. They used the cars to get to and from work. They had all come home for lunch.

As the writer drove away from that farm he wondered was it really the government's responsibility to subsidize the farm production of a family into which the income from three nonfarm jobs was flowing?

At what point did a man stop being a farmer or stop being entitled to government aid?

That Wisconsin farmhouse was not exceptional. In every state the division between the farmer and nonfarm worker is being blurred. Ten years ago one could stop at almost any house by the road and the occupant was almost certain to be a farmer.

Now a person has to hunt up silos, or look for cows and pigs to be able to locate a farmhouse.

Who is a farmer has become one of the great unsolved mysteries of our economy.

Chapter 14A

BORIS C. SWERLING

Stanford University

Positive Policies
for American Agriculture

HOW A SOCIETY deals with its agriculture can be crucial to its economic progress and political structure. Nineteenth century England, in choosing the route of cheap food imports, and Denmark, in sacrificing domestic food grains to imported feedstuffs, made decisions affecting the entire course of their future economic development. Despite widespread emphasis on industrialization at the present time, the success of economic programs currently being undertaken in underdeveloped countries will depend in large measure on their handling of the farm sector: their ability to squeeze capital out of agriculture to finance off-farm activities; the extent to which labor can be released from farming for employment in other enterprises; the development of a rural market for the products of local industry; and a high rate of expansion in domestic food supply as a prime offset to domestic inflationary pressures or balance-of-payment difficulties. The Communists exploit legitimate aspirations for land reform, but their longer-term strategy is to destroy an independent peasantry in order to assert political control over the countryside and economic control over the cities. Indeed, Khrushchev has described "the shift of the peasantry to co-operation" as "the crucial problem of socialist development."[1]

At home, there are comparable references to the American "farm problem" as the major domestic issue of the day, and it is not at all surprising that the independent farm operator and his counterpart in small business enterprise should enjoy favored treatment in societies that place a high value on private proprietorship. But economic change continually involves advantage to some economic groups and disadvantage to others. Whereas the newly independent countries typically give undue political influence to the town, historical systems of representation in the

[1] N. S. Khrushchev, Control Figures for the Economic Development of the USSR for 1959-1965. Moscow, 1959, p. 81.

older democracies seriously overweigh the interests of the countryside. One of the less pleasant manifestations of countervailing power in any democratic society is that an important group
whose economic status is deteriorating may exact excessive political conditions as the price of progress. In periods of rapid
change, the social challenge is twofold: on the one hand, to resist extravagant claims made in the name of any vested interest,
and on the other, to invent instrumentalities that ease the impact
of necessary adjustment on injured parties without serious damage to the efficiency of the economic system. This is essentially
an issue of social justice and the challenge confronts not only
farm policy but also public action in such fields as minerals,
tariffs and depressed areas, to mention only a few.

Artificial market support for individual commodities, which
is a distinguishing feature of American farm programs, is the
typical means of aiding groups adversely affected by economic
change. This commodity emphasis is in line with comparative
endowments of economic data, the structure of congressional
committees and the organization of special interest groups. The
commodity approach is in favor among political liberals and conservatives alike. On the one hand, a higher price for wheat or
cotton is defended by those whose natural inclination is to favor
the disadvantaged. By contrast, among those whose allegiance to
private business enterprise is most vociferous, intervention in
or even elimination of commodity markets[2] are somehow more
respectable than direct income transfers that interfere less ar-
bitrarily with the price system. Similarly, many can argue
strongly for states, rights and restraint on federal power while
endorsing commodity devices for redistributing income among
the states. The same people who condemn foreign aid as "give-
aways" can vote heavy expenditures for foreign disposal of surplus farm products. It is not too much to say that Congress
speaks the language of free enterprise, but interferes more extensively with the price system than would be appropriate in a
completely socialist state.

Programs for raising farm income by artificially supporting
the prices of major crops have relied heavily upon a particular
rationale: the apparent unresponsiveness of market demand to
changes in prices of agricultural commodities; the short-term
inflexibility of agricultural supplies, and particularly the difficulty of reducing total farm output when market prices fall; the
vulnerability of primary producers in times of economic

---

[2]For a defense of futures trading in onions, see H. Working, Price Effects of
Futures Trading. Food Research Institute Studies, Stanford, I:3-27, 1960.

depression; and the assumption that federally-organized restriction of farm output would be advantageous to agricultural producers. Respectable econometric investigations can be enlisted in defense of these propositions. The marked contrast between the high professional competence of the agricultural economist and the sordid state of present farm policy does nevertheless lead one to ask whether the failure is entirely one of implementing unchallengeable economic findings, or whether there may also have been serious shortcomings of analysis and prescription. There are certainly other fields of public policy in which the recasting of our economic knowledge, the adaptation of public attitudes and the adjustment of liberal institutions lag seriously behind the rapid pace at which the structure of modern economic life is changing.

If one is impressed by the malfunctioning of commodity programs, conscious of economic realities that have contributed to recent difficulties and cool to the merits of policy proposals most widely discussed, he is under some obligation to devise alternative arrangements. May I presume to restate here a different and much more modest approach for protecting the income of farm operators.[3] The measure attempts to apply standard principles of social insurance, along the following lines:

1. As with unemployment insurance, benefits would be related to the income experience of the individual farm operator during the recent past.
2. Social security practices would be followed in establishing an upper limit on the amount of insured income, and there would accordingly be a modest ceiling on the total benefits enjoyed by a particular individual.
3. Benefits would accrue only to growers who suffer an abnormal reduction in income, not to prosperous and distressed individuals indiscriminately.
4. Specifically, a grower would draw benefits if his farm earnings in a given year fell more than, say, 25 per cent below the average of the preceding 5 years. The maximum base income would be set at $4,800, net, equivalent to some $15,000, gross.
5. The right to benefits would attach to the person, not to farm land or to the farm enterprise, and would accordingly not be transferable.
6. Benefits would not be conditional upon the production of particular commodities or even upon continued employment in agriculture.

---

[3] B. C. Swerling, Income Protection for Farmers: A Possible Approach. Jour. Pol. Econ. LXVII:173-86, 1959.

7. Benefits would be scaled downward as off-farm sources of income rose, but at the same time contingent protection would be afforded to persons shifting from farming to other occupations.
8. The plan would be contributory and compulsory, but the federal government would subsidize the program by making premium payments on some matching basis.

The merits and the deficiencies of this particular proposal warrant careful exploration, and this audience is well qualified to evaluate them. But the presentation has the broader purpose of high-lighting criteria that any agricultural reform should satisfy under present-day conditions. Let us explore some of the issues the proposal raises.

THE INCOME TARGET

To be sure, the degree of protection afforded would be considerably less generous than is aimed at under present statutory standards. But much frustration has hitherto arisen from the attempt to attain the unattainable. Pursuit of purchasing power parity for agricultural commodities ignores real gains in productive efficiency and human well-being. The goal of an historically based fair share of the national income for a conglomerate agriculture defies the inevitable decline in that sector's relative position in a progressing economy. Efforts are made to remove the disparity between the absolute level of per capita income on and off the farm despite the evidence that such differentials are well-nigh universal,[4] and their meaning is far from clear. Those who stress market development for particular field crops can take little satisfaction in falling per capita consumption of wheat or potatoes, well-demonstrated indicators of dietary improvement. An American secretary of agriculture can hardly seek to promote a heavy in-migration to agriculture, an increase in farm population as a percentage of the total or a steady decline in the average size of farm, but neither can he point with unmitigated pride to trends in a contrary but more appropriate direction.

Outside agriculture, income-maintenance programs have typically been guided by the principle of a social minimum or have sought to pool risks in order to soften the distress caused by adverse economic developments beyond any individual's control. In this spirit Congress has enacted minimum wage,

---

[4] J. R. Bellerby, Agriculture and Industry Relative Income. Macmillan, London, 1956.

unemployment insurance and social security legislation. Remember that the urban labor force does well if unemployment insurance covers half a man's earnings for a 26-week period, and recall also the considerable number of farm people who now enjoy this degree of protection on the off-farm portion of their earnings. By standards of social insurance, 75 per cent of base represents a generous level of income support, but even higher figures would avoid adverse side effects that result from corresponding percentages of statutory parity.

THE RELIEF OF REAL DISABILITIES

Confusion and misunderstanding arise from the failure to consider certain alleged disabilities of farm people in proper perspective. The plight of the small-scale farmer is exaggerated if we ignore evidence that rising off-farm earnings appear to have more than offset his reduced earnings from agriculture.[5] Mechanization and new technology ought not to be considered as merely independent sources of disturbance, for they have helped agriculture adjust to the drain of labor into the cities[6] and have placed a larger scale of enterprise within the competence of a single farm family. Recent trends in farm indebtedness need to be interpreted against the low level of overhead charges attained during the past two decades. The farmer's satisfaction with his current cash position is seriously underestimated unless account is taken both of the rising volume of depreciation charges built into official estimates of net farm income, and also of concurrent changes in the value of his assets.

A more careful identification of the special disadvantages to which farm people are subject and the special disabilities from which they suffer is necessary if we are to specify appropriate fields for public policy. Only a few decades ago, the isolation of the rural hinterland, the immobility of rural people and the arduousness of farm life and work took high places on the list. Merely to identify the traditional items is to call attention to the considerable degree of success in overcoming them. Electrification and mechanization, much of it internally financed out of farm

---

[5]N. M. Koffsky and E. W. Grove, The Current Economic Position of Commercial Farms. In U.S. Congress, Joint Economic Committee, Policy for Commercial Agriculture. 85th Congress, 1st Session, Nov. 22, 1957. Pp. 79-90. According to the AMS-Census Survey of Farmers' Expenditures in 1955, operators' combined expenditures for family living and production purposes in 1955 are estimated at $40 billions, one third higher than that year's cash receipts from farm marketings and government payments.

[6]C. Clark, Afterthoughts on Paley. Rev. Econ. & Stat. XXXVI:267-73, 1954, p. 272.

earnings, have eased hard chores in homestead and fields. The rural electrification program was widely supported, on the principle that a public interest attached to extending transmission lines to sparsely settled rural areas. Farm-to-market roads and an extensive highway network are at least as important for having increased the mobility of farm people, including their access to town jobs and city medical facilities, as they are for having eased the shipment of farm produce. The sweeping changes involved in these improvements in the manner of living are little reflected in official indexes of level of living calculated for farm-operator families.

Income variability — whether the result of natural hazards, changing market circumstances or special commodity cycles — does remain a real hazard of commercial agriculture, and public policy can reasonably seek to moderate its impact upon the individual farmer. Commodity price supports have been discredited in part because they superimposed upon this appropriate objective an excessive income target.

THE CONCERN FOR SOCIAL JUSTICE

The proposal disavows any social responsibility for protecting the market fortunes of higher-income farmers. Clearly the traditional practice of allocating public benefits in strict proportion to volume of marketings does not follow equitable principles of income distribution. Congressional and administration actions accordingly reflect an increasing inclination to limit total benefits to individual growers. Such ceilings are restraints upon privilege, not upon opportunity. Indeed, under present tax structures and with the high proportion of federal nonmilitary expenditures now absorbed by agricultural programs, it seems likely that price supports involve an essentially regressive redistribution of income. In other respects as well, past programs and present proposals fall short of what social justice would dictate. More attention is paid to bargaining weakness in the markets where farm products are sold than to bargaining strength in the markets where farm labor is hired. Rising wages of farm workers, reflecting improvement in the real well-being of a significant component of the farm labor force, enter the statutory parity ratio as a distinct increase in costs, and suggest only deterioration in average farm conditions. Gains to operating farmers are highly transitory if programs defended on grounds of higher income for an underprivileged group serve instead to bid up the price of land and burden succeeding generations of farmers with a higher cost structure. There is a real danger of accentuating this tendency if acreage allotments become freely negotiable or we move to an overt system of marketing certificates. Rights attached to the person are not open to the same criticism.

The relatively large number of low-income farm people has hitherto served to depress per capita estimates of farm income and has afforded a statistical justification for commodity programs ill suited to relieving agricultural poverty. Relating benefits to the individual's income experience would be similarly ineffective as an aid for the poor in agriculture; nor can unemployment insurance eliminate urban slums. Yet the insurance route improves the orientation of public policy in two dimensions. In the first place, there can be a frontal attack on the real problems of low-income farm areas, with full recognition of the demographic, regional and racial factors involved. Secondly, many low-income folk of rural origin are now themselves confronted with unwholesome living conditions in the cities. The public interest in relieving their serious disadvantages of health, training and community facilities has hardly terminated merely because they have moved to new constituencies. The enormous internal migration of recent decades warrants far more public attention than it has received. Slum clearance can well stand larger public expenditures and commodity programs less if we are to face up to genuine social problems of low-income farm families.

CYCLICAL CONSIDERATIONS

Price supports are commonly regarded as part of our battery of built-in economic stabilizers,[7] but that view is not entirely justified. The long time lags that separate announcement of support levels from date of crop harvest, resort to support loans, actual federal expenditures and subsequent federal receipts from disposal operations are far too long to allow nice adjustment to the requirements of contra-cyclical policy. Study of these processes in the recent past indicates that the consequent pattern of federal spending is as likely to accentuate general economic fluctuations as it is to moderate them.[8] Heavier call on the

---

[7] Karl Fox, The Contribution of Farm Price Support Programs to General Economic Stability. In National Bureau of Economic Research, Policies to Combat Depression, Princeton, 1956. Pp. 295-349.

[8] Boris C. Swerling, Agriculture and Recent Economic Conditions: Experience and Perspective. Federal Reserve Bank of San Francisco, 1959.

agricultural loan programs of the federal government during periods of general credit restraint have similarly perverse effects.
The behavior of agriculture, and not just of program instrumentalities, has differed during recent cycles from what we have
customarily expected. Consumer spending has been sufficiently
maintained that industrial recessions appear to have affected
rural America as much by drying up opportunities for off-farm
employment as by effects on commodity markets. The traditional
view that economic recessions are transmitted in magnified fashion from the general economy to the agricultural sector certainly
requires serious reconsideration. With the 1958 demonstration
that farm income can rise sharply in the face of industrial weakness, indicators other than the level of general economic activity
can best guide the timing of financial aid to farm people. Granted
the diversity of income experience within farming during conditions short of major commodity inflation or serious recession,
the behavior of the actual earnings of the individual farm operator affords a more serviceable guide for action. Moreover, with
production charges now absorbing so large a share of marketing
receipts, commodity programs are a particularly expensive
method of supporting farm income, and the alternative of overt
transfer payments becomes increasingly attractive. [9]

INCENTIVES ON THE FARM

One need not be oversold on the normative virtues of competitive equilibrium and yet be impressed by the usefulness of the
price system for coaxing rather than coercing appropriate adjustments. A great failure of the inherited farm program is the
perverse inducements it sets before the individual farm operator.
Federal aid has been attached to the continued production of unneeded commodities, with heavy emphasis on field crops least
associated with a high-consumption society. Marginal incentives
to produce have remained high, whereas marginal public returns
from surplus output have been exceedingly low. Growers have
felt impelled to plant unneeded acreages of surplus crops in
order to maintain a production history and insure entitlement to
future allotments. High price supports, capitalized into the high
value of allotments, required high payments in order to idle land
under the acreage reserve program, with the public treasury in

[9]A curious by-product of present procedures is that the value of agricultural
production and accordingly Gross National Product tend to be overstated in the national economic accounts, and a significant transfer payment is completely hidden.

effect bidding against itself. The vote by corn farmers to abandon acreage allotments on the 1959 crop was widely advertised
as a decision favoring lower prices with more freedom to plant;
but a price structure combining higher average supports for corn
and a 10-point cut in supports on minor feed grains had predictable consequences. Indeed, a price-support structure reflecting
the application of various statutory formulas and freezes, percentages of average market price and sundry lesser criteria,
verges on the chaotic.

As an instrument of social control, does the resultant price
system really serve as well as prices more free to reflect
changes in market demand and in real costs? Or could one hope
for anything better if various commodity groups were given fuller
autonomy in handling their own affairs? One can answer both
those questions in the negative without placing farmers' income
entirely at the mercy of the free market. Subsidy payments that
do not vary directly with output are less likely to distort desirable price signals. An income-insurance plan avoids marginal incentives to expand output, and the contingent assistance it provides ought to have little effect on the grower's decision to plant.

MATTERS OF AGRICULTURAL INPUTS

It is of course widely recognized that farm productivity is increasingly responsive to inputs purchased from outside agriculture. But neither public policy nor economic analysis seems to
have taken the implications of this situation into proper account.
Public measures for restricting output continue to concentrate on
limiting acreage alone; the alternative of limiting use of such
highly productive inputs as fertilizer and irrigation water is not
seriously considered; and practices that evoke prompt increases
in yields are subsidized under cover of legitimate conservation
practices. While land-use adjustments as reflected in the Great
Plains program may be desirable for their own sake, even a
massive program of land retirement does not by itself promise
to be an effective route towards production control under present
technological conditions.

On the other hand, technical explanations of the "farm problem" in terms of excess labor supply[10] do not always make it
clear that labor outflow cannot reduce surplus capacity if over-
compensated by capital inflow. Earlier notions of "capital

---

[10]D. G. Johnson, The Dimensions of the Farm Problem. In Iowa State University
Center for Agricultural Adjustment, Problems and Policies of American Agriculture.
Iowa State University Press, Ames, 1959. P. 47.

rationing" were popular during a period of massive capital investment in agriculture.[11] More recent studies of capital intensity in various sectors of the American economy indicate that, if account is taken of factors directly and indirectly employed, a dollar's worth of field crops now absorbs more capital relative to labor than do major products of the iron and steel industry.[12]

Because farmers' propensity to invest is high, programs intended to improve farm levels of living can and do lead instead to higher production expenditures and enlarged surplus capacity. There is certainly evidence that soil bank payments have had precisely that effect.[13] With capital as well as land and labor being devoted to agriculture in excessive amounts, subsidized agricultural credit needs to be disbursed sparingly and judiciously. The legacy of unwarranted investment is of various undesirable sorts: the operator becomes committed to a higher level of cash expenditures in subsequent periods; computed depreciation charges rise, with adverse effects on subsequent estimates of net farm income; and problems of excess capacity are transmitted to agricultural supply industries. Excessive capital formation in agriculture will lead to low returns on farm capital just as surely as high birth rates in rural areas will depress returns to farm labor.

Considerations such as these speak strongly for public measures more likely to have their impact directly on farm consumption and the conditions of family living, including access to medical services, educational facilities and community services generally. Income payments that offset shortfalls in earnings seem far less likely to be dissipated in production expenditures than are the windfall gains, unrestricted in total amount, that frequently accrue under present programs.

EFFICIENCY OF ADMINISTRATIVE CONTROL

Present programs frequently make impossible claims upon the administrative capabilities of the responsible agencies. This occurs when major activities must be initiated too quickly, like

---

[11] T. W. Schultz, The Economic Organization of Agriculture, McGraw-Hill, New York, 1953. P. 306.

[12] W. Leontief, Factor Proportions and the Structure of American Trade: Further Theoretical and Empirical Analysis. Rev. Econ. & Stat. XXXIX:386-407, 1956.

[13] Contrast the behavior of net farm income with that of the monthly index of value of shipments of farm machinery, equipment, and wheel-type tractors. In U.S. Department of Commerce, Bureau of the Census, Facts for Industry, Series M35 S, December, 1959.

320 BORIS C. SWERLING

the acreage reserve program in 1956; or when enforcement regulations are deemed too onerous, as in the fight against cross compliance; or when there are few standards that can be unequivocally applied, as in various disaster relief measures. Considering the vested interests already built into the purchasing, lending, storage, exporting and importing functions of the Commodity Credit Corporation, and the enormous volume of its business, the surprise is that outright administrative bungles are so infrequent. Program minutiae involving individual agricultural commodities continue to absorb an exhausting amount of congressional energy, long after experience has dictated a less intimate role in such fields as tariff making and public utility regulation. The time pattern of congressional action is at odds with biological lags in agricultural production, and the farm operator cannot know what rules of the game are to be enforced in the period ahead. Whatever reduction may have been made in the degree of economic uncertainty confronting farmers has been offset, in part if not entirely, by rising political uncertainties.

Whether a system of tight marketing controls could be effectively administered remains seriously in doubt. Marketing agreements have hitherto succeeded where the pattern of supply closely approximated conditions of natural monopoly, which is hardly the case for major field crops. The sugar program, frequently cited as a prototype, is facilitated by special relationships between individual growers and a limited number of processors, and the administrative record would be far less satisfactory if foreign sugar supplies did not provide a buffer for the control system. Even a strong advocate of marketing controls is impressed by the difficulty of regulating the feed-grain sector.[14]

Before the extension of social security to farm operators, it would have been quite impractical to suggest initiating a system of income reporting for purposes outlined in this paper. But with comprehensive administrative machinery now in existence, new alternatives are open. Administrative standards are certainly more solidly established for social insurance than for price supports, and income insurance has features that provide a high degree of self-policing against possible abuse. There is good reason to believe that a scale of premiums and benefits could be devised that would be quite as defensible as those now in use for purposes of unemployment insurance and social security itself.

---

[14] Willard W. Cochrane in U.S. Congress, Joint Economic Committee, Policy for Commercial Agriculture, Hearings. December, 16-20, 1957. P. 353.

INTERNATIONAL COMMODITY POLICY

An incidental gain from going the income-insurance route is that here is one approach that may be applied also to the international instability problems of primary producing countries.[15] Consistency between our foreign and domestic practice would be a welcome change from the present state of affairs. Parity between prices paid and received by farmers remains the domestic standard, but at the water's edge we renounce the terms-of-trade approach to stabilizing price relationships between primary products and manufactured goods.

We are prepared to dispose of surplus stocks of imported rubber on an announced schedule, but there is little support for doing likewise with domestic corn or wheat. We endorse historical share of world markets as a rule applicable to cotton but would be considerably embarrassed if it were extended to American exports of soybeans, corn or inedible animal fats. Stocks of wheat and corn on hand are to some degree justified as contingency reserves, but official concern does not extend to the size of mainland stocks of sugar or coffee, the two major foodstuffs shipped in by ocean-going vessels. International commodity agreements are resisted for imported commodities subject to cyclical instability in industrial demand, but are endorsed for an export commodity like wheat and also for an imported one like sugar, lest lower world market prices embarrass our domestic control program. Commodity programs make for difficulties in our trade relations with countries whose political values and economic institutions most closely resemble our own. Here are further good reasons for aiding farm people otherwise than by the commodity route.

A few concluding comments are in order. The professional economist concerned with agriculture, like his colleague in the monetary field, is fortunate in the abundance of empirical data at his disposal, and society enjoys a certain corresponding immunity from irrelevant flights of academic fantasy. It is upon close observation of economic events, rather than upon the customary expertise of the agricultural economist, that many of the judgments in this paper are based. The discussion does not lead to a full-scale prescription for policy, an agenda for research or a program for extension, and perhaps the path of advocacy has been pursued beyond the limits of good scholarship.

The exercise of ingenuity is far more respectable in fields

---

[15] United Nations, Dept. of Economic and Social Affairs. World Economic Survey, 1958, New York, 1959. P. 128.

like mathematics and technology than in the area of social institutions; and it is easier to prescribe institutional reforms for the
agriculture of underdeveloped lands abroad than to cast off discredited agricultural policies at home. But upon America's capacity to adapt domestic social arrangements in keeping with
contemporary needs and in the spirit of Western liberalism,
much depends. Whatever the defects of the precise mechanism
here outlined, it does meet the challenge to devise institutional
arrangements appropriate to present-day circumstances.

Chapter 14B

JOHN A. SCHNITTKER

Kansas State University

Positive Policies
for American Agriculture

TIME IS SHORT for those who would propose significant social and economic innovations for United States agriculture for the early 1960's. A new administration, popularly chosen and with a character molded to some degree by the public will, should open the way for us to learn much about the dominant goals and values — the aspirations — of the American people with respect to economic and farm policy.

Not all the years of the decade of the sixties will be equally important from the standpoint of farm policy. The character of a new administration — the key ingredients of which are the personality of the President, the predispositions of his party and the demands of the times — is formed early in its tenure. Witness the immediate and unrelenting opposition of the Coolidge and Hoover administrations to public intervention in the economy, the consistent and sometimes almost malignant interventionism of the Roosevelt era once its pattern was set and the diligent search for new and tenable justifications for chosen and virtually unchangeable farm policy commitments by the Eisenhower Administration.

These are critical years for economic and social policy. The elements of the farm policy likely to prevail for much of the next decade will be decided in the years 1960 to 1962. Those are the harvest years — years in which social scientists who aspire to modest influence in the course of history ought to make themselves heard as never before in language which can be understood.

I do not suggest that all of us ought to turn our attention to short-range problems and to direct an urgent communication with policy makers in the 87th Congress. U. S. agriculture is not at the brink of catastrophe. Farm policy is not, as some argue, the crucial domestic issue of the 1960's. The terms of the next armistice in farm policy are, nonetheless, important. I am deeply impressed by the demands of policy makers for knowledge and insight and means of innovation, and by the sharp contrast between those public officials who succeed in marshalling

323

intelligence in the solution of public policy problems and those
who do not. I am convinced that the process of social innovation
is chiefly, although not exclusively, a succession of short-run
improvisations with a long-run objective in mind. The proper
strategy in public affairs as in mortal combat is to plan the en-
gagements to win the war, not to try to end the conflict in one
great encounter.

In the face of the farm policy contradictions of the 1950's and
the needs of the 1960's, economists ought not, in the words of
W. H. Auden's poem, be found: "Lecturing on navigation while
the ship is going down."

We are less than citizens and less than scholars if we count
ourselves as mere spectators at a political circus, and cynically
deplore each successive act. The times demand engagement and
commitment, not withdrawal and neutrality.

The elements of farm policy which I will propose are essentially short-run and conventional, in line with my conviction that
the path of progress in the next decade is to build on the present.
We are too prone to forget, in the current public agony over large
surpluses and indefensible public expenditures for farm programs, that there have been successes as well as failures in a
generation of farm policy. Some say it is too late to throw out
the whole system of federal farm programs. I believe it is too
early. The seven years since 1953 have been poor but not disastrous years for agriculture. There is no genuine and general farm
crisis — only a modest urgency, a puzzling over successive events
and a persistent foreboding of worse to come. Lacking the elements of revolution, we must build on what we have.

Before turning to public policy prescriptions which would improve on the present yet be consistent with dominant aspirations
and values of the American people, I want to cite seven areas of
economic and social analysis in which there is now substantial
agreement — to point out where argument is either unnecessary
or is largely ceremonial. Some are questions of fact, others of
goals and values.

1. In the absence of enabling legislation (permitting marketing agreements and orders, for example) and direct government
intervention in farm price determination, the average level of
farm prices in the 1960's would be substantially below the price
level of the late 1950's, if research and discovery were to continue at a fairly rapid pace. The average level of income of
commercial farmers would be sharply reduced as the decline in
the number of farmers would be too slow in a decade or less to
offset reduced margins per unit, as slightly increased

disappearance of products with inelastic demands failed to offset price declines and as other prices continue to rise.

Free market farm prices averaging perhaps as much as one-fourth below the late 1950's are, in fact, the expected norm for the 1960's, even if the rest of the economy is exceptionally pros-perous and slightly inflationary. Under those conditions the prices and incomes of farm operators from farming would not, as in an earlier era, be closely correlated with business con-tractions and expansions. Nor would they be so correlated in the 1960's if we have subtantial price support programs. Ours is no longer an agriculture in an unstable economy — one subject to wild swings in employment and income. It is an agriculture in an economy rather successfully stabilized if not quite fully employed by a combination of public and private actions. Explanations of the level and stability of farm prices and incomes — once couched in terms of an unstable economy — must be revised accordingly for the coming decade.

It is no longer very controversial to argue that the equilib-rium average free market level of farm product prices would be much below 1960 levels, both for the short run of 1960-63 and the longer run of 1960-70. A few farm leaders and an occasional economist can be found to state a contrary opinion — that price supports hold farm prices down, not up. I believe the evidence runs strongly against them.

2. It is increasingly apparent that such prices for farm products would be intolerable to many of the people who man commercial agriculture — faced with a threat to survival — and to the whole society. The price system which would yield such re-sults has indeed been given to us by historic circumstances. But the essence of democratic society is that it is a product of reason and moral strength. Man need not submit equally to the benevo-lence and the tyranny of history. He has devised pricing institu-tions — for labor, for industry, for public utilities — with conse-quences more acceptable than with pricing under pure competition. It would be a violation of consistency (and therefore of order), as well as a violation of justice, to argue that having substantially modified other product and factor pricing institutions, we must now stop short even though we recognize the main weaknesses of the structure and the price system common to agriculture.

3. A third area of agreement follows from the first two: an active role by government — that is, by political society — in eco-nomic affairs in the 1960's is not only legitimate but also neces-sary if we are to program — to plan — changes in key institutions at rates we wish to accept and at costs we choose to pay.

To understand this bipartisan, if somewhat unequal,

commitment, we must understand the final, true aim of political society. It is, in the words of Maritain[1] (and in my opinion):

... to better the conditions of human life itself, or to procure the common good of the multitude, in such a manner that each concrete person, not only in a privileged class but throughout the whole mass, may truly reach that measure of independence which is proper to civilized life and which is ensured alike by the economic guarantees of work and property, political rights, civil virtues, and the cultivation of the mind.

In this view of democratic life, the state — the public service corporation of the body politic — is the servant of man, not man the slave of the state or of the inherited establishment. This is, I believe, the dominant American view.

Opposition to the principle of frank government action in economic affairs in the U. S. is increasingly ceremonial. Despite occasional incantation to the contrary, both political parties and all major farm organizations accept it as a permanent part of the national life of this generation, at least. As Galbraith[2] wrote in 1954:

On two of the most important subjects of controversy in our time, labor and farm policy, the real issue has been resolved. A struggle, which once involved a great change in the power relationships in the American economy has subsided into a skirmish over the terms of the ultimate accommodation.

What relationship is there between national goals and a role for government in economic events? The relationship is that of ends to means. Other chapters have dealt chiefly with ends; my assignment is to discuss means. The means of public agricultural policy are statutes, administrative regulations and precedent. Means ought not debase ends — to keep man in the very process of becoming, from reaching that to which he aspires. So while we speak of a growing national agreement on the propriety of public economic policy, of the need and even the duty to reshape our institutions and thus to better their results, we must remind ourselves also of the dangers. They are not negligible. Tocqueville's warning a century ago is doubly relevant today.[3]

It must not be forgotten that it is especially dangerous to enslave men in the minor details of life.... Subjection in minor affairs breaks out every day, and is felt by the whole community indiscriminately. It does not drive men to resistance, but it crosses them at every turn, till they are led to surrender the exercise of their will.

[1] Jacques Maritain, Man and the State. University of Chicago Press. 1951. P. 54.
[2] John K. Galbraith, Economics and the Art of Controversy. Rutgers University Press. 1955.
[3] As quoted by Saul Alinsky, Reveille for Radicals. University of Chicago Press. 1946. Pp. 68-69.

Farm policy in the 1960's can meet this test but not without effort, for the possibilities for proliferation of minutiae in farm programs are endless.

There is some trace of Utopia — of a naive faith in human and institutional perfectibility — in our reliance on government to alter circumstances no longer tolerable to the majority. But the alternative to Utopianism is not despair. Even in a realistic, pessimistic democracy, man is not without hope. He knows that change does not always turn out to be progress, but he keeps trying, in pursuit of his own true nature, to improve the mutual adaptation of environment and self. It is thus in pursuit of high human aspirations that man sets himself the task of improving the institutions by which farm products are priced and the owners of farm resources compensated for their labor.

Is it equality of opportunity and equality before the law to grant collective bargaining rights to labor but to decline even to search for similar innovations in farm markets? Is there justice in overt selection or tacit acceptance of output and employment policies, and price and wage policies for much of industry and labor but rejection of similar price and output policies (if they can be devised) for agricultural producers? Do we designate as just a pricing system which tells us that the value of 800 million bushels of wheat a year is $1.5 billion, but the value of a billion bushels accidentally produced in the same year would have been perhaps half a billion dollars less? Is it a contribution to order and stability — to harmonious relationships among human activities — to accept an economic structure for agriculture with distinctly different characteristics than the dominant economic structure and results if not unique, at least unusual?

Obviously, a certain kind of freedom is lost in the pursuit of order (stability) and justice. But the sources of personal freedom for some have always been in its partial denial to others. Those who have mourned in the 1950's the farmers' loss of freedom to plant indiscriminately — whatever the consequences to himself and his neighbors — would also have predicted disaster when the public utilities and the grain exchanges were regulated. These people seem not to understand that the exercise of personal freedom is and must be less than an absolute right. Yet I think the proper explanation of their actions is that they value pure individualism at all costs more than do the rest of us and they wish to substitute their objectives for ours.

It is also important to distinguish between democratic and totalitarian restraints upon individual freedom. There is little evidence that the modest limits upon farmers' actions to date have been broadly unpopular. Witness the continued popularity

of milk marketing orders, wheat marketing quotas and even conservation reserve.

There is much evidence that farmers who have experienced
both low prices and restrictions on marketings in a framework of
almost complete freedom to innovate and to compete for control
over the means of production — to be acquisitive — do not view as
a genuine dilemma the choice between unrestrained freedom of
proprietary power and collective restraints on private actions to
insure them an equitable share in the fruits of their labor.

4. We can agree that our national goal of full employment,
grounded in justice and in the dignity of the individual, extends to
rural as well as urban people. There is a firm consensus among
economists that improvement in the conditions of life of the forgotten half of agriculture is essentially a problem in economic
growth and public welfare, not of farm policy. Conflicts of goals
and values in this matter have been largely resolved. Having
chosen the objective, we have implicitly dedicated ourselves to
the search for means appropriate to the goal of full employment,
and we have been fairly successful.

It is interesting to discuss and discover reasons for the high
incidence of genuine poverty in agriculture. But I do not see why
we should surround this matter with so much mysticism. Jobs in
industry and trade attract people from agriculture. We can agree
that changes in occupation and residence caused by the attraction
of the city and not by coercive push from farms are by definition
desirable. Excessive unemployment on farms as in the cities is
by definition a shortage of jobs relative to workers. Since we
cannot reduce the number of workers in the immediate future, but
instead, must employ a labor force growing at an increasing rate,
we shall have to increase the number of jobs in pursuit of our
national aspirations.

To this end, public policy to discover and achieve the rate of
growth needed in the technological and organizational context of
the 1960's to fully employ all who wish to work is completely
straightforward. We cannot nor do we wish to remake the steel
industry into a textbook example of pure competition so that it
would cut prices, not employment, when demand declines. We do
not expect to pursue our full employment policies by making
wages flexible downward, thus employing all at lower wages in
recession. We can perhaps discover and create conditions under
which trade and industry will fully employ the labor force in the
1960's even though the former are increasingly concentrated and
all are increasingly powerful. We do not need to know precisely
how much of our redundant farm labor is the result of the market
structure of labor and industry combined, in order to strike

boldly at unemployment and resulting human debasement wher-
ever it exists.

5. We can agree, I believe, that even though the price system is not omnipotent, it is a useful ally in resource allocation.
Although aggregate farm output responds sluggishly at best to
lower prices, it responds considerably more quickly to higher
prices. Substantially higher prices for many farm commodities
in the early 1960's are, therefore, contradictory to our resource
allocation objectives. They would make direct output restriction
slightly more difficult and land retirement more costly. Even so,
if the public is in a mood to accept slightly higher food prices as
it accepts other price increases, the case against modest increases in farm prices is not a strong one. It should not be much
more difficult to administer a price of 80 per cent of parity for
wheat than one of 75 per cent, for example.

6. There is almost no dissent to the idea that the present
commodity storage situation is wasteful of public money. It is in
obvious conflict with our goals of efficiency and needs to be cut
back sharply. No one is expected to come forward with an acceptable justification for carrying over 1.5 billion bushels of corn
or wheat each year although some will try. Termination of open-
ended price support commitments and systematic carry-over reduction keyed to equitable treatment of farm producers who would
be directly affected and to the grain trade will merit the approval
of both parties and nearly all voters in the early 1960's.

7. We have the knowledge now as never before to debunk the
mythology and the shibboleths which clutter farm policy debate
and impede farm policy reform. There is enough research,
enough knowledge, to place ignorance and partisan or pressure
group demagoguery clearly out of bounds in serious discussion.

If scholars will only speak up, they can put across these facts
and many more:

a. That depressions are not farm-led, even though agriculture is
   important to the economy.
b. That 100 per cent of parity farm prices are not axiomatically
   fair, even though parity prices and incomes, like just wages,
   are meaningful ideas.
c. That the pricing system implicitly termed "natural" (because
   its opposite is termed "artificial") was not made in Heaven,
   and has no more claim to transcendence or permanence than
   any other.
d. That the race between population and food supply in the next
   generation in the U. S. is probably no contest. Talk of the im-
   minent need for more land to feed the U. S. population — and

we hear this every day — is likely to be irresponsible unless
highly qualified.

e. That many essential elements of genuine competition remain
in an economy substantially modified by government action.
Price supports and acreage allotments did not spell the end of
efforts to increase efficiency and income nor would a 100-
million acre soil bank. Effective marketing quotas for wheat
would not end the competition individual producers engage in.
The error of confusing "pure competition" with competition
among producers for control over resources is a serious one.

With these elements of agreement, we proceed to more specific elements of farm policy for the 1960's, consistent with
dominant aspirations of the American people. As noted, the general direction of farm policy may well be decided in the next
year or two. Its shape and scope will reflect the way the winning
political party and the successful candidate for the presidency interpret the desires of their supporters for farm policy. Inevitably then, farm policy in the 1960's would not be the same when a
Democrat is president as it would be if a Republican were president.

It may appear, however, from the foregoing recital of agreement, that it will not matter (for farm policy) which party is in
power. This is not the case. As Rossiter[4] notes, Republicans
and Democrats are still "at least a city block apart" on farm
policy and other matters. If the gap closes, it is the Democrats
who are most likely to open it again. Most of the agreement I
have cited and the elements of acceptable future farm policy I
will cite involve institutional innovation, and Democrats innovate
less reluctantly than Republicans. Faster action toward even
those elements on which there is substantial agreement is likely,
therefore, under Democrats. To some this is virtue — to others
vice. It is, I think, a statement of fact, not of value.

RESEARCH FOR THE FUTURE

What would be a positive policy for agricultural research and
education in the 1960's? There are few signs that the American
people would support efforts to reduce research effort in food
production technology. Critical inquiry in this area is necessary,
for farm production research is not self-justified. It may be
met, with hostility, not only by research administrators and

---

[4]Clinton Rossiter, Parties and Politics in America. Cornell University Press.
1960. P. 127.

scientists, but by a public sensitive to the possible food needs of future generations in the U. S. and the world. Food production research is no longer justifiable on grounds that it is chiefly for the farmers. This observation is trite by now; yet the clamor goes on to justify such research expenditures for obsolete reasons. Food research in the 1960's is chiefly for the consumers of 1970 to 2000. On those grounds it should stand or fall.

The most pressing food problems are those outside the U. S. The research programs of land grant colleges and universities and the USDA have not yet addressed themselves seriously to the problems of adapting the advanced technologies of the western world to the elemental needs of the rest of the world. If, upon reflection, we find ourselves ready to permit a slowdown in the rate at which our scientists create new technologies to make our own future food supply more secure and our farm adjustment problems ever more difficult, there is surely no higher priority than to turn their attention to massive technical assistance for the less-developed nations. This could not be done in the present framework of support, heavily based on state appropriations. But with appropriate vision, it could be done somehow.

EDUCATION

The key to effective employment of the population is not only job availability but adaptation of the labor force to the increasingly complex opportunities for work. Justice to each new generation requires us to prepare it for the future, not the past. Justice to those who are unemployed and, to a degree, technologically unemployable requires us to recognize that if the people of the depressed rural and urban areas and the expatriates from commercial agriculture are to be full partners in the prosperity of the 1960's, they must be educated, trained and informed.

This will require a thorough rehabilitation of our educational structure — academic and vocational, federal and state. It will mean large contributions by most developed regions of the U. S. to the education and the economic repatriation of people in other regions. The federal-state employment service will have to extend its services and its imagination far beyond its present scope.

Impressive arguments will be marshalled against these proposals. Some will say, with William G. Sumner,[5] that "A free man in a free society has no duty whatever toward other men of

---

[5]W. G. Sumner, What Social Classes Owe to Each Other. Harper & Brothers, New York. 1883.

the same rank and standing except respect, courtesy, and good will." Others will deny that administrators can be convinced, that bureaus can be reorganized or that financing can be arranged.

The people of the U.S. are ready for striking innovations in education, even if public officials are not. They are prepared to have vocational education for agriculture put into proper perspective relative to vocational education for industry, trades and services. Economic opportunity for most of the millions of young and mobile people on farms today is in nonfarm employment. I do not know the ideal relative expenditures, but I doubt that it is appropriate to spend nearly twice as much for agricultural and home economics vocational education as for trade, industry and distributive education.

Action Programs

The significant feature of agricultural policy in the 1960's will be the convergence of the two parties and all major farm organizations on either reluctant acceptance or wholehearted approval of a restrictive farm output policy. Agreement on this score is far advanced but is obscured by the rituals of day-to-day political and pressure group disputation, and by diversity of means.

Let there be no mistake about the reasons for this convergence on output policy. Output policy — whether pursued through land retirement, selective direct marketing controls or by bargaining associations, private or public — has price policy as its chief end. Price policy has income policy as its objective.

Resource owners, farm and nonfarm, covet market arrangements which show promise of doing justice to individual and corporate performance, not modest insurance against disaster. We are gradually achieving such arrangements in the U.S. Unemployment insurance is important, but it is not a substitute for collective bargaining against a backdrop of full employment. Farm income insurance may be an appropriate supplement to farm output and price policies but is not likely to be a substitute for them.

Farm output and price policy for the 1960's — whatever the means — need not be deeply concerned with the distribution of the benefits of publicly or privately administered farm prices in order to be consistent with society's concept of justice. We tolerate and even encourage a degree of administered prices in other sectors of the economy irrespective of the distribution of ownership of corporation stock. We thus foster acquisitiveness, and protect equally the access of persons to the law and their unequal capacities to acquire property. It would be inconsistent to deny through price supports keyed to farm size, similar treatment to owners of farm resources. It is not very satisfying to deny the operator of a large farm proportional access to land retirement funds, but to grant him full access to the price-increasing effects of land retirement.

But we can, in good conscience, support farm prices and thus returns to farm resources indiscriminately only if we expose to ourselves the sham that it is the poor in agriculture whom we aim to assist through price policy. There will be intense pressure to continue this mockery if genuine agricultural poverty is not in sharp decline in the 1960's. But if unemployed and low-income farmers are being rapidly absorbed through education and economic growth, the argument that price policy should be designed to help the poor, and should discriminate against those who have gained control of large quantities of farm resources, will become exceedingly transparent. It is jobs and wage policy, not commodities and price policy, which can attract the attention of two million or more underemployed farmers.

What of the farm price level for the 1960's? Once the problem of economic growth and unemployment is on the way to solution, the argument for a farm price level substantially higher than in the 1950's largely dissolves. There is a bit of good sense in arguing for a farm price level of 100 per cent of parity or higher when there are a million nearly full-time farm producers with gross incomes below $2,500 whose incomes could be raised perhaps one-third by such a move. With these people employed elsewhere, or with their farms improved or their incomes supplemented, the scene changes. Most of the truly commercial farm producers of the 1960's will not require that level of prices for rather profitable operation.

Discrimination on the part of commercial agriculture in its price aspirations cannot be overstressed. Society is already convinced — or can be convinced by a strong president — that it is reasonable to provide price and output policies for farm products despite ideological conflicts. But two self-interests are opposed to each other in the choice of a price level. The general public, not farmers, will likely decide upon the elusive but very real "fair farm prices" of the future.

Finally, public credit policies adapted to the agriculture of the future, with larger farms and greater capital needs, is exceptionally important. Planning to facilitate changes in farm size is commendable and in line with norms of order and efficiency.

The dominant values of the U. S. public are congenial to broad expansion of marketing agreements and orders with or without supply-control features to commodities with suitable characteristics, and to limited extension of treasury payments to maintain farm income (as for wool). Radical opposition notwithstanding, these are neither totalitarian aims, nor are they to be pursued by totalitarian means.

In short, I do not see the need for revolution in the 1960's. We can build on what we have. We need a pluralistic farm policy approach to cope with political reality.

J. CARROLL BOTTUM
Purdue University

Discussion

THE INSTRUCTIONS which I received were as follows: "Given the framework provided by preceding authors, what should be the agricultural policy elements for the 1960's in respect to research, education and action programs, relative to goals, values and economic interests of farm people; relative to goals and values of American society; short-run and long-run policy elements." Therefore, I shall appraise these papers from these viewpoints.

In essence, if I interpret Dr. Swerling correctly, he has accepted the equilibrium model with free prices supplemented by a relief program for agricultural producers when their incomes fall more than 25 per cent below the preceding five years. He also suggests that maximum payments might be limited to $4,800 or some such figure. He does not go into detail on how such a program might be administered or for how long these payments should be made. It seems to me that inevitably such a program would be of greater protection to the small farms than to the larger farms. The $4,800 limitation proposal emphasizes this.

Such a program is fraught with many difficulties concerning which one might raise many questions. Nevertheless I, too, believe society's goals might allow for the acceptance of such a program if suitable protections against abuses can be worked out. As Dr. Swerling points out, we have developed a relief program for other sectors of society when incomes fall, and this would be somewhat consistent with other national policies.

However, I do not believe that he has fully delineated the problem. I believe the commercial farm families' goals call for something more in the way of farm policy in this present period than a relief program. As more and more farmers are operating businesses in which the investment is $100,000 to $200,000, they are interested in policies that keep agriculture in adjustment and provide prospects for reasonable incomes. The laborer or the businessman is not satisfied with the relief programs alone. Farmers want some assurance of a price program that gives them a chance to succeed if they are efficient in their businesses. This the free market does promise in the immediate period ahead.

Society likewise has a stake in programs which make possible maintenance of efficient commercial family-size farms. Programs that only maintain the smaller low-income farmer are not in society's economic interests. Therefore, I accept Dr. Swerling's paper as far as it goes, but I would argue that it does not fully deal with the goals and values of farm people in the price and income area.

I do not find much to differ with in his general comments except on page 318, where he states, "While land use adjustments as reflected in the Great Plains program may be desirable for their own sake, even a massive program of land retirement does not by itself promise to be an effective route towards production control under present technological conditions." I would argue that if sufficient payments are made, and sufficient land is taken out of production, it will control output. The question is whether or not society wants to take this approach. When land is taken out, labor and capital on that land are also taken out, and as the rate of technology increases, it means that more land must be shifted out of production.

Dr. Swerling has not chosen to deal extensively with the education or the research phase. Rather he went directly to a proposed program and then discussed values in connection with this program.

Dr. Schnittker has more specifically directed his discussion to education, research and action programs. In connection with his discussion of the role of the agricultural economist, I would in general agree, but I also think that there is a place for some economist to continue to lecture on "navigation" and keep the long-run goals in front of us, even at times when it may appear to some that the ship is going down. Our society is tougher and can stand more abuses than some of us sometimes think. I do not quite believe it is "now or never."

In regard to technological research, it seems to me that Dr. Schnittker implies a program of full steam ahead. With this I believe society agrees. From his tone I believe, although he did not emphasize it, that he also would accept a stepped-up research

program in the adjustment area, which our rapid rate of technological progress makes desirable.

It is when he comes to the action programs and the philosophy
concerning them, that I am most disturbed. Under his section of
substantial agreement, he states, "It no longer is very controversial to argue that the equilibrium average free market level
of farm product prices would be much below 1960 levels, for the
short run of 1960-63, or the long run of 1960-70." I am inclined
to agree that there is considerable agreement relative to the
level of prices in the short run, but I do not believe that there is
much general agreement relative to prices in the longer run.
Many adjustments are now taking place, and if agricultural
prices were to fall to the indicated levels in the short run, and
this situation was accompanied by a growing general economy,
considerable adjustment and realignment of prices would take
place in the longer run. However, this is a question of projection
or forecasting, and not a question of values, therefore I will not
pursue it further.

Under point three Dr. Schnittker states, "Where do we find
justice in a price system which tells us that the value of 800 million bushels of wheat a year is $1.5 billion, but the value of a bil-
lion bushels is perhaps half a billion less." Later he says under
point four, "We can agree that even though the price system is
not all-powerful, it is a useful ally in agricultural resource allocation." In the first case he is appraising the free price system
on the basis of justice, and in the second case, as an adjuster of
resources. I don't think anyone would argue that free prices always render justice. This situation simply illustrates the problem of finding a point of compromise between two goals.

I think his point on the necessity of having a growing economy
which will employ our people and the excess people from agriculture is an important one. I mention it only to emphasize his
point.

In connection with his proposed action programs, it seems
that he has committed himself to administered price controls,
certificates, quotas, etc., more than he needs to. I am not sure
that society has taken such a position. I do not believe that he
needs to commit himself to one or the other of these approaches
to discuss values or the merits of the programs. People are
willing, probably within broad limits, to accept either approach.
The real question is which will work best. It therefore comes
down mainly to economic evaluation of what each program will do
for them.

I would agree that a program which allows prices to guide
production, and in which the emphasis is on increasing the

mobility of the resources, is quite different from one which calls for administered prices, and then attempts to move the resources by other means, but the real issue is what would be the consequences of each.

In closing, I should like to add that it is my belief that society wants aggressive programs in technological research and education, supplemented more vigorously than in the past with research and educational programs which provide information to our people on how they may adjust and how their institutions may adjust to our changing, more scientific age.

In the action areas, it appears to me that the movement of human and cultivated land resources out of agricultural production is the inevitable consequence of economic progress in agriculture. Therefore, to have a prosperous agriculture, these adjustments must take place under whatever type of action program we have. These consequences flow from the acceptance of progress as a goal. The real issue in the policy field is which bundle of action programs can most effectively bring about these changes and at the same time adequately protect farmers' incomes and the welfare of those who must adjust, and which also most nearly stays within the social economic framework of our values.

Chapter 15

GEORGE L. MEHREN

University of California

Positive Policies
for American Agriculture:
From Values to Goals
to Analyses to Means

M ATERIAL PRESENTED IN PRECEDING CHAPTERS
provided background for the two concluding papers.[1] Authors Swerling and Schnittker were charged doubly. First,
the discussions were to be based upon all of the preceding material. Second and more important, the authors were asked to try
"to formulate agricultural policy elements for the 1960's which
are most consistent with the basic economic and social values for
agriculture" — whatever that is — and "to formulate agricultural
policy elements which are most consistent with the basic economic and social values for the total society" — whatever that is.[2]
The papers are appraised here within those missions and in the
context of the book as a whole.

Four questions seem explicitly to have been engaged by the
contributing authors:

1. What are, or perhaps what should be, the values or preference
   systems of individuals and groups in formulating agricultural
   policy?

2. How can values or preference systems be translated into
   workable or operational goals of farm policy?

3. What must be known about the determinants of changes in goal
   or target variables in order systematically to link values and
   means?

4. What alternatives of administration or control are consistent
   with given combinations of goals for farm policy?

Other and perhaps more important questions are engaged but
not answered. How does one reconcile hostile value structures,

---

[1] Boris C. Swerling, Positive Policies for American Agriculture. This book.
and John A. Schnittker, Positive Policies for American Agriculture. This book.
[2] Earl O. Heady and Lee G. Burchinal, The Concern With Goals and Values in
Agriculture. This book.

338

or should they be reconciled? What values should serve as bases for operating targets? What are the causal relationships of values to goals — and of means and achievement of targets to values and thus back again to goals and means?

It seems to be agreed that it is not yet possible directly to specify or to weight the value constructs that may well be the bases for administrative action in farm policy and that there are incompatibilities of values that preclude translating values into operational goals. Yet, without such translation, rational program activity is clearly impossible.

There seems to be only one major source of disagreement between Dr. Swerling and Dr. Schnittker: The two studies at issue here reach exactly opposite conclusions. Yet, each engage precisely the same question and within the same background and identical missions. Both studies are internally consistent in linking values to goals, thence to analysis, and finally to administrative proposals. Both authors apply analytical methods responsibly and within accepted rules. They start with basically opposite value constructs. Dr. Swerling seems to believe that price support of commodities is wrong — morally wrong, and wrong by the norms of efficiency. Dr. Schnittker believes differently.

Who is right? Should the differences be reconciled? If so, what compulsion of logic or other analysis can achieve reconciliation? If there is to be an agricultural adjustment program of real substance during the 1960's, one or the other of these value constructs must yield. Which one?

To appraise these two papers in the reference terms laid down in their mission and in the context of contributed discussions requires specification of the major attributes of values or preference systems; of operational goals; of the analytical determinants of such targets; and of operating programs. No violence to the values of the writers is intended. They seem to show their values plainly.

Value Constructs or Preference Systems

Farm policy ultimately involves management designed to yield some combination of targets presumed to be consistent with underlying value or preference norms. These broad and often vaguely specified value constructs must ultimately be defined in terms of optimal levels or other attributes of operational targets. Then, in the action or program phases of policy, consistent means of obtaining the goals must be prescribed.   John M. Brewster discusses this in Chapter 6.[3] It is apparently impossible to quantify most values. The value constructs to which reference was made in nearly every presentation remained unidentified. Yet, preference systems have long been specified in demand and welfare theory. Here it has not been necessary actually to measure such values. Effective empirical work — including definition of goals, analysis and management or policy — has long been possible without measurement or aggregation of individual preference maps. Preference patterns and goals therein consistent with observed behavior are identified ex post to observed adjustments in demand. In this sense, value constructs for farm policy could be defined generally in terms of substitution relationships just as they are defined in demand theory in order to be made operational. Perhaps values might be approximated by postulation ex post to observed behavior of those involved in farm policy.

There was difficulty in determining whether operating targets or administrative mechanisms taken alone have any value component. There seemed to be general agreement that methods for deriving targets and setting and keeping their optimum values were causal determinants of subsequent value systems. At least implicitly, some contributing authors seemed to believe that norms could be made conceptually operational even if only by defining preference systems and goals that might be uniquely consistent with what people appear actually to do.

Differences among individuals with respect to particular attributes or weight of a preference system do not appear to be resoluble by adherence to any generally accepted procedures of logic or testing.

Yet, the authors held that these constructs are and perhaps should be the primary determinants of farm policy. Controversy, therefore, centered upon appropriate expression of values, of operating targets and of means to achieve such goals. It seems generally agreed that it is now difficult or impossible to specify the methods for translating values into goals. It also seems agreed that means for weighting such values have not been developed, since the values themselves are not identified. Thus, while there is no fatal conceptual difficulty in developing complex preference or value systems for individuals, the major present difficulty in formulating targets is the virtual impossibility of aggregation. Even if the thus-far-unattained specification of individual preference systems were given, still there would be no compelling constraints which would assure agreement or even

[3] John M. Brewster, Society Values and Goals in Respect to Agriculture. This book.

limit permissible controversy with respect to weighting. There are, of course, many other computational difficulties. Additionally, weighting seems impossible if there be substantial interdependencies among alternative value systems for individuals and groups. In short, value constructs, even if defined ex post as logical concepts consistent with observed behavior, are not yet fully operational guides nor are they bases either for appraisal or adjustments either of actions or of values themselves.

Yet, somehow, participants seemed to agree that changes in values or in weights lead to changes in the optimum prescriptions for farm programs. Somehow, there was implicit assumption that all farm programs should be consistent with some set of weighted value constructs.

With this apparent agreement, the authors seemed, in effect, to conclude that programs are right only if they be consistent with some set of values thus far unspecified and possibly beyond specification. Yet, there seemed also to be agreement that values actually can be defined in terms of differing levels of specificity. Values, as defined or undefined, therefore seemed not to be goals but in some sense to be the determinants of operating targets or goals. However, values did seem to be considered as primary governors or guides in choosing among alternative actions through which targets might be achieved. They seemed also to be considered the final bases for consistent administration and also for consequent adjustments by individuals or groups of their own value systems.

Little if any reference was made to the determinants of preference systems. Little was said of any systematic or causal relationship of value constructs — however defined — to operating goals and actions. But it seemed clearly to be agreed that values — whatever they may be or however they may be weighted — are the bases for all other parts of policy programs. They were held to be governors of a continuing process ranging from values to targets to analysis to programs, back to values, and so on, ad infinitum. Implicitly or otherwise, it seemed to be agreed that values must be represented by surrogates or carrier variables derived by methods not once defined.

Operational Goals — Surrogates for Values

If administrative action is not to be "wrong" — where "wrong" means inconsistent with accepted values — then there is clear necessity for operational definition of value surrogates as targets. Absent this, there is no basis for rational action, for appraisal, or

for adjustment of program. Most participants seemed to agree
that means and ends are not discrete. They also agreed, apparently, that in fact there are many different groups, often with different values and often selecting different but always complex con-
glomerates of goals to be optimized. Professor Maddox defined
farm policy as a "continuous process of group and individual
compromise with temporary armistices" only.[4] Yet, even here
there was agreement with respect to the necessity for operational
goals, even if underlying value constructs and their linkage to
targets remained undefined.

An operational definition of a conglomerate of targets involves specification of the operations required or the procedures
used in the identification process itself. Optimally, value constructs should be translated to operational targets in quantitative
form as <u>carriers</u> for values. In this sense, the farm <u>problem</u> or
any other <u>problem</u> can be defined as a situation in which the
magnitudes or other attributes of weighted target variables are
undesirable or inconsistent with accepted value constructs. A
solution of a problem then can be defined as changing the variables representing the values to more highly desired magnitudes
or other attributes.

The transition from the general underlying value system to
quantitative carrier variables serving as targets could conceivably
be achieved by successive decreases in generalization of expression of values. This could lead to ultimate agreement that certain
quantitative targets shall, during the operating period, be taken to
represent the underlying value constructs and thereby to serve as
guides in administration, as bases for appraisal of achievement,
and possibly as bases for readjustment of the entire interrelated
sequence running from values to administration. Similarly, it
should be possible so to narrow group preference systems to
represent goals of individuals or units in reasonably homogeneous
institutions. There appear to be no other ways whereby the consistency of value constructs and administrative actions may be
appraised.

Achievement of target levels or qualities in carrier variables
can be taken at least as a best possible approximation to optimi-
zation adjustments for given creeds. Goals or targets specified
this way are free of the crippling difficulties of the typical unspecified preference construct. Targets are susceptible of operational definition. Values — as used by these participants — are
not. Conceptually, it is possible to weight and therefore to

---

[4] James G. Maddox, discussing The Concern with Goals and Values in Agriculture.
This book.

aggregate targets so defined. It is not possible to aggregate or even rationally to assign weights to creeds or values as defined by the participants. It is possible to measure interdependencies among targets. This could not be done with broadly generalized value constructs.

However, as Professor Maddox pointed out, it is actually necessary to specify goal magnitudes simultaneously in a variety of carrier variables. Nearly always, the value objectives of individuals or groups, even if narrowly defined, involve a multiplicity of creeds or values. Nearly always, these creeds and values appear to be interrelated with respect to their major determinants. Yet, as Dr. Foote noted, "If we are to get out of the realm of clashing platitudes, the best way to do so is to start transforming our values into goals, our words into numbers. . . . Intentions thus become intended effects. . . ."[5] With a multiplicity of targets, interrelations may be competing, or hostile, or involve substitutability.

Targets at best, it would seem from the conclusions of the participants, can be little more than approximations, and perhaps not good approximations, to basic values. There seems yet to be no method whereby the systematic or causal interrelations, if any, of generalized "values" and specific operating targets can be linked. It may be possible, as in some phases of demand theory, to specify the kind of value construct which would appear to be consistent on an ex post basis with observed behavior. The difficulties of this kind of specification are clearly understood. Most compelling, there is an operating necessity for explicit quantification of target goals if they are to guide action, guide appraisal, guide adjustment of administrative activity, and serve to amend underlying values themselves. Goals must be weighted so that they are mutually consistent or possible of simultaneous achievement within some pattern or system of interrelationship.

There is also necessity to introduce constraints or limitations impinging upon the goals. Achievement of targets may be limited or even precluded by constraints far beyond the power of persons involved in the value-means system. These constraints or limitations may emerge from many value sources — legal, institutional and budgetary. They may be physical in origin. Limits or constraints could be introduced into the definition of the target variables, into analysis of such variables or even into the administrative phases of policy. However, in policy, constraints often appear in the definition of the target variables which are taken to approximate the values themselves.

---

[5]Nelson N. Foote, Goals and Values and Social Action: A Model With Complications. This book.

Little is known of how operating goals can or should be derived from the apparently underlying values. Little is known of how acceptance of values can or should be reached. The goals must be operationally defined to involve explicit questions conceivably answerable without reference to values. Weights are also drawn, apparently, out of underlying value constructs. Constraints, side conditions or limits may also be drawn from value constructs, relative or otherwise. Whether they are or whether they should be, or how they might be, are questions left unanswered by the contributing authors. Yet, it seemed agreed that if rationality is to be obtained in action, targets must be defined and weighted to provide basis for selection of optimum means. The difficult issue of expression of values through targets or carriers does not appear to have been resolved to the satisfaction of all participants.

The Analytical Component of Policy

If values must be expressed through surrogates or goals, the analytical component of policy — farm or otherwise — is the next logically necessary link between values and means. Analysis is the single component of the policy process appearing to be free of any normative content. In this phase, it is first necessary to specify the alternative variables of alternative forms of relationship through which it is conceivably possible to obtain or to keep the optimum magnitudes or other qualities of the goals.

It seemed to be agreed by the participants that efforts to represent preference systems are not "scientific" or "theory-measurement" processes. In fact, the papers and discussions seem to indicate that participants do not know how values develop; how they may be specified; how they may be weighted; how their interrelations may be measured; how they can be related to goals; and how these goals can be related simultaneously to values and administration. It appeared agreed that there is no compulsion for competent and responsible people to reach agreement with respect to the relative desirability of values or goals. Ultimately, selection among values may rest upon aesthetic, ethical or other considerations not susceptible of resolution by accepted rules of analysis. These attitudes, which seemed to be general, support the generally accepted viewpoint that "scientific method" is a narrowly specified mechanism applicable only to narrowly defined questions. Fundamentally, questions must be structured to involve nothing more than patterns of co-variation if the arbitrary procedures of "scientific method" are to be applied. No value or normative questions may be engaged by these devices.

Creeds and carrier targets are indeed "Siamese twins" with
respect to administrative operations, but they can only be joined
together by means of "scientific" analysis of variation in target
carriers. It seemed widely agreed that neither goals nor administrative actions have separate operational rationality aside from
their underlying value constructs.

Perhaps even the analytical phase of policy is ultimately an
arbitrary process involving rigid conventions based on aesthetic
norms. It was widely agreed that value and action questions are
not resolved separately nor are they susceptible of standard
hypothesis-testing procedures. Most participants seemed ready
to agree with John Brewster that "in organizational terms, this
problem is a question of what alternative to customary rules can
be spelled out and its results quantified... and... in value terms,
the problem is a question of what new weightings of competing
creeds would be required by the alternatives to our customary
ways... and... the ideal models of scientific theory and measurement are not to be equated with so-called normative systems."[6]
This means that to achieve targets consistent with values, action
must be consistent with the determinants of goals. A given conglomerate of goal attributes might well be gotten by manipulation
of a battery of alternative combinations of determining variables,
magnitudes and relationships or forms of relationships. Thus, the
basic purpose of the analytical phase is to specify those variables
and relationships closely and systematically related to targets
which might be susceptible of administrative manipulation. They
may also provide the basis for choice among the different alternative administrative organizations and operations through which the
goal conglomerate conceivably could be achieved. Thus, goals
cannot be gotten except through analysis of the narrowest "scientific" or "hypothesis-testing" type. Consistent relationships of
administrative operations and goals cannot otherwise be gotten.

This phase is really what Brewster calls "scientific method"
or "theory-measurement" and serves as a major link in the chain
from values to goals to means. Values and goals are normative
and their generation does not directly involve analytical processes.
There is no direct reference to norms in selecting or weighting
carriers. But, for given weighted variables, the procedure of
analysis which links values to means is a straightforward "scientific" operation. At issue are carefully structured questions, involving issues of naked co-variation and nothing else, designed to
"explain" variation in the weighted goal or target system. The results are the necessary information to set up an administrative

---

[6]Brewster, op. cit.

mechanism which can yield optimum results in terms of weighted
goals subject to the constraints or limits introduced in the system.

Both the variables and the interrelations which might serve as
administrative bases for control are identified. Alternatives
through which different variables or different relationships might
be changed in different ways to get given ends can also be identified. It is also possible to develop the side conditions not directly
introduced in the identification of the goals themselves.

There was little discussion of this analytical component and
occasional disparagement of its function. Yet, there seemed to be
implicit understanding that this phase is indeed the necessary link
between values, goals and means. While there are no apparent
rules to resolve conflicts with respect to values or their deriva-
tives — goals — there seemed to be implicit agreement that the
analytical component was tenable only if values or goals were presented on a disjunctive basis. Thus, it is consistent with accepted
conventions of analysis to state that "if the goals are taken to be
some conjuncture of target variables, then optimal administration
must be based on analysis of the system explaining variation in the
goal conglomerate." This does not mean that the goal is necessarily accepted as a surrogate of the value or that there be any
logical or other compulsion for general acceptance of the value
constructs themselves.

While there are many ways of presenting the relationship of
the analytical component to the total value-means continuum, three
main attributes must be known in order to develop the appropriate
means to achieve goals. These involve the variables causally related to the goals, their net interrelationships, and the total system
of co-variation. Given this information, it then becomes possible
to know those variables and relationships susceptible of manipulation; the alternatives among various relations and control variables
through which a given combination of goal attributes might be gotten; and, in some cases, all of the possible alternatives for optimal
administration.

The Administrative Phase of Policy

Administration means development of an operating mechanism
to impose optimum magnitudes or other attributes upon the determining variables or relationships which govern the goals. Explaining variation in the targets requires at least an approximation to
straightforward "scientific" analysis. This may be an ideal procedure, but efficiency of administration for given goals is otherwise impossible. With a complex of goals, it is likely that there

will be alternative ways to get and to keep the desired target attributes. There are fundamental differences between the analytical
component and the administrative processes. First, analysis can
specify the alternatives of relationships or variables to be manip-
ulated to obtain given targets. Administration is designed to
achieve the optimal magnitudes of determining variables or relationships. Second, the analytical processes are at least superfi-
cially free of value connotation. However, there are elements of
the administrative phase in which normative components are explicitly introduced.

An administrative mechanism may be defined in terms of units,
methods, variables or relationships involved in control centers
through which executive authority is expressed; parallel mechanisms designed to induce such adjustment without expression of
authority, and consistent accounting, reporting and appraisal centers. Most important, provision for equity or distribution of burdens and benefits is an explicit reintroduction of normative judgments. The contributing authors seemed generally to agree that
selection among alternative operational procedures could lead in-
definitely over time to changes in accepted values, thence to targets, thence to analytical procedures, and again to administrative
mechanisms and actions.

This continual adjustment of the value-means mechanism over
time might be attributable to inconsistency of selected targets with
basic creeds or of weights assigned to targets. Failure to introduce constraints or outright error in the analytical component of
the process could lead to inconsistency between values and administrative operations. Inconsistency of administrative operations
with the analytical component would lead almost inevitably to similar inconsistency of means with goals and therefore with values.
There could be unforeseen side effects not introduced in target
specification or in the analysis of the target variables. Finally,
there could be change over time in the underlying creed structures
from changes in other determinants and therefore in the targets,
analysis and administrative operation.

With alternative "explanations" of variation in targets, there
could also be alternative administrative mechanisms for given
goals involving different interrelationships and constraints and
perhaps yet be of equal "efficiency" in optimizing in the norms.
Choice among these possible administrative alternatives must apparently rest on aesthetic, ethical or other "unscientific" bases.
Thus, while targets and means are simultaneously defined through
the analytical component of policy, there are usually alternative
means to achieve given ends. Accordingly, the ultimate choice of
means for given ends may also be normative and lead to readjustment over time in all phases of the entire process.

As indicated, the analytical operations involved in defining targets and in explaining determination of target variation differ
sharply in nature from administrative operations designed to set
up an optimal administrative machine to get and to keep the optimal attributes in the determinants of target variables or goals.
There is a growing body of theory and measurement with respect
to optimal organization and operations. Consistent administration
can be defined in terms of optimal attributes of centers of authority, inducement, accounting, reporting and appraisal. Equity provisions bring value constructs back into the administrative process. "Efficient" administration is consistent with the goals, the
analytical determinants of the goals, and the constraints of operation.

Apparently, the whole process of policy formulation and execution is agreed to be a continuum whereby all four components of
the process — values, goals, analysis and operation — may change
over time.

THE APPRAISAL

Wishfully or otherwise, some measure of consensus seems to
have been found in the viewpoints of many participants in this
presentation of values and goals. Appraisal of the Swerling and
Schnittker proposals is based upon apparent consensus of major
attributes and relationships in the process by which values are
linked to means of action through targets and analysis. First, the
values upon which Messrs. Swerling and Schnittker base their recommendations are identified. Next, there is identification of the
goals representing their values. Then, there is appraisal of the
analytical procedures through which Swerling and Schnittker identify the variables and interrelationships incident to their goal system. Finally, the proposed administrative procedures are related
to the analytical component, which in turn is specified by the targets which can be taken as representative of their underlying value
systems.

Insofar as it is possible, effort has been made to determine the
assumed relationships through which the targets are taken to represent the underlying value or preference constructs; to appraise
the consistency of the analytical systems they have developed; to
identify internal difficulties — which indeed seem minor; and, where
possible, to indicate the sequential implications of their recommendations. This in a sense is an unaesthetic procedure grossly
inconsistent with many of the norms explicitly accepted by professional analysts. To depart into the first person, I have never

checked — and do not now dare to check — my own work to determine the apparently underlying values; to measure the procedures
whereby values are translated into goals; and to check the consistency of goal analysis to targets and to means. Here, the four major questions engaged in this presentation could be paraphrased as
follows and addressed to Messrs. Swerling and Schnittker:

1. What do you believe to be right or desirable?

2. How do you specify operationally that which you believe to be
   valuable or preferred?

3. What must you know about variation in that which you believe to
   be preferred?

4. What must you do to achieve your targets?

The results are remarkable. Again, Swerling and Schnittker
are competent and professionally responsible. Yet, engaging an
identical question with an identical mission and in the context of
the same basic discussion, opposite conclusions are reached. The
two authors have conformed carefully to accepted conventions of
logical derivation and empirical testing. Again, the fundamental
difference appears to be the implicit assumption by Dr. Swerling
that direct-interventionist programs or price support is wrong.
The implications of this divergence are not clear. The possibilities of, or the necessities for, resolution are not clear. Only this
much is clear: agreement could be reached only by resolution of
the fundamental difference in their values. There appear to be no
errors of logic or analysis. The basic divergence of value constructs does not appear to be subject to any agreed compulsion for
resolution.

Positive Policies for American Agriculture: Swerling

This dissection of the conclusions of an able economist was
undertaken, among other reasons, because Dr. Swerling is an old
and valued friend who is aware that he is held in high professional
regard. Yet, like all people born of Adam, he uses many value-
loaded terms, operationally undefined, but giving some index of the
value basis for his proposals. In effect, Dr. Swerling has explicitly restricted a "positive farm policy" to limited insurance payments and by indirection has indicated a value preference for substantially "free market" values. He has engaged all of the four
questions. His values and targets are hostile to the present program and favorable to his proposals. He has analyzed the old

programs and his own proposals in basically non-normative terms.
He has proposed administrative procedures consistent with his
negative case against the present proposals and his affirmative
case for the limited unemployment or income-insurance device.

The Value Constructs

Dr. Swerling attributes to the "general public" certain values
deemed to be hostile to present farm programs. He believes that
the American people hold high in their value system such notions
as private proprietorship, small farms and small business enterprises generally. He believes that country values are held higher
than urban preferences. He holds that price support programs are
advocated within value systems where the constructs of preference
for open and free markets, state's rights and free enterprise are
blandly, blithely and inconsistently amalgamated with advocacy of
direct price intervention. He believes that the regressive effects
of these programs violate prevailing notions of equity. He looks
upon use of the power and the treasury of government to increase
returns to farmers, in the absence of any protection for agricultural labor, as directly hostile to prevailing notions of "social
justice."

Dr. Swerling further sets out his own views. He indicates that
there is no compulsion from any construct of justice to protect
higher income farmers who may be temporarily distressed. He
believes that the present system is "malfunctioning," "inconsistent
with economic realities," and thus apparently inconsistent with
some efficiency norm. He believes that the value of "consistency"
— the foundation for nonagricultural income-maintenance programs
to decrease or to pool individual income risks and to set minimum
protection for events beyond individual control — should be extended
to agriculture on the same bases as in other industries. Dr.
Swerling develops two explicit value constructs leading him to
reject present policies and to substitute a proposal for a relatively
small-scale income protection insurance. He believes that "justice" requires resistance to the extravagant claims of a declining
sector of the economy but that "justice" also requires that adjustment be eased if it can be done without damage to general "efficiency." Both these values — affirmative and negative — are derived from his own construct of justice.

The Targets

Dr. Swerling has developed two operational goals closely akin to his stated values. First, he proposes the elimination of the present system of direct intervention and of all collateral programs required by the standard side effects of direct price support. He seems to imply that income disparity and instability in agriculture have been overstated; that the universality of these two difficulties in all agricultural economies involves some inevitable sequence perhaps beyond amelioration; that returns from noncommercial low-income farms have been included in data taken to support the income disparity and instability cases; that off-farm earnings of small-scale agriculture have not been adequately represented; that the real welfare increments from rising levels of farm living are not effectively shown in current parity calculations; that mechanization and other technological change have eased adjustment to the outflow of farm labor and have increased the typical scale of the farm; that the cash and debt positions of farmers are better than those shown; that price support superimposes an "excess" income target, which in turn generates a damaging capital inflow, offsetting the salutary labor outflow; that there is gross value and operational inconsistency of farm programs with other domestic and foreign policies; and, finally, that the pressure groups who set present farm goals have set fair-share income targets which cannot conceivably be attained in a declining sector of an expanding economy. Thus, the argument for price support as a means of achieving income support to agricultural people is held to be inconsistent with social justice and would be obviously so were it not for the peculiarities of data availability, congressional organization, and similar factors.

With respect to his own affirmative proposal, Dr. Swerling implies that income insurance meets the value criteria of social justice and efficiency in that it is counter to uncontrollable personal income variation while avoiding inconsistent side effects.

In short, Dr. Swerling seems to say that the present system is morally wrong and operationally inconsistent with its own nominal goals. He holds that his own proposal is right and consistent. There seems to be no internal inconsistency in his proposals. His targets can be derived systematically and consistently from his values. There is no way to know whether his values should be accepted.

The Analytical Component

Dr. Swerling analyzes the determinants of variation in income levels and distribution with respect to the present and his own proposed program. First, he lays out the analytical bases for price support operations. He does not directly attack the analytical validity of the standard price support argument involving low price and supply elasticities; the difficulties of a decreasing output with a declining farm price; the sensitivity of agricultural income to depression; and output restrictions leading to price and income increases. He believes, however, that orthodox economic analysis supporting these conclusions may be, in fact, invalid. He also points out quite properly that many low-income difficulties are analytically unrelated to price maintenance. He believes that there may be a possible perverse relationship to cyclic policy and that such intervention may counter the necessary labor outflow required to obtain stable and reasonably equal incomes in agriculture.

There is no difficulty in the affirmative analysis associated with his own target variables. He believes that his proposal cannot possibly lengthen or worsen present agricultural maladjustments. He considers that the "free market" is left with no price distortion and that expansion incentives are avoided. There may be implicit agreement by Dr. Swerling that his income-insurance proposal is basically palliative and not in itself a solution directly affecting income determinants but that it is not hostile to a free market solution. His "free market efficiency" and his "social justice" creeds therefore appear to be consistent.

Administrative Operations

Dr. Swerling quite effectively buttresses his argument by noting the severe administrative difficulties involved in present programs, given their nominal goals. He holds that there are occasionally quite impossible administrative burdens; that it is far too costly a method of intervention; and that these programs introduce political uncertainty through burdening Congress with direct administrative activity. There is little direct reference to administrative attributes of his own proposals except correctly to note that workable analogies are available by reference to similar programs in nonagricultural industries.

The Conclusions

Thus, Dr. Swerling in effect rejects present programs and any programs similar to them. He suggests in effect a free market solution eased by protection of minimum income levels for all people in the economy. He has stated his goals quite explicitly and has analyzed them well. He has buttressed his analytical conclusions with references to the administrative consistency of his affirmative proposals and the inconsistency of those policies the rejection of which he recommends. Given his values, the conclusion again seems tenable that Dr. Swerling believes that programs of the present type are "wrong" and that programs like those he suggests are "right." These are moral judgments. There does not seem to be any way to reconcile such judgments with opposite conclusions based upon acceptance of different values.

Positive Policies for American Agriculture: Dr. Schnittker

The Value Constructs

Like Dr. Swerling, this reviewer, and virtually all of his colleagues, Dr. Schnittker also uses some value-loaded terms which are not precisely defined. Even so, he has quite carefully and systematically laid out the value constructs underlying his own qualified endorsement of a program that Dr. Swerling rejects outright.

Dr. Schnittker explicitly postulates certain beliefs with respect to the "nature of man." He believes that man is not a slave of the state and that all individuals are of equal worth and dignity; that man has risen above the tyranny of history with respect to control of other markets and can and should do so with respect to agricultural markets; that people are more important than commodities; that each generation quite properly is most interested in its own welfare; and that no individual should be unnecessarily harrassed by the program operations of government. Quite explicitly, and as an important element in his argument, he rejects any naive acceptance of perfectibilism of man or his institutions.

He posits certain axioms with respect to the "nature of man's government." He holds that the American people generally accept the obligation by, or at least through, government to reshape our own institutions; that democracy is a product of what he calls reason and moral strength; that government intervention is necessary and legitimate if change is to be achieved at a desired rate and cost; and that the "final, true aim of political society" is to improve

the lot of the individual as a means to assure the proper individual
independence built upon guarantees of work, property, political
rights, civil virtues and the cultivation of the mind.

Dr. Schnittker sets out axioms of "equality" and "justice." He
believes that the norms of equality of opportunity and equality before the law require exploration of innovations in farm policy if
collective bargaining is to be allowed to labor. Then he holds that
justice requires formulation of government policies designed to
manipulate farm prices, output, wages and employment if the same
programs are used in other industries; that something be done
about the inelasticity of demand for wheat; and accelerated research and action with respect to future needs for foods, foreign
aid and assistance for the unemployed or unemployable.

There are norms called "consistency," "order," "stability,"
and "harmony." Part of the price paid for order and justice is
held to be some loss of decision-making freedom by farmers.
There are implications that indiscriminate planting or other individual decisions can be injurious to neighbors; that persons holding
divergent values may place greater preference upon "individualism"
than "society" does; that those who believe that diminished freedom of decision is hostile to social order and stability may in fact
desire to impose their own values upon society; that the freedom
of decision making is yielded by democratic methods, which presumably renders it consistent with one or more of the governing
norms; but that order and consistency require continued development of innovations in farm markets, since product and factor
pricing institutions already have been changed.

Finally, he sets out axioms to which the "people" — whatever
that may be — are presumed to agree. It is held that the general
public agrees that farm policy is not presently the most crucial
domestic issue but would consider a 25 per cent relative price decrease during the decade beginning 1960 "intolerable" — whatever
that is — to "agriculture" — whatever that is — and to "general society" — whatever that is. Full employment in all sectors is taken
to be a generally acceptable value. The norms relevant to the
low-income problem in agriculture are held not to be in conflict
with the system of values justifying price intervention as a means
to solace other ills. Dr. Schnittker holds that the low-income
problem involves growth and welfare, substantially different issues
than those to which price support should properly be directed.
Finally, he believes that political campaigns disclose the basic
values of the American public with respect to a positive policy for
farming and perhaps identify a "fair farm price" — which is a "real
thing."

As in all cases of value statements, it is difficult to know the bases upon which this comprehensive set of guides and governors to public policy rests. It is also difficult to know how they can be effectively related to goals and programs, even assuming that they are in fact the preference structures of the people to whom they are here attributed.

The Targets

Consistent with these values attributed by Dr. Schnittker to man, his government and the public, a comprehensive set of operational goals is specified. First, Dr. Schnittker holds that a target of a slight increase in price without reference to distribution of gains is tenable under his values only if it be understood that this goal is not related to the noncommercial, low-income enterprises in farming. His second goal is the improvement of conditions for farm product pricing so that owners of farm resources are compensated fairly for their labor. This presumably means alteration of the structural attributes of markets. Then, as a third goal, he specifies national full employment in all sectors, or at least a decrease in all unemployment including rural. He proposes changes in the attributes of agricultural labor to fit with nonagricultural demands. He proposes to decrease price support in agriculture if underemployment declines in consequence of increasing general employment opportunity. Then, there are several collateral goal proposals involving decreases in storage operations; unemployment insurance, which is taken to be no substitute for price and output policies but perhaps a supplement thereto; and inquiry into appropriate goals for long-run food needs, foreign aid, credit, and scale of operation.

These are respectable targets. They are certainly susceptible of analytical inquiry, and they seem to follow from the broad value systems specified by Dr. Schnittker.

The Analytical Component

As in the case of Dr. Swerling, Dr. Schnittker's analytical processes seem to be consistent with his proposals. First, Dr. Schnittker states quite properly that there is an operating necessity to build upon present programs rather than to introduce fundamentally new ones. He states that price support operations are a necessary counter to declines in farm price attributable to the excessively slow decline in the number of farms, to demand inelasticities and to continuing increases in factor prices. He also

holds that price and incomes in farming are insulated from general
economic fluctuations if price supports are used. He sees no possibility of remedial effect through population growth alone. He
feels that there is ample scope for competition sufficient to maintain efficiency in farming in the face of price support operations.

Dr. Schnittker points out with respect to possibilities of increasing employment of agricultural labor in nonagricultural industries that it is impossible to decrease the present and prospective labor force, and therefore effort must be made to increase
jobs. He believes that the situation reflects a pull to the nonagricultural industries rather than a push away from farming. He
holds that further analysis of the determinants of demand for labor
in all industries during the 1960 decade is needed. He believes
that unemployment insurance does not in any analytical sense touch
upon the determinants of the real income problems in agriculture.
It cannot be taken as a substitute for collective bargaining and
surely is no causal determinant of demand for farm labor.

Administrative Operations

Administrative compulsion to build upon present operations is
stressed. Dr. Schnittker notes the pressure of time in determining
values and goals which, if rendered operational in 1960-62, would
in all likelihood color operating activities for a long time ahead.
He stresses the good effect of providing adequate information to
intelligent policy makers. He feels that it is necessary to strike at
agricultural underemployment even prior to full development of
goals or analytical information. Dr. Schnittker places minor emphasis on administrative mechanisms, since he is in effect suggesting short-run improvisations built upon present administrative
machinery, yet guided by a long-run objective.

The Conclusions

Dr. Schnittker has laid out constructs of justice and equality
which differ substantially from those to which Dr. Swerling seems
to adhere. It is quite impossible to reconcile these differences.
From these different values, Dr. Schnittker supports a positive
program almost diametrically opposed to that proposed by Dr.
Swerling.

THE CONCLUSIONS

Two able and responsible people, operating within the same context of discussion, have engaged essentially the same general question. They have used essentially similar procedures in considering the same four major questions discussed in this book. Substantial exception can be taken to only one phase of the development of these conclusions. One may find values unacceptable. Their goals are clear, and they are operational. The analytical procedures are consistent. Both men know how programs are administered. They have set out their values quite explicitly. Here, and here alone, seems to be the major reason for the opposite conclusions. This difference leaves certain questions unanswered. What, if anything, is the importance of the difference; how could it be reconciled; and if it could be reconciled, should it be so resolved?

Two conclusions seem to be clear. If one structures his questions solely to the naked issues of co-variation and if he conforms meticulously to narrowly defined rules of analysis, compelling answers to certain types of questions can be gotten. Those questions can and must be relevant only to co-variation. They cannot encompass the really important questions faced by most people. It is impossible effectively to engage issues of ethics, metaphysics, epistemology, aesthetics or theology by the use of the arbitrary and ultimately normative devices of scientific method. Yet, it is wantonly wasteful to disparage this method or to fail to realize that it is the crucial link between ends and means.

Second, it seems obvious that we cannot now answer the important questions of value posed in these papers. An action or means is "right" if it be consistent with an accepted precept or norm. It is "wrong" if it be inconsistent. There is no real difficulty in appraising consistency. Some norms are held by some people to be relative and by others to be absolute and eternal, independent of human consciousness or acceptance. Different groups have tortured and killed because intransigent and therefore wicked people held different absolutes for which they would torture and kill. There is no real difficulty in defining "right" farm policy if agreement can be reached with respect to governing values. No compulsion to agree upon norms seems yet to have emerged. What is right to Swerling may still be wrong to Schnittker.

Index